CARRIAGE OF GOODS BY SEA

PAYNE AND IVAMY'S CARRIAGE OF GOODS BY SEA

TENTH EDITION

BY

E. R. HARDY IVAMY
LL.B., Ph.D., LL.D.

OF THE MIDDLE TEMPLE, BARRISTER; PROFESSOR OF LAW
IN THE UNIVERSITY OF LONDON

LONDON
BUTTERWORTHS
1976

ENGLAND: BUTTERWORTH & CO. (PUBLISHERS) LTD.
LONDON: 88 Kingsway, WC2B 6AB

AUSTRALIA: BUTTERWORTHS PTY. LTD.
SYDNEY: 586 Pacific Highway, Chatswood, NSW 2067
Also at Melbourne, Brisbane, Adelaide, and Perth

CANADA: BUTTERWORTH & CO. (CANADA) LTD.
TORONTO: 2265 Midland Avenue, Scarborough M1P 4S1

NEW ZEALAND: BUTTERWORTHS OF NEW ZEALAND LTD.
WELLINGTON 1: T. & W. Young Building,
77–85 Customhouse Quay, CPO Box 472

SOUTH AFRICA: BUTTERWORTH & CO. (SOUTH AFRICA) (PTY.) LTD.
DURBAN: 152/154 Gale Street

USA: BUTTERWORTH & CO. (PUBLISHERS) INC.
BOSTON: 19 Cummings Park, Woburn, Mass. 01801

©

Butterworth & Co. (Publishers) Ltd.
1976
Reprinted 1978

ISBN Casebound: 0 406 64056 4
Limp: 0 406 64057 2

Preface

SINCE the last edition was published in 1972 considerable changes have occurred in the law relating to the carriage of goods by sea.

Charter-parties by demise as in *Marmara Transport A.S. v. Mobil Tankers S.A.: The "Mersin"*, [1973] 1 Lloyd's Rep. 532 and *Skibsaktieselskapet Snefonn, Skibsaksjelskapet Bergehus und Sig. Bergesen D.Y. & Co. v. Kawasaki Kisen Kaisha Ltd.: The "Berge Tasta"*, [1975 1 Lloyd's Rep. 422, have shown a revival as indicated in Chapter 2 ("Charter-parties"). In this chapter the most marked development has occurred in connection with the vexed question of the shipowner's right to withdraw a vessel from the charterer's service because the hire has not been paid, and is illustrated by *Tenax S.S. Co., Ltd. v. The "Brimnes" (Owners): The "Brimnes"*, [1974] 2 Lloyd's Rep. 241, *Mardorf Peach & Co., Ltd. v. Attica Sea Carriers Corp. of Liberia: The "Laconia"*, [1975] 1 Lloyd's Rep. 634 and *Oceanic Freighters Corp. v. M.V. Libyaville Reederei und Schiffahrts G.m.b.H.: The "Libyaville"*, [1975] 1 Lloyd's Rep. 537. Also included in this Chapter are the most recent cases concerning the "off-hire" clause, e.g. *Canadian Pacific (Bermuda) Ltd. v. Canadian Transport Co., Ltd.: The "H.R. Macmillan"*, [1974] 1 Lloyd's Rep. 311, and the "employment and indemnity" clause, e.g. *The "Berkshire"*, [1974] 1 Lloyd's Rep. 185. *Alma Shipping Corp. of Monrovia v. Mantovani: The "Dione"*, [1975] 1 Lloyd's Rep. 115 and *Marbienes Compania Naviera S.A. v. Ferrostaal A.G.: The "Democritos"*, [1975] 1 Lloyd's Rep. 386 are further authorities on the right to send a vessel on a last voyage which is reasonably expected to be completed during the period of the time charter-party.

Chapter 3 ("Bills of Lading") has been expanded to take account of a number of American and Canadian cases which have interpreted the Hague Rules.

Chapter 7 ("The Exclusion and Limitation of a Shipowner's Liability") has been revised in the light of *New Zealand Shipping*

Co., Ltd. v. *A. M. Satterthwaite & Co., Ltd.* : *The "Eurymedon"*, [1974] 1 All E.R. 1015 (right of third party to rely on limitation of liability clause in a bill of lading) and especially of the cases decided in the United States and Canada on the interpretation of "package" and "unit" in Art. IV, r. 5 of the Hague Rules.

Revision of Chapter 9 ("General Average") has been rendered necessary by the York-Antwerp Rules 1974, which are set out in full in Appendix G.

Chapter 10 ("Demurrage and Despatch Money") takes account of *E. L. Oldendorff & Co., G.m.b.H.* v. *Tradax Export S.A.* : *The "Johanna Oldendorff"*, [1973] 3 All E.R. 148, which has adopted a new rule as to what constitutes an "arrived ship" in a port charter-party.

In Appendix B the "Gencon" charter-party and the "Baltime 1939" charter-party are reproduced by the courtesy of the Baltic and International Maritime Conference.

I should like to thank the staff of Butterworths for undertaking the arduous job of preparing the Index and the Tables of Cases and Statutes, and for seeing the book through the press.

E. R. HARDY IVAMY

University College London
March 1976

Contents

CHAPTER 4.—THE CONSTRUCTION OF CHARTER-PARTIES AND BILLS OF LADING

CHAPTER 5.—THE PRELIMINARY VOYAGE

CHAPTER 6.—LOADING, DISCHARGE AND DELIVERY

Table of Statutes

References in this Table to "*Statutes*" are to Halsbury's Statutes of England (Third Edition) showing the volume and page at which the annotated text of the Act will be found. Page references printed in bold type indicate where the Act is set out in part or in full.

List of Cases

CHAPTER 1

Commercial Practice

The branch of the law of contract which relates to the carriage of goods by sea will be better understood if the student knows something of the general practice of merchants, shipowners, and bankers who carry on the commerce of the world. For the benefit, therefore, of those who have not had the advantage of practical experience in such matters it is proposed to examine, in very brief form, some of the steps which are usually taken by those wishing to transport goods from one portion of the globe to another. In the course of such examination familiarity with common shipping terms will also be gained.

When a manufacturer, exporter, or other person has sold goods to a customer overseas and has decided, on the grounds of cost and convenience, which shipping line will best carry them for him to their destination, he can obtain from the offices of that line, or from printers who make it their business to supply them, three or four copies of a document known as a **bill of lading**. Almost all shipping lines have their own special forms of bills of lading. These serve as (1) *documents of title* to the goods, once they are shipped; (2) *a receipt for the goods* delivered to the shipowner or **carrier**; and (3) *evidence of the contract* which has been entered into between the **shipper** of the goods and the **shipowner**.

Under modern conditions when a shipment is made by a regular line, there are usually agents on each side intervening between the shipper and the shipowner.[1] The shipper frequently employs a **forwarding agent** and the shipowner a **loading broker**. The forwarding agent's normal duties are to ascertain the date and place of sailing, obtain a space allocation if that is required, and fill in the blank spaces in the printed bills of lading, each one in

---

[1] See *Heskell* v. *Continental Express, Ltd.*, [1950] 1 All E. R. 1033.

1

identical terms, indicating the name of the **consignee**, or person to whom the goods are to be delivered; a description of the goods, including the **shipping marks** which have been put on the bales, cases, or bags for the purpose of identification; stipulations as to the time and place of payment of **freight** (*i.e.* the remuneration payable to the shipowner for the carriage of the goods), and various other details. The three or four copies (the practice varies) of the bill of lading thus filled in are known as a **set**. The forwarding agent sends these documents to the loading broker for signature. He also arranges for the goods to be brought **alongside**, *i.e.* within reach of the ship's tackle, and he makes the customs entry and pays any dues on the cargo. After shipment he collects all the copies of the bill of lading except one, and he sends them to the shipper. The remaining copy is handed to the shipowner and forms part of the **ship's papers** for the voyage. The ship's **manifest** is made up from all the bills so collected.

All the regular shipping lines operating from the United Kingdom appear to employ a **loading broker**. His duties are normally as follows. He advertises the dates of sailings, and he supervises the arrangements for loading, though the actual **stowage**, or packing of the goods in the ship's holds, is decided on by the **cargo superintendent**, who is in the direct service of the shipowner. The loading broker will also sign the bills of lading and issue them in exchange for the freight. He is paid by way of commission on the freight, and that doubtless induces him to carry out his primary function of securing enough cargo to fill the ship.

It will be realised from this account of their duties that the loading broker and the forwarding agent perform well-defined and separate functions. Nevertheless, in practice, the same firm is often both the loading broker and the forwarding agent. A firm usually acts as loading broker for only one shipping line and does all that line's business. It is free in respect of other business to act as it will.

The shipper normally insures the goods against marine and, sometimes, war risks, breakage or leakage. The consideration paid by him to the insurers is a **premium**, and the document embodying the contract is a **policy**. He then has the complete set of **shipping documents** consisting of a bill of lading, the policy of insurance, and the **invoice** (which shows the details of the goods bought and the price payable). In nearly all cases the documents are attached to a **draft** or bill of exchange drawn on the consignee or on a bank named by him[1] either at sight or at so many days or months. Almost invariably the shipper does one of three things with these documents:

(1) He may send them direct to the consignee of the goods. This is most frequently done when the consignee is his agent or employee.

(2) He may hand them to his banker with a covering letter asking the banker to collect from the consignee, or the bank named by the consignee, the amount indicated on the invoice against delivery of the documents. This the banker will do in consideration of a small commission.

(3) He may **discount** the bill of exchange with his banker, *i.e.* the banker credits him at once with the amount of the bill, less a small commission.

The consignee himself may be a merchant, or a **factor** (a selling agent), who wishes to resell the goods. Often he is able to do so before they are landed at their destination. In such a case he makes the documents over by a suitable form of **endorsement** or signature on the reverse side of the bill of lading to the new owner of the goods, who becomes an **endorsee for value.** An endorsement of the bill of lading made with the intention of transferring the ownership of the goods named therein to the endorsee has the effect of actually making such endorsee owner of such goods. An **endorsement in blank** is merely the signature of the shipper written on the back of the bill of lading. A **special endorsement** is made up of the shipper's signature and a direction to deliver to a particular person; for example, if a bill of lading is in favour of "A. B. & Co. or order" and the goods are bought from them by C. D. & Co., a suitable special endorsement would be "Deliver to C. D. & Co. or order. (Signed) A. B. & Co."

Various forms of contract for the sale of goods to an overseas

---

[1] The transaction is arranged by means of a Bankers' Commercial Credit. See generally C. M. Schmitthoff, *The Export Trade* (6th edn. 1975), pp. 215–237; H. C. Gutteridge and M. Megrah, *The Law of Bankers' Commercial Credits* (4th Edn. 1968).

buyer have become stereotyped by usage, of which the commonest are the following:

(1) A **C. I. F. contract.**[1] These letters stand for "cost, insurance, and freight". Here the seller contracts to deliver the goods to the buyer on the quay, or, where special terms are included in the contract, at the railway station, of the place named by the buyer as their destination, the seller paying the insurance premium and the freight. Sometimes the seller fulfils the contract by buying goods already afloat which are bound for the proper destination, and transferring the ownership of them to the buyer.

(2) An **F. O. B. contract.**[2] These letters stand for "free on board". Here the seller's obligation is to deliver the goods over the ship's rail. The buyer must pay the insurance premium and the freight and any other expenses which may be incurred by the goods in transit, and the goods travel at the buyer's risk.

(3) An **exwarehouse contract.** In this case the buyer purchases the goods on the understanding that he will be responsible for their removal from the warehouse in which they are lying at the time of sale, and for their transportation to their destination.

It may be that during the voyage the ship or some of the cargo suffers damage. Subject to various exceptions, any loss so sustained must be borne by the shipowner or by the cargo-owner (or by their respective insurers) as the case may be. Such a loss, known as **particular average**, lies where it falls.

The most important exception to this rule is where a grave peril, *e.g.* a hurricane, threatens the whole adventure and some sacrifice is made intentionally for the benefit of everyone concerned. Perhaps some of the cargo will be **jettisoned** or thrown overboard. When such a sacrifice, known as a **general average sacrifice**, has been made, the loss, called a **general average loss**, is imposed upon all those for whose benefit the sacrifice was made.

---

[1] See generally D. M. Sassoon, *C.I.F. and F.O.B. Contracts* (2nd Edn. 1975) (published as *British Shipping Laws*, vol. 5).

[2] See generally *ibid.*

They must all bear the loss rateably, in proportion to the value of their respective interests.

On arrival at the port of destination the master will, provided that the freight has been paid, deliver the goods to the first holder of a proper bill of lading who presents himself and demands them. It would appear at first sight that the existence of a set of bills involves great risk of fraud. In practice, however, the cases of persons who have no right to the goods becoming possessed of them are extremely rare. Without a copy of the bill of lading the consignee is usually unable to obtain delivery of the goods from the carrier, though sometimes, *e.g.* where the documents have been delayed in transmission, the carrier consents to deliver against an **indemnity**. This will be given by some person or company of high standing, *e.g.* a bank, and will cover the carrier in respect of any loss which he may suffer by handing over the goods without the production of a bill of lading.

As soon as the consignee accepts delivery of the goods on the quay, if he suspects that they have suffered any loss or damage covered by the policy of insurance, he calls in the local agent of the insurers and asks him to make an official **survey** of the parcel and furnish a signed certificate. The consignee may also seek the assistance of an independent surveyor. He may then make his claim against the insurers themselves. The importance of marine insurance to the merchant lies in the fact that by certain clauses in the bill of lading known as **exceptions** the shipowner avoids responsibility for a multitude of **excepted perils** or mishaps which may befall the cargo; but for the risks undertaken by the insurers, the merchant would be faced with the impossibility of trading with anything like a prospect of gain. A person whose business it is to work out the respective liabilities of the parties concerned, where average has been incurred, is an **average adjuster**.

It may be, however, that for some reason, such as delay or neglect, the consignee fails to take delivery. In such a case the master may land and warehouse the goods, or, if that is impracticable, may elect to carry them, in the interests of their owner, to some other place.

We must now glance at alternative methods frequently employed by shippers of goods in place of the simple process, already noticed, of entering into a contract with a shipowner which is evidenced by a bill of lading.

It often happens that a shipper wishes either

(1) to hire a ship for a fixed time;
or (2) to hire a ship, or a portion of a ship, for a certain voyage;
or (3) to become for the time being the owner of a ship, by causing her to be leased to him.

The contract entered in any of these three cases is a **charter-party**. In case

(1) it is known as a **time charter,**
(2) as a **voyage charter,**
(3) as a **charter by demise.**

In some instances the shipper who has entered into the charter-party wishes himself to fill the ship with his own goods; in others he advertises that he has a certain amount of space and, for a consideration, ships other merchants' goods; sometimes he even charters a ship as a speculation, having no cargo himself to ship in her, hoping to make a profit by the demands of others for such space as he can offer.

Where a ship is used, either by the shipowner or by her charterer, to carry the goods of a number of persons under different bills of lading, she is said to be employed as a **general ship**.

This brings us to a consideration of the variations of the term "freight", as commonly used. **Advance freight** is often agreed upon, *i.e.* freight to be paid before the goods are delivered by the carrier to the consignee; for example, it may be agreed that payment is to be made on shipment. Again, sometimes a charterer agrees to pay **lump sum freight**; this means that he binds himself to pay a fixed sum for the whole voyage or series of voyages covered by the charter-party, irrespective of the amount of goods carried. **Pro rata freight** is freight which may become payable proportionately to the part of the voyage accomplished or to the part of the cargo delivered. **Dead freight** is the name given to the damages payable, in certain circumstances, by a charterer who has failed to load a **full and complete cargo,** that is to say a cargo which will fill the holds of the ship as far as they can be filled with safety; for, except where lump sum freight is agreed upon, the shipowner generally stipulates for the loading of the largest cargo he can carry. The shipowner's remuneration for carrying the goods beyond their original destination, where the consignee has failed to take delivery or to forward instructions as to the disposal of the goods, is **back freight**.

Finally, acquaintance should be made with the following terms:

Barratry is any act of fraud or violence done by the master or crew, without the consent or privity of the shipowner, which either results in, or necessitates the risk of, loss of or damage to the ship or cargo.

A contract whereby in an emergency both ship and cargo are given as security for a loan to enable the ship to complete her voyage is a **bottomry bond**; where only the cargo is given as security, the document is known as a **respondentia bond**. Both transactions are very rare at the present day.

The letters **D. W. C.** stand for dead-weight capacity. This phrase, when it appears in a charter-party without any restrictive explanatory words, means the gross weight of goods of any kind which the ship can carry.

A charter-party generally fixes a number of days, called **lay-days**, within which the ship is to be loaded or discharged, as the case may be. **Demurrage** is a sum named in the charter-party to be paid by the charterer as liquidated damages for delay beyond such lay-days. When the lay-days have expired and demurrage has not been provided for, *or* when the time for loading or discharge is not agreed, *or* where demurrage is only to be paid for an agreed number of days and a further delay takes place, the shipowner is entitled to **damages for detention**; for clearly the earning-power of a ship depends upon her continuous employment with as little delay as possible between voyages. A charter-party sometimes provides that **despatch money** will be payable to the charterer if he loads or discharges the vessel in a time which is shorter than the number of lay-days.

Apart from special customs, **working days** are all days on which work is generally done at the particular port in question; **weather working days** are all working days on which the weather allows of work of the particular kind in question being done; and **running days** are all days on which a ship might be sailing at sea, that is to say every day in the year.

Deviation means departure from the prescribed or ordinary trading route which the ship should follow in fulfilment of a contract of carriage.

Inherent vice is a term applied to goods signifying any fault or characteristic of the goods or their packing which of itself causes them to be damaged or to deteriorate, without any negligence or wrong-doing by anyone.

A **mate's receipt** is a temporary form of receipt given by the mate of a ship for goods which have been received on board. This receipt is subsequently handed to the shipowner—or more usually to the loading broker—in exchange for the bills of lading.

Pilferage is a general term covering thefts of goods at any time during transit, or while lying in a warehouse.

Salvage is the remuneration payable to persons outside the contract of carriage who have saved the ship or cargo from loss or damage.

Wharfage is a charge made for receiving goods on a wharf, or for storing them there, or for removing them from the wharf.

CHAPTER 2

Charter-parties

THE TYPES OF CHARTER-PARTY

Unlike a bill of lading, a charter-party is always a contract (not merely evidence of a contract) and never anything more.[1]

There are three types of charter-party:

(1) *a voyage charter-party, i.e.* where the vessel is chartered for a certain voyage;

(2) *a time charter-party, i.e.* where the vessel is chartered for a certain period of time[2];

(3) *a charter-party by demise, i.e.* a lease of the vessel.

A voyage or time charter-party confers on the charterer simply the right to have his goods carried by a particular vessel. Here the possession and control of the ship are not transferred to the charterer. The shipowner exercises these rights through the master and crew who are employed by him.

---

[1] As to the functions of a bill of lading, see pp. 55-66, *post*.

[2] Another form of time charter-party is a "consecutive voyage" charter-party under which a vessel is chartered for a period of time for a number of consecutive voyages. See, *e.g., Sanko S.S. Co., Ltd.* v. *Propet Co., Ltd.,* [1970] 2 Lloyd's Rep. 235, Q.B.D. (Commercial Court); *Suisse Atlantique Société d'Armement Maritime S.A.* v. *N.V. Rotterdamsche Kolen Centrale,* [1966] 2 All E. R. 61; [1967] 1 A. C. 361, H. L.; *Agro Co. of Canada, Ltd.* v. *Richmond Shipping, Ltd.: The "Simonburn",* [1973] 1 Lloyd's Rep. 392, C. A., which concerned the question whether an arbitrator had been appointed within the time stated in the charter-party; *"Yoho Maru" (Owners)* v. *Agip S.p.a. c/o S.N.A.M. S.p.a.,* [1973] 1 Lloyd's Rep. 409, Q.B.D., where the question was the rate of freight payable; *Marmara Transport A.S.* v. *Mobil Tankers S.A.: The "Mersin",* [1973] 1 Lloyd's Rep. 532, Q.B.D. (Commercial Court), where the issue was as to the amount of freight payable; *Skibsakiteselskapet Snefonn, Skibsaksjelskapet Bergehus and Sig. Bergesen D.Y. & Co.* v. *Kawasaki Kisen Kaisha, Ltd.: The "Berge Tasta",* [1975] 1 Lloyd's Rep. 422, Q.B.D. (Commercial Court), where the question was whether redelivery of the vessel was late.

9

But in the case of a charter-party by demise the charterer puts his own stores, fuel oil, etc. on board and hires the crew. The master and crew are the charterer's servants, and the possession and control of the ship vest in him. Consequently, the shipowner has no responsibility in connexion with goods shipped while the vessel is thus leased.

Whether the possession and control of the vessel are to pass to the charterer depends on the intention of the parties.

The main test for discovering their intention is whether the master is to be the servant of the charterer or of the shipowner.[1]

Contracts whereby the possession and control of a ship vest in the charterer are becoming more common to-day especially in the oil tanker trade, and MACKINNON, L.J.'s *dictum* that "a demise charter-party has long been obsolete"[2] is, therefore, too sweeping.[3]

The importance of the distinction between a charter by demise and a charter-party proper is that under the former the master is the agent of the charterer, not of the shipowner. Thus, in *Sandeman* v. *Scurr*,[4]

a ship was chartered to proceed to Oporto and there load a cargo. The charter-party gave the master power to sign bills of lading at any rate of freight without prejudice to the charter. Goods were shipped at Oporto by persons ignorant of the charter-party, under bills of lading signed by the master. *Held*, the charter did not amount to a demise. Consequently, the master's signature to the bill of lading bound the shipowner.

---

[1] *Page* v. *Admiralty Commissioners*, [1921] 1 A. C. 137.

[2] *Re An Arbitration between Sea and Land Securities Ltd. and Dickinson & Co., Ltd., The Alresford*, [1942] 1 All E. R. 503, at p. 504; [1942] 2 K. B. 65, at p. 69.

[3] See, e.g. *R.M. & R. Log, Ltd.* v. *Texada Towing Co., Ltd., Minnette and Johnson, The Coast Prince*, [1967] 2 Lloyd's Rep. 290, where it was held that the charterer was in breach of an express and implied undertaking to redeliver the chartered vessel in as good a condition as when received; *Falmouth Docks and Engineering Co.* v. *Fowey Harbour Commissioners: The "Briton"*, [1975] 1 Lloyd's Rep. 319, where a dredger was let out under a demise charter-party; *Attica Sea Carriers Corporation* v. *Ferrostaal-Poseidon Bulk Reederei G.m.b.H.* (1975) *Times*, November 25, C.A., where a clause in the charter-party stated that the vessel was to be redelivered in the same good order and condition as on delivery, and that before redelivery, the charterer must effect all repairs found to be necessary, and it was held that the charterer was entitled to redeliver her even though the repairs had not been effected, and that the shipowner's remedy lay in damages.

[4] (1866), L. R. 2 Q. B. 86. Chorley and Tucker's *Leading Cases* (4th edn. 1962), p. 290.

But, in *Baumwoll* v. *Furness*,[1]

where the charter-party provided for the hire of the ship for four months, the charterer to find the ship's stores and pay the master and crew, insurance and maintenance of the ship to be paid by the shipowner who reserved power to appoint the chief engineer, it was *held* that the charter amounted to a demise because the possession and control of the ship vested in the charterer. Hence the shipowner was *not* liable to shippers ignorant of the charter for the loss of goods shipped under bills of lading signed by the master.

In view of the relative unimportance of charter-parties by demise, the following pages will deal only with those charter-parties which do not deprive the owner of possession of his ship.

VOYAGE CHARTER-PARTIES

(1) The Principal Clauses in Voyage Charter-parties

The shipowner and charterer are quite free to make their contract in any form that they choose. But usually they use charter-parties in a standard form, *e.g.* one of the many which are approved by the Documentary Committee of the Chamber of Shipping of the United Kingdom. The terms found in them vary according to the type of trade concerned. The approved forms are usually referred to by their "code names", *e.g.* "Gencon",[2] "Russwood". The parties are, of course, entitled to make such amendments to the terms to be found in the printed forms as they think fit.[3]

In general, the following provisions are found in most voyage charter-parties:

(1) The shipowner agrees to provide a ship and states her position, her capacity and class on the register.

---

[1] [1893] A. C. 8. Chorley and Tucker's *Leading Cases* (4th edn. 1962), p. 290.

[2] The "Gencon" Form is reproduced in Appendix B by the courtesy of the Baltic and International Maritime Conference.

[3] On the relation between the printed and the written words, see p. 102, *post*.

(2) As to the preliminary voyage to the port of loading, the ship-owner promises that the ship shall proceed with reasonable despatch.[1]

(3) The shipowner makes certain representations of fact regarding the ship, *e.g.* that she is "tight, staunch, and in every way fitted for the voyage".[2]

(4) The shipowner undertakes to carry the goods to their destination.

(5) The charterer agrees to provide a full cargo.[3]

(6) The charterer agrees to pay freight.[4] This is usually so much per ton of goods or per cubic foot of space.[5]

(7) A list of excepted perils. These exceptions are often made mutually operative.[6]

(8) Provisions regulating the manner of loading and discharge,[7] and especially the time to be allowed for these operations,[8] and the rate of demurrage.[9]

(9) A cancelling clause, giving the charterer the right to cancel the contract in the event of non-arrival of the ship by a certain day at a certain port.[10]

(10) A "general paramount clause", the purpose of which is to incorporate the Hague Rules.[11]

(11) The "amended Jason clause".[12]

(12) A "both-to-blame collision clause".[13]

---

[1] See pp. 110–111, *post.*
[2] See pp. 17–18, *post.*
[3] See pp. 119–122, *post.*
[4] See pp. 221–229, *post.*
[5] *Ibid.*
[6] See pp. 147–155, *post.*
[7] See pp. 118–119, 130–131, *post.*
[8] See pp. 205–206, *post.*
[9] See pp. 217–218, *post.*
[10] See pp. 111–112, *post.*
[11] See p. 67, *post.*
[12] See pp. 192–193, *post.*
[13] See pp. 152–153, *post.*

(13) An arbitration clause.[1]
(14) A clause concerning payment of commission to the ship-broker for negotiating the charter-party.
(15) A "cesser" clause.[2]
(16) A war clause.
(17) A clause incorporating the York-Antwerp Rules 1974 relating to general average.[3]

The interpretation and effect of the above clauses are discussed in this chapter and the ones which follow, but first it is necessary to consider what undertakings are implied by law.

(2) Implied Undertakings in Voyage Charter-parties

It is a general rule of law that the courts will not imply a particular term in a contract merely because it would have been reasonable for the parties to have inserted such a term. Nevertheless, it is well recognised, as Lord WRIGHT has said,[4]

---

[1] See *e.g., Liberian Shipping Corporation* v. *A. King & Sons, Ltd.,* [1967] 1 All E. R. 934; [1967] 2 Q. B. 86, C. A., where the clause stated: "Any claim must be made in writing and Claimants' Arbitrator appointed within 3 months of final discharge, and where this provision is not complied with the claim shall be deemed to be waived and absolutely barred"; *A/S Det Dansk-Franske Dampskibsselskab* v. *Compagnie Financière d'Investissements Transatlantiques S.A. (Compafina), The Himmerland,* [1965] 2 Lloyd's Rep. 353, where it was held that an arbitration clause in the above form barred a claim even though the cause of action giving rise to the claim had not arisen or come to the knowledge of the claimant until too late to enable him to comply with the clause; *Tradax Export S.A.* v. *Volkswagenwerk A.G.,* [1970] 1 All E. R. 420; [1970] 1 Q. B. 537, C. A., where it was held that a person was not "appointed" as an arbitrator where he had only been nominated and had not been actually informed of the nomination (*see* p. 140, *post*); *Astro Vencedor Compania Naviera S.A. of Panama* v. *Mabanaft G.m.b.H.,* [1971] 2 All E. R. 1301; [1971] 3 W. L. R. 24, C. A., where the arbitration clause was held to be wide enough to cover a dispute arising out of the arrest of a vessel. For a case where a third party guaranteed that the charterers would pay such amount as was awarded by an arbitrator, see *Compania Sudamericana de Fletes S.A.* v. *African Continental Bank, Ltd.: The "Rosarina",* [1973] 1 Lloyd's Rep. 21, Q. B. D. (Commercial Court).
[2] See pp. 218–219, *post.*
[3] See Chapter 9, *post.*
[4] In *Luxor (Eastbourne), Ltd.* v. *Cooper,* [1941] 1 All E. R. 33, at p. 52; [1941] A. C. 108, at p. 137.

"that there may be cases where obviously some term must be implied if the intention of the parties is not to be defeated, some term of which it can be predicated that 'it goes without saying,' some term not expressed but necessary to give to the transaction such business efficacy as the parties must have intended."

(A) *On the part of the Shipowner*

In the case of a voyage charter-party the shipowner impliedly undertakes:

(1) to provide a seaworthy ship;
(2) that she shall proceed with reasonable despatch; and
(3) that she shall proceed without unjustifiable deviation.

These undertakings may, however, be varied or excluded by clear and unambiguous terms in the contract.

(1) *Seaworthiness*. The implied undertaking is that the ship shall, when the voyage begins, be seaworthy for that particular voyage and for the cargo carried.[1] Thus, the standard varies with every adventure. The shipowner undertakes not merely that he has taken every precaution, but that in fact the ship is seaworthy. It is no defence that he did not know of the existence of a defect.[2] But his undertaking relates merely to the ordinary perils likely to be encountered on such a voyage with the cargo agreed on. He does not guarantee that the ship will stand any weather, however stormy. The following test has been laid down:[3] Would a prudent owner have required the defect to be remedied before sending his ship to sea if he had known of it? If he would, the ship was unseaworthy.

Unseaworthiness includes lack of sufficient bunker fuel for the voyage, or, where the voyage is a long one and the ship will fuel at ports of call, for the particular stage of the journey during which the loss occurs.[4] It also includes an avoidable excess of coal which makes it necessary for the ship to incur expenses for lightening.[5]

---

[1] *Stanton* v. *Richardson* (1874), L. R. 9 C. P. 390.
[2] *The Glenfruin* (1885), 10 P. D. 103.
[3] *McFadden* v. *Blue Star Line*, [1905] 1 K. B., at p. 706.
[4] *The Vortigern*, [1899] P. 140. See also *Northumbrian Shipping Co., Ltd.* v. *Timm (E.) & Son, Ltd.*, [1939] 2 All E. R. 648; [1939] A. C. 397.
[5] *Darling* v. *Raeburn*, [1907] 1 K. B. 846.

Even though a shipowner has not installed the latest appliances, the vessel may still be held to be seaworthy.[1]

The shipowner's duty to provide a seaworthy ship comprises a duty to have her loading and discharging tackles available for the ordinary purposes of loading and discharging.[2]

Although a charter-party provides that stowing, trimming and discharging are to be performed and paid for by the charterers, the shipowner is still under an obligation to have the ship's gear available for their use.[3]

Since the ship must be seaworthy with reference to the cargo agreed on, proper appliances to deal with special cargoes are necessary.

Thus, it will be seen that in reality the undertaking is twofold:

(1) That the ship is fit to receive the particular cargo at the time of loading. A defect arising after the cargo has been shipped is no breach of this undertaking.[4]
(2) That she is seaworthy at the time of sailing.[5]

The effect of unseaworthiness. The undertaking to provide a seaworthy vessel is one of a complex character which cannot be categorised as being a "condition" or a "warranty". It embraces obligations with respect to every part of the hull and machinery, stores, equipment and the crew. It can be broken by the presence of trivial defects easily and rapidly remediable as well as by defects which must inevitably result in a total loss of the vessel. Consequently the problem is not soluble by considering whether the undertaking is a "condition" or a "warranty". The undertaking is an undertaking one breach of which may give rise to an event which relieves the charterer of further performance of his

---

[1] *Virginia Carolina Chemical Co.* v. *Norfolk and North American S.S. Co.,* [1912] 1 K. B. 229, C. A.

[2] *Hang Fung Shipping and Trading Co., Ltd.* v. *Mullion & Co., Ltd.,* [1966] 1 Lloyd's Rep. 511, where the shipowner did not make the necessary gear available, and the charterers were held entitled to claim reimbursement of the expenses which they had incurred in hiring additional labour.

[3] *Ibid.*

[4] *McFadden* v. *Blue Star Line,* [1905] 1 K. B. 697.

[5] *Cohn* v. *Davidson* (1877), 2 Q. B. D. 455.

part of the contract if he so elects, and anoth₍ breach of which entitles him to monetary compensation in the form of damages.[1]

If the charterer or shipper discovers that the ship is unseaworthy before the voyage begins, and the defect cannot be remedied within a reasonable time, he may throw up the contract. Thus, in *Stanton* v. *Richardson*,[2]

a ship was chartered to take a cargo including wet sugar. When the bulk of the sugar had been loaded, it was found that the pumps were not of sufficient capacity to remove the drainage from the sugar, and the cargo had to be discharged. Adequate pumping machinery could not be obtained for a considerable time, and the charterer refused to reload. *Held*, the ship was unseaworthy for the cargo agreed on, and, as she could not be made fit within a reasonable time, the charterer was justified in refusing to reload.

After the voyage has begun, the charterer is no longer in a position to rescind the contract, but can claim damages for any loss caused by initial unseaworthiness.

Further, although the vessel is unseaworthy, the shipowner can still rely on the exception clauses in the charter-party, if the loss has not been caused by unseaworthiness. Thus, in *The Europa*,[3]

a ship was chartered for the carriage of a cargo of sugar from Stettin to Liverpool, and one of the excepted perils in the charter-party was "collision". On entering the dock at Liverpool the ship struck the dock wall; a water-closet pipe was broken and water got through it into the 'tween decks, and some sugar stowed there was damaged. In the 'tween decks near to the water-closet pipe were two scupper holes. The pipes which had originally been affixed to, and led from, these two scupper holes for the purpose of carrying off water from the 'tween decks to the bilges had been removed, and the scupper holes had been imperfectly plugged, with the result that water from the broken closet-pipe got through the scupper holes and passed into the sugar stowed in the lower hold. It was not disputed that this imperfect plugging existed before the cargo was loaded, and that thereby the ship was unseaworthy. The owners of the *Europa* did not therefore dispute their liability for the

---

[1] *Hong Kong Fir Shipping Co., Ltd.* v. *Kawasaki Kisen Kaisha, Ltd.*, [1962] 1 All E. R. 474, C. A., at pp. 487–488 (*per* DIPLOCK L.J.). See also the judgment of UPJOHN, L.J., *ibid.*, at pp. 483–484.

[2] (1874), L. R. 9 C. P. 390.

[3] [1908] P. 84. Chorley and Tucker's *Leading Cases* (4th edn. 1962), p. 303. See also *Smith, Hogg & Co., Ltd.* v. *Black Sea and Baltic General Insurance Co., Ltd.*, [1940] 3 All E. R. 405; [1940] A. C. 997; *Monarch S.S. Co., Ltd.* v. *A/B Karlshamns Oljefabriker*, [1949] 1 All E. R. 1; [1949] A. C. 196.

damage to the sugar in the lower hold, admitting that it was caused by the unseaworthiness. But they did dispute their liability for the damage to the sugar in the 'tween decks. *Held*, that they were not liable for this damage. It was true that the undertaking as to seaworthiness was a condition precedent, but once the cargo had been loaded the owners could be made responsible only in damages. The breach of the condition did not displace the terms of the contract. The damage to the sugar in the 'tween decks was caused not by unseaworthiness, but by the collision, and so the owners were entitled to rely on the exception clause.

Where the ship is seaworthy when she sails, but becomes unseaworthy while at sea, the incidence of liability will be determined not by reference to the undertaking (of which, of course, there has been no breach) but by reference to the cause of the loss. If the loss was due to an excepted peril, the shipowner will be protected, otherwise he will not.

It should, however, be observed that where fire results from unseaworthiness, the owner of the ship may be able to invoke the Merchant Shipping Act 1894, s. 502,[1] and so excape liability.[2]

Express and implied undertakings as to seaworthiness. A clause in a charter-party that the ship is to be "tight, staunch, and strong, and in every way fitted for the voyage", relates to the preliminary voyage to the port of loading. It refers to the time at which the contract is made[3] or to the time of sailing *for* the port of loading. The undertaking of seaworthiness implied by law, on the other hand, relates to the time of sailing *from* the port of loading.

The express undertaking, therefore, does not displace the undertaking implied by law. Thus, in *Seville Sulphur Co.* v. *Colvils*,[4]

under a charter containing the above clause the ship was to proceed to Seville and there load. The ship was unseaworthy on leaving Seville, and this was *held* to be a breach of the undertaking implied by law.

A breach of the implied undertaking of seaworthiness at the port of loading entitles the charterer to refuse to load;[5] but a breach of the express undertaking does not, unless it is such as to

---

[1] See pp. 160–161 and Appendix D, *post.*
[2] *Louis Dreyfus & Co.* v. *Tempus S.S. Co.,* [1931] A. C. 726.
[3] *Scott* v. *Foley* (1899), 5 Com. Cas. 53.
[4] (1888), 25 Sc. L. R. 437.
[5] *Stanton* v. *Richardson, p.* 16, *ante.*

frustrate the object of the charter.[1] This difference arises from the different times to which the express and the implied undertakings relate. The charterer's obligation to load is conditional upon the ship being seaworthy at the port of loading, not upon her being seaworthy at the time the contract was made.

Burden of proving unseaworthiness. The burden of proving unseaworthiness is upon those who allege it, and there is no presumption of law that a ship is unseaworthy because she breaks down or even sinks from an unexplained cause. Nevertheless in rare cases the facts may raise an inference of unseaworthiness and so shift the burden of proof. Thus, in *Fiumana Societa di Navigazione* v. *Bunge & Co., Ltd.,*[2]

it was *held* that an unexplained fire in the coal bunkers afforded a reasonable presumption that this was due to unfitness of the bunker coal at the time of loading of the cargo which amounted to a breach of the warranty of seaworthiness.

Excluding liability for unseaworthiness. The shipowner can, however, exempt himself from liability for unseaworthiness, but if he wishes to do so, he must use clear and unambiguous language.[3]

Thus, in *Nelson Line (Liverpool), Ltd.* v. *James Nelson & Sons, Ltd.,*[4]

Frozen meat had been shipped under an agreement which stated that the shipowner would not be liable for any damage "which is capable of being covered by insurance". The meat arrived in a damaged condition on account of the unseaworthiness of the vessel. *Held*, that the clause was not sufficiently clear to exempt the shipowner from being liable to supply a seaworthy ship.

(2) *Reasonable despatch.* The shipowner undertakes that the ship shall proceed on the voyage with reasonable despatch. Thus, in *M'Andrew* v. *Adams,*[5]

By the terms of a charter-party dated 20th October, 1832, a vessel was to proceed from Portsmouth where she was then lying to St. Michaels (in the Azores) and there load a cargo of fruit and return to London. On

---

[1] *Tarrabochia* v. *Hickie* (1856), 26 L. J. Ex. 26.
[2] [1930] 2 K. B. 47.
[3] See further for similar clauses in bills of lading, pp. 83–84, *post.*
[4] [1908] A. C. 16; [1904-7] All E. R. Rep. 244, H. L.
[5] (1834), 1 Bing. N. C. 29.

7th November, instead of proceeding direct to St. Michaels she went on an intermediate voyage to Oporto, and returned later to Portsmouth, from where she finally sailed for St. Michaels on 6th December. *Held,* that the shipowner was liable to the charterer for breach of the implied undertaking that the voyage should be commenced within a reasonable time.

Further, in the case of a consecutive voyage charter-party the shipowner's obligation to proceed with despatch applies to every voyage made under it.[1]

If he fails to carry out this undertaking, the shipper's remedy depends upon whether the failure is such as to frustrate the venture as a commercial enterprise. If it is, he may repudiate the contract;[2] if it is not, he has an action for damages for the delay, but to this the plea of excepted perils is a good answer.[3]

It should be noted that this rule of law is distinct from the doctrine which we shall notice,[4] whereby a contract of affreightment may be dissolved by implication on account of the frustration of the adventure due to unforeseen events *totally unconnected with any breach* of the contract by either party. For the effect of the frustration is different in the two cases: where there has been a breach of the implied undertaking of reasonable despatch resulting in frustration, only the shipper is released from his obligations; but where the frustration is independent of any breach, *e.g.* where war subsequently breaks out, the release is mutual.

The one rule is a particular application of the general principle that a failure to perform his part of the contract by one contractor may, according to the circumstances, be of so serious a nature as to justify the other contractor in treating it as a repudiation of the entire contract; the other rule is a modification[5] of an ancient and rigorous doctrine which excluded the grafting upon a contract, under any circumstances, of an exception which would operate as an excuse for its non-performance.[6]

---

[1] *Suisse Atlantique Société d'Armement Maritime S.A.* v. *N.V. Rotterdamsche Kolen Centrale,* [1966] 2 All E. R. 61; [1967] 1 A. C. 361, H. L.

[2] *Freeman* v. *Taylor* (1831), 1 L. J. C. P. 26.

[3] *Barker* v. *M'Andrew* (1865), 18 C. B. N. S. 759.

[4] See pp. 47–54, *post.*

[5] First clearly stated in *Taylor* v. *Caldwell* (1863), 3 B. & S. 826.

[6] The rule in *Paradine* v. *Jane* (1647), Aleyn. 26.

(3) *No deviation.* It is an implied condition precedent in every voyage charter-party that the ship shall proceed on the voyage without departure from her proper course. If the route is not prescribed in the contract, the proper course is the ordinary trade route. "If no evidence be given, that route is presumed to be the direct geographical route, but ... evidence may always be given to show what the usual route is, unless a specific route be prescribed by the charter-party or bill of lading. .... In some cases there may be more than one usual route."[1]

It must, however, be observed that "the essence of deviation is the voluntary substitution of another voyage for the contract voyage": hence, where the master, who was ill, unintentionally steered a wrong course, it was *held* that there had been no deviation.[2]

When deviation is justified at Common Law. In certain cases deviation will be justified, apart from any express terms of the contract, and will, therefore, not expose the shipowner to liability. These are:

(1) For purposes necessary for the prosecution of the voyage or for the safety of the adventure.

One of the main duties of the master is to use all reasonable care to bring the adventure to a successful conclusion, protecting the ship and cargo from undue risks, as agent for the shipowner. Considerable latitude is thus given to him in the matter of taking the ship off her proper course. If the ship sustains such damage that repairs are necessary, he must put into the nearest port at which such repairs can be effected.[3] The same doctrine applies in the case of any other grave peril threatening the ship *or* her cargo,[4] *e.g.* pirates, hurricanes, icebergs or heavy fog.

The deviation is still justified, even though necessitated by the ship's unseaworthiness at the commencement of the

---

[1] *Reardon Smith Lines, Ltd.* v. *Black Sea and Baltic General Insurance Co., Ltd., The Indian City,* [1939] 3 All E. R. 444, at p. 457, *per* Lord PORTER; [1939] A. C. 562, at p. 584.

[2] *Rio Tinto Co.* v. *Seed Shipping Co.* (1926), 42 T. L. R. 381.

[3] *James Phelps & Co.* v. *Hill,* [1891] 1 Q. B. 605.

[4] *The Teutonia* (1872), L. R. 4 P. C. 171.

voyage, if in fact it would be dangerous to keep her at sea without effecting such repairs.[1]

Thus, in *Kish* v. *Taylor*,[2]

The master of a vessel took on board an excessive load of deck cargo to such an extent that she was rendered unseaworthy. As a result of the unseaworthiness she was obliged to deviate from her normal route in order to proceed to a port for repairs. *Held*, that the deviation was justifiable.

Lord ATKINSON said:[3]

"Must the master of every ship be left in this dilemma, that whenever, by his own culpable act, or a breach of contract by his owner, he finds his ship in a perilous position, he must continue on his voyage at all hazards, or only seek safety under the penalty of forfeiting the contract of affreightment? Nothing could, it would appear to me, tend more to increase the dangers to which life and property are exposed at sea than to hold that the law of England obliged the master of a merchant ship to choose between such alternatives."

(2) To save human life.

Deviation to save human life is always justified, but not to save property, unless this is expressly stipulated. Thus, in *Scaramanga* v. *Stamp*,[4]

where a ship deviated to assist another in distress, but instead of merely saving the crew, attempted to earn salvage by towing the distressed vessel into port, and, in the attempt, went ashore herself and was lost with her cargo, it was *held* that the shipowner was liable for the loss of the cargo although it was partly caused by "perils of the sea" which were excepted by the charter.

Express clauses permitting deviation. The terms of the contract often give the shipowner the right to call at ports off the ordinary trade route. Vague general terms, however, will not be taken to confer an unlimited right to turn aside.

A clause[5] often gives liberty to the vessel to tow or assist vessels, or both, in all situations, and also to deviate for the purpose of

---

[1] *Kish* v. *Taylor*, [1912] A. C. 604. Lord PORTER expressed the opinion that the rule does not apply if the owners *knew* of the vessel's state on sailing: *Monarch S.S. Co., Ltd.* v. *A/B Karlshamns Oljefabriker*, [1949] 1 All E. R. 1, at p. 5. This, with respect, seems open to question.

[2] *Supra.*

[3] [1912] A. C., at pp. 618–19.

[4] (1880), 5 C. P. D. 295.

[5] For an example, see the "Gencon" charter-party, clause 10 (Appendix B).

saving life or property, or both, and to comply with any orders given by the government of the nation under whose flag she sails or by any other government.[1]

The effect of unjustifiable deviation. In a leading case, Lord ATKIN observed:[2]

"I venture to think that the true view is that the departure from the voyage contracted to be made is a breach by the shipowner of his contract, a breach of such a serious character that, however slight the deviation, the other party to the contract is entitled to treat it as going to the root of the contract, and to declare himself as no longer bound by any of the contract terms. . . . If this view be correct, then the breach by deviation does not automatically cancel the express contract, otherwise the shipowner by his own wrong can get rid of his own contract."

The charterer, however, can elect to treat the contract as subsisting, and if he does this with knowledge of his rights, he must, in accordance with the general law of contract, be held bound.[3] But there must be acts which plainly show that he intended to treat the contract as still binding.[4]

Where there has been unjustifiable deviation, the shipowner cannot rely on the exception clauses in the charter-party, and is then only entitled to the benefit of the exceptions available to a common carrier, *e.g.* Act of God, loss by the Queen's Enemies, if he can prove that the loss would have occurred even if no deviation had taken place.[5]

Further, the shipowner cannot claim the contractual rate of freight payable under the charter-party, but may be entitled to a

---

[1] See *Luigi Monta of Genoa* v. *Cechofracht Co.*, [1956] 2 All E. R. 769; [1956] 2 Q. B. 552.

[2] *Hain S.S. Co., Ltd.* v. *Tate and Lyle, Ltd.*, [1936] 2 All E. R. 597, H. L., at p. 601.

[3] *Hain S.S. Co., Ltd.* v. *Tate and Lyle, Ltd.* (*supra*). This doctrine has been applied to a case where, upon the true construction of the charter-party, there was one indivisible contract for "two consecutive voyages": deviation on the first voyage was held to have entitled the charterers to elect to treat the entire contract as repudiated and so to free themselves from liability in respect of the second voyage. See *Re An Arbitration between Compagnie Primera de Navagaziona de Panama and Compania Arrendataria de Monopolio de Petroleos S.A. The Yolanda*, [1939] 4 All E. R. 81; [1940] 1 K. B. 362.

[4] *Hain S.S. Co., Ltd.* v. *Tate and Lyle, Ltd.* (*supra*).

[5] *James Morrison & Co., Ltd.* v. *Shaw, Savill and Albion Co., Ltd.*, [1916] 2 K. B. 783.

reasonable sum if the goods are carried to their destination safely.[1] Again, he cannot claim a general average contribution from the charterer unless the breach of contract by the deviation has been waived.[2]

(B) *On the part of the Charterer Not to Ship Dangerous Goods*

The charterer impliedly undertakes that he will not ship dangerous goods.[3] Even if the master accepts them on board, the charterer will be liable for any loss or damage they may cause,[4] unless the master has acted unreasonably in carrying them.[5]

Sometimes charter-parties expressly prohibit the loading of dangerous goods, but sometimes a charterer is entitled by an express term to load them provided that due notice is given to the master.

Goods may be "dangerous" not merely by reason of the fact that they may endanger the safety of the vessel, *e.g.* (i) iron ore concentrate with a high moisture content;[6] (ii) copper concentrate,[7] but also because they are liable to cause her to be detained.

Thus, in *Mitchell, Cotts & Co.* v. *Steel Brothers & Co., Ltd.*[8]

The charterers loaded a cargo of rice on board a vessel, and sent her to a port where they knew that it could not be discharged without the permission of the British Government. They did not inform the shipowners of this. Permission was refused and the ship was delayed. *Held*, that the charterers were liable for damages for the delay.

---

[1] *Hain S.S. Co., Ltd.* v. *Tate and Lyle, Ltd. (supra).*
[2] *Ibid.*
[3] For the meaning of "dangerous goods", see *infra.*
[4] *Chandris* v. *Isbrandtsen-Moller*, [1950] 1 All E. R. 768; [1951] 1 K. B. 240.
[5] *Compania Naviera Maropan S/A* v. *Bowaters Lloyd Pulp and Paper Mills*, [1955] 2 All E. R. 241; [1955] 2 Q. B. 68, C. A. (similar principle applied concerning safe port).
[6] *Micada Compania Naviera S.A.* v. *Texim*, [1968] 2 Lloyd's Rep. 57, Q. B. D. (Commercial Court). For the evidence on this point, see the judgment of DONALDSON, J., *ibid.*, at pp. 60, 62.
[7] *Heath Steele Mines, Ltd.* v. *The "Erwin Schroder"*, [1969] 1 Lloyd's Rep. 370, Exchequer Court of Canada., Nova Scotia Admiralty District. For the evidence on this point, see the judgment of POTTIER, J., *ibid.*, at p. 373.
[8] [1916] 2 K. B. 610; [1916–17] All E. R. Rep. 578.

Statutory provisions concerning dangerous goods. The following statutes make provision with regard to dangerous goods:

(1) The Merchant Shipping Act 1894, ss. 446–50.[1] By s. 446 a consignor of dangerous goods must indicate the nature of the goods on the outside of the packages, and he must give notice of the nature of the goods to the master or owner of the vessel at or before the time of shipment.

(2) The Merchant Shipping (Safety Convention) Act 1949, s. 23 enables rules to be made by the Secretary of State for the Environment for regulating in the interests of safety the carriage of dangerous goods.[2] Goods declared by the rules to be dangerous are deemed to be "dangerous goods" for the purposes of the 1894 Act.

(3) The Explosive Substances Act 1883, s. 8 enables the master or owner of a vessel to search the cargo for dangerous goods, if he has reasonable grounds for suspecting that such goods are concealed on board.

TIME CHARTER-PARTIES

(A) The Principal Clauses in Time Charter-parties

Although the parties are entitled to make their contract in any manner that they like, it is usual for them to adopt one of the forms of time charter-party approved by the Documentary Committee of the Chamber of Shipping of the United Kingdom, *e.g.* the "Transitime" form or the "Baltime" form,[3] and then amend it as they think fit.

In general the following provisions are found in most time charter-parties:

---

[1] See Appendix D, *post.*

[2] The relevant rules are the Merchant Shipping (Dangerous Goods) Rules, 1965, S. I. 1965, No. 1067, as amended by the Merchant Shipping (Dangerous Goods) (Amendment) Rules, 1968, S. I. 1968, No. 322, the Merchant Shipping (Dangerous Goods) (Amendment) Rules 1972, S. I. 1972, No. 666 and by the Hovercraft (Application of Enactments) Order 1972, S. I. 1972, No. 971.

[3] The "Baltime" form is reproduced in Appendix B by the courtesy of the Baltic and International Maritime Conference.

(1) The shipowner agrees to provide and pay for the insurance of a vessel[1] for a period of time[2], and states her size, speed, fuel consumption, and amount of fuel on board;

(2) the port of delivery and the time of delivery of the vessel to the charterer are stated;

(3) The charterer agrees to engage only in lawful trades and carry lawful merchandise,[3] and only use good and safe ports where the vessel can "safely lie always afloat"[4];

(4) the shipowner agrees to pay for the crew's wages, for the vessel's insurance and her stores, and promises to maintain her in a thoroughly efficient state;[5]

(5) the charterer agrees to provide and pay for fuel, to pay dock

---

[1] A clause sometimes provides that the shipowner is entitled to substitute another vessel during the currency of the charter-party: *Niarchos (London), Ltd.* v. *Shell Tankers, Ltd.*, [1961] 2 Lloyd's Rep. 496. See also *S.A. Maritime et Commerciale of Geneva* v. *Anglo-Iranian Oil Co., Ltd.*, [1954] 1 All E. R. 529; [1954] 1 W. L. R. 492, C. A. (charter-party for series of voyages). For a case where the shipowners agreed to insure a vessel against war risks and the charterers were to reimburse them if an extra premium were paid in respect of such risks, see *World Magnate Shipping Ltd.* v. *Rederi A/B Soya*, [1975] 2 Lloyd's Rep. 498, Q. B. D. (Commercial Court).

[2] Sometimes the period of time is at the charterers' option as in *Empresa Cubana de Fletes* v. *Aviation and Shipping Co., Ltd.*, [1969] 2 Lloyd's Rep. 257, Q. B. D. (Commercial Court) ("24/30 calendar months in charterers' option declarable at the end of the 22nd month with a margin of 15 days more or less at charterers' option from the time the vessel is delivered"), where it was held that the period of 22 months after which the option was to be declared was not affected by another clause in the charter-party concerning time lost through circumstances beyond the charterers' control. (See the judgment of ROSKILL, J., *ibid.*, at p. 261). Sometimes the period is expressed in a different way, e.g. "the period necessary to perform one time charter trip via safe port(s) East Coast Canada within [specified] trading limits": *Segovia Compagnia Naviera S.A.* v. *R. Pagnan and Fratelli: The "Aragon"*, [1975] 2 Lloyd's Rep. 216, Q. B. D. (Commercial Court).

[3] See p. 120, *post*.

[4] This phrase is concerned exclusively with the marine characteristics of the loading or discharging place and requires that the vessel shall at all times be water-borne and shall be able to remain there without risk of loss or damage from wind, weather or other craft which are properly navigated. Thus, a place which dries out or one in which she might in certain winds or tides lie across the fairway would not be within the requirements of the clause: *Vardinoyannis* v. *Egyptian General Petroleum Corporation, The "Evaggelos Th."*, [1971] 2 Lloyd's Rep. 200, Q. B. (Commercial Court), at p. 204 (*per* DONALDSON J.). As to "safe ports", see pp. 107-108, *post*.

[5] See p. 30, *post*.

and harbour dues, and arrange and pay for loading and discharge;

(6) the charterer agrees to pay a named sum for the hire of the vessel;[1]

(7) a clause concerning the redelivery of the vessel;[2]

(8) certain events are stated on the occurrence of which hire will cease to be payable;[3]

(9) the master is to be under the orders of the charterer;[4]

(10) a list of "excepted perils";[5]

(11) the charterer agrees to indemnify the shipowner for loss or damage to the vessel by careless loading or discharge;[6]

(12) a cancelling clause;[7]

(13) a clause incorporates the York-Antwerp Rules 1974 relating to general average;[8]

(14) an arbitration clause;

(15) a clause concerning payment of commission to the ship-broker for negotiating the charter-party;[9]

(16) a war clause.[10]

Some of the above clauses will now be examined in more detail.

Seaworthiness of Vessel

A clause in a charter-party often states:

"The Owners let, and the Charterers hire the Vessel . . . she being in every way fitted for ordinary cargo service."[11]

---

[1] See p. 30, *post.*   [2] See pp. 40–42, *post.*
[3] See pp. 33–35, *post.*   [4] See pp. 35–38, *post.*
[5] See pp. 38–39, *post.*   [6] See p. 39, *post.*
[7] See pp. 111–112, *post.*   [8] See Chapter 9, post.

[9] See, *e.g., Les Affreteurs Réunis Societe Anonyme* v. *Leopold Walford* (*London*), *Ltd.,* [1919] A. C. 801; *Christie and Vesey* v. *Maatschappij Tot Exploitatie van Schepen en Andere Zaken, The Helvetia,* [1960] 1 Lloyd's Rep. 540.

[10] See, *e.g., Ocean Tramp Tankers Corporation* v. *V/O Sovfracht,* [1964] 1 All E. R. 161; [1964] 2 Q. B. 226, C. A., where a vessel was trapped in the Suez Canal during the Suez crisis of 1956.

[11] See, *e.g.,* "Baltime 1939" form, clause 1 (Appendix B). Sometimes, however, there is no absolute duty to provide a seaworthy vessel, for the clause may state: "Vessel on delivery shall be, in so far as due diligence can make her so, seaworthy, tight, staunch, strong and in every way suitable . . .". See, *e.g. United States of America* v. *The "Marilena P" and Marilena Compania Naviera S.A.,* [1969] 2 Lloyd's Rep. 641, U.S. Court of Appeals, Fourth Circuit.

A vessel is not in every way fitted for cargo service if at the time of her delivery to the charterers her engine room staff is incompetent and inadequate, and accordingly she is unseaworthy.[1]

Again, shipowners were held to be in breach of the clause set out above if at the time of the delivery of the vessel to the charterers she had not a deratisation certificate from the port health authorities or a deratisation exemption certificate, for without the certificate she could not trade as the charter-party provided or for the contemplated purpose.[2]

If the vessel is delivered in a damaged condition, the evidence may show that the charterers have waived any claim which they may have against the shipowners.[3]

Use of Safe Ports Only

A usual clause states :[4]

"The vessel to be employed . . . between good and safe ports or places where she can safely lie always afloat . ".

If the charterer sends a vessel to an unsafe port,[5] and she is damaged as a result, he will have to indemnify the shipowner. Thus, in *Grace (G. W.) & Co., Ltd.* v. *General Steam Navigation Co., Ltd.,*[6]

a vessel under time charter was directed to Hamburg. The master complied with the charterer's order and she was damaged by ice in the approaches to the port. *Held*, the charterer was liable for such damage.

---

[1] *Hong Kong Fir Shipping Co., Ltd.* v. *Kawasaki Kisen Kaisha, Ltd.*, [1962] 1 All E. R. 474; [1962] 2 Q. B. 26, C. A.

[2] *Cheikh Boutros Selim El-Khoury* v. *Ceylon Shipping Lines, Ltd.* ; *The "Madeleine,"* [1967] 2 Lloyd's Rep. 224.

[3] See *e.g. Marbienes Compania Naviera S.A.* v. *Ferrostal A.G. : The "Democritos"*, [1975] 1 Lloyd's Rep. 386, Q. B. D. (Commercial Court), where the case was remitted to the arbitrators so that they could consider whether there had been a waiver by the charterers. (See the judgment of KERR, J., *ibid.*, at p. 398.)

[4] "Baltime 1939" form, clause 2. See Appendix B, p. 251, *post*. Sometimes a charter-party states that the wharf or place of loading or discharge must be safe. See *e.g. Venore Transportation Co.* v. *Oswego Shipping Corporation; Banco do Brasil (Third Party): The "Santore"*, [1974] 2 Lloyd's Rep. 236, U.S. Court of Appeals, Second Circuit, where a berth at which there was only one pontoon was held to be unsafe (see the judgment of LUMBARD, Ct. J., *ibid.*, at p. 239).

[5] See pp. 125–126, *post*.

[6] [1950] 1 All E. R. 201; [1950] 2 K. B. 383; *Lensen Shipping Co.* v. *Anglo-Soviet Shipping Co.* (1935), 40 Com. Cas. 320.

Again, in *Tage Berglund* v. *Montoro Shipping Corporation, Ltd.: The "Dagmar"*,[1]

a vessel was directed to Cape Chat, Quebec. While she was loading there the wind and swell increased and she was driven aground. The ship-owners claimed damages on the ground that the port was unsafe in that the pier gave no shelter from a northerly wind, that there was no means of communicating an adverse weather forecast to the vessel, and that the charterers had failed to warn the master of the approach or risk of bad weather.

Held, that the port was unsafe unless the vessel was warned (a) that she would receive no weather information from the shore and must rely on her own resources for obtaining weather forecasts; and (b) that in strong winds and seas the port was unsafe for her to remain in it. The action succeeded because the charterers had given warning (b) but not (a), and had passed on no weather forecasts.[2]

But if the master has acted unreasonably, *e.g.* knowing of the danger in the port has still proceeded to enter it, and damage results, the charterer will not be liable.[3]

Where the charter-party requires the vessel to use safe ports only, the port must not only be safe when she is ordered to it but safe when she arrives there although a temporary obstacle which will merely involve her in non-frustrating delay will not render the port unsafe.[4] In judging the safety of a port at the time of nomination and of arrival account must be taken of reasonably foreseeable changes in conditions.[5]

Sometimes the charter-party specifies that the vessel must only use safe ports within a certain area, *e.g.* "vessel to perform one time charter trip via safe port(s) East Coast Canada within . . .

---

[1] [1968] 2 Lloyd's Rep. 563, Q. B. D. (Commercial Court).

[2] See the judgment of MOCATTA, J., *ibid.*, at p. 586.

[3] *Grace (G. W.) & Co., Ltd.* v. *General Steam Navigation Co., Ltd. (supra).* The same principle is applied in the case of voyage charter-parties: *Compania Naviera Maropan S/A* v. *Bowaters Lloyd Pulp and Paper Mills*, [1955] 2 All E. R. 241; [1955] 2 Q. B. 68, C. A.; *Reardon Smith Line, Ltd.* v. *Australian Wheat Board*, [1956] 1 All E. R. 456; [1956] A. C. 266, P. C.

[4] *Vardinoyannis* v. *Egyptian General Petroleum Corporation: The "Evaggelos Th."*, [1971] 2 Lloyd's Rep. 200, Q. B. (Commercial Court), at p. 204 (*per* DONALDSON, J.).

[5] *Ibid.*, at p. 206 (*per* DONALDSON, J.).

trading limits", the trading limits being defined as "always within Institute Warranty Limits East Coast Canada, U.S.A. East of Panama Canal, U.K. Continent Gibraltar-Hamburg Range, Mediterranean . . .".[1]

Detention of Vessel

A usual clause provides that:

"In the event of the Vessel being driven into port or to anchorage through stress of weather, trading to shallow harbours or to rivers or ports with bars or suffering an accident to her cargo, any detention of the Vessel and/or expenses resulting from such detention is to be for the Charterers' account even if such detention and/or expenses, or the cause by reason of which either is incurred, be due to, or be contributed to by, the negligence of the Owners' servants."[2]

The word "bars" in the above clause applies to rivers and ports, *i.e.* the clause relates to trading to rivers with bars and to trading to ports with bars.[3]

The River Plate is no less a river for the purpose of the clause because it is made up of the River Uruguay and the River Parana.[4]

The Martin Garcia Bar in the River Plate is a "bar", and the mere existence of a passageway or channel cut by artificial means through the barrier of sand or silt or whatever else the bar may be made of, does not prevent the bar from being a bar.[5]

To render the charterers liable under the clause, the shipowners must show that the proximate cause of detention or expense was trading to a river with a bar or to a port with a bar. It is not enough

---

[1] *Segovia Compagnia Naviera S.A.* v. *R. Pagnan and Fratelli : The "Aragon"*, [1975] 2 Lloyd's Rep. 216, Q. B. D. (Commercial Court), where it was held that the expression "U.S.A. East of Panama Canal" meant that part of the U.S.A. which could be reached from Europe westbound without passing through the Panama Canal or going round Cape Horn. (See the judgment of DONALDSON, J., *ibid.*, at p. 222.)

[2] "Baltime 1939" form, clause 11 (B). See Appendix B, p. 252, *post.*

[3] *Court Line, Ltd.* v. *Finelvet, A.-G. : The Jevington Court,* [1966] 1 Lloyd's Rep. 683, at p. 691 (*per* ROSKILL, J.).

[4] *Ibid.,* at p. 690 (*per* ROSKILL, J.).

[5] *Ibid.,* at p. 695 (*per* ROSKILL, J.).

that the charterers should be trading geographically and in point of time to a river with a bar or to a port with a bar.[1]

Maintenance of Vessel in an Efficient State

Under the usual type of clause[2] the shipowner is not under a duty to see that the vessel is absolutely fit at all periods of her service under the charter-party, but he must take reasonable steps to rectify defects as soon as they are brought to his notice.[3] But if he does not keep the vessel in an efficient state, this only entitles the charterer to sue him for damages, and not to repudiate the charter-party,[4] though sometimes the failure to remedy the defect within a reasonable time may amount to frustration of the contract.[5]

The Payment of Hire

The charter-party usually states the amount of hire which must be paid, *e.g.*

"The charterers to pay as hire £2.50 per deadweight ton."

Sometimes, however, the rate is calculated according to a standard scale such as the International Tanker Nominal Freight Scale. Thus, in the case of a consecutive voyage charter-party a clause stated that the hire was to be calculated "in accordance

---

[1] *Ibid.*, at p. 697 (*per* ROSKILL, J.).

[2] See "Baltime 1939" form, clause 3. See Appendix B, p. 251, *post*. In *Splosna Plovba of Piran* v. *Agrelak S.S. Corporation: The "Bela Krajina"*,]1975] 1 Lloyd's Rep. 139, Q. B. D. (Commercial Court) the shipowners were held not to have broken the obligation to keep the vessel in a thoroughly efficient state, for it had not been shown that they had failed to ensure that her holds were ready to receive a cargo of grain.

[3] *Tynedale S.S. Co.* v. *Anglo-Soviet Shipping Co.*, [1936] 1 All E. R. 389, C. A.

[4] *Hong Kong Fir Shipping Co., Ltd.* v. *Kawasaki Kisen Kaisha, Ltd.*, [1962] 1 All E. R. 474; [1962] 2 Q. B. 26, C. A.

[5] *Ibid.* As to frustration, see pp. 47–54, *post*.

with the dollar rates provided in the International Tanker Nominal Freight Scale minus 31¼ per cent".[1]

A clause in a charter-party sometimes provides that the hire may be increased or decreased if there is an alteration in the wages paid to the crew.[2] Further, there may be a clause to the effect that hire will be reduced if the vessel cannot accommodate all the goods intended to be shipped.[3]

The terms of the contract usually provide that hire must be paid monthly in advance, and in cash. If, however, the shipowner has regularly accepted payment by cheque, he is not entitled to withdraw the vessel from the service of the charterer for not paying the next instalment in cash, unless he first gives him notice that payment must once again be made in this way.[4] Although the contract usually gives the shipowner the right to withdraw the vessel for non-payment of hire, and determine the charter-party,

---

[1] *Achille Lauro fuo Gioacchino & C* v. *Total Societa Italiana per Azioni*, [1969] 2 Lloyd's Rep, 65, C. A., where the question was whether hire was to be based on a national ballast voyage via the Cape of Good Hope or via the Suez Canal; *Agenor Shipping Co., Ltd.* v. *Société des Petroles Miroline*, [1968] 2 Lloyd's Rep. 359, Q. B. D., where the question was whether the accounting currency was the Pound Sterling or the United States Dollar; *Total Societa Italiana per Azioni* v. *Liberian Transocean Navigation Corp.: The "Alexandra I"*, [1972] 1 Lloyd's Rep. 399, C. A., where a similar question arose in the case of a consecutive voyage charter-party; *"Yoho Maru" (Owners)* v. *Agip S.p.a. c/o S.N.A.M. S.p.a.*, [1973] 1 Lloyd's Rep. 409, Q. B. D., where the question in a consecutive voyage charter-party was whether the 1971 or the 1972 "Worldscale" schedule of rates should be applied; *Marmara Transport A/S* v. *Mobil Tankers S.A.: The "Mersin"*, [1973] 1 Lloyd's Rep. 532, Q.B.D. (Commercial Court), which concerned an amendment to the "Intascale" rate after a consecutive voyage charter-party had been entered into.

[2] *W. Bruns & Co. of Hamburg* v. *Standard Fruit and S.S. Co. of New Orleans: The "Brunsrode"*, [1975] 2 Lloyd's Rep. 74, Q. B. D. (Commercial Court).

[3] *Oceanic Freighters Corporation* v. *M.V. Libyaville Reederei und Schiffahrts G.m.b.H.: The "Libyaville"*, [1975] 1 Lloyd's Rep. 537, Q. B. D. (Commercial Court), where there was a dispute as to the number of trailers a "roll-on roll-off" vessel could carry on her trailer deck, and a new clause was added to the charter-party to the effect that if she was only able to accommodate 16 trailers (as against 17), the daily hire was to be reduced by 1½ per cent.

[4] *A/S Tankexpress* v. *Compagnie Financière Belge des Petroles S.A.*, [1948] 2 All E. R. 939; [1949] A. C. 76, H. L.; *Zim Israel Navigation Co. Ltd.* v. *Effy Shipping Corporation: The "Effy"*, [1972] 1 Lloyd's Rep. 18, Q. B. D. (Commercial Court).

he should exercise this right quickly, because if he does not, he may be deemed to have waived his right to do so.[1]

A right to withdraw the vessel from the service of the charterers "in default of payment of hire" is lost if payment is tendered before notice of withdrawal is communicated to the charterers even if the tender is late and is refused by the shipowners.

Thus, in *Empresa Cubana de Fletes* v. *Lagonisi Shipping Co., Ltd. : The "Georgios C"*,[2]

A charter-party in "Baltime 1939" form stated that "In default of payment of hire the owners have the right of withdrawing the vessel from the service of the charterers . . ." The charterers should have paid the hire on October 2, 1964. On October 5 at 9.35 a.m. the shipowners radioed the master stating "Charterers did not pay hire therefore ship withdrawn", but did not inform the charterers. The charterers paid the hire at 2.50 p.m. At 5.45 p.m. the shipowners cabled them saying that the vessel was withdrawn. *Held*, that the purported withdrawal was ineffective because it had not been communicated[3] to the charterers before the hire was paid. The words "in default of payment" meant "in default of payment and so long as default continues".

But a right to withdraw the vessel "failing the punctual and regular payment of the hire" cannot be defeated by a late tender of the hire which is refused by the shipowners because such a tender would still leave a situation in which they could say that there had been a default in punctual payment.[4] On the other hand, if the shipowners or their agents accept the tender before the charterers receive notice of withdrawal, the right to withdraw the vessel is waived.[5]

A clause in a charter-party sometimes states that where there is any failure to make regular and punctual payment, the ship-

---

[1] *Nova Scotia Steel Co.* v. *Sutherland S.S. Co.* (1899), 5 Com. Cas. 106.

[2] [1971] 1 Lloyd's Rep. 7, C. A.

[3] Lord DENNING, M. R., however, said *obiter* (*ibid.*, at p. 14) that in exceptional cases communication of withdrawal might be excused, *e.g.* where the charterer had disappeared.

[4] *Tenax S.S. Co., Ltd.* v. *The "Brimnes" (Owners): The "Brimnes"*, [1974] 2 Lloyd's Rep. 241, C. A.

[5] *Ibid.*: *Mardorf Peach & Co., Ltd.* v. *Attica Sea Carriers Corporation of Liberia: The "Laconia"* (1976), *Times*, February 27, C. A.; *Oceanic Freighters Corporation* v. *M.V. Libyaville Reederei und Schiffahrts G.m.b.H.: The "Libyaville"*, [1975] 1 Lloyd's Rep. 537, Q. B. D. (Commercial Court).

owners must give a number of days' written notice to rectify the failure. If no such notice is given, there is no right of withdrawal.[1]

Where hire is payable in advance at so much per ton on the deadweight capacity of the vessel, there is an implied obligation on the shipowner to inform the charterer correctly as to the deadweight capacity.[2]

A cross-claim by the charterers cannot be set off against a claim by the shipowners for unpaid hire.[3]

Where hire remains unpaid, the Court may grant an ex parte application by the shipowners for an interim injunction to restrain the charterers from removing any of their assets out of the jurisdiction.[4]

The "Off-Hire" Clause

A usual clause[5] provides that:

"In the event of drydocking[6] or other necessary measures to maintain the efficiency of the vessel, deficiency of men or Owners' stores, breakdown of machinery, damage to hull or other accident, either hindering or

---

[1] *Oceanic Freighters Corporation* v. *M.V. Libyaville Reederei und Schiffahrts G.m.b.H.: The "Libyaville"* (*supra*), where MOCATTA, J., said (*ibid.*, at p. 554) that the clause showed a praiseworthy effort to reduce the technicalities inappropriate to a commercial relationship which so often arose in connection with the right to withdraw a ship under a time charter-party.

[2] *Kawasaki Kisen Kabushiki Kaisha* v. *Bantham Shipping Co., Ltd.*, [1938] 3 All E. R. 690; [1938] 2 K. B. 790.

[3] *Seven Seas Transportation, Ltd.* v. *Atlantic Shipping Co. S.A.*, [1975] 2 Lloyd's Rep. 188, Q. B. D. (Commercial Court), where DONALDSON, J., pointed out (*ibid.*, at p. 191) that if any alleged claim for breach of a time charter-party could, if subsequently proved, be set off against hire, there would be otal confusion as to when hire was overdue and a vessel could be withdrawn frotm the services of the charterer.

[4] *Nippon Yusen Kaisha* v. *G. and J. Karageorgis*, [1975] 2 Lloyd's Rep. 137, C. A.; *Mareva Compania Naviera S.A.* v. *International Baulkcarriers S.A.*, [1975] 2 Lloyd's Rep. 509, C. A.

[5] For similar clauses in American forms of charter-party, see *Heinrich C. Horn* v. *Cia de Navegacion Fruca S.A. and J.R. Atkins* (*Trading as Alabama Fruit and Produce Co.*), *The "Heinz Horn"*, [1970] 1 Lloyd's Rep. 191, U. S. Ct. of Appeals, Fifth Circuit; *United States of America* v. *The "Marilena P" and Marilena Compania Naviera S.A.*, [1969] 2 Lloyd's Rep. 641, U. S. Ct. of Appeals, Fourth Circuit.

[6] For a drydocking clause in a tanker time charter-party, see *A.K. Fernstroms Rederi* v. *Transportes Maritimos Internacionals, Ltda.*, [1960] 1 Lloyd's Rep. 669.

preventing the working of the vessel and continuing for more than 24 consecutive hours, no hire to be paid in respect of any time lost thereby during the period in which the vessel is unable to perform the service immediately required."[1]

"Deficiency of men" relates to the numerical deficiency and not their unwillingness to work, *e.g.* refusal to proceed to sea in time of war except in convoy.[2] The word "men" means "crew", and not additional gunners needed to protect a merchant ship in time of war against attacks by enemy submarines.[3]

Although damage to the ship's machinery may have been sustained at an earlier date, it will not be held to have "broken down" within the meaning of the clause until it is necessary for her to proceed to port for repairs to be effected.[4]

"Or other accident" includes running aground in a river,[5] but if a crew refuses to sail except in convoy, that is not an "accident", and hire continues to be payable.[6]

Where a charter-party stated that hire was to be reduced in the event of a breakdown of a Munck crane or cranes, with which the vessel was fitted, "by reason of disablement", and the trolley of No. 1 crane fell overboard, and No. 2 and No. 3 cranes were taken out of service for examination, hire was held not to be payable in respect of No. 1 crane but was payable in respect of the other two cranes, for there had not been a breakdown "by reason of disablement".[7]

---

[1] "Baltime 1939" form, clause 11 (A). See Appendix B, p. 252, *post*. For a case where the charterers were held liable to pay overtime to the officers and crew even when the vessel was off-hire, see *Court Line, Ltd.* v. *Finelvet A.G., The Jevington Court,* [1966] 1 Lloyd's Rep. 683, at p. 698. For a case where the vessel was not off-hire on account of rust in her holds, see *Splosna Plovba of Piran* v. *Agrelak S.S. Corporation: The "Bela Krajina"*, [1975] 1 Lloyd's Rep. 139, Q. B. D. (Commercial Court).

[2] *Greek Government* v. *Minister of Transport, The Ilissos,* [1949] 1 All E.R. 171; [1949] 1 K. B. 525, C. A.

[3] *Radcliffe* v. *Compagnie Generale* (1918), 24 Com. Cas. 40, C. A.

[4] *Giertsen* v. *Turnbull* (1908), S. C. 1101.

[5] *S.S. Magnhild* v. *McIntyre Brothers & Co.,* [1921] 2 K. B. 97; [1921] All E. R. Rep. 359.

[6] *Greek Government* v. *Minister of Transport, The Ilissos,* [1948] 1 All E. R. 904; [1949] 1 K. B. 7 (at first instance).

[7] *Canadian Pacific (Bermuda), Ltd.* v. *Canadian Transport Co., Ltd.: The "H.R. Macmillan"*, [1974] 1 Lloyd's Rep. 311. (See the judgment of Lord DENNING, M.R., *ibid.*, at p. 314.)

"The working of the vessel" is considered to be hindered even if there is only a partial interference with her working. Thus, in *Hogarth* v. *Miller Brothers & Co.*,[1]

the vessel's high-pressure engine broke down. But she managed to get into port with the assistance of a tug and partly by using her own low-pressure engine. *Held*, hire was not payable during this period, because the working of the vessel had been hindered.

But as long as she is capable of performing the service immediately required, hire will continue to be payable, *e.g.* if the vessel is discharging and fit for that purpose, it does not matter if she was not in a fit state to put to sea.[2]

If the vessel breaks down and puts into port for repairs, hire will cease to be payable, but will become payable again when she is fit to sail again from that place, and not from the time when she reaches again the spot at which the breakdown occurred.[3]

A further clause[4] usually sets out the position if the vessel is lost, *e.g.*

"Should the vessel be lost or missing, hire to cease from the date when she was lost. If the date of loss cannot be ascertained, half hire to be paid from the date the vessel was last reported until the calculated date of arrival at the destination. Any hire paid in advance to be adjusted accordingly."[5]

The "Employment and Indemnity" Clause

A clause usually provides that:

"The master to be under the orders of the charterers as regards employment, agency or other arrangements. The charterers to indemnify the owners against all consequences or liabilities arising from the master . . . signing bills of lading or otherwise complying with such orders."[6]

Under the "employment and indemnity" clause the charterers

---

[1] [1891] A. C. 48, H. L.

[2] *Ibid.*, See further, *Court Line, Ltd.* v. *Finelvet A.-G., The Jevington Court*, [1966] 1 Lloyd's Rep. 683, where a vessel which was refloated after grounding still remained able to perform the service required, *viz.* to unload and reload the charterers' cargo. See the judgment of ROSKILL, J., *ibid.*, p. 698.

[3] *Vogemann* v. *Zanzibar S.S. Co.* (1902), 7 Com. Cas. 254, C. A., unless there is a clause to the contrary.

[4] "Baltime 1939" form, clause 16.

[5] For a case where a clause stated that "money paid in advance and not earned" was to be repaid to the charterers, see *Melling* v. *Minos Shipping Co., Ltd.: The "Oliva"*, [1972] 1 Lloyd's Rep. 458, Q. B. D. (Commercial Court).

[6] "Baltime 1939" form, clause 9. See Appendix B, *post*.

are entitled to present to the master for signature by him on behalf of the shipowners bills of lading which contain or evidence contracts between the shippers of goods and the shipowners provided that the bills of lading do not contain extraordinary terms or terms manifestly inconsistent with the charter-party. The master is obliged, on presentation to him of such bills of lading, to sign them on the shipowners' behalf.[1]

The charterers, however, may, instead of presenting the bills of lading to the master for signature by him on behalf of the shipowners, sign them themselves on the same behalf. In either case the signature binds the shipowners as principals to the contract contained in or evidenced by the bills of lading.[2]

In *Milburn* v. *Jamaica Fruit Importing and Trading Co. of London,*[3]

The master had signed bills of lading which omitted a clause excepting liability for negligence. The vessel was damaged and by reason of the absence of the clause, the shipowners could not obtain a general average contribution from the owners of the cargo. *Held,* since the charterers had ordered the master to sign the bills, they must indemnify the shipowners for the loss they had suffered in not recovering the contribution.

The shipowner, however, is entitled to an indemnity under the "Employment and Indemnity" clause only if he can show that there was a causal connexion between the loss and his compliance with the charterer's instructions.

Thus, in *The White Rose: A/B Helsingfors S.S. Co., Ltd.* v. *Rederiaktiebolaget Rex,*[4]

---

[1] *The "Berkshire"*, [1974] 1 Lloyd's Rep. 185, Q. B. D. (Admiralty Court) at p. 188 (*per* BRANDON, J.).

[2] *Ibid.,* at p. 188 (*per* BRANDON, J.).

[3] [1900] 2 Q. B. 540, C. A. See further *Gesellschaft Burgerlichen Rechts* v. *Stockholms Rederiaktiebolag Svea* (*S.S. Brabant*), [1966] 1 All E.R. 961; [1967] 1 Q. B. 588, where it was held that the shipowners could not claim an indemnity from the charterers in respect of damage to the owners of cargo caused by coal dust because the charter-party contained a clause stating: "The decks and holds and other spaces to be properly cleaned at Owners' risk and expense before loading."

[4] [1969] 2 Lloyd's Rep. 52, Q. B. (Commercial Court). See the judgment of DONALDSON, J., *ibid.,* at p. 59. See further, *Vardinoyannis* v. *Egyptian General Petroleum Corporation, The "Evaggelos Th.",* [1971] 2 Lloyd's Rep. 200, Q. B. (Commercial Court), where the question was whether the charterers were responsible for the loss of a vessel by shell fire at Suez in the war between Egypt and Israel in 1967.

Under a time charter-party containing the usual "Employment and Indemnity" clause the charterers ordered the vessel to Duluth, Minnesota to load a cargo and arranged for the loading to be carried out by a stevedoring company. One of the company's employees was injured when he fell through a 'tween deck hatch. The shipowners settled his claim against them, and now claimed an indemnity from the charterers under the "Employment and Indemnity" clause. It was proved that the accident was caused partly by the employee's failure to have regard for his own safety and partly because there was no fencing round the hatch, and that the charterers had not been negligent. *Held*, that the action failed, for, on the evidence, there was no causal connexion between the order to load the cargo and the loss incurred by the shipowners.

The meaning of the expression "to indemnify against all liabilities" is that it imposes the obligation to indemnify against the incurring of a liability, not the discharge of that liability by payment or determination of that liability by judicial process.[1]

Consequently the shipowner should make certain that his claim against the charterer is not statute-barred under the Limitation Act 1939, s. 2, which allows him 6 years in which to sue.[2]

Thus, in *Bosma* v. *Larsen*,[3]

A charter-party contained a clause stating that the charterers would indemnify the shipowners "against all liabilities arising from the master signing bills of lading". The bill of lading was signed by the master on the charterers' orders in respect of some fish carried from Iceland to Italy. The fish arrived damaged on July 17, 1956. On March 10, 1962, the cargo insurers were awarded damages against the shipowners by an Italian Court. On December 17, 1963, the shipowners paid the insurers under a compromise settlement. On March 12, 1965, the shipowners issued a writ claiming to be indemnified under the indemnity clause. *Held*, that the action was statute-barred. The cause of action arose on July 17, 1956. It was not dependent upon the determination of liability by the Italian Court or payment under the compromise settlement.

The clause set out above does not entitle the charterer to give orders concerning navigation. This remains the responsibility of the master, and he is the judge, *e.g.* of whether it is safe for his vessel to proceed to sea, even if directed to do so by the charterer.[4]

It is the duty of the master to act reasonably upon receipt of

---

[1] *Bosma* v. *Larsen*, [1966] 1 Lloyd's Rep. 22. See especially the judgment of McNair, J., *ibid.*, at p. 28.

[2] See p. 138, *post*.

[3] [1966] 1 Lloyd's Rep. 22.

[4] *Larrinaga S.S. Co., Ltd.* v. *R.*, [1945] 1 All E. R. 329; [1945] A. C. 246, H. L.

orders. Some orders are of their nature such that they would, if
the master were to act reasonably, require immediate compliance.
Others would require a great deal of thought and consideration
before a reasonable master would comply with them.[1]

Thus, in *Midwest Shipping Co., Ltd. Inc.* v. *D. I. Henry (Jute),
Ltd.,*[2]

A time charter-party stated that the master was to be "under the orders
and directions of the charterers as regards employment and agency".
The vessel sailed from Chalna on October 10. On October 12 he received
a cable from the charterers ordering him to return there. He informed
them that he could not cross the bar there until October 20, and continued
on his voyage. On October 13 he was again ordered to return and wait
until there was sufficient water over the bar. He still continued on the
voyage because the bills of lading showed that the vessel had sailed for
Singapore instead of for Durban and the port authorities might cause
difficulties if he returned. He pointed this out to the charterers, who on
October 14 again ordered him to return despite the fact that the bills of
lading stated that the vessel was bound for Singapore. The master
turned round and arrived at Chalna on October 19. The charterers
claimed that his failure to return when ordered constituted a breach of
the charter-party and that they were entitled to deduct 5 days while the
vessel was off-hire and the cost of 5 days' fuel which was wasted. *Held*,
that the action failed. There has been no breach of the charterparty,
for, on the evidence,[3] the master had acted reasonably.

If a shipowner threatens to send the vessel on a voyage which is
entirely inconsistent with the terms of the time charter-party, the
charterer is entitled to apply for an injunction to restrain him from
doing so.[4]

Excepted Perils

A usual clause states:

"The owners only to be responsible for delay in delivery of the vessel
or for delay during the currency of the charter and for loss or damage to
goods on board, if such delay or loss has been caused by want of due

---

[1] *Midwest Shipping Co., Ltd. Inc.* v. *D. I. Henry (Jute), Ltd.,* [1971] 1 Lloyd's
Rep. 375, Q. B. D. (Commercial Court), at p. 379 (*per* DONALDSON, J.).

[2] [1971] 1 Lloyd's Rep. 375, Q. B. D. (Commercial Court).

[3] Set out *ibid.,* at pp. 378-380.

[4] *Empresa Cubana de Fletes* v. *Lagonisi Shipping Co., Ltd.: The "Georgios C"*,
[1971] 1 Lloyd's Rep. 7, C. A. The same principle applies in the case of an
intermittent voyage charter-party: *Associated Portland Cement Manufacturers
Ltd.* v. *Teigland Shipping A/S: The "Oakworth"*, [1975] 1 Lloyd's Rep. 581,
C. A. (See the judgment of Lord DENNING, M.R., *ibid.,* at p. 583.)

diligence on the part of the owners or their manager in making the vessel seaworthy and fitted for the voyage or any other personal act or omission or default of the owners or their manager. The owners not to be responsible in any other case nor for damage or delay whatsoever and howsoever caused even if caused by the neglect or default of their servants. The owners not to be liable for loss or damage arising or resulting from strikes, lock-outs or stoppage or restraint of labour (including the master, officers or crew) whether partial or general."[1]

Such a clause exempts a shipowner from liability for additional expenses incurred by a charterer through the master refusing to discharge a part cargo at a nominated port, and the charterer is not entitled to withhold hire in respect of the time lost through the master's refusal.[2]

Careless Loading or Discharge

A clause usually provides that:

"The charterers to be responsible for loss or damage caused to the vessel or to the owners by goods being loaded contrary to the terms of the charter or by improper bunkering or loading, stowing or discharge of goods or any other improper or negligent act on their part or that of their servants."[3]

The indemnity afforded by this clause is wide enough to cover a reasonable settlement of a claim made by a stevedore against the shipowners in respect of injuries sustained by him in loading a vessel, but the charterers are under no liability to indemnify the shipowners unless there has been improper or careless loading on their part and this caused the injuries.[4]

---

[1] "Baltime 1939" form, clause 13. See Appendix B, *post.*

[2] *Nippon Yusen Kaisha* v. *Acme Shipping Corporation: The "Charalambos N. Pateras"*, [1971] 2 Lloyd's Rep. 42, Q.B.D. (Commercial Court). See the judgment of MOCATTA, J., *ibid.*, at p. 46; *affirmed*, [1972] 1 All E.R. 35, C.A.

[3] "Baltime 1939" form, clause 13. See Appendix B, *post.*

[4] *A/B Helsingfors S.S. Co., Ltd.* v. *Rederiaktiebolaget Rex: The "White Rose"*, [1969] 2 Lloyd's Rep. 52, Q. B. D. (Commercial Court). See the judgment of DONALDSON, J., *ibid.*, at p. 60. For a case where a charter-party provided that the charterers were to bear 1s. per gross registered ton "on any one cargo" of claims arising from improper stowage or short delivery, see *Clan Line Steamers, Ltd.* v. *Ove Skou Rederi A/S*, [1969] 2 Lloyd's Rep. 155, Q. B. D. (Commercial Court) where ROSKILL, J., held (*ibid.*, at p. 163) that the words "any one cargo" meant any one parcel of cargo identifiable by a separate bill of lading.

War Clause

A clause in a time charter-party often states:[1]

"The vessel, unless the consent of the owners be first obtained, not to be
ordered nor continue to any place or on any voyage nor be used on any
service which will bring her within a zone which is dangerous as the
result of any actual or threatened act of war, war hostilities, warlike
operations. . . ."

Whether a zone is dangerous is a matter of fact in each case.
Thus, in *Ocean Tramp Tankers Corporation* v. *V/O Sovfracht*,[2]

During the Suez Canal crisis of 1956 the charterers ordered a vessel,
which was chartered under a charter-party containing a war clause in the
form set out above, to Port Said and allowed her to remain in the Canal.
Held, that the zone was "dangerous"[3] and that the charterers were in
breach of the clause.

Redelivery

Usually the charterer has to redeliver the ship in the same good
order as when delivered (fair wear and tear excepted).[4] Often
there is a clause stating the amount of fuel-oil which must be left
in the vessel's bunkers on redelivery. The charterer is usually
required to give notice of the port at which redelivery will be made.

Where a vessel is redelivered to the shipowner and is not in
the same good order as when delivered due to the charterer's
fault, and repairs to her have to be effected in order to restore her
to that condition, the shipowner can claim the cost of the repairs
and any loss of profit whilst she is being repaired. But he cannot
claim hire for this period.[5]

---

[1] See, *e.g.*, "Baltime 1939" form, clause 21 (Appendix B).

[2] [1963] 2 Lloyd's Rep. 381, C. A.

[3] The evidence on this point is set out *ibid.*, at pp. 387–8.

[4] *Chellew Navigation Co.* v. *A. R. Appelquist Kolimport A.G.* (1933), 38 Com.
Cas. 218. Breach of a similar clause in a charter-party by demise was held to
entitle the shipowner to claim damages only, and not to insist on the charterer
effecting the repairs before redelivery: *Attica Sea Carriers Corporation* v.
Ferrostaal-Poseidon Bulk Reederei G.m.b.H., (1975) *Times*, November 25, C. A.

[5] *Wye Shipping Co.* v. *Compagnie Paris-Orleans*, [1922] 1 K. B. 617. See
also *Attica Sea Carriers Corporation* v. *Ferrostaal-Poseidon Bulk Reederei
G.m.b.H.* (*supra*), where the shipowners' remedy where the vessel was let out
under a demise charter-party and redelivered in bad condition lay in damages
only, and they could claim hire until the repairs were effected.

If the charterer sends the vessel on her last voyage at a time when there is no expectation that she will be redelivered within a reasonable time of the end of the period of the charter-party, and she is, in fact, redelivered late, he is guilty of a breach of contract.[1]

When a charter-party is for a stated period, *e.g.* 3 or 6 months, without any express margin or allowance, the Court may imply a reasonable margin or allowance because it is impossible for anyone to calculate exactly the day on which the last voyage may end.[2] But it is open to the parties to provide that there is to be no margin or allowance.[3] It is also open to them to fix expressly what the margin or allowance will be, and then the vessel must be redelivered within the permitted margin or allowance.[4]

If the charterer sends the vessel on a voyage which it is reasonably expected will be completed by the end of the charter period, the shipowners must obey the directions. If she is delayed by causes for which neither party is responsible, hire is payable at the charter rate until redelivery even though the market rate may have gone up or down.[5]

Thus, in *London and Overseas Freighters, Ltd.* v. *Timber Shipping Co. S.A.*,[6]

A vessel was chartered "for 12 months 15 days more or less in charterers' option" from December 29, 1967. Discharge of her cargo was delayed by reason of strikes and she was not redelivered to the shipowners until April 24, 1969. The charterers contended that damages were the only remedy available to the shipowners, and should be assessed on the basis of the current market rate. *Held*, that the charterers were liable to pay the contractual rate of hire from December 29, 1968 until April 24, 1969.

---

[1] *Alma Shipping Corporation of Monrovia* v. *Mantovani: The "Dione"*, [1975] 1 Lloyd's Rep. 115, C. A.: *Marbienes Compania Naviera S.A.* v. *Ferrostaal A.G.: The "Democritos"*, [1975] 1 Lloyd's Rep. 386, Q. B. D. (Commercial Court); affirmed (1976) *Times*, January 27, C. A.; *Skibsaktieselskapet Snefonn, Skibsaksjeselskapet Bergehus and Sig. Bergesen D. Y. & Co.* v. *Kawasaki Kisen Kaisha, Ltd.: The "Berge Tasta"*, [1975] 1 Lloyd's Rep. 422, Q. B. D. (Commercial Court), which concerned late redelivery of a vessel chartered under a consecutive voyage charter-party.

[2] *Alma Shipping Corporation of Monrovia* v. *Mantovani: The "Dione"* (*supra*) at p. 117 (*per* Lord DENNING, M.R.).

[3] *Ibid.*, at p. 117 (*per* Lord DENNING, M.R.).

[4] *Ibid.*, at p. 117 (*per* Lord DENNING, M.R.).

[5] *Ibid.*, at p. 117 (*per* Lord DENNING, M.R.).

[6] [1971] 1 Lloyd's Rep. 523, H. L. See the judgment of Lord REID, *ibid.*, at p. 528, and that of Lord MORRIS OF BORTH-Y-GEST, *ibid.*, at p. 529.

If the charterer sends the vessel on a voyage which cannot reasonably be expected to complete within the charter period, the shipowner is entitled to refuse that direction and call for another one. If the charterer refuses to give it, the shipowner can accept his conduct as a breach going to the root of the contract, fix a fresh charter for the vessel, and sue for damages.[1]

If the shipowner agrees to the voyage originally ordered by the charterer, he is entitled to be paid at the current market rate for the excess period.[2]

Thus, in *Alma Shipping Corporation of Monrovia* v. *Mantovani: The "Dione"*,[3]

A vessel was chartered "for a period of 6 months 20 days more or less in charterers' option" from March 8, 1970. The charterers sent her on her last voyage on August 2. It could not reasonably be expected to be completed until the middle of October. In fact, the vessel was redelivered on October 7. *Held,* by C. A., she should have been redelivered by September 28. Hire was payable at the charter rate until that date, but thereafter at the market rate.

(B) Implied Undertakings in Time Charter-parties

In the case of a time charter-party certain undertakings are implied by law, *viz.*

(1) *On the part of the shipowner :* that the vessel is seaworthy[4] at the commencement of the period of the hiring.[5] But unseaworthiness by itself does not entitle the charterer to repudiate the contract. He can only do so if the delay in putting the defects right is such as to amount to a frustration of the charter-party.[6]

---

[1] *Alma Shipping Corporation of Monrovia* v. *Mantovani: The "Dione"* [1975] 1 Lloyd's Rep. 115, C. A., at p. 118 (*per* Lord DENNING, M.R.).

[2] *Ibid.,* at p. 118 (*per* Lord DENNING, M.R.).

[3] [1975] 1 Lloyd's Rep, 115, C. A.

[4] As to seaworthiness, see pp. 14–18, *ante.*

[5] *Giertsen* v. *Turnbull* 1908, S. C. 1101; *Hong Kong Fir Shipping Co., Ltd.* v. *Kawasaki Kisen Kaisha, Ltd.,* [1962] 1 All E. R. 474; [1962] 2 W. L. R. 474, C. A.

[6] See p. 16, *ante.*

(2) *On the part of the charterer:*

(*a*) that he will only use the vessel between good and safe ports[1].

(*b*) that he will not ship dangerous goods.[2]

REPRESENTATIONS, CONDITIONS AND WARRANTIES

If the charterer has entered into a charter-party on the strength of statements made to him by the shipowner, certain courses are open to him if the statements turn out to be untrue. Certain remedies are also available to him if there has been a breach of condition or a breach of warranty on the part of the shipowner.

The Legal Effect

(1) *Representations.*[3] If the shipowner makes an innocent misrepresentation which induces the charterer to sign the contract, the charterer is entitled to rescind the charter-party.[4]

Where an innocent misrepresentation has been made, the person making it will be liable to pay damages unless he proves that he had reasonable ground to believe and did believe up to the the contract was made that the facts represented were true.[5]

But in lieu of rescission of the contract on the ground of innocent misrepresentation, the Court may declare the contract subsisting and award damages if it is of opinion that it would be equitable to do so, having regard to the nature of the misrepresentation and the loss that would be caused by it if the contract were upheld, as well as to the loss that rescission would cause to the other party.[6]

---

[1] *Vardinoyannis* v. *Egyptian General Petroleum Corporation: The "Evaggelos Th.",* [1971] 2 Lloyd's Rep. 200, Q. B. (Commercial Court), at p. 205 (*per* DONALDSON, J.).

[2] See pp. 23-24, *ante.* The statutes relating to the shipment of dangerous goods there mentioned also apply to time charter-parties.

[3] See generally Chitty, *The Law of Contracts* (23rd edn. 1968), Volume 1, Chapter 6. This subject is primarily a matter of the law of contract, and a full discussion would appear out of place in an introductory book on the carriage of goods by sea.

[4] *Ibid.,* paras. 298–314.

[5] Misrepresentation Act, 1967, s. 2 (1).

[6] *Ibid.,* s. 2 (2).

If the misrepresentation is fraudulent, the charterer can rescind the contract and claim damages for deceit.[1]

No remedy is available to him if the misrepresentation, whether innocent or fraudulent, does not induce him to enter the contract.[2]

(2) *Conditions.* Certain terms in a charter-party go to the root of the contract and amount to a condition. If there has been a breach of a condition, the charterer can refuse to load, and can claim damages as well.[3]

(3) *Warranties.* Some terms in the charter-party do not go to its root, and for breach of them a charterer can claim damages only.[4]

If a representation has been made a term of the contract, then it may amount to a condition or a warranty, as the case may be.[5]

Is the Term a Condition or a Warranty?

Whether the term amounts to a condition or a warranty is a matter of construction, depending on the intention of the parties and the whole of the circumstances.

However, the following express terms are usually held to be conditions:

(i) the position of the ship at the date of the charter-party;

Thus, in *Behn* v. *Burness*,[6]

A charter-party stated that a vessel was "now in the port of Amsterdam". In fact, she was 62 miles away from that port. *Held*, that the statement was a condition and, since it had been broken, the charterer was entitled to refuse to load when the vessel arrived at the port of loading.

(ii) her time of sailing;

Thus, in *Bentsen* v. *Taylor, Sons & Co.* (2),[7]
A vessel was described as "now sailed or about to sail from a Pitch Pine Port to the United Kingdom." The charter-party was dated March 29,

---

[1] Chitty, *op. cit.*, paras. 278–281.
[2] *Ibid.*, paras. 273–274.
[3] *Ibid.*, para. 595.
[4] (1863), 2 B & S. 751. Cf. also *Ollive* v. *Booker* (1847), 1 Exch. 416.
[5] [1893] 2 Q. B. 274, C. A. See also *Glaholm* v. *Hays* (1841), 2 Man. & G. 257.
[6] *Ibid.*, para. 595.
[7] *Ibid.*, para. 583.

but in fact the vessel did not leave the port concerned until April 23. *Held*, that the phrase "now sailed or about to sail" was a condition, and the charterers would have been able to repudiate the charter-party, but were not entitled to do so since, on the evidence, they had waived the breach of the condition.

(iii) her nationality;[1]

(iv) her class on the register;[2]

(v) her capacity for a particular cargo;[3]

(vi) the date when she is "expected ready to load".

Thus, in *Maredelanto Compania Naviera S.A.* v. *Bergbau-Handel G.m.b.H.*: *The "Mihalis Angelos"*,[4]

A vessel was chartered under a charter-party dated May 25, 1965 which stated that she was "expected ready to load" at Haiphong on July 1. She arrived at Hong Kong on June 23 and began discharging, but did not complete it until July 23. In order to maintain her class on the register she would have had to undergo a general examination in less than 2 days. It would have taken her 2 days to get from Hong Kong to Haiphong. The charterers repudiated the charter-party on July 17 on the ground that there had been a breach of the clause set out above, and that the clause was a condition. Evidence was given that on May 25, 1965 the shipowners could not reasonably have estimated that the vessel would arrive at Haiphong "about July 1". *Held*, that the clause was a condition and the charterers were entitled to repudiate the charter-party.

On the other hand, if the shipowner has failed to carry out a

---

[1] *Lothian* v. *Henderson* (1803), 3 Bos. & P. 499. During the currency of the charter-party there is an implied condition that the ship's flag will not be changed, *e.g.* by a British ship being sold to an alien: *Isaacs & Sons, Ltd.* v. *McAllum & Co.*, [1921] 3 K. B. 377. The amount of damages will depend on the circumstances of each case and may only be nominal: *ibid.*

[2] *Routh* v. *Macmillan* (1863), 2 H. & C. 750.

[3] *Louis Dreyfus et Cie* v. *Parnasa Cia Naviera S.A.*, [1960] 1 All E. R. 759; [1960] 2 Q. B. 49, C. A.

[4] [1970] 2 Lloyd's Rep. 43, C. A. See the judgment of Lord DENNING, M.R., at p. 47. See also *R. Pagnan and Fratelli* v. *N. G. J. Schouten N.V.*: *The "Filipinas I"*, Q. B. D. (Commercial Court), [1973] 1 Lloyd's Rep. 349, where an arbitration award was remitted to an arbitrator for him to consider whether the statement that the vessel was expected ready to load by a certain date was based on reasonable grounds. In *Sanday & Co.* v. *Keighley, Maxted & Co.* (1922), 91 L. J. K. B. 624 and *Finnish Government (Ministry of Food)* v. *Ford (H.) & Co., Ltd.* (1921), 6 Ll. L. Rep. 188, which were both cases concerning the sale of goods, the phrase "expected ready to load" was also held to be a condition.

term of a time charter-party whereby he undertakes to maintain the vessel in a seaworthy state, this only entitles the charterer to sue him for damages, and not to repudiate the charter-party.[1] But he can repudiate if the defect cannot be remedied in a reasonable time.[2] Damages were the only remedy where bunkers on board a vessel were "expected to be about 6–700 tons" and in fact amounted to 936 tons.[3] Again, a clause in a charter-party by demise stating that the charterer was to redeliver the vessel to the shipowner in the same good order and condition as on delivery, and before redelivery make all such repairs found to be necessary, was held not to be a condition precedent to the right to redeliver, but merely to give the shipowner a remedy in damages for the cost of the repairs.[4]

In addition, some terms amounting to conditions are implied, *e.g.* in the case of a voyage charter-party it is implied:

    (i) that the vessel is seaworthy;[5]
   (ii) that she will proceed on the voyage with reasonable despatch;[6]
  (iii) that she shall proceed without unjustifiable deviation.[7]

and in the case of a time charter-party that she shall be seaworthy at the commencement of the period of hiring.[8]

The effect of a breach of these conditions has already been mentioned.

Waiver of Breach of Condition

If the party who has a right to repudiate the contract elects to go on with it, so that the position of the parties is changed, he

---

[1] *Hong Kong Fir Shipping Co., Ltd.* v. *Kawasaki Kisen Kaisha, Ltd.*, [1962] 1 All E. R. 474; [1962] 2 Q. B. 26.

[2] *Ibid.*

[3] *Efploia Shipping Corporation, Ltd.* v. *Canadian Transport Co., Ltd., The "Pantanassa"*, [1958] 2 Lloyd's Rep. 449.

[4] *Attica Sea Carriers Corporation* v. *Ferrostaal-Poseidon Bulk Reederei G.m.b.H.* (1975), *Times,* November 25, C. A.

[5] See pp. 14–18, *ante.*

[6] See pp. 18–19, *ante.*

[7] See pp. 20–23, *ante.*

[8] See p. 42, *ante.*

must abide by the contract, but can sue for damages for any loss he has sustained.[1] Thus, in *Pust* v. *Dowie*,[2]

a ship was chartered for a lump sum on condition that she took a cargo of 1000 tons. In the special circumstances of the voyage she could not take that amount, but the charterers loaded her and she sailed. In an action for the freight it was *held* that there was no breach of the condition, and, even if there had been, the charterers had waived their right to repudiate. They must pay the freight subject only to a set-off as damages.[3]

FRUSTRATION OF A CHARTER-PARTY

Both the shipowner and the charterer will be discharged from their obligations under the charter-party if it becomes frustrated.

Causes Giving Rise to Frustration

Frustration of the charter-party may arise from various causes:

(1) impossibility of performance;

(2) delay;

(3) subsequent change in the law.

(1) *Impossibility of performance.* The doctrine of impossibility of performance applies to contracts in general. For present purposes it is sufficient to note that it affects all contracts of affreightment. But its scope is not unlimited; unless certain well-defined circumstances exist the Court will refuse to apply it.

When performance of a contract depends upon the continued existence of a given person, thing or set of circumstances, a condition will generally be implied that if, without the fault of either party, performance becomes impossible owing to the fact that that person, thing or set of circumstances has ceased to exist, each

---

[1] See *Fraser* v. *Telegraph Construction Co.* (1872), L. R. 7 Q. B. 566.
[2] (1864), 5 B. & S. 20.
[3] See also *Bentsen* v. *Taylor*, [1893] 2 Q. B. 274.

of the parties to the contract shall be discharged from liability for further performance.[1]

The fact that a charter-party becomes more expensive for a party to perform is not sufficient to bring about its frustration.

Thus, in

Ocean Tramp Tankers Corporation v. *V/O Sovfracht,*[2]

A vessel had been chartered under a time charter-party in September 1956 "for a trip out to India via Black Sea" from Genoa. The Suez Canal was blocked in the Suez crisis of that year. *Held,* that in the circumstances the blockage of the Canal did not bring about such a fundamentally different situation as to frustrate the adventure for (i) the voyage via the Suez Canal would normally take 108 days, and via the Cape of Good Hope, 138 days; (ii) the cargo would not have been adversely affected by the longer voyage; and (iii) the voyage via the Cape made no great difference except that it would be more expensive.

Again, in *Palmo Shipping Inc.* v. *Continental Ore Corporation: The "Captain George K",*[3]

A vessel was chartered in April 1967 for a voyage from Coatzacoalcos, Mexico, to Kandla, India. At that time the Suez Canal was open. The distance between the two ports via the Canal was 9,700 miles. When the vessel was approaching the Canal in June 1967, war broke out and the Canal was closed. She turned back and went to Kandla via the Cape of

---

[1] On the theory of frustration generally, see Chitty, *The Law of Contracts* (23rd edn. 1968), Volume 1, Chapter 22. *Taylor* v. *Caldwell* (1863), 3 B. & S. 826; *Joseph Constantine S.S. Line, Ltd.* v. *Imperial Smelting Corporation, Ltd., The Kingswood,* [1941] 2 All E. R. 165; [1942] A. C. 154. A somewhat different view of the basis of the rule was expressed by GODDARD, J., in *W. J. Tatem, Ltd.* v. *Gamboa,* [1938] 3 All E. R. 135; [1939] 1 K. B. 132. But the point was left open by Lord WRIGHT in the *Joseph Constantine* case, [1941] 2 All E. R., at p. 186, as being wholly academic. See further, *Davis Contractors* v. *Fareham U.D.C.,* [1956] 2 All E. R. 145; [1956] A. C. 696, H. L.

[2] [1964] 1 All E. R. 161; [1964] 2 Q. B. 226, C. A., overruling *Société Franco Tunisienne d'Armement* v. *Sidermar S.p.A.,* [1960] 2 All E. R. 529; [1961] 2 Q. B. 278.

[3] [1970] 2 Lloyd's Rep. 21, Q. B. D. (Commercial Court). See the judgment of MOCATTA, J., *ibid.,* at p. 32, where he said that the difference between the contemplated voyage via the Canal and the voyage via the Cape amounted only to a difference in expense, and for that reason was insufficient to produce frustration. See also *American Trading and Production Corporation* v. *Shell International Marine, Ltd.: The "Washington Trader",* [1972] 1 Lloyd's Rep. 463, District Court for the Southern District of New York, where the Suez Canal was closed in 1967, and it was held that the added expense involved in the Cape of Good Hope route was insufficient to make out a case of frustration. (See the judgment of TYLER, D.J., *ibid.,* at p. 467.)

Good Hope and sailed 18,400 miles in consequence. *Held*, that in the circumstances the closure of the Canal did not frustrate the charter-party, and the charterers were not liable to the shipowners for the additional costs incurred in sailing via the Cape.

Where, however, the charterer seeks to rely on destruction of the intended cargo as giving rise to frustration, it would seem that he must show that the contract was for shipment of a *specific* cargo and that that cargo has become substantially a total loss and cannot be replaced.[1]

Although, however, this principle is common to the general law of contract, the warning by Viscount SIMON, L.C., in the *Joseph Constantine* case[2] should always be borne in mind:

"Discharge by supervening impossibility is not a Common Law rule of general application, like discharge by supervening illegality; whether the contract is terminated or not depends on its terms and the surrounding circumstances in each case."

It follows that, where an implied term of the kind set out above would be inconsistent with some express term of the contract, the doctrine of frustration cannot be invoked. So, in *Isles S.S. Co.* v. *Theodoridi*,[3]

where the charter-party contained a clause that, in the event of export of grain from the loading port being prohibited, the contract should be null and void, it was *held* that the doctrine of frustration could not be invoked, since impossibility of performance was dealt with in an express clause: *expressum facit cessare tacitum*.

The application of the maxim *expressum facit cessare tacitum* will, however, exclude the doctrine of frustration only in cases where the express term relied on deals with *total* impossibility of performance: where a limited interruption only is contemplated by the express term, the doctrine will not be excluded by that term. Thus, in the *Fibrosa* case,[4]

where the contract contained an express provision that "should dispatch be hindered or delayed by . . . any cause beyond our reasonable control

---

[1] See *E. B. Aaby's Rereri A/s* v. *Lep Transport, Ltd.* (1948), 81 Ll. L. Rep. 465, where the finding of the fact was against the charterers on all three points and the actual decision was negative in form. Whether it is in all circumstances necessary to prove non-replaceability, and if so in what sense, does not appear to have been decided.

[2] [1942] A. C., at p. 163.

[3] (1926), 24 Ll. L. Rep. 362.

[4] *Fibrosa Spolka Akcyjna* v. *Fairbairn Lawson Combe Barbour, Ltd.*, [1942] 2 All E. R. 122 [1943] A. C. 32.

including . . . war . . . a reasonable extension of time shall be granted",
and performance of the contract by an English company to deliver
machinery to a Polish company was rendered impossible by the outbreak
of war in 1939, the argument that that express term precluded the existence
of an implied term was *held* on the facts to be unsound. Viscount SIMON,
L.C., said: "The ambit of the express condition is limited to delay in
respect of which a reasonable extension of time might be granted. That
might mean a minor delay as distinguished from a prolonged and indefinite interruption of prompt contractual performance which the
present war manifestly and inevitably brings about. . . . The principle is
that where supervening events, not due to the fault of either party, render
the performance of a contract indefinitely impossible, and there is no
undertaking to be bound in any event, frustration ensues, even though
the parties may have expressly provided for the case of a limited
interruption."[1]

It will be noted that the doctrine does not apply in cases where
performance becomes impossible by reason of the default of one
of the parties to the contract. When, therefore, one of the parties
relies upon frustration as releasing him from further contractual
liability, the onus of proof as to whether or not the impossibility
was due to his default may be important. Thus, in *Joseph Constantine S.S. Line, Ltd.* v. *Imperial Smelting Corporation, Ltd.*,[2]

where damages for failure to load a cargo were claimed by the charterers,
the shipowners relied on the explosion which had occurred in the ship as
having frustrated the chartered voyage. The cause of the explosion,
however, could not be established. In these circumstances it was *held* by
the House of Lords that the onus was upon the charterers to establish
neglect or default on the part of the shipowners; the latter, having shown
that the voyage was frustrated by the explosion, had established a *prima
facie* defence and were not bound to prove further that neglect or default
on their part had not caused the explosion.

The fact that it has become more onerous or more expensive for
one party than he thought is not sufficient to bring about a
frustration. It must be more than merely more onerous or more
expensive. It must be positively unjust to hold the parties bound.
It is often difficult to draw the line. But it must be done, and it is
for the Courts to do it as a matter of law.[3]

---

[1] [1942] 2 All E. R. 122, at p. 125; [1943] A. C. 32, at p. 40.
[2] [1941] 2 All E. R. 165; [1942] A. C. 154.
[3] *Ocean Tramp Tankers Corporation* v. *V/O Sovfracht*, [1963] 2 Lloyd's Rep.
381, C. A., at p. 390 (*per* Lord DENNING, M.R.).

(2) *Delay*. Discharge from liability on this ground was explained by BAILHACHE, J., thus:

"The commercial frustration of an adventure by delay means, as I understand it, the happening of some unforeseen delay without the fault of either party to a contract, of such a character as that by it the fulfilment of the contract, in the only way in which fulfilment is contemplated and practicable, is so inordinately postponed that its fulfilment when the delay is over will not accomplish the only object or objects which both parties to the contract must have known that each of them had in view at the time they made the contract, and for the accomplishment of which object or objects the contract was made."[1]

The burden of proving that a sufficiently serious interruption has occurred to put an end to the contract is, of course, on the party who asserts it.[2] At one time it was thought that the doctrine did not apply if the contract was partly executed, but it is now well settled that this is not so.[3]

In the leading case of *Jackson* v. *Union Marine Insurance Co.*,[4]

frustration was due to stranding on rocks. The charterers, judging that the delay would be considerable, threw up the charter before the ship was refloated. The Court of Appeal upheld the judgment of first instance in which the charterers were *held* not liable to load the ship, the jury having found that the time necessary for repairing was unreasonably long.

But in *Trade and Transport Inc.* v. *Iino Kaiun Kaisha, Ltd.* : *The "Angelia"*,[5]

A cargo of phosphate rock was not available at the loading port due to lack of transport. The lack of transport existed at the time the voyage charter-party for the carriage of the cargo was entered into. No enquiry was made by the charterers. The charterers failed to supply a cargo and cancelled the charter-party on the ground that the cargo would not be available before the expiry of a frustrating time. *Held*, by Q. B. D. (Commercial Court) that, on the evidence, the delay was not sufficient to frustrate the charter-party.

---

[1] *Per* BAILHACHE, J., in *Admiral S. Co.* v. *Weidner, Hopkins & Co.*, [1916] 1 K. B., at p. 436, cited with approval in the C. A., [1917] 1 K. B., at p. 242.

[2] *Metropolitan Water Board* v. *Dick, Kerr & Co.*, [1917] 2 K. B. 1, *per* SCRUTTON, L.J., at p. 31.

[3] *Embiricos* v. *Reid*, [1914] 3 K. B. 45; *Bank Line, Ltd.* v. *Arthur Capel & Co.*, [1919] A. C. 435, at p. 455.

[4] (1874), L. R. 10 C. P. 125. See further, *Universal Cargo Carriers Corporation* v. *Citati*, [1957] 3 All E. R. 234; [1957] 1 W. L. R. 979, C. A.

[5] [1972] 2 Lloyd's Rep. 154, Q. B. D. (Commercial Court). (See the judgment of KERR, J., *ibid.*, at p. 163.)

The following cases illustrate the doctrine of frustration in relation to time-charters. In *Admiral S. Co.* v. *Weidner Hopkins & Co.*:[1]

a ship was hired under a time charter-party for "two Baltic rounds". She was not allowed to leave a Russian port on account of the outbreak of war between Germany and Russia. The charter contained an exception of "restraints of princes". *Held*, that the delay was such as completely to frustrate the adventure and the charterers were not liable for hire.

On the other hand, it should be noted that the doctrine of frustration:

"does not apply when the time charterer has the use of the vessel for some purpose for which he is, under the terms of the time charter-party, entitled to use her, even though that purpose is not the particular purpose for which he desires to use her."[2]

In other words, the interruption must be such as to destroy the whole basis of the contract. The learned Judge went on to say that as to when a party is entitled to claim that frustration has taken place, the test is the estimate which a reasonable man of business would make of the probable period during which the vessel's services would be lost to the charterer, "and it will be immaterial whether his anticipation is justified or falsified by the event".[3]

Thus, in *Port Line, Ltd.* v. *Ben Line Steamers, Ltd.*,[4]

In November 1954 a vessel was chartered for 30 months. In August 1956 she was requisitioned in view of the Suez Canal crisis, the period of requisition being estimated to be 3 or 4 months. She was released in late November 1956. *Held*, the charter-party was not frustrated.

Further, in *Hong Kong Fir Shipping Co., Ltd.* v. *Kawasaki Kisen Kaisha, Ltd.*,[5]

a vessel was chartered for 24 months from February 1957. Her engines kept breaking down and in June 1957 major repairs had to be effected. These were estimated to take until September, and she was redelivered to the charterers in that month. *Held*, the charter-party was not frustrated.

---

[1] [1917] 1 K. B. 222.
[2] *Per* BAILHACHE, J., in *Anglo-Northern Trading Co., Ltd.* v. *Emlyn Jones and Williams*, [1917] 2 K.B., at p. 84.
[3] [1917] 2 K. B., at p. 85.
[4] [1958] 1 All E. R. 787; [1958] 2 Q. B. 146.
[5] [1962] 1 All E. R. 474; [1962] 2 Q. B. 26, C. A.

(3) *Subsequent change in the law.* Again, both parties are released by a supervening change in the law which renders the contract illegal either by English law or by the law of the country in which performance was to have taken place.[1] It must be stressed that discharge by supervening illegality, unlike frustration by supervening impossibility, abrogates the contract quite independently of its terms, or of the presumed intention of the parties to it.[2]

Effect of Frustration

At Common Law, the effect of frustration upon the rights and liabilities of parties to a contract of affreightment was, in the main, governed by the same rules as applied in the case of other commercial contracts. Those principles, established in 1942 as the result of the decision of the House of Lords in the *Fibrosa* case,[3] may be summarised as follows. Where frustration occurred, the contract automatically came to an end and each of the parties was thereafter released from any further liability to perform his part of the bargain; further, if either party had, in pursuance of the contract, made a payment to the other in respect of a consideration which had wholly failed, the money so paid could be recovered as money had and received.

An important exception to this general proposition, however, is to be found in the Common Law rule that freight paid in advance is not returnable if frustration supervenes. This rule

"should . . . be regarded as a stipulation introduced into such contracts by custom, and not as the result of applying some abstract principle."[4]

The Common Law, however, was radically altered in the case of contracts to which the Law Reform (Frustrated Contracts) Act 1943,[5] applies. That Act does not, however, apply "to any charter-party, except a time charter-party or a charter-party by way of

---

[1] *Ralli Brothers* v. *Compania Naviera*, [1920] 2 K. B. 287.
[2] *Per* Viscount SIMON, L.C., in *Joseph Constantine S.S. Line, Ltd.* v. *Imperial Smelting Corporation, Ltd., The Kingswood,* [1941] 2 All E. R. 165, at p. 171; [1942] A. C. 154, at p. 163.
[3] [1942] 2 All E. R. 122; [1943] A. C. 32.
[4] *Ibid., per* Viscount SIMON, L.C., at pp. 126 and 43 respectively.
[5] 7 Halsbury's Statutes (3rd edn.), 9.

demise, or to any contract (other than a charter-party) for the carriage of goods by sea".[1] It will therefore be seen that the majority of contracts with which this work is concerned are wholly outside the scope of the Act. In connexion with bills of lading and voyage charter-parties the rights and liabilities of the parties in the event of frustration fall to be determined solely in the light of the Common Law principles summarised above: in other words freight paid in advance is still, in the absence of any stipulation to the contrary, an irrecoverable payment.

It should, however, be remembered that in the case of time-charters and charters by demise discharged by frustration, the rights and liabilities of the parties are governed by the provisions of the Act, for a full discussion of which the reader is referred to works dealing with the general law of contract.[2]

RELEASE OF ONE PARTY FROM HIS OBLIGATIONS

We are now on fresh ground. There is no question of frustration. The principle is this: if either party, before the time for performance of the contract, renounces the contract, the other is released; but if that other elects to treat the contract as still subsisting, he will have his remedy for the breach which has been committed;[3] in so electing, however, he runs the risk of the offending party escaping all liability by reason of a subsequent change of circumstances which renders performance within the agreed time impossible.[4]

Again, either party is released if, before the time for performance, the other has by his conduct made it impossible for him to perform his part.[5]

---

[1] *Ibid.*, s. 2 (5) (a).

[2] See Chitty, *The Law of Contracts* (23rd edn. 1968), Volume 1, paras. 1311–1321; Anson, *Principles of the English Law of Contract* (24th edn. 1975), Chapter XIV.

[3] *Danube and Black Sea Rail and Kustenjie Harbour Co., Ltd.* v. *Xenos* (1863), 13 C. B. N. S. 825.

[4] *Avery* v. *Bowden* (1856), 6 E. & B. 953, 962.

[5] *Budgett* v. *Binnington*, [1891] 1 Q. B. 35. See also *Alexander* v. *Akt. Hansa*, [1920] A. C. 88.

CHAPTER 3

Bills of Lading

THE FUNCTIONS OF A BILL OF LADING

A bill of lading has, in the eyes of the law, various aspects:—

(1) It is very good evidence of the contract of affreightment, though not the contract itself, for the contract is usually entered into before the bill of lading is signed.[1]

(2) It is a receipt for the goods shipped and contains certain admissions as to their quantity and condition when put on board.

(3) It is a document of title, without which delivery of the goods cannot normally be obtained.

It is in the second and third of these functions that a bill of lading differs entirely from a charter-party. In the first there is some similarity. A charter-party is always a contract, and nothing more. Where the charterer is also the shipper, the bill of lading is usually only a receipt for the goods and a document of title.[2] In no case, however, docs a proper bill of lading fail to function as a document of title.

---

[1] See *per* Lord BRAMWELL in *Sewell v. Burdick* (1884), 10 App. Cas., at p. 105, and *The Ardennes (Owner of Cargo) v. The Ardennes (Owners)*, [1950] 2 All E. R. 517; [1951] 1 K. B. 55, where evidence was admitted of the contract which was made before the bill of lading was signed and which contained a different term. See also *Rambler Cycle Co., Ltd. v. Peninsular and Oriental Steam Navigation Co., Sze Hai Tong Bank, Ltd. (First Third Party), Southern Trading Co. (Second Third Party)*, [1968] 1 Lloyd's Rep. 42 (Malaysia Federal Court), at p. 47 (*per* THOMSON, L.P.).

[2] See *Rodocanachi v. Milburn* (1886), 18 Q. B. D. 67.

(1) Evidence of the Contract

Where the charterer is also the shipper, the rights of shipowner and charterer as such will be governed by the charter-party
alone.[1] The bill of lading cannot vary or add to the terms of the
charter-party unless it contains an express provision to that effect.

But where the charterer puts the ship up as a general ship, the
contract of carriage will in each case be evidenced by the bill of
lading given to each shipper, irrespective of the terms of the
charter-party, except where there is an express agreement to the
contrary.[2] Further, in the case of a general ship, if a shipper knew
of the existence of a charter-party, he is taken to have contracted
with the charterer and can sue or be sued by him; if he did not,
his contract is with the shipowner.[3]

Where the shipper of goods in the chartered ship indorses a bill
of lading to the charterer, the relations between the shipowner
and the charterer are still governed by the charter-party, at any
rate when the master is only authorized to sign bills of lading
without prejudice to the charter-party.[4]

Where the charterer indorses a bill of lading so as to transfer
the rights and obligations evidenced by it, the indorsee will not
be affected by the terms of the charter-party unless:

(1) there is a clause in the bill of lading incorporating some

---

[1] These statements should be read as painting a general picture in broad
outline only. It seems clear that a charterer who is also the shipper may well
be liable for freight under the bill of lading notwithstanding a cesser clause in
the charter-party: see *Rederi Aktiebolaget Transatlantic* v. *Board of Trade* (1925),
30 Com. Cas. 117, at pp. 125–6; and *Hill S.S. Co.* v. *Hugo Stinnes, Ltd.*, 1941
S. C. 324.

[2] *Pearson* v. *Goschen* (1864), 17 C. B. N. S. 352.

[3] *Sandeman* v. *Scurr* (1866), L. R. 2 Q. B. 86; Chorley and Tucker's *Leading
Cases* (4th edn. 1962), p. 290; *The "Berkshire"*, [1974] 1 Lloyd's Rep. 185,
Q. B. D. (Admiralty Court), where the contract was held to be one between the
shipowners and the shippers. (See the judgment of BRANDON, J., *ibid.*, at p. 188.)

[4] *Love and Stewart, Ltd.* v. *Rowtor Co., Ltd.*, [1916] 2 A. C. 527, H. L.;
President of India v. *Metcalfe Shipping Co., Ltd.: The "Dunelmia"*, [1969]
3 All E.R. 1549; [1969] 1 Q. B. 289, C. A., distinguishing *Calcutta S.S. Co.,
Ltd.* v. *Andrew Weir & Co.*, [1910] 1 K. B. 759.

or all of the terms of the charter-party in itself; such clause must be clear and express;[1]

or (2) the bill of lading is one which the master could not have legally given on account of the terms of the charter-party.

Exceptional terms are sometimes introduced, and the question, familiar in the law of contract, arises: How far is an acceptor of an offer in common form bound by conditions contained in it? The question has arisen mainly in connexion with tickets issued to passengers containing stipulations limiting the liability of the carrying company. The answer is that the acceptor is bound by such terms, whether he read them or not[2] provided reasonable notice of them was given him.[3] "If a shipowner wishes to introduce into his bill of lading so novel a clause as one exempting him from general average contribution . . . he ought not only to make it clear in words, but also to make it conspicuous by inserting it in such type and in such part of the document that a person of ordinary capacity and care should not fail to see it."[4]

(2) The Bill of Lading as a Receipt

Under modern conditions the bill of lading is usually signed by the loading broker,[5] but sometimes by the master, acknow-

---

[1] As to the effect of the clause "all other conditions as per charter-party" see *Serraino* v. *Campbell*, [1891] 1 Q. B. 283, and *Vergottis* v. *Robinson David & Co.* (1928), 31 Ll. L. Rep. 23. Whether the terms of a charter-party have been incorporated into the bill of lading is in each case a matter of construction. See, *e.g.*, *The Merak*, [1965] 1 All E. R. 230; [1965] P. 223, C. A. (arbitration clause in charter-party *held* to be incorporated into bill of lading); *Atlas Levante-Linie Aktiengesellschaft* v. *Gesellschaft Fuer Getreidhandel A.G. and Becher, The Phonizien*, [1966] 1 Lloyd's Rep. 150 (arbitration clause in charter-party *held* not to be incorporated into bill of lading); *The "Annefield"*, [1971] 1 All E. R. 394; [1971] P. 168, C. A. (arbitration clause in charter-party *held* not to be incorporated into bill of lading); *Pacific Molasses Co. and United Molasses Trading Co. Ltd.* v. *Entre Rios Compania Naviera S.A.: The "San Nicholas"*, [1976] 1 Lloyd's Rep. 8, C. A. (charter-party governed by English held to be incorporated into bill of lading, even though blanks were left in charter-party). In *Denny, Mott and Dickson, Ltd.* v. *Lynn Shipping Co., Ltd.*, [1963] 1 Lloyd's Rep. 339, it was held that an arbitration clause in a charter-party had been effectively incorporated into the bill of lading, but that the clause did not apply in the events which happened. As to this point, see p. 139, *post*.

[2] *Watkins* v. *Rymill* (1883), 10 Q. B. D. 178.

[3] *Richardson* v. *Rowntree*, [1894] A. C. 217. See generally H. B. Sales, "Standard Form Contracts", *Modern Law Review*, Vol. 16 (1953), pp. 318–42.

[4] *Per* LUSH, J., in *Crooks* v. *Allan* (1879), 5 Q. B. D., at p. 40.

[5] See p. 1, *ante*.

ledging the quantity and condition of the goods when put on board. The precise effect of this acknowledgment is most important in view of the rule of law that the ship must deliver "what she received as she received it, unless relieved by the excepted perils".[1]

Sometimes the bill of lading refers to the "leading marks" inscribed on the goods, and sometimes there is a statement as to their quality.

(a) Receipt as to quantity

(i) *At Common Law.* The bill of lading is *prima facie* evidence that the quantity of goods alleged to have been shipped has been shipped in fact. But the shipowner is entitled to show that the goods were never shipped.[2] If he does so, he escapes liability in respect of them. Thus, in *Grant* v. *Norway*,[3]

a bill of lading was signed by the master for twelve bales of silk, which the shipowner proved had not been put on board. *Held*, that the master had no authority to sign for goods not shipped, and the holders of the bill of lading had no claim against the shipowner for non-delivery of these bales.

If the bill of lading contains the words "weight and quantity unknown", it is not even *prima facie* evidence, and to succeed in an action for non-delivery the shipper must show that the goods were in fact shipped.[4]

(ii) *Under the Carriage of Goods by Sea Act, 1924.* Under the Carriage of Goods by Sea Act 1924,[5] a shipper can demand that a bill of lading be issued to him showing "either the number of packages or pieces, or the quantity, or weight, as the case may be, as furnished in writing by the shipper".[6] Such bill of lading is *prima facie* evidence of the receipt of the goods as therein

---

[1] *Per* Lord SUMNER in *Bradley* v. *Federal Steam, etc., Co.* (1927), 137 L. T. 266, at p. 267.

[2] *Smith* v. *Bedouin S.N. Co.*, [1896] A. C. 70.

[3] (1851), 10 C. B. 665.

[4] *New Chinese Co.* v. *Ocean S.S. Co.*, [1917] 2 K. B. 664. *A.-G. of Ceylon* v. *Scindia Steam Navigation Co., Ltd.*, [1961] 3 All E. R. 684; [1962] A. C. 60, P. C.

[5] For the circumstances in which the Act applies, see pp. 67–69, *post*.

[6] Sched. Art. III, r. 3 (Appendix E, *post*).

described.[1] The shipper is deemed to have guaranteed the accuracy at the time of shipment of the quantity and weight as furnished by him, and must indemnify the shipowner against all loss, damages, and expenses arising from inaccuracies in such particulars.[2] It should be observed that the master is not bound to show *both* the number of packages *and* the weight; if the number is stated, the phrase "weight unknown" may properly be inserted, and will have full effect.[3]

Thus, In *Oricon Waren-Handels G.m.b.H.* v. *Intergraan N.V.*,[4]

A bill of lading to which the Hague Rules applied acknowledged receipt of 2000 packages containing copra cake. A clause in it stated: "Contents and condition of contents, . . . measurement . . . weight . . . unknown, any reference in this Bill of Lading to these particulars is for the purpose of calculating Freight only." The bill of lading also stated under the heading "Description of Goods": "Said to Weigh Gross, 105,000 Kg. . . ." *Held*, the bill of lading was *prima facie* evidence of the number of packages shipped, but was no evidence whatever of their weight.

(iii) *Under the Carriage of Goods by Sea Act 1971*. Where the Carriage of Goods by Sea Act 1971[5] applies,[6] the position is the same as that under the Carriage of Goods by Sea Act 1924, except that as far as the statement as to the quantity shipped is concerned, proof to the contrary is not admissible when the bill of lading has been transferred to a third party acting in good faith.[7]

(iv) *Under the Bills of Lading Act 1855*. Although he may not have a remedy as against the shipowner, the consignee or indorsee for value of a bill of lading can make use of the Bills of Lading Act 1855, s. 3. This section states that in his hands the bill of lading is conclusive evidence, *as against the master or other person*[8] *signing it,* that the goods represented to have been shipped were actually shipped. But this does not apply where:

---

[1] Sched. Art. III, r. 4 (Appendix E, *post*).
[2] Sched. Art. III, r. 5 (Appendix E, *post*).
[3] *Pendle and Rivet* v. *Ellerman Lines* (1927), 33 Com. Cas. 70.
[4] [1967] 2 Lloyd's Rep. 82.
[5] *This Act is not yet in force.* See p. 76, *post*.
[6] See pp. 77–79, *post*.
[7] Carriage of Goods by Sea Act, 1971, Sched., Art. III, r. 4.
[8] In *V/O Rasnoimport* v. *Guthrie & Co., Ltd.*, [1966] 1 Lloyd's Rep. 1, it was assumed that ship's agents who had signed the bill of lading were "other persons" for the purpose of s. 3. See the judgment of MOCATTA, J., *ibid.*, at p. 18.

(A) the holder of the bill of lading knew when he took it
    that the goods had not been shipped;
or (B) the person signing can show that the misrepresentation
    was due to the fraud of the shipper, the holder of the bill
    of lading, or some one under whom the holder claims.

Section 3 does not make such a person liable for non-delivery
of any goods represented as having been shipped. It only gives the
consignee or indorsee for value a statutory estoppel to rely on to
show that the goods were shipped. It does not give him a separate
cause of action.[1]

The person who signs the bill of lading without the authority
of the shipowner stating that goods have been shipped, and they
have, in fact, not been shipped at all, is liable to an indorsee of the
bill of lading, who has relied on that statement, for damages for
breach of warranty of authority.[2]

(b) *Receipt as to condition.* Where goods are described in the
bill of lading as being "shipped in good order and condition",
the position is as follows:

(1) *As between the shipowner and a charterer who was also the
    shipper.* Here the position is governed by the charter-
    party, which cannot be varied by the bill of lading.[3] Subject
    to this, the position appears to be the same as in (2) *infra.*
(2) *As between the shipowner and a shipper other than the
    charterer.* Here the admissions in the bill of lading, though
    not conclusive, afford some evidence against the shipowner.[4]
    The mere fact, however, that the goods have been delivered
    in a damaged condition does not suffice to render the
    shipowner liable. The shipper must show that the damage
    was due to fault on the part of the shipowner, or else that
    the goods were in fact shipped in good condition internally.[5]

---

[1] *V/O Rasnoimport* v. *Guthrie & Co., Ltd.* (*supra*).
[2] *Ibid.* As to the measure of damages, see *ibid.*, pp. 7, 18.
[3] *Sugar Supply Commission* v. *Hartlepools*, [1927] 2 K. B. 419; *Rodocanachi* v.
Milburn (1886), 18 Q. B. D. 67.
[4] *The Peter der Grosse* (1875), 1 P. D. 414; *Crawford and Law* v. *Allan Line
S.S. Co., Ltd.*, [1912] A. C. 130.
[5] *The Ida* (1875), 32 L. T. 541; *J. Kaufman, Ltd.* v. *Cunard S.S. Co., Ltd.*,
[1965] 2 Lloyd's Rep. 564.

Both (1) and (2) above must be read subject to this qualification, that it is, of course, open to the parties to agree, by an express clause in the document which governs their respective rights, that the statements in the bill of lading shall be conclusive. A "conclusive evidence" clause of this type will bind the shipowner, unless there has been fraud on the part of the shipper.[1]

(3) *As between the shipowner and an indorsee for value of the bill of lading*

    (i) *At Common Law.* Here, unless there is evidence to show that the indorsee did not act to his detriment on the faith of the bill,[2] the shipowner will be estopped by the admissions contained therein.[3]

---

[1] *Crossfield* v. *Kyle S.S. Co.*, [1916] 2 K. B. 885. Cf. *Oricon Waren-Handels G.m.b.H.* v. *Intergraan N.V.*, [1967] 2 Lloyd's Rep. 82, where a clause in a c.i.f. contract which stated "Weighing.—Final settlement shall be made on the basis of gross delivered weight and the goods shall be weighed at place of discharge at port of destination herein named", was not a conclusive evidence clause, but made it mandatory upon the buyers to see that the goods were weighed at the place of discharge. It did not provide that the gross delivered weight should only be arrived at in the manner specified in the clause. See the judgment of ROSKILL, J., on this point, *ibid.*, at p. 95.

[2] *The Skarp*, [1935] P. 134; *Peter Cremer, Westfaelische Central Genossenschaft G.m.b.H. and Intergraan N.V.* v. *General Carriers S.A.: The "Dona Mari"*, [1973] 2 Lloyd's Rep. 366, Q.B.D. (Commercial Court), where it was shown that the bills of lading would have been rejected by the buyers of some tapioca stated to be "shipped in good order and condition" but actually in moist condition, if the bills of lading had been claused. (See the judgment of KERR, J., *ibid.*, at p. 373.)

[3] *Silver* v. *Ocean S.S. Co.*, [1930] 1 K. B. 416; *Cummins Sales and Service Inc.* v. *Institute of London Underwriters: The "Goldenfels"*, [1974] 1 Lloyd's Rep. 292, U.S. Court of Appeals, Fifth Circuit, where the shipowners were estopped from showing pre-shipment damage to some component parts of a pre-fabricated metal building. Sometimes the shipowner is willing to issue to the shipper of the goods a clean bill of lading even though they are not in good condition, provided that the shipper is willing to indemnify him against any claim by a holder of the bill. But he runs the risk of the indemnity being held to be illegal because the bill of lading contains a false representation, and therefore to be unenforceable: *Brown Jenkinson & Co.* v. *Percy Dalton (London), Ltd.*, [1957] 2 All E. R. 844; [1957] 2 Q. B. 621, C. A. See further, *Hellenic Lines, Ltd.* v. *Chemoleum Corp.*, [1972] 1 Lloyd's Rep. 350, New York Supreme Court (Appellate Division), where it was held that a letter of guarantee against a clean bill of lading issued in respect of bagged fertilizer in a leaky condition contravened public policy as expressed in the United States Carriage of Goods Act 1936, s. 3 (8) and could not be enforced.

To found such an estoppel, however, the statement in the bill of lading must be clear and unambiguous: if the words "received in apparent good order and condition" are qualified by other clauses in the document, this may prevent the bill from being a clean bill and in such a case estoppel will not arise. So, in *Canadian and Dominion Sugar Co., Ltd.* v. *Canadian National (West Indies) Steamships, Ltd.*[1]

where the bill, relating to a shipment of sugar, contained the qualifying words "signed under guarantee to produce ship's clean receipt" and the ship's receipt was not clean, in that it contained the phrase "many bags stained, torn and re-sewn", it was *held* that the bill was not a clean bill and the shipowners were not estopped.

An admission as to the condition of goods on shipment will bind the shipowner only as to defects which ought to be apparent on reasonable inspection. Thus, in *Compania Naviera Vazcongada* v. *Churchill*,[2]

timber, although obviously stained with petroleum, was stated in the bill of lading to be "shipped in good order and condition". *Held*, the assignee of the bill of lading could sue the shipowner for damages, and the latter was estopped from denying that the timber was shipped in good condition.

In another case, *The Peter der Grosse*,[3]

a bill of lading acknowledged the receipt of goods "shipped in good order and condition . . . weight, contents, and value unknown". The goods were delivered both externally and internally damaged. *Held*, that the bill of lading was evidence that the goods had been shipped in good condition externally, and that there was no obligation on the consignees to show how the damage had arisen. The shipowners were, therefore, liable.

---

[1] [1947] A. C. 46, P. C. See also *Tokio Marine and Five Insurance Co., Ltd.* v. *Retla S.S. Co.,* [1970] 2 Lloyd's Rep. 91, U.S. Ct. of Appeals, Ninth Circuit, where it was held that no estoppel arose in the case of a bill of lading concerning some steel pipes damaged by rust before shipment for the bill of lading, although stating that the goods were shipped in apparent good order and condition, stated "The term 'apparent good order and condition' when used in this bill of lading with reference to iron, steel or metal products does not mean that the goods, when received, were free of visible rust or moisture". See the judgment of JAMESON, D. J., *ibid.*, at p. 96.

[2] [1906] 1 K. B. 237.

[3] (1875), 1 P. D. 414.

But, if estoppel is established, it will operate in favour of an innocent indorsee even if the master has been induced to sign by the shipper's fraud.[1]

Of course, the fact that an indorsee of the bill of lading happens also to be the charterer will not affect the position; in such circumstances he sues not *qua* charterer, but *qua* indorsee of the bill.[2]

(ii) *Under the Carriage of Goods by Sea Act 1924.* Where the Carriage of Goods by Sea Act 1924 applies,[3] any shipper[4] can insist upon the bill of lading incorporating a statement as to the "apparent order and condition" of the goods.[5]

The effect of the incorporation of these statements in the bill of lading will be the same as that of statements properly inserted by the master at Common Law, *i.e.* they will be *prima facie* evidence in favour of the shipper and conclusive in favour of an innocent indorsee for value.[6]

(iii) *Under the Carriage of Goods by Sea Act 1971.* Where the Carriage of Goods by Sea Act 1971[7] applies,[8] the position is the same as that under the Carriage of Goods by Sea Act 1924 except that as far as the statement as to order and condition of the goods is concerned, proof to the contrary is not admissible when the bill of lading has been transferred to a third party acting in good faith.[9]

---

[1] *Evans* v. *James Webster & Brothers, Ltd.* (1928), T. L. R. 136.

[2] *United Molasses Co.* v. *National Petroleum Co.* (1934), 50 T. L. R. 266.

[3] See pp. 67–69, *post*.

[4] The carrier is under no duty to issue a bill of lading showing the apparent good order and condition of the goods unless the shipper actually demands such a bill of lading: *Canadian and Dominion Sugar Co., Ltd.* v. *Canadian National (West Indies), Ltd.,* [1947] A. C. 46, P. C., at p. 57; *Tokio Marine and Fire Insurance Co., Ltd.* v. *Retla Steamship Co. (supra),* at p. 96.

[5] Sched. Art. III, r. 3. In *Tokio Marine and Fire Insurance Co., Ltd.* v. *Retla Steamship Co. (supra)* it was held that the "rust" clause which qualified the meaning of "apparent good order and condition" was not invalid under Art. III, r. 3.

[6] Sched. Art. III, r. 4.

[7] *This Act is not yet in force.* See p. 76, *post*.

[8] See pp. 77–79, *post*.

[9] Carriage of Goods by Sea Act 1971, Sched. Art. III, r. 4.

(c) *Receipt as to "leading marks"*

(i) *At Common Law.* The Bills of Lading Act 1855, s. 3, does not preclude the person who has signed the bill of lading from showing that the goods shipped were marked otherwise than as stated, unless the marks are material to the description of the goods. Thus, in *Parsons* v. *New Zealand Shipping Co.*,[1]

frozen carcases of lamb were put on board, and the bills of lading, signed by the defendants, described the goods as "622X, 608 carcases. 488X, 226 carcases." On arrival, some carcases were found to be marked 522X and others 388X. The indorsee of the bill of lading argued that the defendants were estopped from denying the statement in the bill of lading and were liable for failing to deliver the carcases shipped. It was *held* by the majority of the Court of Appeal that the marginal description of the goods in the bills of lading and the numbers of packages stated therein did not affect or denote the nature, quality, or commercial value of the goods. The Act protects persons who have acted on a misrepresentation that goods have been shipped when they have not. Here the marks were quite immaterial as far as the purchaser was concerned, because the lambs delivered were of the same character and value as those shipped.

(ii) *Under the Carriage of Goods by Sea Act 1924.* Where the Carriage of Goods by Sea Act 1924 applies,[2] a shipper can insist on the bill of lading showing "the leading marks necessary for the identification of the goods".[3] The master can refuse to show them in the bill of lading if the goods or their containers are not clearly marked "in such a manner as should ordinarily remain legible until the end of the voyage".[4] Further, he can refuse to incorporate them in the bill of lading if he has reasonable grounds for suspecting that the information relating to them supplied by the shipper is inaccurate, or he has had no reasonable means of checking it.[5] If the leading marks are inserted, the bill of lading is *prima facie* evidence of the receipt by the shipowner of the goods as therein described.[6]

---

[1] [1901] 1 K. B. 548.
[2] See pp. 67–69, *post.*
[3] Sched. Art. III, r. 3.
[4] *Ibid.*
[5] *Ibid.*
[6] Sched. Art. III, r. 4.

The Act, however, is careful to provide that the shipper shall be deemed to have guaranteed to the carrier the accuracy at the time of shipment of the information furnished by him, and that he must indemnify the carrier against any loss due to that information being inaccurate.[1] If, therefore, inaccurate information concerning marks or quantities is incorporated in the bill of lading, and an indorsee for value makes a claim against the carrier as a result, the carrier, though liable to the indorsee, has a remedy against the shipper.

(iii) *Under the Carriage of Goods by Sea Act 1971.* Where the Carriage of Goods by Sea Act 1971[2] applies,[3] the position is the same as that under the Carriage of Goods by Sea Act 1924 except that as far as the statement as to the leading marks is concerned, proof to the contrary is not admissible when the bill of lading has been transferred to a third party acting in good faith.[4]

(d) *Receipt as to quality.* A master does not generally bind the shipowners by a description in the bill of lading of the *quality* of the goods. Thus, in *Cox* v. *Bruce,*[5]

bales of jute were shipped with marks indicating the quality of the jute. The bill of lading wrongly described the bales as bearing other marks indicating a better quality. The holders of the bill of lading claimed the difference in value from the shipowner. *Held,* the shipowner was not estopped from denying the statement in the bill of lading as to quality. It is not the captain's duty to insert quality marks; hence, if he states them incorrectly, this does not prevent the shipowner from showing that goods of that quality were not put on board.

(3) The Bill of Lading as a Document of Title

For many purposes possession of a bill of lading is equivalent in law to possession of the goods. It enables the holder to obtain delivery of the goods at the port of destination[6] and, during the transit, it enables him to "deliver" the goods by merely transferring

---

[1] Sched. Art. III, r. 5.
[2] *This Act is not yet in force.* See p. 76, *post.*
[3] See pp. 77–79, *post.*
[4] Carriage of Goods by Sea Act 1971, Sched. Art. III, r. 4.
[5] (1886), 18 Q. B. D. 147.
[6] *Erichsen* v. *Barkworth* (1858), 3 H. & N. 894.

the bill of lading. These rules are particularly important in c.i.f. contracts. Thus, in *Horst* v. *Biddell Brothers,*[1]

a contract was made for the sale of hops to be shipped from San Francisco to London, c.i.f. net cash. The buyer refused to pay for the goods until they were actually delivered. *Held,* that possession of the bill of lading is in law equivalent to possession of the goods, and that, under a c.i.f. contract, the seller is entitled to payment on shipping the goods and tendering to the buyer the documents of title.

In *Sanders* v. *Maclean,*[2]

the buyer refused to pay because only two out of the three bills of lading were tendered to him. *Held,* apart from a special stipulation, the tender of one bill of lading is sufficient.[3]

A bill of lading, unlike a bill of exchange, is not a negotiable instrument. The holder of a bill of lading who indorses it to an indorsee, cannot therefore give a better title than he himself has. Thus, if he has no title, he cannot pass one.

When the word "negotiable" is used in relation to a bill of lading, it merely means transferable.[4]

It has never been settled, however, whether delivery of a bill of lading which is marked "non-negotiable" transfers title at all.[5]

THE CARRIAGE OF GOODS BY SEA ACT 1924

Until 1924, bills of lading were governed by the Common Law and by the express or implied terms of the contract. But a fundamental change was made by the Carriage of Goods by Sea Act 1924, with regard to those bills of lading to which it applies.

---

[1] [1912] A. C. 18.

[2] (1883), 11 Q. B. 327.

[3] See also *Shepherd* v. *Harrison* (1871), L. R. 5 H. L. 116.

[4] *Kum* v. *Wah Tat Bank, Ltd.,* [1971] 1 Lloyd's Rep. 439, P. C., at p. 446 (*per* Lord DEVLIN).

[5] *Ibid.,* where Lord DEVLIN said that this was not surprising for when consignor and consignee were also seller and buyer, as they most frequently were, the shipment ordinarily served as delivery (Sale of Goods Act 1893, s. 32 (1)) and also as an unconditional appropriation of the goods (Sale of Goods Act 1893, s. 18, r. 5 (2)) which passed the property, so as between seller and buyer it did not usually matter whether the bill of lading was a document of title or not.

The Background of the Act

In September 1921 a meeting of the International Law Association was held at The Hague with the object of securing adoption by the countries represented of a set of rules relating to bills of lading, so that the rights and liabilities of cargo-owners and ship-owners respectively might be subject to rules of general application. Previously those rights and liabilities had been differently defined in different countries, with consequent embarrassment to overseas trade.

The rules agreed upon, thenceforth known as the "Hague Rules", were revised and were embodied in the articles of an International Convention signed at Brussels in August 1924. In the same month an Act of Parliament was passed—the Carriage of Goods by Sea Act 1924[1]—which gave statutory force to the Rules so far as this country is concerned.

The Scope of the Act

Briefly, the scope of the Act can be stated as follows: it applies to the carriage of goods, other than (A) live animals or (B) deck cargo so stated, by sea *from* any port in Great Britain or Northern Ireland under a bill of lading from the time of loading on till the goods are discharged from the ship. As the matter is of considerable importance, the various points involved in the above statement are enumerated and separately considered below:—

(1) The Act does *not* apply to the carriage of live animals, nor to cargo which is stated in the contract of carriage as being carried on deck and which is so carried.[2] These are the

---

[1] Printed in Appendix E, *post*.

[2] Carriage of Goods by Sea Act 1924, Sched. Art. I (c). A clause in a bill of lading that the "steamer has liberty to carry goods on deck" does not amount to a statement that the goods *are* carried on deck; therefore the goods so shipped are subject to the Hague Rules: *Svenska Traktor Aktiebolaget* v. *Maritime Agencies (Southampton), Ltd.,* [1953] 2 All E.R. 570; *Encyclopaedia Britannica Inc.* v. *The "Hong Kong" Producer and Universal Marine Corporation,* [1969] 2 Lloyd's Rep. 536, U. S. Ct. of Appeals, Second Circuit. See the judgment of ANDERSON, Ct. J., *ibid.,* at p. 542.

limitations of the scope of the Act so far as the class of
goods is concerned.

(2) It is only when the port of *departure* is situated either in
Great Britain or in Northern Ireland that the Act comes
into operation: the port of *destination* is immaterial for
this purpose.[1]

Although the Carriage of Goods by Sea Act 1924 is
limited in this way, it is important to note that most contracts
for carriage by sea, wherever made, are now covered by the
Hague Rules: measures corresponding to the Act of 1924
have been passed in most Commonwealth countries and
also in many foreign countries.[2]

(3) The Act applies only to contracts of carriage "covered
by a bill of lading or any similar document of title".[3]
It does *not* apply to charter-parties as such; but, if a bill
of lading is issued, the Act applies thereto, whether or not
the ship is under charter.[4]

In practice, where the ship is chartered, the effect of the
Act is not felt until the moment when the bill of lading
first governs the rights of its holder,[5] and this is expressly
stated in the Act.[6]

(4) The Act applies only to that part of the contract which
relates to carriage by sea, and from the time of loading on

---

[1] Carriage of Goods by Sea Act 1924, s. 1.

[2] A list will be found in Appendix F.

[3] Carriage of Goods by Sea Act 1924, Sched. Art. I (b). Whenever a contract of carriage is concluded and it is contemplated that a bill of lading will in
due course be issued, that contract is from its creation "covered" by a bill of
lading. *Hugh Mack & Co., Ltd.* v. *Burns and Laird Lines, Ltd.* (1944), 77 Ll. L.
Rep. 377; *Pyrene Co., Ltd.* v. *Scindia Navigation Co., Ltd.*, [1954] 2 All E. R.
158; [1954] 2 Q. B. 402; *Anticosti Shipping Co.* v. *Viateur St. Amand*, [1959]
1 Lloyd's Rep. 352 (Supreme Court of Canada); *Automatic Tube Co. Pty., Ltd.
and Email, Ltd.—Balfour Buzacott Division* v. *Adelaide S.S. (Operations), Ltd.,
Adelaide S.S. Co., Ltd. and Adelaide S.S. Co. Pty., Ltd.; The "Beltana"*, [1967]
1 Lloyd's Rep. 531, at p. 533 (*per* NEVILE, J.).

[4] Carriage of Goods by Sea Act 1924, Sched. Art. V.

[5] See pp. 56–57, *ante.*

[6] Carriage of Goods by Sea Act 1924, Sched. Art. I (b).

until the time when the goods are discharged from the ship.[1]

The Act does not prevent the carrier or the shipper from entering into any agreement, stipulation, condition, reservation or exemption as to the responsibility and liability of the carrier or the ship for the loss or damage to or in connection with the custody and care and handling of goods prior to the loading on and subsequent to the discharge of the ship on which the goods are carried by sea.[2]

The Principal Provisions of the Act

The principal provisions of the Act are as follows:

(1) *General paramount clause.* Every bill of lading to which the Act applies must contain an express statement that it is subject to the Rules set out therein.[3]

---

[1] *Ibid.*, Sched. Art. I (b) and (e): *Pyrene Co., Ltd.* v. *Scindia Navigation Co. Ltd.*, *(supra)* (loading); *Goodwin Ferreira & Co., Ltd.* v. *Lamport & Holt, Ltd.*, [1929] All E. R. Rep. 623 (discharge); *Rambler Cycle Co., Ltd.* v. *Peninsular and Oriental Steam Navigation Co., Sze Hai Tong Bank, Ltd. (First Third Party), Southern Trading Co. (Second Third Party),* [1968] 1 Lloyd's Rep. 42, Malaysia Federal Court, (discharge); *East and West S.S. Co.* v. *Hossain Brothers,* [1968] 2 Lloyd's Rep. 145, Supreme Court of Pakistan (discharge); *Falconbridge Nickel Mines, Ltd., Janin Construction, Ltd. and Hewitt Equipment, Ltd.* v. *Chimo Shipping, Ltd., Clarke S.S. Co., Ltd. and Munro Jorgensson Shipping, Ltd.,* [1973] 2 Lloyd's Rep. 469, Supreme Court of Canada, where it was held that as the shipowners carried barges on the vessel for use in lightering the cargo and were bound by the contract of carriage to use them, the lightering was part of the operation of "discharge" and the Rules applied to it. See the judgment of RITCHIE, J., *ibid.*, at p. 472.

[2] Carriage of Goods by Sea Act 1924, Sched. Art. VII. See, *e.g. Robert Simpson Montreal, Ltd.* v. *Canadian Overseas Shipping, Ltd.: The "Prins Willem III",* [1973] 2 Lloyd's Rep. 124, Court of Appeal, Province of Quebec, District of Montreal, where the cargo was pilfered after it had been discharged into a shed by the stevedores, and the carrier's liability was held to have been effectively excluded.

[3] Carriage of Goods by Sea Act 1924, s. 3. Failure to comply with this direction, however, does not of itself render the contract illegal: *Vita Food Products Inc.* v. *Unus Shipping Co., Ltd.,* [1939] 1 All E. R. 513; [1939] A. C. 277, P. C.

(2) *Abolition of absolute warranty of seaworthiness.* Where the Act applies, the absolute undertaking of seaworthiness is abolished[1], and in its place there is a provision that the carrier must exercise due diligence to make the ship seaworthy.[2]

(3) *Extension of right to deviate.* Liberty to deviate is given in order to save property or where a deviation is reasonable.[3]

(4) *Particulars to be shown in bill of lading.* On the demand of the shipper the carrier must issue a bill of lading giving certain particulars, *e.g.* quantity of goods shipped, their apparent condition.[4]

(5) *Care of cargo.* The carrier must "properly and carefully load, handle, stow, carry, keep, care for and discharge the cargo".[5]

But he is free to determine by the contract with the shipper which part each has to play in the loading. If, however, the carrier does the loading, then he must do it properly.[6]

There is some doubt as to the meaning of the word "properly".[7]

One view[8] is that "properly" means "in accordance with a sound system". The obligation on the carrier is to adopt a system which is sound in the light of all knowledge which the carrier has or ought to have *about the nature of the goods.*

---

[1] Carriage of Goods by Sea Act 1924, s. 2.

[2] *Ibid.,* Sched. Art. III, r. 1. See p. 84, *post.*

[3] *Ibid.,* Sched. Art. IV, r. 4. See p. 89, *post.*

[4] *Ibid.,* Sched. Art. III, r. 3. See pp. 58, 63, *ante.*

[5] *Ibid.,* Sched. Art. III, r. 2. "Carry" does not mean "transport", and the carriage begins the moment the goods are loaded, and before the ship has moved: *G. H. Renton & Co., Ltd.* v. *Palmyra Trading Corporation of Panama,* [1956] 3 All E. R. 957; [1957] A. C. 149, H. L.

[6] *Pyrene Co., Ltd.* v. *Scindia Navigation Co., Ltd.,* [1954] 2 All E. R. 158, at pp. 163–4; [1954] 2 Q. B. 402, at p. 419 (*per* DEVLIN, J.); *G. H. Renton & Co., Ltd.* v. *Palmyra Trading Corporation of Panama,* [1956] 3 All E. R. 957, at p. 966; [1957] A. C. 149, at p. 170, H. L. (*per* Lord MORTON).

[7] *G. H. Renton & Co., Ltd.* v. *Palmyra Trading Corporation of Panama,* [1956] 3 All E. R. 957; [1957] A. C. 149, H. L.; *Albacora S.R.L.* v. *Westcott and Laurance Line, Ltd.,* [1966] 2 Lloyd's Rep. 53.

[8] *Albacora S.R.L.* v. *Westcott and Laurance Line, Ltd. (supra)* at p. 58 (*per* Lord REID). See further, *G. H. Renton & Co., Ltd.* v. *Palmyra Trading Corporation of Panama,* [1957] A. C. 149, at p. 166 (*per* Viscount KILMUIR, L.C.).

Another view[1] is that the word "properly" presumably adds something to the word "carefully", and means "upon a sound system". A sound system does not mean a system suited to all the weaknesses and idiosyncracies of a particular cargo, but a sound system under all the circumstances *in relation to the general practice of carriage of goods by sea.*

A further view[2] is that the word "properly" means "in an appropriate manner". The word properly adds something to "carefully", if carefully has a narrow meaning of merely taking care. The element of skill or sound system is required in addition to taking care.

Whether the carrier has broken his obligation is a question of fact in each case, *e.g.* (i) whether a cargo of wet salted fish had been negligently stowed and ventilated;[3] (ii) whether a cargo of bags of cocoa had been negligently stowed, dunnaged and protected;[4] (iii) whether a cargo of coco yams had been negligently stowed and ventilated;[5] (iv) whether a cargo of melons, garlic and onions had been negligently stowed and badly ventilated because they had been stowed in a hold containing a cargo of fishmeal;[6] (v) whether an electric shovel had been properly stowed because there were gaps in the stowage;[7] (vi) whether the shipowner by entering a strike-bound port causing delay had damaged a cargo of oranges;[8] (vii) whether a cargo of lumber had been safely stowed;[9] (viii) whether boxes of bananas had been properly

---

[1] *Albacora S.R.L.* v. *Westcott and Laurance Line, Ltd. (supra)*, at p. 62 (*per* Lord PEARCE).

[2] *Ibid.*, at p. 64 (*per* Lord PEARSON).

[3] *Ibid.*

[4] *Jahn (Trading as C. F. Otto Weber)* v. *Turnbull Scott Shipping Co., Ltd. and Nigerian National Line, Ltd., The "Flowergate",* [1967] 1 Lloyd's Rep. 1.

[5] *Chris Foodstuffs (1963), Ltd.* v. *Nigerian National Shipping Line, Ltd.,* [1967] 1 Lloyd's Rep. 293, C. A.

[6] *David McNair & Co., Ltd. and David Oppenheimer, Ltd. and Associates* v. *The "Santa Malta",* [1967] 2 Lloyd's Rep. 391.

[7] *Blackwood Hodge (India) Private, Ltd.* v. *Ellerman Lines, Ltd. and Ellerman and Bucknall S.S. Co., Ltd.,* [1963] 1 Lloyd's Rep. 454.

[8] *Crelinsten Fruit Co.* v. *The "Mormacsaga",* [1969] 1 Lloyd's Rep. 515, Exchequer Court of Canada.

[9] *Charles Goodfellow Lumber Sales, Ltd.* v. *Verreault, Hovington and Verreault Navigation Inc.,* [1968] 2 Lloyd's Rep. 383, Exchequer Court of Canada, Quebec Admiralty District. See the judgment of DUMOULIN, J., *ibid.*, at p. 389; reversed on other grounds, [1971] 1 Lloyd's Rep. 185, Supreme Court of Canada.

stowed;[1] (ix) whether the shipowners were negligent in securing the cargo on a barge to keep it from sliding, and in tethering the barge to the vessel;[2] (x) whether apple concentrate in containers had been properly stowed because no additional dunnage had been used;[3] (xi) whether melons stowed in crates 17 high without air circulating in the hold had been properly stowed;[4] (xii) whether cars had been stowed too closely together;[5] and (xiii) whether a cargo of apples and pears had been properly stowed in a refrigerated vessel.[6]

The fact that the goods arrive damaged does not of itself constitute a breach of the carrier's obligation though it may well be in many cases sufficient to raise an inference of a breach of the obligation.[7]

(6) *Immunities given to carrier.* The Act sets out a list of "excepted perils".[8] If loss or damage to the goods results from them, the carrier will not be liable, provided that he has fulfilled his duties under the Act, *e.g.* has exercised due diligence to make the ship seaworthy, has properly loaded and stowed the cargo. The carrier can increase his liabilities,[9] but cannot add to the list of the "excepted perils".[10]

---

[1] *Heinrich C. Horn* v. *Cia de Navegacion Fruco S.A. and J. R. Atkins* (*trading as Alabama Fruit and Produce Co.*), *The "Heinz Horn"*, [1970] 1 Lloyd's Rep. 191, U.S. Ct. of Appeals, Fifth Circuit. See the judgment of Rives, Ct. J., *ibid.*, at p. 196.

[2] *Falconbridge Nickel Mines, Ltd., Janin Construction, Ltd. and Hewitt Equipment, Ltd.* v. *Chimo Shipping, Ltd., Clarke S.S. Co., Ltd. and Munro Jorgensson Shipping, Ltd.*, [1973] 2 Lloyd's Rep. 469, Supreme Court of Canada.

[3] *Bruck Mills, Ltd.* v. *Black Sea S.S. Co. : The "Grumant"*, [1973] 2 Lloyd's Rep. 531, Federal Court of Canada, Trial Division.

[4] *William D. Branson, Ltd. and Tomas Alcazar S.A.* v. *Jadranska Slobodna Plovidba* (*Adriatic Tramp Shipping*): *The "Split"*, [1973] 2 Lloyd's Rep. 535, Federal Court of Canada, Trial Division.

[5] *Nissan Automobile Co.* (*Canada*), *Ltd.* v. *Owners of the Vessel "Continental Shipper" : The "Continental Shipper"*, [1974] 1 Lloyd's Rep. 482, Federal Court of Canada, Trial Division.

[6] *Crelinsten Fruit Co. and William D. Branson, Ltd.* v. *Maritime Fruit Carriers Co., Ltd.: The "Lemoncore"*, [1975] 2 Lloyd's Rep. 249, Federal Court of Canada, Trial Division.

[7] *Albacora S.R.L.* v. *Westcott and Laurance Line, Ltd.* (*supra*), *at* p. 63.

[8] *Ibid.*, Sched. Art. IV, r. 2. See pp. 162–165, *post.*

[9] *Ibid.*, Sched. Art. V.

[10] *Ibid.*, Sched. Art. III, r. 8. See p. 165, *post.*

(7) *Rights given to carrier.* The carrier is entitled to throw overboard goods which are dangerous.[1] He can obtain an indemnity for loss caused to him by the shipper stating the particulars of the goods inaccurately.[2] But the shipper is not responsible for loss or damage sustained by the carrier arising or resulting from any cause without the act, fault or neglect of the shipper, his agents or his servants.[3]

(8) *Limitation of liability.* The Act[4] limits the liability of the carrier to £100 per package or unit[5] in respect of any loss of or damage to or in connection with the goods.[6]

(9) *Limitation of action.* The carrier is discharged from all liability if the action is not brought within one year from the date of the delivery of the goods or the date when they should have been delivered.[7]

Contracting out of the Act

The Act of 1924 was intended mainly to protect holders of bills of lading, by ensuring to them certain rights of which they could not be deprived. It was, therefore, laid down that, in cases to which the Act applies, the carrier should be able to avoid liability only in certain circumstances defined in the Act.[8]

---

[1] *Ibid.,* Art. IV, r. 6. See p. 162, *post.*

[2] *Ibid.,* Art. III, r. 5. See p. 65, *ante.*

[3] *Ibid.,* Art. IV, r. 3. The words "loss or damage" refer to physical loss or damage and not to loss by delay in discharging: *Hellenic Lines, Ltd.* v. *Embassy of Pakistan,* [1973] 1 Lloyd's Rep. 363, U.S. Court of Appeals, Second Circuit. (See the judgment of TIMBERS, Ct. J., *ibid.,* at p. 368.)

[4] *Ibid.,* Art. IV, r. 5. See pp. 173–176, *post.*

[5] But this limit has been raised by the British Maritime Law Association Agreement of 1950. See p. 175, *post.*

[6] These words are not confined to physical damage, and are wide enough to cover, *e.g.* the loss caused by having to tranship goods because they have been delivered at a different port from that stated in the bill of lading: *G. H. Renton & Co.* v. *Palmyra Trading Corporation of Panama,* [1956] 3 All E. R. 957; [1957] A. C. 149, H. L.

[7] Carriage of Goods by Sea Act 1924, Sched. Art. III, r. 6. But the period has been extended to 2 years under the British Maritime Law Association Agreement of 1950. See p. 143, *post.*

[8] *Ibid.,* Arts. II, III and IV.

It should be observed that the term "carrier", as used in the Act, is defined as meaning "the owner or the charterer who enters into a contract with the shipper",[1] *i.e.* the person liable to be sued by the holder of the bill of lading.

In general, the extent of the carrier's immunity, as laid down by the Act, cannot be increased by contract: any clause or contract purporting to relieve a carrier of his liabilities under the Act is expressly declared to be void and of no effect.[2]

Thus, a clause in a bill of lading stating that the carrier would not be liable for any damage unless the shipper proved negligence or lack of due diligence on the carrier's part was held to be void because it shifted the burden of proof from the carrier to the shipper.[3] Again, a clause excluding the carrier's liability "for bags or bales burst, torn or stained and consequences arising therefrom" was held to be void,[4] as also was a clause excluding liability for "deterioration" of a cargo of melons.[5]

On the other hand, the carrier may, by an express provision in the bill of lading, give up any of his rights under the Act and so increase his liabilities.[6] In order that such a clause may be effective it must be clearly worded: "the surrender of a statutory immunity must be clearly stated".[7]

The Act also contains a provision that where "particular goods" are shipped, and the transaction is not an ordinary commercial shipment in the ordinary course of trade, shipper and carrier may make an agreement in any terms, provided certain conditions are

---

[1] Carriage of Goods by Sea Act 1924, Sched. Art. I (a). The word "carrier" does not include stevedores: *Scruttons, Ltd.* v. *Midland Silicones, Ltd.*, [1962] 1 All E. R. 1; [1962] A. C. 446, H. L. See also *Krawill Machinery Corporation* v. *Robert C. Herd & Co., Inc.* [1959] 1 Lloyd's Rep. 305 (United States Supreme Court). Nor does it include the master: *International Milling Co.* v. *The Perseus*, [1958] 2 Lloyd's Rep. 272 (U.S. District Court of Michigan).

[2] *Ibid.*, Sched. Art. III, r. 8.

[3] *Encyclopaedia Britannica Inc.* v. *The "Hong Kong Producer" and Universal Marine Corporation*, [1969] 2 Lloyd's Rep. 536, U.S. Ct. of Appeals, Second Circuit. See the judgment of ANDERSON, Ct. J., *ibid.*, at p. 543.

[4] *Bruck Mills, Ltd.* v. *Black Sea S.S. Co.: The "Grumant"*, [1973] 2 Lloyd's Rep. 531, Federal Court of Canada, Trial Division.

[5] *William D. Branson, Ltd. and Tomas Alcazar S.A.* v. *Jadranska Slobodna Plovidba (Adriatic Tramp Shipping): The "Split"*, [1973] 2 Lloyd's Rep. 535, Federal Court of Canada, Trial Division.

[6] Carriage of Goods by Sea Act 1924, Sched. Art. V.

[7] *The Touraine*, [1928] P. 58, *per* HILL, J., at p. 66.

complied with.[1] The necessary conditions are that no bill of lading has been or shall be issued, and that the terms agreed shall be embodied in a receipt which is non-negotiable and marked as such.[2] Any such agreement has full legal effect, except in so far as an attempted limitation of the carrier's liability as to sea-worthiness may be contrary to public policy.[3]

The precise meaning of the phrase "particular goods" in this connexion has not so far been judicially determined. The only assistance to be derived from the Act itself is the proviso that contracting out in the case of particular goods shall be allowed "where the character or condition of the property to be carried, or the circumstances, terms and conditions under which the carriage is to be performed are such as reasonably to justify a special agreement",[4] but this proviso itself is somewhat obscure. It is submitted, albeit with some hesitation, that the meaning is that where goods of a particular class are shipped, and the parties agree that the carrier shall perform, in relation to those goods, some service apart altogether from his usual duties as a carrier, then the carrier may insist, if he wishes, on a modification of those usual duties.

In order to avoid hampering the coasting trade around and between the British Isles, the Act provides[5] that where the port of destination is within the British Isles, carrier and shipper shall in connexion with any shipment have freedom to contract on any terms, provided again that certain conditions are fulfilled. Here also the conditions are that no bill of lading has been or shall be issued, and that the terms agreed shall be embodied in a receipt which is non-negotiable and marked as such.[6] Moreover, in this connexion also the freedom of contract permitted does not extend to enable the shipowner to limit his obligations as to seaworthiness in any manner which would be contrary to public policy.

---

[1] Carriage of Goods by Sea Act 1924, Sched. Art. VI.
[2] *Ibid.*
[3] *Ibid.*
[4] *Ibid.*, Sched. Art. VI.
[5] *Ibid.*, s. 4; Sched. Art. VI.
[6] For a case in which advantage was taken of the freedom of contract thus preserved, see *Hugh Mack & Co., Ltd.* v. *Burns and Laird Lines, Ltd.*, [1944] N. I. 106.

Interpretation of the Act

Since the Carriage of Goods by Sea Act 1924 is based on the Hague Rules, it is desirable to seek uniformity of interpretation in the many jurisdictions in which the Rules may arise for consideration. Thus, Lord ATKIN said in *Stag Line, Ltd.* v. *Foscolo, Mango & Co. Ltd.*,[1]

"For the purpose of uniformity it is, therefore, important that the Courts should apply themselves to the consideration only of the words used without any predilection for the former law, always preserving the right to say that words used in the English language which have already in the particular context received judicial interpretation may be presumed to be used in the same sense already judicially imputed to them."

Again, Lord MACMILLAN observed in the same case,[2]

"As these Rules must come under the consideration of foreign Courts it is desirable in the interests of uniformity that their interpretation should not be rigidly controlled by domestic precedents of antecedent date, but rather that the language of the Rules should be construed on broad principles of general acceptance."

THE CARRIAGE OF GOODS BY SEA ACT 1971

The International Convention which was signed at Brussels in 1924 was amended by a Protocol signed there on February 23, 1968. The United Kingdom was a signatory to this Protocol, and the Carriage of Goods by Sea Act 1971[3] was passed in order to give effect to it.

The Act, however, does not come into effect immediately, but only on such date as Her Majesty may by Order in Council appoint.[4]

---

[1] [1932] A. C. 328, H. L., at p. 343.

[2] *Ibid.,* at p. 350.

[3] The text of the Act is set out in Appendix H, *post.*

[4] Carriage of Goods by Sea Act 1971, s. 6 (5). For the purposes of the transition from the law in force immediately before the day appointed under this subsection to the provisions of the Act of 1971, the Order appointing the day may provide that those provisions shall have effect subject to such transitional provisions as may be contained in the Order: *ibid.*

Principal Provisions of the Act

The principal provisions of the Act are as follows:

(1) *Repeal of Carriage of Goods by Sea Act 1924*

The Act of 1971 repeals the earlier Act of 1924 in its entirety.[1]

(2) *Hague Rules set out in revised form*

The Hague Rules as revised by the Protocol are set out in the Schedule to the Act of 1971 and have the force of law.[2]

(3) *General scope of Act*

The Act applies to certain types of contract only. There are special provisions relating to the carriage of live animals and deck cargo. Where a vessel is chartered and a bill of lading is issued under the charter-party, the Act applies only from a certain moment. The Act applies only to certain parts of the contract of carriage.

(a) *Types of contract concerned.* The Act applies to:

(i) any contract for the carriage of goods by sea in ships where the port of shipment is a port in the United Kingdom and the contract expressly or by implication provides for the issue of a bill of lading or any similar document of title.[3]

(ii) any bill of lading if the contract contained in or evidenced by it expressly provides that the Hague Rules shall govern the contract.[4]

(iii) any receipt which is a non-negotiable document marked as such if the contract contained in or evidenced by it is a contract for the carriage of goods by sea which expressly provides that the

---

[1] *Ibid.*, s. 6 (3) (a).
[2] *Ibid.*, s. 1 (2).
[3] *Ibid.*, s. 1 (3).
[4] *Ibid.*, s. 1 (6) (a).

Rules are to govern the contract as if the receipt were a bill of lading.[1]

(b) *Carriage of live animals and deck cargo.* Where the shipment is made from a port in the United Kingdom, the Act does not apply to the carriage of live animals and cargo which by the contract of carriage is stated as being carried on deck and is so carried.[2]

But where the bill of lading expressly provides that the Hague Rules shall govern the contract, or a non-negotiable receipt provides that the Rules are to govern the contract as if it were a bill of lading, the Act applies even though the cargo consists of live animals or deck cargo.[3]

(c) *Bills of lading issued under charter-party.* The Act does not apply at all to a charter-party.[4]

Where a vessel is chartered, a bill of lading issued under the charter-party is merely a receipt and the Act does not apply to it. But the Act does apply "from the moment at which such bill of lading or similar document of title regulates the relations between a carrier and a holder of the same",[5] *i.e.*, if a bill of lading is issued to a charterer, and he indorses it to a third party, the bill of lading is the document which governs the relations between the carrier and the indorsee, and from the moment of indorsement the Act applies.

(d) *Portion of contract to which Act applicable.* The Act applies only to that part of the contract which relates to the carriage

---

[1] *Ibid.*, s. 1 (6) (b). In the case of such a non-negotiable document the Hague Rules apply subject to any necessary modifications and in particular with the omission of the second sentence of r. 4 (concerning the bill of lading as *prima facie* evidence of receipt of the goods by the carrier) and of the omission of the whole of r. 7 (concerning the issue of a "shipped" bill of lading) of Sched. Art. III: *ibid.*

[2] *Ibid.*, Sched. Art. I (c). For the interpretation of this provision, see p. 67, footnote 2, *ante.*

[3] *Ibid.*, s. 1 (7).

[4] *Ibid.*, Sched. Art. V.

[5] *Ibid.*, Sched. Art I (b).

by sea,[1] and only to "the period from the time when the goods are loaded on to the time when they are discharged from the ship".[2]

A carrier or a shipper is entitled to enter into any agreement, stipulation, condition, reservation or exemption as to the responsibility and liability of the carrier or the ship for the loss of or damage to, or in connection with, the custody and care and handling of the goods prior to the loading on, and subsequent to the discharge from, the ship on which the goods are carried by sea.[3]

(4) *Abolition of absolute warranty of seaworthiness*

Where the Act applies, no absolute undertaking by the carrier to provide a seaworthy ship is implied.[4] But the carrier must before and at the beginning of the voyage exercise due diligence to make her seaworthy.[5]

(5) *Extension of right to deviate*

Liberty to deviate is given in order to save property or where a deviation is reasonable.[6]

(6) *Particulars to be shown in bill of lading*

On the demand of the shipper the shipowner must issue a bill of lading giving certain particulars, *e.g.* quantity of goods shipped, their apparent condition.[7]

(7) *Care of cargo*

The carrier must "properly and carefully load, handle, stow, carry, keep, care for and discharge the cargo".[8]

---

[1] *Ibid.,* Sched. Art I (b).
[2] *Ibid.,* Sched. Art I (c).
[3] *Ibid.,* Sched. Art VII.
[4] *Ibid.,* s. 3.
[5] *Ibid.,* Sched. Art. III, r. 1. See p. 88, *post.*
[6] *Ibid.,* Sched. Art. IV, r. 4. See p. 90, *post.*
[7] *Ibid.,* Sched. Art. III, r. 3. See pp. 59, 63, *ante.*
[8] *Ibid.,* Sched. Art. III, r. 2. See pp. 70–72, *ante.*

(8) *Immunities given to carrier*

The Act sets out a list of "excepted perils",[1] and if loss or damage is caused by them, the shipowner will not be liable provided he has fulfilled his duties under the Act.

He is entitled to increase his liabilities,[2] but cannot add to the list of "excepted perils".[3]

The defences provided for in the Act apply in any action against the carrier in respect of loss or damage to the goods whether the action be founded in contract or in tort.[4]

If an action is brought against a servant or agent of the carrier (such a servant or agent not being an independent contractor), such servant or agent is entitled to avail himself of the defences which the carrier is entitled to invoke under the Act.[5]

(9) *Rights given to carrier*

The carrier is entitled to throw overboard goods which are dangerous.[6] He can obtain an indemnity for loss caused to him by the shipper stating the particulars of the goods inaccurately.[7] But the shipper is not responsible for loss or damage sustained by the carrier arising or resulting from any cause without the act, fault or neglect of the shipper, his agents or his servants.[8]

(10) *Limitation of liability*

The Act limits the liability of the carrier to 10,000 francs per package or unit or 30 francs per kilo of gross weight of the goods lost or damaged, whichever is the higher.[9]

The limits of liability provided for in the Act apply in any action brought against the carrier in respect of loss or damage to goods whether the action is founded in contract or tort.[10]

---

[1] *Ibid.*, Sched. Art. IV, r. 2. See p. 167, *post.*
[2] *Ibid.*, Sched. Art. V.
[3] *Ibid.*, Sched. Art. III, r. 8.
[4] *Ibid.*, Sched. Art. IV *bis*, r. 1.
[5] *Ibid.*, Sched. Art. IV *bis*, r. 2.
[6] *Ibid.*, Sched. Art. IV, r. 6. See p. 167, *post.*
[7] *Ibid.*, Sched. Art. III, r. 5. See pp. 59, 63, *ante.*
[8] *Ibid.*, Sched. Art. IV, r. 3.
[9] *Ibid.*, Sched. Art. IV, r. 5 (a). See pp. 176–177, *post.*
[10] *Ibid.*, Sched. Art. IV *bis*, r. 1.

If an action is brought against a servant or agent of the carrier (such servant or agent not being an independent contractor), such servant or agent is entitled to avail himself of the limits of liability set out above.[1]

(11) *Limitation of action*

The carrier is discharged from all liability if the action is not brought within one year from the date of the delivery of the goods or the date when they should have been delivered.[2]

But an action for indemnity against a third person may be brought after the expiration of the year if brought within the time allowed by the law of the Court seized of the case.[3]

(12) *Contracting out of the Act*

Any clause in the contract which purports to relieve a carrier of his liabilities under the Act is expressly declared to be void and of no effect.[4]

But the carrier may by an express provision in the bill of lading surrender his rights and immunities and increase any of his responsibilities and obligations under the Act.[5]

Further, where "particular goods" are shipped and the transaction is not an ordinary commercial shipment in the course of trade, the shipper and the carrier may make an agreement in any terms provided certain conditions are complied with.[6]

SOME USUAL CLAUSES IN BILLS OF LADING

The actual terms of bills of lading vary from company to company. But usually there are provisions in them setting out:

(1) the name of the vessel, port of shipment, port of delivery, and the person to whom delivery is to be made;

---

[1] *Ibid.,* Sched. Art. IV *bis*, r. 2. See p. 177, *post.*
[2] *Ibid.,* Sched. Art. III, r. 6. See p. 143, *post.*
[3] *Ibid.,* Sched. Art. III, r. 6 *bis*. See p. 143, *post.*
[4] *Ibid.,* Sched. Art. III, r. 8. See p. 74, *ante.*
[5] *Ibid.,* Sched. Art. V. See p. 74, *ante.*
[6] *Ibid.,* Sched. Art VI. See pp. 74–75, *ante.*

(2) the number of the goods shipped, their apparent condition, and leading marks;[1]

(3) a General Paramount Clause incorporating the Hague Rules;[2]

(4) a list of "excepted perils;[3]

(5) a "deviation" clause;[4]

(6) the amount of the freight to be paid;[5]

(7) the extent of the shipowner's lien over the goods carried;[6]

(8) how delivery is to be made;[7]

(9) a clause incorporating the York–Antwerp Rules 1974 in relation to general average;[8]

(10) a "Both-to-Blame" Collision Clause;[9]

(11) what law is to govern the contract;[10]

(12) an arbitration clause.[11]

IMPLIED UNDERTAKINGS IN BILLS OF LADING

Various undertakings are implied in bills of lading by Common Law or imposed by statute.

---

[1] See p. 64, *ante*. On the effect of "weight and condition unknown" clauses, see p. 59, *ante*.

[2] See p. 69, *ante*. Even when the Hague Rules do not apply to the bill of lading *proprio vigore*, the parties are entitled to incorporate them into the contract.

[3] See pp. 147–155, *post*.

[4] See pp. 21–22, *ante*.

[5] See pp. 221–229, *post*.

[6] See pp. 234–235, *post*.

[7] See pp. 130–131, *post*.

[8] See pp. 188–189, *post*.

[9] See pp. 152–153, *post*.

[10] See p. 109, *post*.

[11] See. *e.g., Denny, Mott and Dickson, Ltd.* v. *Lynn Shipping Co., Ltd.,* [1963] 1 Lloyd's Rep. 339, where the bill of lading incorporated a clause in a charterparty, which stated: "All claims must be made in writing and the Claimant's Arbitrator must be appointed within twelve months of final discharge, otherwise the claim shall be deemed waived and absolutely barred." See further as to this case, p. 139, *post*.

(A) On the part of the shipowner

The shipowner undertakes:

(1) that his ship is seaworthy;

(2) that she shall proceed with reasonable despatch; and

(3) that she shall proceed without unjustifiable deviation.

(1) Seaworthiness

(a) At Common Law

As we have seen, the duty of a shipowner under a voyage charter-party is to supply a ship which is seaworthy in fact.[1] The same rule applies in the case of a bill of lading. Similarly, seaworthiness includes cargo-worthiness. Thus, in *Cargo per Maori King* v. *Hughes*,[2]

where the contract was to carry frozen meat, the ship was *held* to be unseaworthy unless provided with suitable refrigerating machinery.

The shipowner cannot protect himself by ambiguous and general words.[3] Thus, in *Ingram* v. *Services Maritime du Treport*,[4]

a stipulation was inserted in the bill of lading, absolving the shipowners from every duty, warranty, or obligation, provided they exercised reasonable care in connexion with the upkeep of the ship. *Held*, that this was too ambiguous to exempt the shipowners from the obligation to provide a seaworthy ship.

Further, in *Nelson Line (Liverpool), Ltd.* v. *James Nelson & Sons, Ltd.*,[5]

Frozen meat had been shipped under an agreement which stated that the shipowner would not be liable for any damage "which is capable of being

---

[1] See pp. 14–18, *ante*.

[2] [1895] 2 Q. B. 550.

[3] *Elderslie S.S. Co.* v. *Borthwick,* [1905] A. C. 93.

[4] [1914] 1 K. B. 541.

[5] [1904–7] All E. R. Rep. 244, H. L. See also *The "Rossetti"*, [1972] 2 Lloyd's Rep. 116, Q. B. D. (Admiralty Court), where there was a conflict between the provisions on unseaworthiness in two of the clauses of the bill of lading, and it was held that there was no clear exception of liability for unseaworthiness. (See the judgment of BRANDON, J., *ibid.,* at p. 116.)

covered by insurance". The meat arrived in a damaged condition on account of the unseaworthiness of the vessel. *Held*, that the clause was not sufficiently clear to exempt the shipowners from being liable to supply a seaworthy ship.

Again, limitation of liability to a specified sum,[1] or a clause totally exempting the shipowner from liability if the claim is not made within a given time,[2] cannot avail the shipowner where the loss is due to unseaworthiness unless clear and express words were used to indicate it.

Thus, in *Tattersall* v. *National Steamship Co.*,[3]

cattle were shipped under a bill of lading which provided that the shipowners were not to be responsible for disease or mortality and that in no circumstances should they be held liable for more than £5 for each of the animals. The ship had not been properly disinfected before the cattle were received on board, with the result that they contracted foot-and-mouth disease. *Held*, that the omission to disinfect the ship constituted a breach of the warranty of cargoworthiness, and so the shipowners were prevented from relying on the clause in the bill of lading limiting liability to £5 for each of the cattle.

(b) By Statute

(i) *Under the Carriage of Goods by Sea Act 1924*. Where the Carriage of Goods by Sea Act 1924 applies,[4] no absolute undertaking as to seaworthiness is implied.[5] The carrier has, however, before and at the beginning of the voyage to exercise due diligence (i) to make the ship seaworthy;[6] (ii) to properly man, equip and supply her; and (iii) to make the holds, refrigerating and cool chambers, and all other parts of the ship in which goods are

---

[1] *Tattersall* v. *National S.S. Co.* (1884), 12 Q. B. D. 297.
[2] *Atlantic Co.* v. *Louis Dreyfus & Co.*, [1922] 2 A. C. 250.
[3] *Supra.*
[4] See pp. 67-69.
[5] Section 2.
[6] *The Makedonia, Owners of Cargo Laden on Makedonia* v. *Makedonia Owners,* [1962] 2 All E. R. 614; [1962] P. 190 (failure to instruct engineers in operation of o l fuel system); *Robin Hood Flour Mills, Ltd.* v. *N. M. Paterson & Sons, Ltd., The Farrandoc,* [1967] 2 Lloyd's Rep. 276 (Exchequer Court of Canada) (shipowners not assuring themselves of experience, competence and reliability of second engineer before engaging him).

carried, fit and safe for their reception,[1] carriage and preservation.[2]

The words "before and at the beginning of the voyage" mean the period from at least the beginning of the loading until the vessel starts on her voyage.[3]

The word "voyage" means the contractual voyage from the port of loading to the port of discharge as declared in the bill of lading. Where the voyage is divided into "stages", *e.g.* as regards bunkering, the carrier's obligation is to exercise due diligence before and at the beginning of the voyage to have the vessel adequately bunkered for the first stage, and to arrange for adequate bunkers of the proper kind at intermediate ports so that the contractual voyage may be performed.[4]

Whether due diligence has been exercised is a matter of fact in each case. Cases on this point have related to a failure to provide sufficient bunker fuel,[5] a failure in the ship's steering gear,[6] the blowing out of a boiler tube,[7] a fault in a vessel's design,[8] a failure to see that a valve was properly tightened,[9] thawing out frozen scupper pipes by the use of an acetylene torch,[10] a failure in a vessel's reduction gear,[11] a failure to equip

---

[1] In *The Fehmarn*, [1964] 1 Lloyd's Rep. 355, the bill of lading was not governed by the Hague Rules, but contained a clause in substantially the same terms as those of Art. III, r. 1, and it was held that the carriers were in breach because they had not properly cleaned the vessel's tanks for the reception of the cargo of turpentine, which arrived at the port of discharge in a contaminated condition.

[2] Carriage of Goods by Sea Act 1924, Sched. Art. III, r. 1.

[3] *Maxine Footwear Co., Ltd.* v. *Canadian Merchant Marine, Ltd.* [1959] 2 All E. R. 740; [1959] A. C. 589, P. C.: *Western Canada S.S. Co., Ltd.* v. *Canadian Commercial Corporation*, [1960] 2 Lloyd's Rep. 313 at p. 319 (Supreme Court of Canada).

[4] *The Makedonia (supra)*.

[5] *Northumbrian Shipping Co.* v. *Timm*, [1939] 2 All E. R. 648; [1939] A. C. 397 H. L.: *The Makedonia (supra)*.

[6] *The Assunzione*, [1956] 2 Lloyd's Rep. 468.

[7] *Goulandris Brothers, Ltd.* v. *B. Goldman & Sons, Ltd.*, [1957] 3 All E. R. 100; [1958] 1 Q. B. 74.

[8] *Riverstone Meat Co. Pty., Ltd.* v. *Lancashire Shipping Co., Ltd.*, [1958] 3 All E. R. 261; [1959] 1 Q. B. 74 (at first instance).

[9] *Riverstone Meat Co. Pty., Ltd.* v. *Lancashire Shipping Co., Ltd.*, [1961] 1 All E. R. 495; [1961] A. C. 807, H. L.

[10] *Maxime Footwear Co., Ltd.* v. *Canadian Merchant Marine, Ltd.*, [1959] 2 All E. R. 740; [1959] A. C. 589, P. C.

[11] *Union of India* v. *N. V. Reederij, Amsterdam*, [1963] 2 Lloyd's Rep. 223, H. L.

a tramp vessel with radar and loran,[1] a failure to instruct engineers in the operation of an oil fuel system,[2] the engagement of an incompetent engineer,[3] a failure to provide a plan of the piping in a vessel's engine room,[4] a failure to check a valve in the forward hold suction line and thus causing a hold to be unsafe for the carriage of the cargo,[5] a failure to notice that the coamings of a deep tank hatch were defective,[6] a failure to see that a vessel's sanitary water system was in order,[7] and a failure to have on board the latest Admiralty List of Radio Signals.[8]

The negligence of his servants or agents will be sufficient to affect him with liability; but he will not be responsible for negligence on the part of the shipbuilders in constructing the ship, unless he himself or someone for whose default he is responsible was in some way at fault, as, for example, by negligently passing bad work.[9]

However, he will be liable for negligence on the part of ship repairers to whom the vessel has been sent for repairs.

---

[1] *President of India* v. *West Coast S.S. Co.; The "Portland Trader"*, [1964] 2 Lloyd's Rep. 443, U.S. Court of Appeals, where it was held that the employment of radar and loran in the navigation of tramp vessels was not so essential that their absence would give rise to a finding of unseaworthiness; *American Smelting & Refining Co.* v. *S.S. "Irish Spruce" and Irish Shipping Ltd.*: *The "Irish Spruce"*, [1976] 1 Lloyd's Rep 63, District Court, Southern District of New York.

[2] *The Makedonia, Owners of Cargo Laden on Makedonia* v. *Makedonia Owners*, [1962] 2 All E. R. 614; [1962] P. 190.

[3] *Robin Hood Flour Mills, Ltd.* v. *N. M. Paterson & Sons, Ltd., The Farrandoc*, [1967] 2 Lloyd's Rep. 276, Exchequer Court of Canada. As to this aspect of the case, see the judgment of THURLOW, J., *ibid.*, at pp. 281–2; that of NOEL, J., *ibid.*, at pp. 286–7; and that of GIBSON, J., *ibid.*, at p. 289.

[4] *Ibid.* As to this aspect of the case, see the judgment of THURLOW, J., *ibid.*, at p. 280, that of NOEL, J., *ibid.*, at p. 286, and that of GIBSON, J., *ibid.*, at p. 289.

[5] *Fisons Fertilizers, Ltd. and Fisons, Ltd.* v. *Thomas Watson (Shipping), Ltd.*, [1971] 1 Lloyd's Rep. 141, Mayor's and City of London Court. For the evidence as to when the defect occurred, see *ibid.*, at pp. 142–143.

[6] *Sears Roebuck & Co.* v. *American President Lines, Ltd.*: *The "President Monroe"*, [1972] 1 Lloyd's Rep. 385, District Court, Northern District of California.

[7] *International Produce Inc. and Greenwich Mills Co.* v. *S.S. "Frances Salman", Swedish Gulf Line A/B and Companhia de Navegacao Maritima Netumar: The "Frances Salman"*, [1975] 2 Lloyd's Rep. 355, District Court, Southern District of New York.

[8] *American Smelting & Refining Co.* v. *S.S. "Irish Spruce" and Irish Shipping Ltd.*: *The "Irish Spruce"* (*supra*).

[9] *W. Angliss* v. *P. & O.*, [1927] 2 K. B. 456.

Thus, in *Riverstone Meat Co. Pty., Ltd.* v. *Lancashire Shipping Co., Ltd.,*[1]

a fitter employed by ship repairers negligently refixed some inspection covers on some storm valves. Water entered the valves during the voyage and damaged the cargo. *Held*, the negligence of the fitter was a lack of due diligence for which the carrier was responsible.

He will also be liable for the failure of a compass adjuster to exercise due diligence.[2]

The certificate of a Lloyd's surveyor is likely to be accepted by the Court as conclusive to show that the carrier has exercised due diligence when it relates to a case in which he has built or bought a ship in the first instance.[3] To go behind it "would involve a retrogression beyond the point to which a reasonable (shipowner) can be expected to go".[4] But it is not so likely to be accepted where it relates to his duty as to the day-to-day maintenance and upkeep of his ship.[5]

A clause stating that a survey certificate shall be "conclusive evidence of due diligence" to make the ship seaworthy is void under Article III, r. 8 of the Act.[6]

Under the Act, it has been held that the onus of proving unseaworthiness is upon those who allege it; it is then for the carrier to show, if he can, that in fact he did exercise due diligence.[7]

---

[1] [1961] 1 All E. R. 495; [1961] A. C. 807, H. L.

[2] *Paterson S.S., Ltd.* v. *Robin Hood Mills, Ltd.* (1937), 58 Ll. L. Rep. 33, P. C.

[3] *W. Angliss* v. *P. & O. Co.* (*supra*); *Waddle* v. *Wallsend Shipping Co.,* [1952] 2 Lloyd's Rep. 105; *Riverstone Meat Co. Pty., Ltd.* v. *Lancashire Shipping Co., Ltd.,* [1958] 3 All E. R. 261; [1959] 1 Q. B. 74 (at first instance).

[4] *Waddle* v. *Wallsend Shipping Co.,* [1952] 2 Lloyd's Rep. 105, at p. 130.

[5] *Cranfield Brothers, Ltd.* v. *Tatem Steam Navigation Co., Ltd.* (1939), 64 Ll. L. Rep. 264, at p. 267; *The Assunzione* (*supra*).

[6] *The Australia Star* (1940), 67 Ll. L. Rep. 110, at p. 116.

[7] Carriage of Goods by Sea Act 1924, Sched. Art. IV, r. 1; *W. Angliss and Co.* v. *P. & O.* (*supra*); *Charles Goodfellow Lumber Sales⁹ Ltd.* v. *Verreault Hovington and Verreault Navigation Inc.,* [1971] 1 Lloyd's Rep. 185, Supreme Court of Canada, where it was held that the production of a certificate of seaworthiness signed by an inspector appointed by the Department of Transport was not sufficient to discharge the burden of proof that due diligence had been exercised by the shipowners. See the judgment of RITCHIE, J., *ibid.*, at p. 194.

(ii) *Under the Carriage of Goods by Sea Act 1971.* Where the Carriage of Goods by Sea Act 1971[1] applies[2], no absolute undertaking as to seaworthiness is implied.[3] But the carrier is under the same duty as that imposed on him by the Carriage of Goods by Sea Act 1924, *viz.* before and at the beginning of the voyage he must exercise due diligence (i) to make the ship seaworthy; (ii) to properly man, equip and supply her; and (iii) to make the holds, refrigerating and cool chambers, and all other parts of the ship in which goods are carried, fit and safe for their reception, carriage and preservation.[4]

(2) Reasonable Despatch

As in the case of a voyage charter-party,[5] it is implied in bills of lading that the voyage must be prosecuted with reasonable despatch.

The Carriage of Goods by Sea Act 1924 makes no reference to the implied undertaking as to reasonable despatch. It seems, therefore, that that undertaking forms part of the contract even though the Act applies. The omission to mention the point in the Rules seems to have been due to an oversight, as it was clearly intended that no term other than those laid down by the Act should be implied in a contract governed thereby.

Further, no mention is made in the Carriage of Goods by Sea Act 1971[6] of such an undertaking.

(3) No Deviation

The General Rule

(a) *At Common Law*

As in the case of a voyage charter-party,[7] it is implied in all bills of lading that no deviation will be made from the contractual

---

[1] *This Act is not yet in force.* See p. 76, *ante.*
[2] See pp. 77–79, *ante.*
[3] Carriage of Goods by Sea Act 1971, s. 3.
[4] *Ibid.,* Sched. Art. III, r. 1.
[5] See pp. 18–19, *ante.*
[6] *This Act is not yet in force.* See p. 76, *ante.*
[7] See pp. 20–23, *ante.*

route, unless such deviation is justified, *i.e.* where it is made for purposes necessary for the prosecution of the voyage or for the safety of the adventure, or to save human life.

(b) *By Statute*

(i) *Under the Carriage of Goods by Sea Act 1924.* The most important alteration of the law with regard to deviation effected by the Carriage of Goods by Sea Act 1924 is that, in cases to which that Act applies,[1] deviation for the purpose of saving property at sea is justified and therefore not deemed to be a breach of the contract.[2]

The Act also provides that "any reasonable deviation" is not to be considered a breach of the contract.[3] Whether or not a particular deviation is reasonable is a question of fact in each case.[4]

Thus, in *Stag Line, Ltd.* v. *Foscolo, Mango & Co. Ltd.*,[5]

in the course of a voyage from Swansea to Constantinople a vessel deviated from the contractual route in order to land at St. Ives some engineers who had been testing her fuel-saving apparatus. After leaving St. Ives she struck a rock and was lost. *Held*, not a reasonable deviation.

In that case Lord ATKIN said:[6]

"A deviation may, and often will, be caused by fortuitous circumstances never contemplated by the original parties to the contract, and may be reasonable though it is made solely in the interests of the ship or solely in the interests of the cargo or indeed in the direct interest of neither; as for instance where the presence of a passenger or of a member of the ship or crew was urgently required after the voyage had begun on a matter of national importance; or where some person on board was a fugitive from justice, and there were urgent reasons for his immediate

---

[1] See pp. 67–69, *ante.*

[2] Sched. Art. IV, r. 4.

[3] *Ibid.*,

[4] *Stag Line, Ltd.* v. *Foscolo Mango & Co., Ltd.*, [1932] A. C. 328; [1931] All E. R. Rep. 666, H. L.; *Accinanto, Ltd.* v. *A/S J. Ludwig Mowinckels: The Ocean Liberty*, [1953] 1 Lloyd's Rep. 38, C. A.; *Thiess Bros. (Queensland) Pty., Ltd.* v. *Australian S.S. Pty., Ltd.*, [1955] 1 Lloyd's Rep. 459; *Georgia-Pacific Corporation* v. *"Marilyn L."*, *Elvapores Inc., Evans Products Co. and Retla S.S. Co.: The "Marilyn L."*, [1972] 1 Lloyd's Rep. 418, District Court for the Eastern District of Virginia, Norfolk Division, where the master had not followed the route suggested by the Pacific Weather Analysis.

[5] *Supra.*

[6] [1932] A. C. at p. 343.

appearance. The true test seems to be what departure from the contract voyage might a prudent person controlling the voyage at the time make and maintain having in mind all the relevant circumstances existing at the time including the terms of the contract and the interest of all parties concerned, but without obligation to consider the interests of any one as conclusive."

Again, in *Thiess Brothers (Queensland) Pty., Ltd.* v. *Australian Steamship Pty., Ltd.*,[1]

a vessel was required by the terms of a bill of lading to deliver a cargo at Melbourne. She deviated to Newcastle (N.S.W.) only 4 miles off her course to take on bunkers for her next voyage.
Held, not a reasonable deviation.

Where goods are packed in containers and stowed on the deck of a container ship built for the purpose of carrying deck cargo, such shipment does not constitute an unreasonable deviation.[2]

(ii) *Under the Carriage of Goods by Sea Act 1971.* Where the Carriage of Goods by Sea Act 1971[3] applies,[4] the position is the same as that under the Carriage of Goods by Sea Act 1924.[5]

Express clauses permitting deviation. As in the case of voyage charter-parties,[6] bills of lading often contain a clause which gives the shipowner the right to call at ports off the ordinary trade route. Thus, in *Leduc* v. *Ward*,[7]

where the bill of lading gave "liberty to call at any ports in any order and to deviate for the purpose of saving life or property," the voyage being from Fiume to Dunkirk, the ship was taken out of her course to Glasgow on the shipowner's private business. She was lost in a storm in the Clyde. *Held*, the above clause merely gave a right to call at any ports in the ordinary course of the voyage. The shipowner was therefore liable.

In construing all such clauses as the above, the Court will apply

---

[1] [1955] 1 Lloyd's Rep. 459, Supreme Court of New South Wales.

[2] *Du Pont de Nemours International S.A. and E.I. Du Pont de Nemours & Co. Inc.* v. *S.S. "Mormacvega" etc. and Moore-McCormack Lines Inc.: The "Mormacvega"*, [1974] 1 Lloyd's Rep. 296, U.S. Court of Appeals, Second Circuit. (See the judgment of TIMBERS, Ct. J., *ibid.*, at p. 300.)

[3] *This Act is not yet in force. See p. 76, ante.*

[4] *See pp. 77-79, ante.*

[5] Carriage of Goods by Sea Act 1971, Art. IV, r. 4.

[6] See p. 21-22, *ante.*

[7] (1888), 20 Q. B. D. 475.

the general principle that the main object of the contract must not be defeated. So, even where the deviation clause gives liberty to call at ports *outside* the direct geographical voyage in express terms, such liberty will be limited, by inclusion in the contract of a special description of the voyage undertaken (*e.g.* "Malaga to Liverpool"), to permission to call at ports on the course of that voyage.[1]

On the other hand, a very comprehensive deviation clause protected the shipowner in *Connolly Shaw, Ltd.* v. *Nordenfjeldske S.S. Co.*,[2]

Lemons were shipped from Palermo to London under a bill of lading which provided: ". . . the ship is to be at liberty, either before or after proceeding towards the port of delivery of the said goods, to proceed to or return to and stay at any ports or places whatsoever (although in a contrary direction to or out of or beyond the route of the said port of delivery) once or oftener in any order backwards or forwards for loading or discharging cargo passengers coals or stores or for any purpose whatsoever . . . and also such ports places and sailing shall be deemed included within the intended voyage of the said goods." Before proceeding to London the ship deviated to Hull. In spite of the delay, the lemons arrived in London in good condition, but in the interval the price of lemons had fallen. The indorsees of the bills of lading failed to recover damages against the shipowners, for it was *held* that the deviation to Hull was covered by the clause.

(B) On the part of the Shipper

A shipper impliedly undertakes that the goods he ships are not dangerous when carried in the ordinary way, unless

(1) he expressly notifies the shipowner to the contrary,

or (2) the shipowner knows, or ought to know, that they are dangerous.[3] Thus, in *Brass* v. *Maitland*,[4]

where bleaching powder containing chloride of lime was shipped and damaged other goods on board, the shipowner, having been made liable for the damage, sued the shipper. It was proved that

---

[1] *Glynn* v. *Margetson*, [1893] A. C. 351; *G. H. Renton & Co., Ltd.* v. *Palmyra Trading Corporation of Panama*, [1956] 3 All E.R. 957; [1957] A. C. 149, H. L.

[2] (1934), 50 T. L. R. 418.

[3] *Bamfield* v. *Goole, etc., Transport Co.*, [1910] 2 K. B. 94.

[4] (1856), 6 E. & B. 470.

the latter knew of the character of the goods he had shipped; but, as the master ought to have known that the powder contained chloride of lime, it was *held* that the shipper was not liable.[1]

It seems that the true nature of this implied undertaking is not that of an *absolute* guarantee of the harmlessness of the goods, but only a guarantee that the goods are not dangerous to the knowledge of the shipper, and that he has taken reasonable care to assure himself of that fact.[2]

Where the nature of the goods shipped is liable to cause the forfeiture or detention of the ship, the goods are "dangerous" with the meaning of this principle,[3] subject, of course, to the limitations (1) and (2) set out above.[4]

But the shipper does not impliedly undertake that the cargo can be expeditiously unloaded. Thus, in *Transoceanica Italiana* v. *H. S. Shipton & Sons*,[5]

a cargo of barley contained some sand and stones. The suction pump employed in the discharge of the vessel became choked in consequence, and she was delayed. *Held,* the shipper was not liable for the delay.

The statutes mentioned in the previous chapter relating to the carriage of dangerous goods apply also where they are carried under bills of lading.[6] In addition, where the Carriage of Goods by Sea Act 1924 applies,[7] the carrier or the master is entitled to destroy or render innocuous dangerous goods without being

---

[1] See also *Sebastian S.S. Owners* v. *De Vizcaya,* [1920] 1 K. B. 332; *The Domald,* [1920] P. 56; *Heath Steele Mines, Ltd.* v. *The "Erwin Schroder"*, [1969] 1 Lloyd's Rep. 370, Exchequer Court of Canada, Nova Scotia Admiralty District, where it was held that the master could not have known the danger in carrying a cargo of copper concentrate and what precautions should have been taken. See the judgment of POTTIER, J., *ibid.*, at p. 374.

[2] *Per* ATKIN, J., in *Mitchell, Cotts & Co.* v. *Steel Bros. & Co.,* [1916] 2 K. B. 610, at p. 614; see also Lord ELLENBOROUGH's *dictum* in *Williams* v. *East India Co.* (1802), 3 East, at p. 200.

[3] *Mitchell, Cotts & Co.* v. *Steel Bros. & Co. (supra).*

[4] See *per* SIR HENRY DUKE, P., in *The Lisa,* [1921] P., at pp. 46–47. The decision was reversed on other grounds: (1924), 40 T. L. R. 252.

[5] [1923] 1 K. B. 31.

[6] See p. 24, *ante.*

[7] See pp. 67–69, *ante.*

liable to pay compensation.[1] Where the Carriage of Goods by Sea Act 1971[2] applies[3], the position is the same as under the Carriage of Goods by Sea Act 1924.[4]

TRANSFER OF RIGHTS AND LIABILITIES
UNDER A BILL OF LADING

At Common Law contracts were not assignable. Hence a transfer of a bill of lading with the intention of passing the property in the goods did not transfer the rights and liabilities under the contract of carriage; it merely passed the property in the goods.

But a great change was made by the Bills of Lading Act 1855.[5]

Section 1 provides that:

"Every consignee[6] of goods named in a bill of lading, and every endorsee[7] of a bill of lading, to whom the property in the goods therein mentioned shall pass upon or by reason of such consignment or endorsement, shall have transferred to and vested in him all rights of suit, and be subject to the same liabilities in respect of such goods as if the contract contained in the bill of lading had been made with himself."

The Contract Transferred

The contract transferred is that embodied in the bill of lading[8] including, of course, such terms as are implied by law in all con-

---

[1] Sched. Art. IV, r. 6 (See Appendix E).

[2] *This Act is not yet in force.* See p. 76, *ante.*   [3] See pp. 77–79, *ante.*

[4] Carriage of Goods by Sea Act 1971, Sched. Art. IV, r. 6.

[5] See Appendix C, *post.*

[6] But where a charterer, who has received a bill of lading in respect of goods he has shipped, and has named in it another person as the consignee, he can still hold the shipowner liable on the charter-party: *Gardano and Giampari* v. *Greek Petroleum, George Mamidakis & Co.*, [1961] 3 All E. R. 919.

[7] See e.g. *The "Berkshire"*, [1974] 1 Lloyd's Rep. 185, Q. B. D. (Admiralty Court), where the bill of lading was endorsed by the shippers in blank and transferred by them to the receivers; *Pacific Molasses Co. and United Trading Co. Ltd.* v. *Entre Rios Compania Naviera S.A. : The "San Nicholas"*, [1976] 1 Lloyd's Rep. 8, C. A., where it was held that there was at least a *prima facie* case that the property passed by indorsement.

[8] But once there is a contract for the carriage of goods between a carrier and another party, the other party can always sue on the contract for failure to carry safely, subject, of course, to all relevant exceptions, whether or not at the time of the loss or damage the other party owns the goods or is entitled to immediate possession of them: *Dunlop* v. *Lambert,* (1839) 6 Cl. & F. 600; *Concord Petroleum Corporation* v. *Gosford Marine Panama S.A. : The "Albazero"*, [1975] 2 Lloyd's Rep. 295, C. A. (See the judgment of ROSKILL, L.J., *ibid.*, at p. 309.)

tracts of carriage by sea, *e.g.* not to deviate. If the bill of lading does not contain some term of the original agreement, that term will not be binding as between shipowner and assignee of the bill of lading. Thus, in *Leduc* v. *Ward*,[1]

a ship deviated to Glasgow and was lost. The indorsee of the bill of lading sued for non-delivery of the goods. It was *held* that evidence to show that, before the goods were put on board, the shippers had agreed to the deviation to Glasgow was not, as between the shipowner and the indorsee of the bill of lading, admissible to vary the contract contained therein.

Passing of the Property in the Goods

The Common Law gave effect to the mercantile usage[2] whereby indorsement and delivery of a bill of lading during the transit gave to the indorsee such property in the goods as it was the intention of the parties to transfer. In order that the property in the goods may pass by assignment of the bill of lading, the following conditions must be complied with:

(1) *The bill of lading must be transferable on the face of it.*

(2) *The goods must be in transit.*

They need not be at sea, but they must have been handed over to the shipowner or forwarding agent for carriage and not yet delivered to any person having a right to claim them under a bill of lading.[3]

(3) *The bill of lading must have been put in circulation by one who had a good title to the goods.* (Herein bills of lading differ from negotiable instruments proper, for a *bona fide* holder for value of the latter gets a good title irrespective of prior equities.)

---

[1] (1888), 20 Q. B. D. 475.

[2] See *Lickbarrow* v. *Mason* (1794), 1 Sm. L. C. 13th edn., p. 703; Chorley and Tucker's *Leading Cases* (4th edn. 1962), p. 293.

[3] See the *dictum* of WILLES, J., quoted with approval in *Barber* v. *Meyerstein* (1870), 39 L. J. C. P. at p. 191. See also *Barclays Bank, Ltd.* v. *Commissioners of Customs and Excise*, [1963] 1 Lloyd's Rep. 81, Q. B. D., where DIPLOCK, L.J., said (at p. 88): "So long as the contract is not discharged [*i.e.* by surrendering possession of the goods to the person entitled to them], the bill of lading . . . remains a document of title by indorsement and delivery of which the rights of property in the goods can be transferred."

(4) *There must have been an intention to transfer the property.*

The indorsement and delivery of a bill of lading passes only such property in the goods as the parties intended to pass. Hence it may:

(a) Pass no property at all.

It is common for an unpaid seller to reserve the right of disposing of the goods by taking the bills of lading in his own or his agent's name as consignee.[1] The bill is sent to the agent in order to prevent the buyer obtaining delivery of the goods before payment of the price. Clearly no property in the goods is intended to pass to the agent in such a case.

Other instances of no property passing are where the indorser has no property to pass, or where the goods have already been delivered properly by the shipowner to a third party.

or (b) Pass the property subject to a condition.

The unpaid seller may ensure payment by a conditional indorsement of the bill of lading. This may be effected by forwarding to the buyer one of the bills of lading together with a bill of exchange for the price of the goods. In this connexion the Sale of Goods Act 1893, s. 19 (3) provides that:

> "Where the seller of goods draws on the buyer for the price, and transmits the bill of exchange and bill of lading to the buyer together, to secure acceptance or payment of the bill of exchange, the buyer is bound to return the bill of lading if he does not honour the bill of exchange, and if he wrongfully retains the bill of lading, the property in the goods does not pass to him."

It should be observed, however, that the buyer in this case is a person in possession of a document of title to goods with the consent of the seller. Consequently, if

---

[1] For a case where the seller's agent sent endorsed bills of lading to the buyer by post, and it was held that the property in the goods passed on the posting and not on the receipt of the bills of lading; see *Concord Petroleum Corporation* v. *Gosford Marine Panama S.A. : The "Albazero"*, [1975] 2 Lloyd's Rep. 295, C. A.

he transfers it to a *bona fide* purchaser for value, the latter gets a valid title to the goods under the Factors Act 1889,[1] even though the original buyer has not accepted the bill of exchange.[2]

or (c) Pass the property absolutely.

or (d) Merely effect a mortgage or pledge of the goods as security for money lent.

An instance of this is where a shipper lodges an indorsed bill of lading with a banker who discounts for him the draft attached thereto with a view to providing fresh trading capital at once.

Thus, in *Sewell* v. *Burdick*,[3]

machinery was consigned to Poti deliverable to shipper or assigns on payment of freight. The master pledged the bills of lading with bankers as security for a loan. The shipper having failed to claim the goods, they were sold by the Russian customs authorities, but did not realise more than the amount of the customs duty and charges. The shipowner sought to recover the freight from the bankers as holders of the bills of lading. *Held*, the mere indorsement and delivery of a bill of lading by way of pledge does not pass the property in the goods to the endorsee so as to make the latter liable on the contract in the bill of lading.

Lord SELBORNE'S speech in this case makes it clear that the question is one of the intention of the parties. He said:[4]

"One test is whether the shipper retains any such proprietary right in the goods as to make it just that he should also retain rights of suit against the shipowner under the contract in the bill of lading. If he does, the statute can hardly be intended to take those rights from him and transfer them to the endorsee. If they are not transferred, neither are the liabilities."

But the Act is not restricted to cases of out-and-out sale. It would probably apply to an indorsee of a

---

[1] Section 9. See also Sale of Goods Act 1893, s. 25 (2).
[2] *Cahn* v. *Pockett's, etc., S.P. Co.*, [1899] 1 Q. B. 643; Chorley and Tucker's *Leading Cases* (4th edn. 1962), p. 194.
[3] (1884), 10 App. Cas. 74.
[4] (1884), 10 App. Cas., at p. 84.

bill of lading by way of security "who converts his symbolical into real possession by obtaining delivery of the goods".[1]

Further, it should be observed that the mere fact that an indorsee of the bill of lading has not thereby acquired the general property in the goods does not necessarily mean that he has no remedy against the shipowner. So, in *Brandt* v. *Liverpool S. N. Co.*,[2]

> where a bill of lading was indorsed to pledgees, who on the faith thereof made an advance to the shipper and obtained the goods on presenting the bill of lading and paying the freight, it was *held* that, although they could not invoke the Act, yet a contract to deliver and accept the goods in accordance with the terms of the bill of lading ought to be inferred from the fact that, on the bill of lading being presented and the freight paid, the goods had been delivered and accepted.

Preservation of Shipowner's Right to Freight

The Bills of Lading Act 1855, s. 2 preserves the right of the shipowner to claim freight from the original shipper although the bill of lading may have been assigned by him.

Preservation of Shipper's Right of Stoppage *in Transitu*

The Bills of Lading Act 1855, s. 2, preserves the right of the original shipper to stop the goods *in transitu*.

Besides the right of conditional indorsement and of reserving the *jus disponendi*, the unpaid seller can resume possession of the goods by exercising the right of stoppage in transit. This is defined by the Sale of Goods Act 1893, s. 44, as follows:

> "Subject to the provisions of this Act, when the buyer of goods becomes insolvent, the unpaid seller who has parted with the possession of the goods has the right of stopping them *in transitu*, that is to say, he may resume possession of the goods as long as they are in course of transit, and may retain them until payment or tender of the price."

---

[1] *Ibid.*, at p. 86.

[2] [1924] 1 K. B. 575. See also *Peter Cremer, Westfaelische Central Genossenschaft G.m.b.H. and Intergraan N.V.* v. *General Carriers S.A.: The "Dona Mari"*, [1973] 2 Lloyd's Rep. 366, Q. B. D. (Commercial Court.)

There are four points to be noted in connexion with this right, namely:

(1) *The buyer must be insolvent.* He need not be bankrupt. It is sufficient if he cannot pay his debts as they fall due.[1]

(2) *The right can be exercised only while the goods are in transit.*[2] The question of the duration of the transit is primarily one of the intention of the parties. Ordinarily the transit begins when the goods leave the seller's possession, and ends when they get into the possession of the buyer. Delivery to the buyer's agent for the purpose of forwarding puts an end to the transit if the further destination has not been notified to the seller; otherwise it does not.[3]

Delivery to carriers does not end the transit even though they are employed by the buyer, unless the intention of the parties is clearly to the contrary. Thus, if the buyer charters a ship and sends for the goods, the transit is not terminated by shipment of the goods, although the seller does not know where the goods are being taken.[4] But, where the charter amounts to a demise so that the buyer has complete control of the ship, an unconditional delivery to the master puts an end to the transit.[5] And where the buyer actually owns the vessel, the presumption is even stronger that an unconditional delivery, negativing the right of stoppage, is intended.[6] Again, where the carrier agrees to hold the goods for the consignee, *e.g.* to warehouse them for him, the transit will be considered at an end.[7]

---

[1] Sale of Goods Act 1893, s. 62 (3), which states that: "A person is deemed to be insolvent within the meaning of this Act who either has ceased to pay his debts in the ordinary course of business, or cannot pay his debts in the ordinary course of business, or cannot pay his debts as they become due, whether he has committed an act of bankruptcy or not".

[2] *Lickbarrow* v. *Mason* (1794), 1 Sm. L. C. (13th edn.), p. 703; Chorley and Tucker's *Leading Cases* (4th edn. 1962), p. 293.

[3] *Re Isaacs, Ex parte Miles* (1885), 15 Q. B. D. 39.

[4] *Re Cock, Ex parte Rosevear China Clay Co.* (1879), 11 Ch. D. 560.

[5] *Fowler* v. *M'Taggart* (1801), cited at 1 East 522.

[6] *Merchant Banking Co.* v. *Phœnix Bessemer Co.* (1877), 5 Ch. D. 205.

[7] *Foster* v. *Frampton* (1826), 6 B. & C. 107.

(3) *Its exercise does not rescind the contract of sale, but merely restores possession of the goods to the seller.*[1]

Thus, s. 48 (1) of the Sale of Goods Act 1893 states:

"Subject to the provisions of this section, a contract of sale is not rescinded by the mere exercise by an unpaid seller of his right of . . . stoppage *in transitu*".

(4) *It is defeated by a* bona fide *transfer of the bill of lading for value.*[2] Generally the right of stoppage in transit exists against the buyer and all who claim under him. It is available against a purchaser from him.

Thus, s. 47 of the Sale of Goods Act 1893 states:

"Subject to the provisions of this Act, the unpaid seller's right of . . . stoppage *in transitu* is not affected by any sale or other disposition of the goods which the buyer may have made, unless the seller has assented thereto"

But where such a purchaser takes a bill of lading or other document of title *bona fide* and for value, the right of stoppage in transit is lost, for s. 47 of the Act of 1893 goes on to state:

"Provided that where a document of title to goods has been lawfully transferred to any person as buyer or owner of the goods, and that person transfers the document in good faith and for valuable consideration, then, if such last-mentioned transfer was by way of sale, the unpaid seller's right of . . . stoppage *in transitu* is defeated and if such last-mentioned transfer was by way of pledge or other disposition for value, the unpaid seller's right of . . . stoppage *in transitu* can only be exercised subject to the rights of the transferee."

The indorsee of a bill of lading is thus in a better position than the original consignee, for the latter's title to the goods is subject to the seller's right of stoppage in transit. For instance, in *Lickbarrow* v. *Mason*,[3]

T shipped goods under a bill of lading (in four parts) made out to "T or order or assigns". Two of the bills of lading were endorsed in blank and sent to Freeman, the buyer of the goods.

---

[1] *Kemp* v. *Falk* (1882), 7 App. Cas. 573.

[2] *Lickbarrow* v. *Mason* (1794), 1 Sm. L. C. (13th edn.), p. 703; Chorley and Tucker's *Leading Cases* (4th edn. 1962), p. 293.

[3] *Supra*.

Freeman sold the goods and transferred the two bills of lading to Lickbarrow, a *bona fide* purchaser for value. Freeman became bankrupt. T tried to stop the goods in transit, and sent one bill of lading to Mason, who obtained possession of the goods. It was *held* that T's right to stop the goods had been defeated by the assignment to Lickbarrow, who was therefore entitled to recover the goods.

Effect of Subsequent Re-indorsement

If the indorsee of a bill of lading sells the goods and re-indorses the bill of lading, he ceases to be responsible for liabilities under the contract; but if he retains the bill of lading, a mere re-sale will not free him.[1] And re-indorsement must take place while the goods are in transit and before delivery.

COMPARISON OF BILL OF LADING WITH MATE'S RECEIPT

By way of contrast, the effect of the mate's receipt as conferring rights upon its holder is much more limited. Lord WRIGHT has stated that a mate's receipt

"is not a document of title to the goods shipped. Its transfer does not pass property in the goods, nor is its possession equivalent to possession of the goods. It is not conclusive, and its statements do not bind the shipowner as do the statements in a bill of lading signed within the master's authority. It is, however, *prima facie* evidence of the quantity and condition of the goods received, and *prima facie* it is the recipient or possessor [of the mate's receipt] who is entitled to have the bill of lading issued to him. But if the mate's receipt acknowledges receipt from a shipper other than the person who actually receives the mate's receipt, and, in particular, if the property is in that shipper, and the shipper has contracted for the freight, the shipowner will *prima facie* be entitled, and indeed bound, to deliver the bill of lading to that [shipper]."[2]

A trade custom, however, has been proved to the effect that in trade between Sarawak and Singapore mate's receipts are universally adopted as documents of title in the same way as bills of .ading.[3]

---

[1] *Fowler* v. *Knoop* (1878), 4 Q. B. D. 299.

[2] *Nippon Yusen Kaisha* v. *Ramjiban Serowgee*, [1938] A. C., at pp. 445–6.

[3] *Kum* v. *Wah Tat Bank, Ltd.*, [1971] 1 Lloyd's Rep. 439, P. C. But the custom was held to be inconsistent with the words "not negotiable" in the mate's receipt concerned. See the judgment of Lord DEVLIN, *ibid.*, at pp. 444–445. As to proof of trade custom, see pp. 105–106, *post.*

CHAPTER 4

The Construction of Charter-parties and Bills of Lading

There are well established rules which guide the Courts in the interpretation of charter-parties and bills of lading. But only certain evidence is admissible. Sometimes the particular system of law which governs the contract has to be ascertained. This is a matter of "The Conflict of Laws".

SOME RULES OF CONSTRUCTION

"Questions of construction are very often questions of first impression. They depend immensely upon the circumstances of each individual case and the precise words used in the contracts to be construed. The Court guides itself, of course, by such canons of construction as are available and relevant to the problem in hand."[1]

The following are some of the rules which must be kept in mind:

(1) The primary consideration in construing any contract is the intention of the contracting parties. Thus, a charter-

---

[1] *Marifortuna Naviera S.A.* v. *Government of Ceylon*, [1970] 1 Lloyd's Rep. 247, Q. B. D. (Commercial Court), at p. 256 (MOCATTA, J.).

party or a bill of lading must be construed in the light of the particular undertaking with which it is concerned.[1]

(2) Where there is a conflict between the printed and written[2] parts of the contract owing to an error or to inadvertence, the intention expressed by the written part should, as a general rule, be preferred to that expressed by the printed part.[3]

It is therefore unnecessary, and indeed often impossible, to give full effect to every printed clause.[4]

(3) Any ambiguous term of the contract is to be construed most strongly against the party for whose benefit it is intended, *i.e.* usually against the shipowner.[5] This is known as the *"contra proferentem"* rule.

(4) The rule of interpretation known as the *"ejusdem generis"* rule is often applied. That is to say, general words which are tacked on to specific words are to be construed as referring

---

[1] *Glynn* v. *Margetson*, [1893] A. C. 351; *Australian Oil Refining Pty, Ltd.* v. *R. W. Miller & Co., Ltd.*, [1968] 1 Lloyd's Rep. 448, High Court of Australia, where BARWICK, C. J., said (*ibid.*, at p. 452): "Thus, although the contract which the parties made was called a charter-party and contained many provisions commonly found in contracts merely to the carriage of goods, that contract must, in my opinion, be construed having regard to the whole relationship in which the parties stood and to all the rights and obligations they sought to create or to accept"; *Segovia Compagnia Naviera S.A.* v. *R. Pagnan and Fratelli: The "Aragon"*, [1975] 2 Lloyd's Rep. 216, Q. B. D. (Commercial Court), where DONALDSON, J., said (*ibid.*, at p. 221): "Charter-parties are like any other contract and must be construed as such. Their true construction is a matter of law not fact. The duty of the Court is to ascertain the presumed common intention of the parties, to be deduced from the words used and the background to the transaction. Their actual, but uncommunicated, intentions are irrelevant".

[2] Or typed.

[3] *Hadjipateras* v. *Weigall & Co.* (1918), 34 T. L. R. 360; *Gesellschaft Burgerlichin Rechts* v. *Stockholms Rederiaktiebolag Svea, The Brabant,* [1965] 2 Lloyd's Rep. 546, Q. B. D. (Commercial Court). (See the judgment of McNAIR, J., *ibid.*, at p. 553); *Ismail* v. *Polish Ocean Lines: The "Ciechocinek"*, [1975] 2 Lloyd's Rep. 170, Q. B. D. (Commercial Court). (See the judgment of KERR, J., *ibid.*, at p. 186); *reversed* on other grounds: (1976) *Times*, February 5, C. A.

[4] *Gray v Carr* (1871), L. R. 6 Q. B. 522.

[5] *Burton* v. *English* (1883), 12 Q. B. D. 218; *Diana Maritime Corporation of Monrovia* v. *Southerns, Ltd.*, [1967] 1 Lloyd's Rep. 114, Q. B. D. (Commercial Court), at p. 123 (*per* MEGAW, J.); *Encyclopaedia Britannica Inc.* v. *The "Hong Kong Producer" and Universal Marine Corporation*, [1969] 2 Lloyd's Rep. 536, U.S. Ct. of Appeals, Second Circuit, at p. 542 (*per* ANDERSON, Ct. J.).

only to things or circumstances of the same kind as those described by the specific words. Thus, in *Tillmans* v. *Knutsford,*[1]

> the words "war, disturbance or any other cause" were *held* not to cover ice, despite the universality of the general words "any other".

In some cases, however, the general words are the governing words, and the specific words are subordinate. Thus, in *Ambatielos* v. *Anton, etc., Works,*[2]

> where the clause ran ". . . vessel detained by causes over which the charterers have no control, viz. quarantine, ice, hurricanes . . . etc.; no demurrage payable," it was *held* that the general words were the governing words and that a strike was therefore within the exception. It should be observed that the specific words were, in this case, tacked on to the general words, and not *vice versa*.

But doubt has been expressed as to whether the *ejusdem generis* rule or the discussion of it in relation to different words is really of much assistance where the clause to be construed contains the words "such as".[3]

Thus, in *Diana Maritime Corporation of Monrovia* v. *Southerns, Ltd.*[4]

> A bill of lading stated that if a vessel was prevented from entering the port of discharge or was likely to be delayed there for an unreasonable time "owing to causes beyond the carrier's control such as blockade, interdict, war, strikes, lockouts, disturbances, ice, storms or the consequences thereof", the carrier was entitled to proceed to a convenient port to discharge. The vessel discharged at a convenient port because of delay being anticipated

---

[1] [1908] A. C. 406.

[2] [1923] A. C. 175.

[3] *Diana Maritime Corporation of Monrovia* v. *Southerns, Ltd.,* [1967] 1 Lloyd's Rep. 114, Q. B. D. (Commercial Court), at p. 122 (*per* MEGAW, J.).

[4] [1967] 1 Lloyd's Rep. 114, Q. B. D. (Commercial Court). See the judgment of MEGAW, J., *ibid.*, at p. 123. Cf. *Micada Compania Naviera S.A.* v. *Texim*, [1968] 2 Lloyd's Rep. 57, Q. B. D. (Commercial Court), where a clause in a time charter-party stated that "no live stock nor injurious inflammable or dangerous goods (such as acids, explosives, calcium carbide, ferro silicon, naptha, motor spirit, tar, or any of their products) to be shipped", and it was held that the proper construction of the words in brackets was that they were merely intended by way of exemplification and were not intended by way of restriction. See the judgment of DONALDSON, J., *ibid.*, at p. 61.

at the contractual port of discharge. The cargo owners brought an action against the carrier for breach of contract, claiming damages for the forwarding expenses which they had paid to get the cargo to the contractual port of discharge.

Held, the carrier was liable. The parties never intended to include all causes beyond the carrier's control, but only such causes beyond his control as those specified. Accordingly, the vessel should not have discharged at a port other than the contractual port.

(5) It is not settled whether the Court is entitled to refer to a clause which has been deleted from the document.[1]

(6) The whole of the document must be looked at.

(7) The grammatical construction should be adopted except where there is a clear intention to the contrary.

(8) The words must be construed in their ordinary meaning, but technical words must be given their technical meaning.

(9) The meaning must be limited by the context in which the words are used.

(10) The words of the document must, if possible, be construed liberally, so as to give effect to the intention of the parties.

(11) Where the words are capable of two constructions, the reasonable construction is to be preferred as representing the presumed intention of the parties.

(12) An express term in a document overrides any implied term which is inconsistent with it.

---

[1] Cases where it was held that it was *not* legitimate to refer to a deleted clause include: *Ambatielos* v. *Anton Jurgens Margarine Works*, [1923] A. C. 175, at p. 185, H. L. (*per* Viscount FINLAY); *M. A. Sassoon & Sons, Ltd.* v. *International Banking Corporation*, [1927] A. C. 711, at p. 721, P. C. (*per* Viscount SUMNER); *Firzel, Berry & Co.* v. *Eastcheap Dried Fruit Co.*, [1962] 1 Lloyd's Rep. 370, at p. 375 (*per* McNAIR, J.), affirmed, [1962] 2 Lloyd's Rep. 11; *Compania Naviera Termar S.A.* v. *Tradax Export S.A.*, [1965] 1 Lloyd's Rep. 198, at p. 204 (*per* MOCATTA, J.); *Hang Fung Shipping & Trading Co., Ltd.* v. *Mullion & Co., Ltd.*, [1967] 1 Lloyd's Rep. 511, at p. 526 (*per* McNAIR, J.). Cases where it was held that it was legitimate to refer to a deleted clause include: *Baumwoll Manufactur Von Scheibler* v. *Gilchrest & Co.*, [1892] 1 Q. B. 253, at p. 256 (*per* Lord ESHER, M.R.); *Anastassia S.S. (Owners)* v. *Ugle-Export Charkow* (1933), 46 Ll. L. Rep. 1, at p. 6 (*per* SCRUTTON, L.J.); *Louis Dreyfus et Cie.* v. *Parnaso Cia. Naviera S.A.*, [1959] 1 Q. B. 498, at p. 513 (*per* DIPLOCK, J.).

The Evidence which is Admissible

Where a contract has been reduced to writing, the general rule is that oral evidence is inadmissible to add to, vary or contradict the written instrument.[1] There is, however, a presumption that the parties to a mercantile contract entered into it with reference to the customs prevailing in the particular trade or locality to which the contract relates, provided such customs are reasonable, certain and notorious.[2] This presumption can be rebutted only by showing that the parties intended to exclude the custom, and the most effective way of doing this is by showing that the express terms of the contract are inconsistent with the usage

---

[1] *Goss* v. *Nugent (Lord)* (1833), 5 B. & Ad. 58, at p. 64; *Jacobs* v. *Batavia and General Plantations Trust, Ltd.,* [1924] 1 Ch. 287, at p. 295; *Northern Sales, Ltd.* v. *The "Giancarlo Zeta", "The Giancarlo Zeta",* [1966] 2 Lloyd's Rep. 317 (Exchequer Court, British Columbia Admiralty District), where the Court refused to admit evidence to show that a broker had informed the plaintiff that the plaintiff had an option to load 11,000 tons, although the freight contract stated that the cargo was to consist of "10,000 tons, 10 per cent. more or less quantity at owners' option", for such evidence attempted to add, vary or contradict the terms of the contract. See the judgment of Norris, J., at pp. 326–7.

[2] As in *Kum* v. *Wah Tat Bank, Ltd.,* [1971] 1 Lloyd's Rep. 439, P. C., where a trade custom to the effect that in trade between Sarawak and Singapore mate's receipts were universally adopted as documents of title in the same way as bills of lading was established, but was held to be applicable because the mate's receipt contained the words "not negotiable". See the judgment of Lord Devlin, *ibid.,* at pp. 444–445. As to mate's receipts, see p. 100, *ante.* In *Encyclopaedia Britannica Inc.* v. *The "Hong Kong Producer" and Universal Marine Corporation,* [1969] 2 Lloyd's Rep. 536, U.S. Ct. of Appeals, Second Circuit, an alleged custom in the shipping industry of carrying containerized cargo on deck, regardless of the provisions of the bill of lading, was not established. See the judgment of Anderson, Ct. J., *ibid.,* at p. 544. In *Du Pont de Nemours International S.A. and E.I. Du Pont de Nemours & Co. Inc.* v. *S.S. "Mormacvega" etc. and Moore-McCormack Lines Inc.: The "Mormacvega",* [1973] 1 Lloyd's Rep. 267, District Court, Southern District of New York, it was held that an alleged practice to ship containers on deck was not sufficiently old to make it a trade custom. (See the judgment of Brieant, D.J., *ibid.,* at p. 270.) (The decision was subsequently affirmed on a different point: [1974] 1 Lloyd's Rep. 296, U.S. Court of Appeals, Second Circuit.) In *Nissan Automobile Co. (Canada) Ltd.* v. *Owners of the Vessel "Continental Shipper": The "Continental Shipper",* [1974] 1 Lloyd's Rep. 482, Federal Court of Canada Trial Division, it was proved that it was the practice of the trade for cars to be shipped uncrated.

which it is sought to incorporate.[1] "Any custom of the port to the contrary notwithstanding" is a good example of such an express term.[2]

Thus, in *A/S Sameiling* v. *Grain Importers (Eire), Ltd.*,[3]

a charter-party provided that shipowners' stevedores were to be employed in discharging grain cargo. At the discharging port of Cork there was a custom that the receivers of the cargo had the right to fill the grain into bags or buckets *before* discharge and do debit the shipowners with half the cost. *Held*, that this custom was not inconsistent with the express term of the charter-party and so was effective.

"To fall within the exception of repugnancy the [usage] must be such as if expressed in the written contract would make it insensible or inconsistent".[4] Therefore, while the usage may regulate the mode of performance, it must not be such as to change the intrinsic character of the contract.[5] In the case of a bill of lading, evidence of usage will be more readily admitted than in the case of a charter-party; whereas the charter-party is the contract, the bill of lading is merely a memorandum of the contract.

THE CONFLICT OF LAWS[6]

The parties to a bill of lading or a charter-party are often domiciled in different countries, and the place or places where the contract is to be performed are often different from the place where the contract was made. Hence it is important to find out which system of law is applicable to any particular contract. This is called the "governing" or "proper" law of the contract. Lord ATKIN

---

[1] See, *e.g. Kum* v. *Wah Tat Bank, Ltd. (supra)*.

[2] *Brenda Co.* v. *Green*, [1900] 1 Q. B. 518.

[3] [1952] 2 All E. R. 315; See also *Aktieselkab Helios* v. *Ekman*, [1897] 2 Q. B. 83.

[4] *Per* Lord CAMPBELL, C. J., in *Dale* v. *Humfrey* (1857), 7 E. & B., at p. 275.

[5] *Les Affréteurs Réunis* v. *Walford*, [1919] A. C. 801.

[6] See generally Cheshire, *Private International Law* (9th edn. 1974), pp. 201–218; Dicey and Morris, *Conflict of Laws* (9th edn. 1973), pp. 721–762.

explained the rules determining the proper law of a contract thus:[1]

"The legal principles which are to guide an English court on the question of the proper law of a contract are now well settled. It is the law which the parties intended to apply. Their intention will be ascertained by the intention expressed in the contract, if any, which will be conclusive. If no intention be expressed, the intention will be presumed by the court from the terms of the contract and the relevant surrounding circumstances. In coming to its conclusion, the court will be guided by rules which indicate that particular facts or conditions lead to a *prima facie* inference, in some cases an almost conclusive inference, as to the intention of the parties to apply a particular law, *e.g.* the country where the contract is made, the country where the contract is to be performed, if the contract relates to immovables the country where they are situated, the country under whose flag the ship sails in which goods are contracted to be carried. But all these rules only serve to give *prima facie* indications of intention: they are all capable of being overcome by counter indications, however difficult it may be in some cases to find such."

Further, in a case decided by the House of Lords, it was stated that the proper law of the contract was the system of law by reference to which the contract was made or that with which the transaction had its closest and most real connexion.[2]

In another leading case Lord WRIGHT, when delivering the judgment of the Privy Council, again stressed the fact that the proper law of the contract depends upon the intention of the parties "to be ascertained in each case on a consideration of the terms of the contract, the situation of the parties, and generally on all the surrounding facts".[3]

---

[1] *R.* v. *International Trustee for the Protection of Bondholders Aktiengesellschaft*, [1937] 2 All E. R. 164, at p. 166; [1937] A. C. 500, at p. 529, applied in *The Metamorphosis*, [1953] 1 All E. R. 723, at p. 726 in relation to a bill of lading as evidence of a contract of carriage; and in *The Assunzione*, [1954] 1 All E. R. 278; [1954] P. 150, C. A.

[2] *Re United Railways of Havana and Regla Warehouses, Ltd.*, [1960] 2 All E. R. 332, at p. 364 (*per* Lord MORRIS). See also *Rossano* v. *Manufacturers Life Insurance Co., Ltd.*, [1962] 2 All E. R. 214; [1963] 2 Q. B. 352; [1962] 1 Lloyd's Rep. 187, Q. B. D. (Commercial Court) (life insurance); *Bonython* v. *Commonwealth of Australia*, [1951] A. C. 201, P. C.; *Compagnie d'Armement Maritime S.A.* v. *Compagnie Tunisienne de Navigation S.A.*, [1970] 3 All E.R. 71; [1971] A. C. 572, H. L.

[3] *Mount Albert Borough Council* v. *Australian Temperance and General Mutual Life Assurance Society, Ltd.*, [1937] 4 All E.R. 206, at p. 214; [1938] A. C. 224, at p. 240.

It will have been noticed that in the case of contracts of carriage by sea Lord ATKIN referred to the *prima facie* rule that the law of the ship's flag shall apply. There are many illustrations of this rule. Thus, in the leading case of *Lloyd* v. *Guibert*,[1]

a French ship was chartered by a British subject in the Danish West Indies for a voyage from Hayti to Liverpool. She put into a Portuguese port for repairs, and the master was obliged to borrow money on a bottomry bond to pay for the repairs. As the value of the ship and freight proved insufficient to repay the loan, the cargo had to contribute. The plaintiff, as owner of the cargo, claimed an indemnity from the shipowner. To this he was entitled by Danish, Portuguese, and English law, but not by French law. It was *held* that the master's authority was limited by the law of the ship's flag, and consequently the cargo-owner was not entitled to an indemnity.

However, the *prima facie* rule that the law of the flag governs contracts of carriage by sea is, as we have seen, subject to the paramount rule of the intention of the parties, which may be express, or implied from the circumstances of the case. Thus, in *The Industrie*,[2]

London merchants negotiated a charter-party in London with English brokers for the carriage of rice from India to England in a ship belonging to a German owner and flying the German flag. The contract was made upon an ordinary English charter-party form, which contained phrases peculiar to English law and stipulated that freight should be payable in sterling. It was *held* that the deliberate choice of English legal expressions, together with the fact that the contract was made in London between two English firms, indicated a clear intention to make an English contract.

There appears to be some doubt as to the law governing a contract for through carriage partly by land and partly by sea. Probably the best view is that as regards the land journey the law of that country applies, while the law of the flag governs the sea transit, unless a contrary intention is expressed in, or can be implied from, the contract.[3]

---

[1] (1865), L. R. 1 Q. B. 115; *Coast Lines, Ltd.* v. *Hudig and Veder Chartering N.V.* [1972] 1 Lloyd's Rep. 53, C. A., where it was *held* that if, in the determination of the proper law of the contract, the scales were evenly balanced, the law of the flag could be taken as a last resort. (See the judgment of Lord DENNING, M.R., *ibid.,* at p. 57.)

[2] [1894] P. 58. See also *The Adriatic,* [1931] P. 241; *The Njegos,* [1936] P. 90; *The Assunzione,* [1954] 1 All E. R. 278; [1954] P. 150, C. A.

[3] See *Moore* v. *Harris* (1876), 1 App. Cas. 318; *The Patria* (1871), 41 L. J. Adm. 23.

Where there is an express statement by the parties of their intention to select the law of the contract, it is difficult to see what qualifications are possible, provided that the intention expressed is *bona fide* and legal, and provided there is no reason for avoiding the choice on the ground of public policy.[1]

---

[1] *Vita Food Products Inc.* v. *Unus Shipping Co., Ltd.,* [1939] 1 All E. R. 513, at p. 521; [1939] A. C. 277, at p. 290 (*per* Lord WRIGHT), P. C.

The Preliminary Voyage

The Undertaking to proceed to the Port of Loading

The undertaking of the shipowner as to the ship's proceeding to the port of loading affords a good example of a clause which the Court may, according to the particular surrounding circumstances of each case, find to be a condition precedent or merely a warranty.[1] For it will be *either*:

(1) An absolute undertaking to sail for, or arrive at, such port by a fixed date;

or (2) an undertaking merely to use reasonable diligence, *e.g.* "proceed with all convenient despatch."

In the former case, it is a condition precedent to the charterer's liability to load that the ship shall sail or arrive by the date named. Thus, in *Glaholm* v. *Hays*,[2]

a charter-party provided that the vessel was to sail from England for the port of loading on or before February 4. She did not sail until February 22. *Held*, the charterer was not bound to load.

But where no definite time is fixed, the undertaking is to proceed in a reasonable time. In that case (if the delay does not defeat the charterer's object in engaging the ship) he must load, and seek his remedy for any loss caused by the delay in an action for damages.[3] If, however, the undertaking to use diligence is broken in such a way as to frustrate the object of the adventure, the charterer will be entitled to refuse to load. Thus, in *Freeman* v. *Taylor*,[4]

---

[1] For an example, see the "Gencon" charter-party, clause 1, line 8 (Appendix B).

[2] (1841), 2 Man. & G. 257.

[3] *Forest Oak* v. *Richard* (1899), 5 Com. Cas. 100.

[4] (1831), 1 L. J. C. P. 26.

the ship was to go to Cape Town and then proceed with all convenient speed to Bombay. By reasonable diligence she might have arrived at Bombay six weeks earlier than she did arrive. *Held*, the charterer was justified in refusing to load.[1]

Cancelling Clauses

A cancelling clause may exist in the charter-party, in which case the charterer has the option, under the terms of his contract, of repudiating, in certain stipulated circumstances.[2]

The fixing of a cancelling date in a charter-party merely gives warning to the shipowner that non-arrival by the cancelling date may go to the root of the contract so as to entitle the charterer to rescind. It does not relieve the shipowner of his primary obligation to proceed with all convenient speed to the port of loading, or of his secondary obligation in the event of non-performance of that primary obligation to make reparation in money to the charterer for any loss sustained by him as a result of such non-performance.[3]

A cancelling clause is a forfeiture clause and "so not to be applied lightly".[4]

A cancelling clause may even be so strict as not to give the charterer any choice.[5]

The shipowner is under a duty to send the vessel to the port of loading even though it is impossible for her to get there by the cancelling date. If he does not do so, the charterer can sue for any damage which may have resulted.[6]

Where the charterer is late in exercising his option to cancel,

---

[1] See also *Jackson* v. *Union Marine Insurance Co.* (1874), L. R. 10 C. P. 125.

[2] For an example of cancelling clauses, see the "Gencon" charter-party, clause 6 (Appendix B) and the "Baltime 1939" charter-party, clause 22 (Appendix B). See also *Johs. Thode* v. *Vda De Gimeno y Cia. S.L.* (*The Steendiek*), [1961] 2 Lloyd's Rep. 138, C. A. For a case where the charterers were held not to be entitled to cancel the charter-party because they were in breach in ordering the vessel to the port of delivery as and when they did, see *Shipping Corporation of India, Ltd.* v. *Naviera Letasa S.A.*, [1976] 1 Lloyd's Rep. 132, Q. B. (Com. Ct.).

[3] *C. Czarnikow, Ltd.* v. *Koufos,* [1966] 1 Lloyd's Rep. 595, C. A., at p. 610 (*per* DIPLOCK, L.J.).

[4] *Noemijulia S.S. Co., Ltd.* v. *Minister of Food,* [1951] 1 K. B. 223, at p. 228 (*per* DEVLIN, J.). See further, *Cheikh Boutros Selim El-Khoung and Others* v. *Ceylon Shipping Lines, Ltd.: The "Madeleine",* [1967] 2 Lloyd's Rep. 224, Q. B. D. (Commercial Court), at p. 237 (*per* ROSKILL, J.).

[5] See *Adamson* v. *Newcastle Association* (1879), 4 Q. B. D. 462.

[6] *Moel Tryvan Ship Co., Ltd.* v. *Andrew Weir & Co.,* [1910] 2 K. B. 844, C. A.; *Bucknall Bros.* v. *Tatem & Co.* (1900), 83 L. T. 121, C. A.

the shipowner can still accept a notice of cancellation, and waive any rights he may have in respect of the delay.[1]

There is no *contractual* right to rescind a charter-party unless and until the date specified in the clause has been reached.[2]

But where the charterer seeks to say that the contract has been frustrated or that there has been an anticipatory breach which entitles him to rescind, then he has such rights as are given him *at Common Law.*[3]

In such a case all the attendant uncertainties as to the right to claim rescission, whether the right is said to arise from alleged frustration or alleged anticipatory breach, will no doubt arise, and the commercial certainty accorded by a cancelling clause will not exist.[4]

The Application and Scope of Exception Clauses

The exception clauses in a charter-party may apply to the preliminary voyage to the port of loading.

Hence if a chartered ship is prevented from, or delayed in, getting to the loading port by a peril excepted "during the voyage", the exception applies.[5] This, however, is the case only when the preliminary voyage is clearly incidental to, and therefore is considered as part of, the charter voyage. If the ship is disabled by excepted perils while completing a voyage on which she was engaged at the time of chartering, the shipowner will not be excused.[6]

Where the exceptions relate to the whole of the charter-party, the fact that the delay was caused by an excepted peril is a good

---

[1] *Den Norske Afrika Og Australie Linie* v. *Port Said Salt Association, Ltd.* (1924), 20 Ll. L. Rep. 184, C. A.

[2] *Cheikh Boutras Selim El-Khoury and Others* v. *Ceylon Shipping Lines, Ltd.; The "Madeleine"*, [1967] 2 Lloyd's Rep. 224, Q. B. D. (Commercial Court), at p. 245 (*per* ROSKILL, J.).

[3] *Ibid.*, at p. 245 (*per* ROSKILL, J.).

[4] *Ibid.*, at pp. 245–6 (*per* ROSKILL, J.). His Lordship suggested that if it was desired to introduce certainty into these matters, it would be necessary to alter the clause ("Baltime 1939" charter-party, clause 22), though it appeared to have existed in very much its present form for many years: *ibid.*, at p. 245.

[5] *Harrison* v. *Garthorne* (1872), 26 L. T. 508.

[6] *Monroe Bros.* v. *Ryan*, [1935] 2 K. B. 28: *Evera S.A. Comercial* v. *North Shipping Co., Ltd* , [1956] 2 Lloyd's Rep. 367.

defence by a shipowner to an action for damages for failure to start for the loading port by an agreed date; but this will not affect the charterer's right to rescind the contract if the ship does not sail or arrive by the agreed date. The latter right is an absolute one and is not subject to the exceptions.[1] In other words, the excepted perils only operate to relieve from liability; they do not enable the shipowner to plead that he has performed an obligation which he has not performed.

Frustration of the Preliminary Voyage

Either party may be discharged on the ground of impossibility of performance or on the ground of delay, *where no breach of contract by either party has taken place.*[2]

---

[1] *Harrison* v. *Garthorne* (*supra*); *Smith* v. *Dart* (1884), 14 Q. B. D. 105.
[2] For "Frustration", see pp. 47–54, *ante*.

CHAPTER 6

Loading, Discharge and Delivery

LOADING

The Duties of the Shipowner

It is the shipowner's duty to send the ship to the agreed,[1] or, in the absence of special agreement, to the usual place of loading. He must then give notice to the charterer that the ship is ready to load.[2] If he fails to do so, and delay in commencing to load is thereby caused, the charterer will not be responsible, as he is not bound to look out for the ship.[3] If the place named for loading be simply a port or dock, notice may be given as soon as the ship arrives in the port or dock although she is not in the particular spot where the loading is to take place; but this cannot be done when the place is more particularly indicated.[4]

The duties of the shipowner, charterer and master as regards loading were explained by Lord WRIGHT as follows:[5]

---

[1] Once the selection of a berth in a port charter-party has been notified to the shipowner, it cannot be changed unilaterally by the charterer: *Venizelos A.N.E. of Athens* v. *Société Commerciale de Cereales et Financiere S.A. of Zurich: The "Prometheus"*, [1974] 1 Lloyd's Rep. 350, Q. B. D. (Commercial Court). (See the judgment of MOCATTA, J., *ibid.*, at p. 355.)

[2] For a case where the charter-party stated that the shipowner was to be responsible for all expenses incurred by the charterer if the vessel was not ready in accordance with the notice of readiness to load which had been given, see *Marifortuna Naviera S.A.* v. *Government of Ceylon*, [1970] 1 Lloyd's Rep. 247, Q. B. D. (Commercial Court).

[3] *Stanton* v. *Austin* (1872), L. R. 7 C. P. 651.

[4] *Nelson* v. *Dahl* (1879), 12 Ch. D., at p. 581.

[5] *Canadian Transport Co., Ltd.* v. *Court Line, Ltd.*, [1940] 3 All E. R. 112, at pp. 118–9; [1940] A. C. 934, at pp. 943–4. See further, *Mannix, Ltd.* v. *N. M. Paterson & Sons, Ltd.*, [1966] 1 Lloyd's Rep. 139 (Supreme Court of Canada), *per* RITCHIE, J., at pp. 142–3.

"Apart from special provisions or circumstances, it is part of the ship's duty to stow the goods properly. . . . In modern times, the work of stowage is generally deputed to stevedores, but that does not generally relieve the shipowners of their duty, even though the stevedores are, under the charter-party, to be appointed by the charterers, unless there are special provisions which either expressly or inferentially have that effect."

Lord WRIGHT then referred to the terms of the charter-party before the Court. It contained a clause, which is often employed, that the charterers were to load, stow and trim the cargo at their expense.[1] His Lordship continued:

"I think that these words necessarily import that the charterers take into their hands the business of loading and stowing the cargo. It must follow that they not only relieve the ship of the duty of loading and stowing, but, as between themselves and the shipowners, relieve them of liability for bad stowage, except as qualified by the words 'under the supervision of the captain'. . . . These words expressly give the master a right which I think he must in any case have—namely, a right to supervise the operations of the charterers in loading and stowing. . . . To the extent that the master exercises supervision, and limits the charterers' control of the stowage, the charterers' liability will be limited in a corresponding degree."

It has also been held in one case that, in the absence of any provision in a charter-party making the charterers responsible for the stowage of a mechanical shovel, the inspection made by the ship's officers of the way in which the shovel was placed and secured on deck and their approval of it was evidence negativing any implied agreement to relieve the shipowner of the obligation implied by law "to receive the goods and carefully arrange and stow them in the ship."[2]

In another case a clause stating "dunnaging and stowage instructions given by the charterers to be carefully followed but to be executed under the supervision of the master and he is to

---

[1] In *Blandy Brothers & Co., Lda.* v. *Nello Simoni, Ltd.,* [1963] 2 Lloyd's Rep. 393, C. A., the charterers failed to prove a custom of the fruit and vegetable trade that the shipper was responsible for loading and stowing charges. The shipowners failed to prove a custom of the port of Funchal that the shipper paid for bringing the cargo alongside, and that the ship paid for the labour employed on board, *i.e.* in loading and stowing.

[2] *Mannix, Ltd.* v. *N. M. Paterson & Sons, Ltd.,* [1966] 1 Lloyd's Rep. 139 (Supreme Court of Canada).

remain responsible for proper stowage and dunnaging" was held not to relieve the shipowners from their duty to stow the cargo safely.[1]

Where a clause in a charter-party stated "charterers to have full use of the ship's gear as on board", it was held that this did not imply that the charterers were to be responsible for stowage.[2]

Since *prima facie* the stowage of cargo is the ship's responsibility, it is within the authority of a ship's agent to arrange for and pay for the work of stowage.[3]

The Duties of the Charterer

Various duties have to be performed by the charterer:

(1) He must procure a cargo.

(2) He must bring it alongside the vessel.

(3) He must load a full and complete cargo.

(4) He must load in the time stipulated.

(1) *Procuring the cargo.* The charter does not as a rule contain provisions as to how the cargo is to be procured. It presupposes that the charterer has the cargo in readiness on the quay.

The fact that it has become impossible to provide a cargo does not, as a rule, relieve the charterer of liability.

Where the shipowner himself undertakes to procure a cargo, he is under the same strict liability as usually falls on the charterer. Thus, in *Hills* v. *Sughrue*,[4]

---

[1] *Ismail* v. *Polish Ocean Lines: The "Ciechocinek"*, [1975] 2 Lloyd's Rep. 170, Q. B. D. (Commercial Court). (See the judgment of KERR, J., *ibid.*, at p. 185); *reversed* on other grounds: (1976) *Times*, February 5, C. A. For a case where it was held that the sole responsibility for loading rested with the charterers without interference by the master except that he could have required them to alter the loading process for securing the seaworthiness, safe trim and stress of the vessel, see *Georgia-Pacific Corporation* v. *"Marilyn L.", Elvapores Inc., Evans Products Inc. and Retla S.S. Co.: The "Marilyn L."*, [1972] 1 Lloyd's Rep. 418, District Court for the Eastern District of Virginia, Norfolk Division.

[2] *Ibid.*

[3] *Blandy Brothers & Co., Lda.* v. *Nello Simoni, Ltd.*, [1963] 2 Lloyd's Rep. 393, C. A.

[4] (1846), 15 M. & W. 253.

the shipowner agreed to proceed to Ichaboe and there find and load a full cargo of guano. There was no guano to be found there within a reasonable time after the ship's arrival. *Held*, the shipowner was none the less liable to the charterer.

In some cases, however, the charterer will be excused from the liability to provide a cargo, or, if he has one, from the liability to load it:

(a) Where events have rendered performance of the contract illegal either by English Law,[1] or by the law of the country in which performance was to have taken place.[2] Thus, in *Esposito* v. *Bowden*,[3]

> a cargo of wheat was to be loaded at Odessa. Before the ship arrived there, war broke out between England and Russia. *Held*, the charterer was relieved from liability to load a cargo, since performance of the contract would have been contrary to English law as to trading with an enemy.

(b) Where the shipowner has broken a condition precedent. For example, we have already seen that the undertaking as to seaworthiness is a condition precedent.[4]

(c) Where there are express provisions in the contract which relieve the charterer. Thus, in *Gordon S.S. Co.* v. *Moxey*,[5]

> a ship was chartered to carry coal from Penarth to Buenos Aires. The charter-party provided that, in the event of a strike or lock-out causing a stoppage among coal workers, the charter was to be void if the stoppage lasted six running days from the time when the vessel was ready to load. On April 4, 1912, the ship was ready to load; but, owing to a coal strike, no coal arrived at Penarth for shipment until April 11. *Held*, although the strike itself ended on April 9, the stoppage was due to it, and the charterers were entitled to cancel the charter.

(d) Where the whole adventure has been frustrated.

The doctrine of frustration has been explained in an earlier chapter.[6]

---

[1] (1857), 27 L. J. Q. B. 17.
[2] *Ralli Brothers* v. *Compania Naviera*, [1920] 2 K. B. 287.
[3] *Supra*.
[4] *Stanton* v. *Richardson* (1874), L. R. 9 C. P. 390; for the facts, see p. 16, *ante*.
[5] (1913), 18 Com. Cas. 170.
[6] See pp. 47–54, *ante*.

(e) Where the failure to load a cargo is due to the shipowner's default[1] provided that he has no legal excuse for such default.[2]

In this case the charterer can recover from the shipowner any damages sustained as a direct result of the shipowner's default.

Where the shipowner has repudiated the contract, the charterer is not only discharged from his obligation to provide and load a cargo, but need not do so even if the shipowner subsequently declares his willingness to accept it.[3]

(2) *Bringing the cargo alongside.* Where the contract stipulates that the cargo is to be brought "alongside" by the charterer, the expense and risk of doing so is transferred to him. He must actually bring the cargo to the ship's side, and, if necessary, bear the cost of lighterage.

Thus, a usual clause states:

"Cargo to be brought alongside in such a manner as to enable vessel to take the goods with her own tackle . . . Charterers to procure and pay the necessary men on shore or on board the lighters to do the work there, vessel only heaving the cargo on board".[4]

Where a custom as to loading obtains at the port, it will bind even persons ignorant of it unless it is inconsistent with the written contract. Provided such a custom is reasonable, certain, and not contrary to law, there is a presumption that the parties contracted with reference to it. This can be rebutted only by the inconsistency of the custom with the express terms of the contract.[5]

---

[1] *Seeger* v. *Duthie* (1860), 8 C. B. N. S. 45.

[2] See *Phosphate, etc., Co.* v. *Rankin, etc., Co.* (1916), 86 L. J. K. B. 358.

[3] *Danube and Black Sea Rail, and Kustenjie Harbour Co., Ltd.,* v. *Xenos* (1863), 13 C. B. N. S. 825.

[4] "Gencon" form, clause 3. See Appendix B, p. 249. See e.g. *Skibs A/S Trolla and Skibs A/S Tautra* v. *United Enterprises and Shipping (Pte.) Ltd.: The "Tarva",* [1973] 2 Lloyd's Rep. 385, Singapore High Court, where, on the true construction of the charter-party, the responsibility for heaving the cargo on board was that of the charterers but in that operation they were to have the free use of the vessel's derricks, winches, gins and falls. (See the judgment of CHUA, J., *ibid.,* at p. 388.)

[5] *The Nifa,* [1892] P. 411.

Moreover, such matters as strikes, ice, and so on, though they may be individually named in the charter-party as exceptions, will afford no excuse to the charterer if he was prevented from, or delayed in, bringing the cargo down to the ship by one or more of them. He will only be protected if the actual loading is interfered with.[1] If loading was rendered *commercially* impossible by an excepted peril, the charterer will be excused, even though it was not *absolutely* impossible to load.[2] In *Grant* v. *Coverdale*,[3]

a ship was to proceed to Cardiff and load iron. The time for loading was to commence as soon as the vessel was ready to load except in cases of strikes, frosts, or other unavoidable accidents preventing loading. Owing to frost, delay occurred in bringing the cargo *to the dock*. *Held*, the charterer was liable.

At some ports, however, there is no storage accommodation, and goods have to be brought from storing places at some distance from the actual place of loading. In such cases, the charterer will be entitled to the benefit of the excepted perils during the transit from the storing places, provided such transit substantially forms part of the operation of loading, for the parties are taken to have contracted with that reservation in mind.[4]

(3) *Loading a full and complete cargo.* Where the ship has been chartered, the charterer's undertaking is to load a full cargo, not one equal to the ship's burden as stated in the charter-party. Consequently, in *Hunter* v. *Fry*,[5]

where the ship was described as "of the burden of 261 tons or thereabouts", but could have carried 400 tons of the agreed cargo, the shipowner obtained damages for loss of freight arising from the fact that only 336 tons were shipped.

Similarly, in *Windle* v. *Barker*,[6]

where the ship was described as "of the measurement of 180 to 200

---

[1] *Grant* v. *Coverdale* (1884), 9 App. Cas. 470; see, however, Lord SELBORNE'S remarks, *ibid.*, at p. 477.

[2] *SS. Matheos* v. *Louis Dreyfus & Co.*, [1925] A. C. 654.

[3] (1884), 9 App. Cas. 470.

[4] *Hudson* v. *Ede* (1868), L. R. 3 Q. B. 412; see *Grant* v. *Coverdale* (*supra*), at p. 477.

[5] (1819), 2 B. & Ald. 421.

[6] (1856), 25 L. J. Q. B. 349.

tons or thereabouts", the charterer was not entitled to refuse to load her because in fact she measured 257 tons.

The obligation to load a full and complete cargo is subject to the operation of the *de minimis* rule. The test of performance of the obligation is whether the departure from the precise terms of the obligation was so trivial as to be negligible or whether it had some significance.[1]

Each case depends on its own facts. Thus, in one case, a cargo of 12,588 tons 4 cwt. was held not commercially equivalent to 12,600 tons and was not in a commercial sense a full and complete cargo, for the quantity was, on the facts, outside the limits of the *de minimis* rule.[2]

The reason for the obligation to load a full cargo is that otherwise the shipowner would lose freight on account of some part of the ship's carrying capacity not being utilised. Hence, if a full cargo is not loaded, the charterer must pay not only freight on the goods actually shipped but also dead freight,[3] and the obligation to pay it is sometimes transferred to holders of the bills of lading by means of a "cesser" clause which gives a lien for dead freight on the goods shipped.[4]

Sometimes, however, the charter-party states that the amount of cargo to be loaded is to be decided by the shipowners, *e.g.* "10,000 tons of 2,240 lbs., 10% more or less at owners' option".[5]

A charter-party often provides that only "lawful merchandise" must be loaded. This term means such goods as are ordinarily shipped from the port of loading. Furthermore, it has been decided that to be "lawful merchandise", goods loaded under the charter-party must not only be such as can be loaded without

---

[1] *Margaronis Navigation Agency, Ltd.* v. *Henry W. Peabody & Co. of London, Ltd.*, [1964] 2 Lloyd's Rep. 153, C. A.

[2] *Ibid.* DIPLOCK, L. J., said (*ibid.*, at p. 159) that the application of the *de minimis* rule was simple, though difficulties might arise in borderline cases on particular facts. He considered it to be a matter of mixed law and fact (*ibid.*, at p. 160).

[3] See p. 229, *post.*

[4] See pp. 218–219, 231, *post.*

[5] *Northern Sales, Ltd.* v. *The "Giancarlo Zeta" ; The "Giancarlo Zeta"*, [1966] 2 Lloyd's Rep. 317 (Exchequer Court, British Columbia Admiralty District).

breach of the law in force at the port of loading, but must also be such as can lawfully be carried and discharged at the port of discharge.[1]

Sometimes the charter-party authorises the loading of several types of cargo. In this event the charterer may load a full cargo of any one or more of them, unless there is a contrary stipulation, although that cargo may not produce as much freight as the cargo anticipated. Thus, in *Moorsom* v. *Page*,[2]

the charter-party provided for a cargo of "copper, tallow, and hides or other goods." Tallow and hides were tendered, but the shipowner demanded copper as well. It was *held* that the option was with the charterer even though ballast was required as a consequence of his selecting the lighter articles.

Where the charterer is under an obligation to load a full cargo and has the option of loading several kinds of goods, he cannot choose to load goods which leave broken stowage and no others; he is obliged to fill up the spaces. Thus, in *Cole* v. *Meek*,[3]

where the charterer was to provide "a full and complete cargo of sugar or other lawful produce", he loaded mahogany logs, which were produce of the port of loading, but left spaces between the logs. *Held*, he was bound to provide sugar or other produce of the port of loading to fill the spaces, and must pay damages for not doing so.

But the charterer may be excused from liability for broken stowage by a custom of the port of loading. Thus, in *Cuthbert* v. *Cumming*,[4]

a charter-party provided for a "full and complete cargo of sugar, molasses and/or other lawful produce". It was customary at the port of loading to load sugar and molasses in hogsheads and puncheons. This was done; but spaces were left large enough to take small packages of sugar, cocoa, etc. *Held*, it was sufficient for the charterer to load in the customary way.

So also, where the cargo to be carried can be loaded in two different ways, one of which is more economical of space than the

---

[1] *Leolga Compania de Navigacion* v. *John Glynn & Son, Ltd.*, [1953] 2 All E. R. 327.
[2] (1814), 4 Camp. 103.
[3] (1864), 33 L. J. C. P. 183.
[4] (1855), 11 Exch. 405.

other, but each of which is a usual method of loading cargo of the relevant type, the charterer can load in whichever of these ways he pleases, unless he is expressly forbidden so to do by the charter-party. The mere fact that he is under a duty to load a full and complete cargo will not suffice to deprive him of this choice, or to render him liable for dead freight as the result merely of adopting the less economical method.[1]

If the charter-party states that the charterer is entitled to load an alternative cargo, *e.g.* wheat and/or maize and/or rye, and after the loading of the wheat has commenced the export of wheat is prohibited, it is implied that he should be given a reasonable time to determine how to deal with the altered conditions and make arrangements to ship a cargo which can be loaded.[2] What is a reasonable time is a matter of fact. If the prevention of loading arises from a strike, a similar rule will be applied.[3]

Sometimes there will be an *obligation* on the charterer to load an alternative cargo, but sometimes he has an unfettered *option* to do so. In each case it turns on the interpretation of the particular words used in the charter-party.[4]

Thus, in *Reardon Smith Line Ltd.* v. *Ministry of Agriculture, Fisheries and Food,*[5]

A charter-party provided that the charterer was to load "a full and complete cargo . . . of wheat in bulk . . . and/or barley in bulk and/or flour in sacks". The charterer had the option "of loading up to one-third cargo of barley and one-third cargo of flour" at an increased rate of freight. The charterer began to load wheat, but a strike occurred and further loading was delayed. *Held*, that the primary obligation under the charter-party was to load wheat, and the charterer was under no liability to load an alternative cargo of barley and flour which were not affected by the strike.

---

[1] *Angfartygs* v. *Price and Pierce, Ltd.,* [1939] 3 All E. R. 672.

[2] *H. A. Brightman & Co.* v. *Bunge y Born, Limitada Sociedad Anonima Commercial Financiera y Industrial of Buenos Aires,* [1924] 2 K. B. 619, C. A.

[3] *South African Despatch Line* v. *Owners of the Panamanian Steamship Niki,* [1960] 1 All E. R. 285; [1960] 1 Q. B. 518.

[4] *Reardon Smith Line, Ltd.* v. *Ministry of Agriculture, Fisheries and Food,* [1963] 1 All E. R. 545; [1963] A. C. 691, H. L.

[5] *Supra.*

(4) *Loading in the Stipulated Time.* The cargo must be loaded in the stipulated time. If it is not, the charterer will have to pay demurrage or damages for detention, as the case may be.[1]

Again, where a consecutive voyage charter-party is for a total of "two years' consecutive voyages", each time the vessel is tendered for to the charterers for loading during that period they must load her within the laytime provisions.[2]

DISCHARGE

Naming the Port of Discharge

In the case of a general ship the port of discharge is stated in the bill of lading, but where the ship is chartered two cases arise which must be carefully distinguished:–

(1) *Where the port is agreed on and named in the charter-party.* Here, unless limited by other clauses, the obligation to go to the port named is absolute.

(2) *Where the port is not named in the charter-party.* In this case the charterer must name a safe port, and the obligation is the same whether an express provision to that effect is inserted or not. If the charterer names a port which is not safe, the shipowner is discharged from liability to unload there; he can earn the freight by delivering at the nearest safe port.

But once the port has been named and accepted by, or on behalf of, the shipowner (*e.g.* by the master in signing bills of lading), he cannot afterwards refuse to go there on the ground that it is not safe. He can, however, claim damages for injury to the ship by reason of the port not being safe.[3]

---

[1] Demurrage and damages for detention are considered in Chapter 10, *post.*

[2] *Suisse Atlantique Société d'Armement Maritime S.A.* v. *N.V. Rotterdamsche Kolen Centrale*, [1966] 2 All E. R. 61; [1967] A. C. 361; [1966] 1 Lloyd's Rep. 529, H. L.

[3] See p. 128, *post.*

If the ship is delayed by reason of the charterer's failure to name a port, the charterer will be liable in damages.[1] And if, by refusing to name a place of discharge, he prevents the shipowner from earning the freight, he will have to pay it as damages for breach of contract.[2]

Whether the instructions given to the master by the charterer do amount to an order to proceed to a named port of discharge depends on the circumstances.[3]

Where the charter-party provides that the ship is to proceed to a named port for orders, and that the charterer is to give such orders within a specified time after the master has given notice of the ship's arrival, the contract is construed as meaning that, even though the orders do not arrive within the time specified, the master must await their arrival for a reasonable time. He is not at liberty to leave the port of call as soon as the time specified has elapsed, though the charterer may, if the contract so provides, be liable to compensate the owners for the delay.[4]

Where the charterer is given an option as to the ports at which the vessel is to discharge, the Court may construe the clause as meaning that the ports must be taken in geographical order.

Thus, in *Pilgrim Shipping Co., Ltd.* v. *State Trading Corporation of India, Ltd.: The "Hadjitsakos"*,[5]

A vessel was chartered for a voyage from British Columbia to "one or two safe ports India". She proceeded via Singapore, and the charterers nominated Bombay and Calcutta as the discharging ports in that order.

---

[1] *Zim Israel Navigation Co., Ltd.* v. *Tradax Export S.A.: The "Timna"*, [1971] 2 Lloyd's Rep. 91, C. A., where the charterers were held liable in damages from the time when the order for the port of discharge should have been given to the time when it was in fact given.

[2] *Stewart* v. *Rogerson* (1871), L. R. 6 C. P. 424.

[3] *Zim Israel Navigation Co., Ltd.* v. *Tradax Export S.A.: The "Timna"* (*supra*), where the charterers sent a message to the master stating: "The vessel allocated for discharging/lightering at Brake and we suggest tendering [the] notice of readiness anew upon vessel's arrival at Brake", and it was held that this message did not amount to an order to go to Brake. See the judgment of Lord DENNING, M.R., *ibid.*, at p. 94, and that of MEGAW, L.J., *ibid.*, at p. 95.

[4] *Procter, etc., Ltd.* v. *Oakwin S.S. Co.*, [1926] 1 K. B. 244.

[5] [1975] 1 Lloyd's Rep. 356, C. A. (See the judgment of Lord DENNING, M.R., *ibid.*, at p. 360 and that of Sir JOHN PENNYCUICK, *ibid.*, at p. 367.)

Held, by C. A., that they were not entitled to do so for, on the true construction of the charter-party, the parties did not contemplate that the vessel would be asked to discharge, first, at a port on the west coast and, secondly, at an east coast port.

What Constitutes a "Safe Port"

The port specified by the charterer must be "safe". "A 'safe port' means a port to which a vessel can get laden as she is and at which she can lay and discharge, always afloat".[1]

Thus, in *Leeds Shipping Co., Ltd.* v. *Société Française Bunge,*[2]

A charter-party stated that the vessel was to proceed to "one or two safe ports in Morocco". The charterer directed her to Mogador. In this port there was a lack of shelter and a liability to the sudden onset of a high wind which could not be predicted, and which might quickly cause an anchor to drag. The port was very near some rocks and the anchorage was very restricted. *Held,* that the port was unsafe.

Moreover, it must be a port from which she can safely return.[3] If a port is in fact unsafe, it is irrelevant that well-informed men might erroneously have pronounced it to be safe.[4]

The safety of the port should be viewed in respect of a vessel properly manned and equipped, and navigated and handled without negligence and in accordance with good seamanship.[5]

The port must be safe for the particular vessel carrying the cargo she has on board. And it must be politically as well as physically safe, this being a question of fact in each case;[6] *e.g.* the shipowner is not bound to risk confiscation by entering a port which has been declared closed.[7] Again, if the named port is one at which no tugs are ever obtainable, and the chartered vessel cannot, by reason of her size, reach that port without the assistance of tugs, that port is not safe.[8] If the ship with all her cargo cannot safely get into the place named, the ship-owner is entitled

---

[1] *Per* SANKEY, J., in *Hall Brothers* v. *Paul, Ltd.* (1914), 111 L. T., at p. 812.

[2] [1958] 2 Lloyd's Rep. 127, C. A.

[3] *Limerick S.S. Co.* v. *Stott,* [1921] 1 K. B. 568; affirmed, [1921] 2 K. B. 613.

[4] *G. W. Grace & Co., Ltd.* v. *General Steam Navigation Co., Ltd.,* [1950] 1 All E. R. 201.

[5] *Leeds Shipping Co., Ltd.* v. *Société Française Bunge* (*supra*), at p. 131 (*per* SELLERS, L.J.).

[6] See *Palace Shipping Co.* v. *Gans,* [1916] 1 K. B. 138.

[7] *Ogden* v. *Graham* (1861), 31 L. J. Q. B. 26.

[8] *Axel Brostrom* v. *Dreyfus* (1932), 38 Com. Cas. 79.

to unload at the nearest safe place. He is not bound by a custom to unload partly outside and partly inside the port.[1]

A temporary condition of danger, however, will not make the port unsafe, provided that such condition will not last an unreasonable time.[2] It has been said, however, that it does not follow "that the converse is true, that any port which is safe at the moment, but which is liable to become dangerous at short notice, is necessarily a safe port within the meaning of a [particular] charter-party".[3]

"Or so near thereto as she may safely get"

The clause "Or so near thereto as she may safely get" is often added after the name of the port of discharge. Its effect is to limit what would otherwise be an absolute obligation on the shipowner to enter the port named in spite of sand, bars, ice, blockade, etc. The clause is also used even where the port is not named in the charter-party.

The clause relates only to obstacles which are regarded as permanent, not to such as were contemplated as ordinary incidents of the voyage. A temporary obstacle, such as an unfavourable state of the tide or insufficient water to enable the ship to get into dock, will not make the place unsafe so as to discharge the shipowner from liability to unload there, unless the terms of the contract indicate otherwise;[4] and the mere presence of the clause under consideration is not sufficient to indicate otherwise. We have seen that the ship must wait until a temporary obstacle is removed; but the master, though bound to allow a reasonable time to elapse before having recourse to the clause,[5] is not bound to wait an unreasonable time. Thus, in *Dahl* v. *Nelson*,[6]

it was *held* that the voyage was not performed merely by bringing the goods to the entrance of the named dock, which was so crowded that

---

[1] *The Alhambra* (1881), 6 P. D. 68.
[2] See *per* CROMPTON, J., in *Parker* v. *Winlow* (1857), 26 L. J. Q. B., at p. 53; *Dahl* v. *Nelson* (1881), 6 App. Cas. 38.
[3] *Per* ROWLATT, J., in *Johnston* v. *Saxon Queen S.S. Co.* (1913), 108 L. T., at p. 565.
[4] *Allen* v. *Coltart* (1883), 11 Q. B. D. 782.
[5] *The Varing*, [1931] P. 79, *per* SCRUTTON, L.J., at p. 87.
[6] *Supra.*

the vessel could not get in for an indefinite period. Nevertheless, the charterer, having refused to name another place of discharge, it was *held* that the shipowner was not bound to wait an unreasonable time in order to get into the dock.

In *Metcalfe* v. *Britannia Ironworks Co.*,[1]

delivery was to be made at Taganrog, on the Sea of Azof. The charter-party stipulated that the ship should go "to Taganrog, or so near as she could safely get and deliver the cargo afloat". In December, when the vessel arrived, the Sea of Azof was closed by ice and would not be open for five months. It was *held* that the shipowner was not entitled to freight by delivering as near as he could get. The question whether an obstacle is temporary or permanent is not so much one of length of time as of what may be regarded as contemplated incidents of the voyage. That the Sea of Azof should be frozen at that time of the year was regarded as reasonably within the contemplation of the parties.

Again, in *The Athamas* (*Owners*) v. *Dig Vijay Cement Co., Ltd.*,[2]

By the terms of a charter-party a vessel was to discharge her cargo at Pnom-Penh or "so near thereto as she may safely get". She could not get to Pnom-Penh, and had to discharge at Saigon which was 250 miles away. *Held,* that in the circumstances of the case the discharge at Saigon was sufficient compliance with the terms of the charter-party.

PEARSON, L.J., said[3] that the parties should be deemed to have general maritime knowledge and therefore to know that that part of the world was sparsely provided with ports, so that there might well be a long distance between the named port and any possible substitute. That differentiated the present case from one in which the named port was on the west coast of Europe or in the Mediterranean or in the Black Sea. The question was one of degree and to be decided on a basis of commercial knowledge and experience.

Frequently, the words "always afloat" are incorporated in the clause. Many modern ships would be injured by taking the ground, and these words serve to limit the shipowner's obligation. Thus, in *Treglia* v. *Smith's Timber Co.*,[4]

where the bill of lading contained these words and the ship could not

---

[1] (1877), 2 Q. B. D. 423.
[2] [1963] 1 Lloyd's Rep. 287, C. A.
[3] *Ibid.*, at p. 302.
[4] (1896), 1 Com. Cas. 360.

discharge at the port named without taking the ground, it was *held* that the master was entitled to unload at the nearest safe place.

But this clause will not allow the shipowner to refuse to draw into a berth where the ship cannot lie continually afloat, if she can do so for a certain time.[1]

Damage Caused by Entering Unsafe Port

If the charterer nominates an unsafe port and the ship is damaged through going there, he will be liable for the damage, subject, of course to possible questions of remoteness, or *novus actus interveniens, e.g.* if the master, knowing that the port is unsafe still insists on going there and the vessel suffers damage in consequence.[2] The test is: did the master act reasonably in going there? If he acted unreasonably, the charterer is not liable.

Thus, in *Reardon Smith Line, Ltd.* v. *Australian Wheat Board*,[3]

The charterer directed the vessel to a port in Western Australia. The vessel arrived at the port and while loading was being carried out, the wind freshened and soon increased to gale force, and she was severely damaged. *Held*, that the port was unsafe and that the master of the vessel had acted reasonably in going there. The damage to the vessel flowed from the breach of the charter-party, and consequently the charterer was liable.

Notice of Readiness to Discharge

When the ship has arrived at the place of discharge, the consignee or indorsee of the bill of lading must take steps to receive the goods. In the absence of a custom or special contract to the contrary, the shipowner is not bound to notify the consignees that

---

[1] *Carlton S.S. Co.* v. *Castle Co.*, [1898] A. C. 486.

[2] *Compania Naviera Maropan S/A* v. *Bowaters Pulp and Paper Mills, Ltd.*, [1955] 2 All E. R. 241; [1955] 2 Q. B. 68, C. A.; *Reardon Smith Line, Ltd.* v. *Australian Wheat Board*, [1956] 1 All E. R. 456; [1956] A. C. 266, P. C.; *Leeds Shipping Co., Ltd.* v. *Société Française Bunge*, [1958] 2 Lloyd's Rep. 127, C. A. The same rule is applied in the case of time charter-parties. See p. 27, *ante*.

[3] [1956] 1 All E. R. 456; [1956] A. C. 266, P.C.

he is ready to unload,[1] though, if he is intending to have recourse
to the clause "or so near thereto as she may safely get", he must
inform them of the place to which he intends to proceed.[2] In
general, however, it is the duty of the holders of the bills of lading
to look out for the arrival of the ship. The reason for this rule
is that the bills of lading may have been assigned during the voyage,
and the master may not know who is entitled to the goods. But
where the consignee's ignorance of the ship's arrival is due to
some default on the part of the shipowner, such as entering the
ship at the customs-house under a wrong or misleading name,
he will not be liable for delay occasioned thereby.[3] For it is
the shipowner's duty to go through all the proper formalities on
arrival, *i.e.* notification at the customs-house, delivery of papers,
or whatever else local regulations may demand.

Discharging in the Stipulated Time

If the vessel is not discharged in the time stipulated, the
charterer renders himself liable to pay demurrage or damages for
detention, as the case may be.[4]

Again, where a consecutive voyage charter-party is for a total of
"two years' consecutive voyages", each time the vessel is tendered
to the charterers for discharging during that period, they must
discharge her within the laytime provisions.[5]

Cost of Discharging

As to whether the shipowner or the charterer is to bear the cost
of discharging will depend on the terms of the charter-party.

Thus, in *S. G. Embiricos, Ltd.* v. *Tradax Internacional S.A.:
The "Azuero"*,[6]

---

[1] *Harman* v. *Mant* (1815), 4 Camp. 161; *R. Pagnan and Fratelli* v. *Tradax
Export S.A.*, [1969] 2 Lloyd's Rep. 150, Q. B. D. (Commercial Court), at
p. 154 (*per* DONALDSON, J.).

[2] *The Varing* (*supra*).

[3] *Bradley* v. *Goddard* (1863), 3 F. & F. 638.

[4] Demurrage and damages for detention are considered in Chapter 10, *post*.

[5] *Suisse Atlantique Société d'Armement Maritime S.A.* v. *N.V. Rotterdamsche
Kolen Centrale*, [1966] 2 All E.R. 61; [1967] 1 A. C. 361, H. L.

[6] [1967] 1 Lloyd's Rep. 464, Q. B. D. (Commercial Court).

A clause in a charter-party stated: "Charterers' stevedores to be employed by vessel at discharge port and discharge to be free of expense to the vessel." The stevedores at the port of discharge opened and closed the hatches during discharge. The shipowners alleged that the cost (other than the first opening and last closing) was part of cost of discharging vessel, whilst the charterers contended that the cost was part of the cost of the ship fulfilling her duty to take proper care of the cargo during discharge. *Held*, that the opening and closing of the hatches were part of the operation of discharge, and that therefore the charterers were liable.

A charter-party sometimes provides that the charterer is to have the option declarable on or before completion of loading free of expense to the vessel.[1]

"Seaworthy Trim"

Where the vessel is to discharge at more than one port, the charter-party may provide that the vessel is "to be left in seaworthy trim to shift between ports".

The term "seaworthy trim" means that she must be in trim to meet the perils of the passage by sea to the next port not only in the sense that she should be left with an adequate amount of cargo to keep her on an even keel, but also that where necessary part of her cargo should be bagged to stop it shifting while out at sea.[2]

DELIVERY

Where Delivery must be made

Unless otherwise agreed, the consignee must take the goods from alongside, though this obligation may be varied by a custom of

---

[1] *Belships Co. Ltd. Skibs A/S* v. *President of India: The "Belfri"*, [1972] 1 Lloyd's Rep. 12, Q. B. D. (Commercial Court), where it was held that the option had been exercised in time. (See the judgment of MOCATTA, J., *ibid.*, at p. 17.)

[2] *Britain S.S. Co., Ltd.* v. *Louis Dreyfus & Co.* (1935), 51 Ll. L. Rep. 196, at p. 199 (*per* MACKINNON, J.); *J. C. Carras & Sons (Shipbrokers), Ltd.* v. *President of India: The "Argobeam"*, [1970] 1 Lloyd's Rep. 282, Q. B. D. (Commercial Court), at p. 291 (*per* MOCATTA, J.).

the port which is not inconsistent with express terms of the contract. The general rule, however, is that the shipowner is only bound to deliver over the ship's side. Thus, in *Petersen* v. *Freebody*,[1]

a cargo of spars was to be discharged "overside into lighters". The consignee provided lighters at the ship's sides, but did not employ sufficient men in the lighters to take delivery within the time fixed for unloading. The shipowner sued for damages in respect of the delay. It was *held* that the shipowner was not bound to put the spars on board the lighters. His duty was simply to put them over the rail of the ship and within reach of the men on board the lighters. Consequently the consignee was liable for the delay in unloading.

Production of Bill of Lading by Consignee

The master is justified in delivering the goods to the consignee named in the bill of lading on production thereof, or to the first person who presents a properly endorsed bill of lading, provided the master has no notice of dealings with other bills of the same set. In the leading case of *Glyn* v. *East and West India Dock Co.*,[2]

goods were deliverable "to Cottam and Co., or assigns". They deposited one bill of lading with the plaintiffs as security for a loan, and with a second bill they obtained delivery from the dock company. The plaintiffs sued the dock company for wrongful delivery; but it was *held* that they were entitled to deliver on presentation of a proper bill of lading.

If the master has notice of other claims to the goods, he delivers at his peril. His proper course is to interplead,[3] or deliver to one party on tender of an indemnity against the consequences should it turn out that another person was entitled to the goods.

---

[1] [1895] 2 Q. B. 294.

[2] (1882), 7 App. Cas. 591.

[3] Interpleader is a process by which a person in possession of property claimed by two or more persons is able to be relieved from liability by compelling them to bring their claims before a Court at their own expense, thereby securing for himself the protection of the Court's order as to the disposal of the property.

Conversely, the master is not justified in delivering to any person who does not produce the bill of lading. Thus, in *The Stettin*,[1]

barrels of oil were shipped under bills of lading making them deliverable "to Mendelsohn or assigns". The shipper retained one bill of lading and sent the other to his agents to secure payment of the price. The master of the ship delivered the oil to Mendolsohn without production of the bill of lading. *Held*, the shipowner was liable to the shipper for so delivering.

Delivery to Consignee personally

The goods must be handed over to the consignee or his agents. Thus, in *Bourne* v. *Gatliff*,[2]

goods were consigned under a bill of lading to the plaintiff or his assigns. They were discharged at a wharf on the day after the ship's arrival. The consignees were not aware of the ship's arrival, and they were not at the wharf to take delivery. Within twenty-four hours of the discharge the goods were accidentally destroyed by fire. The jury found that delivery at the wharf did not constitute proper delivery by reason of any special custom of the port. *Held*, the shipowner was liable for their value. A reasonable time must be allowed for claiming the goods, and, until that time has elapsed, the shipowner's liability as a carrier continues. "The contract was to deliver to the consignee in the port of London; instead of a delivery to the consignee, the goods were placed on Fenning's wharf".[3]

But where the custom of the port of delivery recognises another mode of delivery, personal delivery is not necessary.[4] Thus delivery to a dock company, where it is usual for the dock company to take cargo and store it until claimed, has been held sufficient.[5] And where the regulations of the port required the consignee to employ harbour porters to receive cargo, delivery to them was

---

[1] (1889), 14 P. D. 142. See also *Sze Hai Tong Bank, Ltd.* v. *Rambler Cycle Co.*, [1959] 3 All E. R. 182; [1959] A. C. 576, P. C.; *Barclays Bank, Ltd.* v. *Commissioners of Customs and Excise*, [1963] 1 Lloyd's Rep. 81, Q. B. D., at p. 88 (*per* DIPLOCK, L.J.); *Rambler Cycle Co., Ltd.* v. *Peninsular & Oriental Steam Navigation Co., Sze Hai Tong Bank Ltd.* (*First Third Party*), *Southern Trading Co.* (*Second Third Party*), [1968] 1 Lloyd's Rep. 42 (Malaysia Federal Court).

[2] (1844), 7 M. & G., 850.

[3] *Per* Lord LYNDHURST in *Bourne* v. *Gatliff* (*supra*), at p. 865.

[4] *Petrocochino* v. *Bott* (1874), L. R. 9 C. P. 355.

[5] *Grange* v. *Taylor* (1904), 9 Com. Cas. 223.

held sufficient to excuse the shipowner from liability for damage subsequently accruing to the goods.[1]

The shipowner may also be excused by statute or by express contract from his liability to make personal delivery. Thus, in *Chartered Bank of India* v. *British India S.N. Co.*,[2]

goods were shipped to Penang to be delivered there "to order or assigns' under bills of lading which contained the condition that "in all cases and under all circumstances the liability of the Company shall absolutely cease when the goods are free of the ship's tackle, and thereupon the goods shall be at the risk for all purposes and in every respect of the shipper or consignee". The landing agents appointed by the defendants fraudulently delivered the goods to persons other than the consignees. *Held*, that, although there had been no delivery under the bill of lading, the above clause was operative and effectual to protect the shipowner.

Apportionment of Cargo

Where goods have become mixed and unidentifiable on the voyage, it seems that two classes of cases must be distinguished:

(1) *Where this has resulted from excepted perils.* Here the consignees become tenants in common of the mixed goods in proportion to their respective interests, and the shipowner must deliver to them proportionately.[3] But the provisions of the bills of lading or a custom of the port of delivery may relieve him of this duty.[4]

(2) *Where the cause of the mishap was not an excepted peril.* Here the shipowner is liable to any particular bill of lading

---

[1] *Knight Steamship Co.* v. *Fleming* (1898), 25 R. (Ct. of Sess.), 1070.

[2] [1909] A. C. 369; *Pacific Milk Industries (M) Bhd.* v. *Koninklinjke (Royal Interocean Lines) and Federal Shipping and Forwarding Agency: The "Straat Cumberland"*, [1973] 2 Lloyd's Rep. 492, State of Selangor, Kuala Lumpur Sessions Court, where the clause in the bill of lading stated: "Wherever it is compulsory or customary at any port to deliver the cargo to the custom or port authorities, . . . delivery so made shall be considered as final delivery". But see *Sze Hai Tong Bank, Ltd.* v. *Rambler Cycle Co. (supra)*, where the action of the master in delivering the goods without production of the bill of lading was held to be a "fundamental breach" of contract.

[3] *Spence* v. *Union Marine Insce. Co.* (1868), L. R. 3 C. P. 427. See further, *Gill and Duffus (Liverpool)* v. *Scruttons, Ltd.*, [1953] 2 All E. R. 977; [1953] 1 W. L. R. 1407.

[4] *Grange* v. *Taylor (supra)*.

holder, and the mere delivery of a proportion of the mixed goods will not relieve him of it,[1] though, of course, a special provision in the bills of lading *might* do so if its terms were wide enough.

In the leading case of *Sandeman* v. *Tyzack, etc., Co.*,[2]

bales of jute were consigned to various persons. The bills of lading provided that the number of packages signed for should be binding on the shipowner. The bales were specifically marked, but the shipowner was exempted from liability for obliteration or absence of marks. When the cargo was unloaded, fourteen bales were missing and eleven others could not be identified as belonging to any particular consignment. All but four of the consignees received the full number of bales, and the shipowner claimed to apportion the eleven bales among these four. It was *held* that, as the shipowner had failed to deliver the full number of bales shipped, he was not entitled to claim the benefit of the exemption as to obliteration of marks; and he was liable for the full value of the missing bales and of those which could not be identified.

Where goods are shipped in bulk under different bills of lading covering undivided portions of the bulk, and the cargo is damaged on the voyage, the shipowner is under no obligation to apportion the loss, or the damaged goods, between the various holders. He is entitled to make complete delivery of sound goods to the first consignee to take delivery. This is so even where there is a special provision in the various bills of lading that each bill is to bear its proportion of shortage and damage; for this provision has been held merely to regulate the rights of the holders *inter se*.[3]

Landing and Warehousing Unclaimed Goods

At Common Law and under the powers given to him by the Merchant Shipping Act, 1894, the master, as agent of the shipowner, has the right to land and warehouse unclaimed goods.[4]

---

[1] *Sandeman* v. *Tyzack, etc., Co.*, [1913] A. C. 680.
[2] *Supra.*
[3] *Grange* v. *Taylor (supra).*
[4] See Chapter 8, p. 183, *post.*

The Cessation of the Shipowner's Responsibility

The shipowner continues liable as a carrier until by the contract, or in the usual course of business, the transit is terminated and the goods have been warehoused for their owner until he is ready to receive them.[1] The mere fact that the goods have reached their destination is not enough to discharge the shipowner. The carrier may limit his liability to that of a bailee by giving notice that he has warehoused the goods and will no longer be responsible for their safe custody, provided the consignee accepts such notice.[2] The consignee's refusal to take delivery, or failure to do so within a reasonable time, also puts an end to the shipowner's liability as a carrier.

When the shipowner has warehoused the goods under s. 493 of the Merchant Shipping Act 1894,[3] he is no longer responsible for their safety. The warehouseman is not an agent for the shipowner for the purpose of ensuring the safety of the goods. He is under an obligation "to deliver the goods to the same person as the shipowner was by his contract bound to deliver them, and is justified or excused by the same circumstances as would justify or excuse the master".[4]

The contract sometimes provides that the shipowner's liability ceases once the goods have been transhipped.[5]

---

[1] See *Bourne* v. *Gatliff* (1844), 7 Man. & G. 850.

[2] *Mitchell* v. *Lancashire and Yorkshire Railway Co.* (1875), L. R. 10 Q. B. 256.

[3] See Appendix D, *post*.

[4] *Per* Lord BLACKBURN in *Glyn* v. *East and West India Dock Co.* (1882), 7 App. Cas. at p. 614. The *dictum* refers to the Merchant Shipping Act 1862, s. 66, but applies to the later Act.

[5] *The "Berkshire"*, [1974] 1 Lloyd's Rep. 185, Q. B. D. (Admiralty Court), where the clause in the bill of lading stated: "Whenever the goods are consigned to a point where the ship does not expect to discharge the carrier or master may without notice forward . . . the goods . . . by any vessel . . . whether operated by the carrier or others . . . this carrier in making arrangements for any transshipment . . . shall be considered solely the forwarding agent of the shippers and without any responsibility whatsoever."

The Measure of Damages

The rule laid down in a leading case is as follows:[1]

"Where two parties have made a contract which one of them has broken, the damages which the other party ought to receive in respect of such breach of contract should be, either such as may fairly and reasonably be considered arising naturally, *i.e.* according to the usual course of things, from such breach of contract itself, or such as may reasonably be supposed to have been in the contemplation of both parties at the time they made the contract, as the probable result of the breach of it."

The problems which have arisen in applying these principles are very numerous, and they cannot be discussed in detail in an elementary work. But the following illustrations will serve to show how the Courts have applied the general principles to the breach of contracts for carriage of goods by sea.

(1) *Where goods are lost or damaged.* Apart from special circumstances, the value of the goods for which compensation must be made, if they have been lost or damaged, is that which they would have had at the time and place at which they ought to have been delivered in proper condition.[2]

(2) *Where goods are delivered short of their destination.* The measure of damages was considered by the House of Lords in *Monarch S.S. Co., Ltd.* v. *A/B Karlshamns Oljefabriker* where Lord PORTER said:[3]

---

[1] *Per* ALDERSON, B., in *Hadley* v. *Baxendale* (1854), 9 Exch. 341. See also *Victoria Laundry (Windsor), Ltd.* v. *Newman Industries, Ltd.*, [1949] 1 All E. R. 997; [1949] 2 K. B. 528.

[2] *The Arpad*, [1934] P. 189. See also *Ceylon Government* v. *Chandris*, [1965] 2 Lloyd's Rep. 204, Q. B. D. (Commercial Court), at p. 216 (*per* MOCATTA, J.). See also *Club Coffee Co., Ltd.* v. *Moore-McCormack Lines Inc., Moore-McCormack Lines (Canada), Ltd., and Eastern Canada Stevedoring (1963), Ltd.*, [1968] 2 Lloyd's Rep. 103, Exchequer Court of Canada, Ontario Admiralty District, where it was held that the measure of damages included Canadian customs duty which the holder of the bill of lading had had to pay on the undelivered goods. See the judgment of THURLOW, J., *ibid.*, at p. 106.

[3] [1949] 1 All E.R. 1, at p. 9.

"the direct and natural consequence is that the merchant should arrange for the carriage forward and charge the shipowner with the reasonable cost of doing so".

In that case,

a British ship was chartered to carry soya beans from Manchuria in April, 1939, and in June the charterers were given bills of lading in respect of them and nominated Karlshamn in Sweden as the port of discharge. Under the terms of the charter-party the owners were under contract to supply a seaworthy ship. The ship was unseaworthy, and the voyage was thereby delayed. Soon after the outbreak of war in September, 1939 the ship was ordered by the Admiralty to proceed to Glasgow, where the beans were discharged. They were then forwarded by the consignees (to whom the charterers had transferred the bills of lading which incorporated the terms of the charter-party) to Karlshamn in neutral ships at a cost of over £21,000. The House of Lords *held* that the consignees were entitled to recover the cost of transhipment from the shipowners by way of damages.

(3) *Where there has been delay in carrying goods.* In this event, the measure of damages is generally the difference between the market value of the goods at the time when they ought to have been delivered and the time when they were in fact delivered.[1]

Thus, in *The Ardennes (Owner of Cargo)* v. *The Ardennes (Owners)*,[2]

Exporters of mandarin oranges shipped a cargo of them relying on an oral promise by the shipowners' agent that the ship would go straight from Cartagena to London. In fact she went first to Antwerp, with the result that when the cargo arrived in London there had been an increase in the import duty on mandarins, and other cargoes of mandarins had arrived, causing a fall in price. *Held*, that as the parties must have been aware that the earlier the goods arrived the better would be the price, the shipowners were liable in damages in respect of the increased import duty which the shippers had had to pay, and to the extent that the delayed arrival had caused them loss of market.

Again, in *The Heron II, Koufos* v. *C. Czarnikow, Ltd.*,[3]

---

[1] *Dunn* v. *Bucknall Brothers*, [1902] 2 K. B. 614; *The Heron II, Koufos* v. *C. Czarnikow, Ltd.*, [1967] 3 All E. R. 686, H. L.

[2] [1950] 2 All E. R. 517; [1951] 1 K. B. 55. See also *Heskell* v. *Continental Express, Ltd.*, [1950] 1 All E. R. 1033.

[3] [1967] 3 All E. R. 686, H. L., not applying *The Parana* (1877), 2 P. D. 118.

A vessel was chartered for a voyage from Constantza to Basrah for the carriage of sugar. She deviated to Berbera to load livestock for the shipowner. If she had not deviated, she would have arrived at Basrah 10 days earlier than she did in fact. The charterers claimed damages for the difference between the market value of the sugar at the due date of delivery and at the actual date of delivery. *Held* by the House of Lords, that they were entitled to this sum.

In determining whether a particular type of loss or damage such as consequential loss of profit, is recoverable as damages for breach of a contract of carriage of goods by sea, the crucial question is whether, on the information available to the carrier when the contract was made, the loss or damage was sufficiently likely to result from the breach of contract to make it proper to hold that the loss or damage flowed naturally from the breach or that loss or damage of that kind should have been within his contemplation.[1]

Limitation of Liability

As we shall see, the shipowner may be entitled to limit his liability for loss of or damage to the goods under the Merchant Shipping Act 1894, s. 503.[2] Further, where the Carriage of Goods by Sea Act 1924 applies, he can limit his liability in accordance with Art. IV, r. 5 of the Schedule to that Act.[3] Liability may also be limited under the Carriage of Goods by Sea Act 1971.[4]

Time for bringing Claims

(i) *Under terms of contract.* If the goods are not delivered, or delivered in a damaged condition, a claim may be made within a period of six years[5] unless, as is common, there is a clause to the contrary in the charter-party or bill of lading. The time allowed

---

[1] *The Heron II, Koufos* v. *C. Czarnikow, Ltd.* (*supra*), at p. 691 (*per* Lord REID).

[2] See pp. 170–173, *post.*

[3] See pp. 173–176, *post.*

[4] See pp. 176–177, *post. This Act is not yet in force.* See p. 76, *ante.* As to the cases in which it applies, see pp. 77–79, *ante.*

[5] Limitation Act 1939, s. 2. See, *e.g., Bosma* v. *Larsen,* [1966] 1 Lloyd's Rep. 22, Q. B. D. (Commercial Court), where the claim was made nearly nine years after the discharge of the goods, and was held to be statute barred.

is usually a short one, *e.g.* the arbitration clause in the "Centro-con" charter-party states:

"All disputes from time to time arising out of this contract[1] shall . . . be referred to the final arbitrament of two arbitrators carrying on business in London. . . . Any claim must be made in writing and Claimants' Arbitrator appointed within 3 months of final discharge, and where this provision is not complied with the claim shall be deemed to be waived and absolutely barred. . . ."[2]

But where there is an arbitration clause in this form, and the goods are never "discharged" because they have been totally lost when the vessel carrying them founders, the clause has no application and the period of six years applies. The word "discharge" must not be read as referring to the date when the cargo "should have been discharged in due performance of the contract".

Thus, in *Denny Mott and Dickson, Ltd.* v. *Lynn Shipping Co., Ltd.*,[3]

Goods were shipped at Munksund, Sweden, on a vessel bound for London. The bill of lading incorporated clause 32 of the charter-party which contained an arbitration clause stating "All claims must be made in writing and the claimant's arbitrator must be appointed within 12 months of the date of final discharge, otherwise the claim shall be deemed waived and absolutely barred". The vessel carrying the goods was a total loss on 18 June, 1959. The indorsees of the bill of lading brought an action against the shipowners on 17 June, 1961. The shipowners contended that the claim was time-barred as the arbitrator was not appointed within 12 months of the date when the cargo should have been discharged.
Held, that the action was not time-barred, for clause 32 did not apply, since the cargo had never been discharged as it had been totally lost.

---

[1] A claim for a general average contribution constitutes a "dispute" for the purpose of the arbitration clause set out above: *E. B. Aaby's Rederi A/S* v. *Union of India: The "Evje"*, [1974] 1 Lloyd's Rep. 57, H. L.; *Alma Shipping Corporation* v. *Union of India and the Chief Controller of Chartering, Ministry of Transport of India: The "Astraea"*, [1971] 2 Lloyd's Rep. 494, Q. B. D. (Commercial Court).

[2] See. *e.g.*, *Liberian Shipping Corporation* v. *A. King & Sons, Ltd.*, [1967] 1 All E. R. 934; [1967] 2 Q. B. 86, C. A.; *Alma Shipping Corporation* v. *Union of India and the Chief Controller of Chartering, Ministry of Transport of India: The "Astraea"* (*supra*); *E. B. Aaby's Rederi A/S* v. *Union of India: The "Evje"* (*supra*).

[3] [1963] 1 Lloyd's Rep. 339, Q. B. D. (Commercial Court). See the judgment of MEGAW, J., *ibid.*, at p. 345.

The words "date of final discharge" did not mean the date when the cargo "was discharged or should have been discharged".

Where a consecutive voyage charter-party incorporates the "Centrocon" arbitration clause, the words "within 3 months of final discharge" mean within 3 months of final discharge under the voyage in respect of which a dispute arises, and do not mean within 3 months of completion of discharge of the last cargo carried under the charter-party.[1]

Where a charter-party states that a claim will be barred unless the claimant appoints an arbitrator within a specified period, the nominated arbitrator must be actually informed within that period that he has been appointed. Otherwise the claim will be barred. Thus, in *Tradax Export S.A.* v. *Volkswagenwerk A.G.*,[2]

A charter-party contained the "Centrocon" arbitration clause, which stated that if any dispute arose, each party should "appoint an arbitrator within 3 months of final discharge". Discharge of the cargo took place on 15 December, 1963. A dispute had arisen between the parties and the charterers nominated their arbitrator on 27 January, 1964, but did not inform him that they wished him to act as their arbitrator until 24 July. The shipowners, who had appointed their arbitrator on 17 February, contended that the charterers' claim was time-barred under the clause because the charterers had not effectively appointed their arbitrator in time.
Held, that the claim was barred. Appointment meant an effective appointment. A mere nomination unknown to the appointee was not an appointment of him.

(ii) *Under the Carriage of Goods by Sea Act 1924.* This Act provides that, where it applies,[3] in any event the carrier is dis-

---

[1] *Agro Co. of Canada, Ltd.* v. *Richmond Shipping, Ltd.: The "Simonburn"*, [1973] 1 Lloyd's Rep. 392, C. A. (See the judgment of Lord DENNING, M.R., *ibid.*, at p. 394.)

[2] [1970] 1 Lloyd's Rep. 62, C. A. See the judgment of SALMON, L.J., *ibid.*, at p. 65.

[3] See pp. 67–69, *ante*. For a case where the charter-party purported to incorporate into its provisions the limitation period provided by the Carriage of Goods by Sea Act 1924, and it was held that, as a matter of construction, it did not do so, see *Overseas Tankship (U.K.), Ltd.* v. *B.P. Tanker Co., Ltd.*, [1966] 2 Lloyd's Rep. 386, Q. B. D. (Commercial Court). For a case where a charter-party effectively incorporated the limitation period stated in the Act of 1924, and it was held that the charterer's claim was time-barred, see *Henriksens Rederi A/S* v. *T. H. Z. Rolimpex: The "Brede"*, [1973] 2 Lloyd's Rep. 333, C. A. (See the judgment of Lord DENNING, M.R., *ibid.*, at p. 338.)

charged from all liability in respect of loss or damage unless suit is brought within one year after the delivery of the goods or the date when they should have been delivered.[1]

The commencement of arbitration proceedings is "suit brought" within the meaning of the above provision.

Thus, in *The "Merak"*,[2]

A cargo owned by the plaintiffs was shipped under a bill of lading subject to the Hague Rules, and was discharged on 21 November, 1961, in a damaged condition. The bill of lading contained a clause stating that any dispute had to be referred to arbitration within 12 months of final discharge. The plaintiffs issued a writ on 15 November, 1962, and the case came on for trial on 28 July, 1964, when the trial Judge stayed the action on the ground that the parties had agreed to refer the dispute to arbitration. By 28 July, 1964, the time limit under the arbitration clause had long since passed. The plaintiffs appealed, and claimed that the arbitration clause was void in that it conflicted with Art. III, rr. 6 and 8, of the Hague Rules, and that they were still entitled to bring an action within one year of final discharge, as they had done in fact.

---

[1] Sched. Art. III, r. 6. In *Automatic Tube Co., Pty., Ltd. and Email, Ltd.—Balfour Buzacott Division* v. *Adelaide S.S. (Operations), Ltd., Adelaide S.S. Co., Ltd. and Adelaide S.S. Co. Pty., Ltd.; The "Beltana"*, [1967] 1 Lloyd's Rep. 531 (Supreme Court of Western Australia) it was held that delivery was made for the purposes of Art. III, r. 6, either when the goods were landed on the wharf and freed from the ship's tackle, or at the latest, when they were placed in a warehouse and immediately became available to the consignee. See the judgment of NEVILLE, J., *ibid.*, at pp. 540–1. In *National Packaging Corp.* v. *Nippon Yusen Kaisha (N.Y.K. Line)*, [1973] 1 Lloyd's Rep. 46, District Court, Northern District of California, it was held that the time-bar period started running after discharge plus notice to the consignee plus a reasonable opportunity to receive the goods. But in *American Hoesch Inc. and Riblet Products Inc.* v. *Steamship "Aubade" and Maritime Commercial Corp., Inc.*, [1971] 2 Lloyd's Rep. 423, District Ct. of South Carolina (Charleston Division), it was held that "delivery" was not synonymous with discharge and denoted a two-party transaction in which the consignee would have an opportunity to observe defects. See the judgment of HEMPHILL, D. J., *ibid.*, at p. 425; *Pacific Milk Industries (M) Bhd.* v. *Koninklinjke Jaya (Royal Interocean Lines) and Federal Shipping and Forwarding Agency: The "Straat Cumberland"*, [1973] 2 Lloyd's Rep. 492, State of Selangor, Kuala Lumpur Sessions Court.

[2] [1965] 1 All E. R. 230; [1965] P. 223, C. A., not following the decision of the U.S. Federal Court of Appeals in *Son Shipping Company, Inc.* v. *De Fosse and Tanghe*, [1952] A. M. C. 1931. DAVIES, L. J., said ([1964] 2 Lloyd's Rep., at p. 535) that if "suit" excluded arbitration, then the Hague Rules would seem to discourage, if not actually to prevent, the inclusion of an arbitration clause in a bill of lading.

Held, that the action must be stayed. The arbitration clause was effective, and since the matter had not been referred to arbitration within 12 months, the plaintiffs were without a remedy. The word "suit" in Art. III, r. 6, included the commencement of arbitration proceedings.

The words "unless suit is brought within one year" mean "unless the suit *before the Court* is brought within one year". They do not mean "unless suit is brought *anywhere* within one year".

Thus, in *Compania Colombiana de Seguros* v. *Pacific Steam Navigation Co.,*[1]

A cargo of electric cables loaded on the defendants' vessel was insured by the plaintiffs for a voyage from Buenaventura, Colombia, and was delivered in a damaged condition on 12 December, 1954. The plaintiffs indemnified the cargo owners, who assigned to them their rights to sue the defendants. The plaintiffs brought an action in the Supreme Court of New York on 2 November, 1955, against the defendants, but it was dismissed for lack of jurisdiction. The plaintiffs then brought the present action against the defendants on 7 January, 1960, in the English Courts.
Held, that the action was statute-barred, under Art. III, r. 6. The fact that the New York proceedings were brought within the period of one year was immaterial.

Further, the mere inclusion of an arbitration clause in a bill of lading to which the Hague Rules apply as a matter of contract does not deprive the carrier of the one-year time limit.[2]

Where the "Centrocon" arbitration clause is incorporated into a bill of lading to which the Act of 1924 applies, it is void in so far as it states that an arbitrator must be appointed within three months of final discharge, because such a provision is in conflict with the one year period of limitation stated in the Act.[3]

But where the loss or damage takes place after the goods are discharged, the one year period of limitation does not operate, and the six year period applies because the Act of 1924 does not relate to anything happening to the goods after their discharge.[4]

---

[1] [1963] 2 Lloyd's Rep. 479, Q. B. D. (Commercial Court). See especially the judgment of ROSKILL, J., *ibid.*, at pp. 494–6.

[2] *Denny, Mott and Dickson, Ltd.* v. *Lynn Shipping Co. Ltd.* (*supra*), at p. 344 (*per* MEGAW, J.).

[3] *Unicoopjapan and Marubeni-Iida Co., Ltd.* v. *Ion Shipping Co.: The "Ion"*, [1971] 1 Lloyd's Rep. 541, Q. B. D. (Commercial Court).

[4] *Rambler Cycle Co., Ltd* v. *Peninsular & Oriental Steam Navigation Co., Sze Hai Tong Bank Ltd.* (*First Third Party*), *Southern Trading Co.* (*Second Third Party*), [1968] 1 Lloyd's Rep. 42 (Malaysia Federal Court).

The Act also states that unless notice of loss or damage is given to the carrier or his agent at the port of discharge before or at the time of the removal of the goods into the custody of the person entitled to delivery of them, or, if the loss or damage be not apparent, within three days, such removal shall be *prima facie* evidence of the delivery of the goods described in the bill of lading.[1]

But Clause 4 of the British Maritime Law Association Agreement[2] extends the period for bringing claims and provides:

"The shipowners will, upon the request of any party representing the cargo (whether made before or after the expiry of the period of twelve months after the delivery of the goods or the date when the goods should have been delivered as laid down by the Hague Rules) extend the time for bringing suit for a further twelve months unless (A) notice of the claim with the best particulars available has not been given within the period of twelve months, or (B) there has been undue delay on the part of consignees, receivers or underwriters in obtaining the relevant information and formulating the claim."

The parties themselves are also entitled to agree that the period should be extended.[3]

(iii) *Under the Carriage of Goods by Sea Act 1971.* The Carriage of Goods by Sea Act 1971[4] states that where it applies,[5] in any event the carrier is discharged from all liability in respect of loss or damage unless suit is brought within one year after the delivery of the goods or the date when they should have been delivered.[6] The period may, however, be extended if the parties so agree after the cause of action has arisen.[7]

---

[1] *Ibid.*

[2] See p. 175, *post.*

[3] See, *e.g. Canadian Klockner, Ltd.* v. *D/S A/S Flint, Willy Kubon and Federal Commerce and Navigation Co., Ltd.: The "Mica"*, Federal Court of Canada, Trial Division. For further proceedings in this case, see [1975] 2 Lloyd's Rep. 371.

[4] *This Act is not yet in force.* See p. 76, *ante.*

[5] See pp. 77–79, *ante.*

[6] Carriage of Goods by Sea Act 1971, Sched. Art. III, r. 6.

[7] *Ibid.*, Sched. Art. III, r. 6.

An action for indemnity against a third person may be brought even after the expiration of the year if it is brought within the time allowed by the law of the Court seized of the case.[1] But the time allowed shall not be less than three months, commencing from the day when the person bringing the action for indemnity has settled the claim or has been served with process in the action against himself.[2]

---

[1] *Ibid.*, Sched. Art. III, r. 6 *bis.*
[2] *Ibid.*, Sched. Art. III, r. 6 *bis.*

CHAPTER 7

The Exclusion and Limitation of a Shipowner's Liability

Although goods have been lost or damaged whilst in the custody of the shipowner, he is not necessarily responsible, for his liability in respect of them may have been excluded by the rules of the Common Law or by the express terms of the contract or by statute. Further, even if he is liable, his liability may have been limited by a clause in the contract or by statute, so that the owner of the cargo will be unable to recover the full amount of his loss.

THE EXCLUSION OF LIABILITY

(A) At Common Law

The view usually accepted. It seems that, in spite of the disapproval of one eminent Judge,[1] the correct view of the law is

(1) that the liability of a shipowner at Common Law varies according as he is a common carrier or not;[2]

(2) that a shipowner is deemed to be a common carrier only in respect of such ships (and, it is submitted, where a *portion* of a ship is chartered, in respect of such *other portion* of that ship) as are employed as general ships;[3] and

---

[1] BRETT, J. (afterwards Lord ESHER, M.R.), in *Liver Alkali Co.* v. *Johnson* (1874), L. R. 9 Exch., at p. 344; and (as an *obiter dictum*) in *Nugent* v. *Smith* (1875), 1 C. P. D., at p. 33.

[2] It may be that a shipowner who carries goods for another is never, strictly speaking, a common carrier, but only under a liability akin to that of a common carrier. This question is not one which can be discussed at length in a preliminary treatise.

[3] See *Scrutton on Charter-parties* (18th edn. 1974), Article 102, p. 198; and Halsbury's Laws of England, 3rd edn., vol. 35, p. 286, para. 426.

(3) that the liability, at Common Law, of a shipowner is as follows:

(A) *If he is a common carrier*, he is absolutely responsible to the owner of the goods carried for any loss or damage to them unless caused by:

(i) an act of God;
or (ii) an act of the Queen's enemies;
or (iii) inherent vice in the goods themselves;
or (iv) the negligence of the owner of the goods;
or (v) a general average sacrifice.

The severity of this rule of the Common Law is said to have had its origin in the danger of theft by the carrier's servants or collusion between them and thieves. To prevent this, the responsibility of an *insurer* for the safe delivery of the goods was imposed on the carrier in addition to his liability as a bailee for reward.[1]

(B) *If he is not a common carrier*, his liability is only that of a bailee for reward; *i.e.* he need only exercise due care and diligence.[2]

It will thus be seen that the liability of a shipowner to a charterer of his ship is not the same as his liability to a shipper when the vessel is not under charter. For in the former case the ship is not a general ship; in the latter she is.

The alternative view. As has been indicated, however, the view of the law stated above is by no means universally accepted. The alternative view, which is preferred by many,[3] is to the effect that, at Common Law, the shipowner is *always* under a liability to deliver the goods received by him in the same condition as they were in when shipped, unless he has been prevented from so doing by one of the five causes mentioned above: in other words, that apart from special contract or statute every shipowner

---

[1] *Per* Lord HOLT in *Coggs* v. *Bernard* (1703), 2 Ld. Raym., at p. 918.
[2] *Per* COCKBURN, C.J., in *Nugent* v. *Smith* (1876), 45 L. J. Q. B., at pp. 700 *et seq.*
[3] See *e.g.* Carver's *Carriage of Goods by Sea* (13th edn. 1971), paras. 4–7; and Halsbury's *Laws of England* (3rd edn.), vol. 35, pp. 424–5, para. 604.

is under a liability akin to that of a common carrier, irrespective of whether the goods were shipped by a charterer or on a general ship.

The absence of a binding decision on the point is no doubt due, at least in part, to the fact that, in practice, goods are invariably shipped in pursuance of a contract the terms of which are set out in a bill of lading or in some other document. In such circumstances the position at Common Law is of no more than academic interest.

It has, however, been pointed out[1] that, in principle, there is no good reason for imposing upon the shipowner whose ship carries the goods of one person only a less strict liability with regard to those goods than he would have incurred had they been shipped by several persons; the reasoning applicable in the one case seems equally applicable in the other.

(B) By the Express Terms of the Contract

In the case of charter-parties and those bills of lading to which the Carriage of Goods by Sea Act 1924, or the Carriage of Goods by Sea Act 1971 (when that Act replaces the Act of 1924),[2] does not apply,[3] a shipowner is quite free to exclude his liability for loss or damage in any way that he thinks fit.

Whether an exclusion clause has been effectively incorporated into the contract so as to form part of it is in each case a matter of construction.[4]

Some usual exceptions

Most of the exceptions commonly met with have been the subject of judicial decisions delimiting their scope.

(1) *Act of God.* This exception, though one of the Common Law exceptions, is almost invariably put into a charter-party or a bill

---

[1] Carver, *op. cit.*, para. 5.

[2] See pp. 76–81, *ante.*

[3] See pp. 67–69, *ante.*

[4] *McCutcheon* v. *David Macbrayne, Ltd.*, [1964] 1 All E. R. 430; [1964] 1 Lloyd's Rep. 16, H. L., where it was held that the plea by the carriers that they were exempted from liability by their conditions of carriage failed, because, as a matter of construction, the conditions had not been effectively incorporated into the contract.

of lading. It covers any accident due to natural causes directly and exclusively, without human intervention, which no reasonable foresight could have avoided.[1] Damage caused by lightning, a storm, or even a sudden gust of wind, may be within this exception. But an accident arising from the navigation of a vessel in a fog would not be within the exception, because partly due to human intervention.[2]

(2) *The Queen's enemies.* This exception also is nearly always expressed in the contract. It does not cover acts done by robbers,[3] but only those done by public enemies. It is said[4] to have arisen from the fact that the bailee who had lost the goods had no remedy against public enemies because they were not within the jurisdiction of our courts. Probably the exception does not cover pirates.[5] It certainly covers enemies of the State to which the carrier belongs.[6] As to enemies of the State to which the shipper belongs, it does not appear that the carrier *requires* protection. If the goods are not contraband, they are not liable to seizure; if they are, this would amount to "inherent vice" in them, and the carrier is not responsible.

It *seems* that if there is an express contract which does not stipulate for the Common Law exceptions of "act of God" and "the Queen's enemies", the shipowner will not be entitled to the benefit of them.[7] But he will not be liable for damage arising from inherent defects in the goods or from negligence of the shipper.[8]

---

[1] *Per* JAMES, L.J., in *Nugent* v. *Smith* (1875), 45 L. J. Q. B., at p. 708; *Falconbridge Nickel Mines, Ltd., Janin Construction, Ltd. and Hewitt Equipment, Ltd.* v. *Chimo Shipping, Ltd., Clarke S.S. Co., Ltd. and Munro Jorgensson Shipping, Ltd.,* [1973] 2 Lloyd's Rep. 469, Supreme Court of Canada, where the loss of the cargo could have been guarded against by the vessel's crew and the exercise of reasonable care and precautions. See the judgment of RITCHIE, J., *ibid.,* at p. 474.

[2] *Liver Alkali Co.* v. *Johnson* (1874), L. R. 9 Exch. 338.

[3] *Mors* v. *Sluce* (1672), T. Raym. 220.

[4] *Southcote's Case* (1601), Cro. Eliz. 815.

[5] *Per* BYLES, J., in *Russell* v. *Niemann* (1864), 34 L. J. C. P., at p. 14.

[6] *Russell* v. *Niemann* (1864), 34 L. J. C. P. 10.

[7] The question is discussed at length in Carver, *op. cit.,* para. 97, but it is largely academic because the usual practice is expressly to insert these exceptions.

[8] *Per* WILLES, J., in *Lloyd* v. *Guibert* (1865), L. R. 1 Q. B., at p. 121. See also *Baxendale* v. *G. E. Rly. Co.* (1869), L. R. 4 Q. B. 244.

(3) *Restraints of princes or rulers.* Besides the case falling within the previous exception, "restraints of princes" includes any acts done, even in time of peace, by the sovereign power of the country where the ship may happen to be. It covers any restrictions imposed by order of an established government on importation or exportation, *e.g.* quarantine regulations, embargoes, blockades or seizure of contraband goods.

It does not cover a seizure resulting from ordinary legal proceedings,[1] nor acts done by a body of persons who are not authorised by an established government.

The exception excuses the shipowner from his obligation to deliver at the port of destination where to do so would expose the ship to real danger of seizure. Thus, in *Nobel's Explosives Co.* v. *Jenkins,*[2]

goods were shipped in England for Japan under a bill of lading excepting "restraints of princes". On the day the ship reached Hong Kong, war was declared between Japan and China. The captain, therefore, landed at Hong Kong such part of the cargo as was contraband. *Held*, the delivery of the contraband goods in Japan was prevented by the excepted peril.

Even where the restraint affects the person of the shipowner only and not the ship, the exception will protect him from liability.[3]

(4) *Seizure under legal process.* Though not, as we have seen, included under the previous exception, the benefit of this exception is often expressly provided by the terms of the contract.

(5) *Pirates or robbers by sea or land.* The word "robbers" does not cover secret theft,[4] but only robbery by violence from outside the ship. Often the word "thieves" is added to this exception, but such word only covers thieves operating from outside the ship.[5]

---

[1] *Crew* v. *G. W. Steamship Co.*, [1887] W. N. 161.
[2] [1896] 2 Q. B. 326.
[3] *Furness, Withy & Co.* v. *Rederiaktiebolaget Banco*, [1917] 2 K. B. 873.
[4] *Taylor* v. *Liverpool S.S. Co.* (1874), L. R. 9 Q. B. 546.
[5] *Ibid.*

(6) *Strikes or lock-outs.* This exception only covers stoppages arising out of trade disputes.[1] It has been held, for example, that a dismissal of labourers to save expense is not covered.[2]

In 1915 in one case it was held that the true definition of the word "strike", though not an exhaustive one, was a general concerted refusal by workmen to work in consequence of an alleged grievance.[3]

But in a case[4] in 1966 it was pointed out[5] that the matter has not rested in that stable condition since then. It might be that since then one has had the great development of sympathetic strikes and the General Strike of 1926 when many of those out on strike had no grievance at all against an employer.

Thus, in *J. Vermaas' Scheepvaartbedrijf N.V.* v. *Association Technique de L'Importation Charbonnière: The "Laga"*,[6]

A charter-party provided that "any time lost through strikes" was not to count for the purpose of the lay days.[7] The chartered vessel was carrying coal and went to a French port for unloading. But the stevedores refused to unload her and all other ships carrying coal, thereby hoping to assist

---

[1] Sometimes the extent of a strike clause is limited to a strike by certain persons only. See *e.g. Caltex Oil (Australia) Pty., Ltd.* v. *Howard Smith Industries Pty., Ltd.: The "Howard Smith"*, [1973] 1 Lloyd's Rep. 544, Supreme Court of New South Wales, Common Law Division, where the charter-party stated that the demurrage rate should be reduced for time lost "through strike action by tugboat crews or pilots".

[2] *Re Richardsons and M. Samuel & Co.*, [1898] 1 Q. B. 261.

[3] *Williams Brothers (Hull), Ltd.* v. *Naamlooze Vennootschap W. H. Berghuys Kolenhandel* (1915), 21 Com. Cas. 253, at p. 257 (*per* SANKEY, J.).

[4] *J. Vermaas Scheepvaartbedrijf N.V.* v. *Association Technique de L'Importation Charbonniere, The "Laga"*, [1966] 1 Lloyd's Rep. 582, Q. B. D. (Commercial Court).

[5] *Ibid.*, at p. 590 (*per* McNAIR, J.).

[6] [1966] 1 Lloyd's Rep. 582, Q. B. D. (Commercial Court). (See especially the judgment of McNAIR, J., *ibid.*, at pp. 590–1.) See also the judgment of Lord DENNING, M.R. in *Tramp Shipping Corporation* v. *Greenwich Marine Inc.: The "New Horizon"*, [1975] 2 Lloyd's Rep. 314, C. A., where he said (*ibid.*, at p. 317): "I think a strike is a concerted stoppage of work by men done with a view to improving their wages or conditions, or giving vent to a grievance or making a protest about something or other, or supporting or sympathising with other workmen in such endeavour. It is distinct from a stoppage which is brought about by an external event such as a bomb scare or by apprehension of danger."

[7] *I.e.*, the time allowed for loading or discharge, as the case may be. See pp. 205–206, *post*.

French miners who were on strike. The stevedores had no grievance against their employers, nor against the shipowners, charterers or receivers of coal cargoes. *Held*, that the sympathetic strike of the stevedores was a strike within the meaning of the charter-party, and the time during which it lasted did not count as part of the lay time.

A refusal to work part of the day only may be held to be a strike, even though such refusal is not in breach of contract.

Thus, in *Tramp Shipping Corporation* v. *Greenwich Marine Inc.: The "New Horizon"*,[1]

A strike clause in a charter-party stated that time was not to count if the cargo could not be discharged by reason of a strike. The vessel arrived at St. Nazaire where the crane and suction workers refused to work except on day work. There was a custom for them to work 24 hours if asked. *Held*, by the Court of Appeal, that their refusal was a strike even though the form of abstention was limited to a portion of the day only, and even though they were not in breach of their contracts of employment in insisting on day work only. Accordingly, the time during which they refused to work did not count as lay time.

(7) *Barratry.* Every deliberate act of wrongdoing by the master or any of the crew against the ship or the cargo, without the authorisation or privity of the shipowner or his agent, is barratrous. It must be a wilful act deliberately done, and to the prejudice of the owners.[2] Thus, if the master scuttles the ship[3] or fraudulently sells the cargo,[4] or fraudulently deviates,[5] his act is barratrous. Where there is a charter by demise, the master is a servant of the charterer and not of the shipowner; so his acts may be barratrous as against the charterer, although done with the shipowner's consent.[6]

---

[1] [1975] 2 Lloyd's Rep. 314, C. A.
[2] *Compania Naviera Bachi* v. *Henry Hosegood & Co., Ltd.*, [1938] **2** All E. R. 189, where the refusal of the crew to discharge a vessel was held **to be** barratry.
[3] *Ionides* v. *Pender* (1873), 27 L. T. 244.
[4] *Havelock* v. *Hancill* (1789), 3 Term Rep. 277.
[5] *Mentz Decker & Co.* v. *Maritime Co.*, [1910] 1 K. B. 132.
[6] *Soares* v. *Thornton* (1817), 7 Taunt. 627.

(8) *Jettison.*

(9) *Collision.* It has been decided[1] that a collision due to any cause other than the negligence of the shipowner or his servants is a "peril of the sea". This exception appears, therefore, to have little or no value where the contract excepts "perils of the sea".

Where "perils of the sea" are excepted, the shipper may have one of the following remedies for damage caused by collision:

(1) If the collision was due solely to the negligence of the carrying ship, he can sue on the bill of lading, for negligence defeats the exceptions.

(2) If another ship alone was in fault, he can sue its owner in tort.

(3) If both ships were to blame, he can recover a portion of the damage from each in proportion to the degree of blame attributable to each.[2]

A "Both to Blame" collision clause is very frequently used, except in the Short Sea and Near Continental trades where goods are carried by shipowners who have no vessels which are likely to visit ports in the United States. Contrary to the practice in most European countries, an American shipowner whose ship is involved in a collision can attach in an American port *any* ship in the same ownership as the one with which he has collided, in spite of the fact that the collision may have occurred in some distant part of the world. The release of the attached ship can be secured only by provision of bail, usually a very large sum.

When the bail has been deposited by the owners of the attached ship, the American shipowner proceeds with the collision action in a court in the United States. By the law of that country, where cargo is lost or damaged in a collision for which both ships are to blame, the cargo-owner may recover in full against the non-carrying ship.[3] Then the non-carrying ship may claim one-half of

---

[1] *The Xantho* (1887), 12 App. Cas. 503.

[2] Maritime Conventions Act 1911, s. 1 (1); 31 Halsbury's Statutes (3rd edn.), 475; Law Reform (Contributory Negligence) Act 1945 (23 Halsbury's Statutes (3rd edn.), 791), by s. 3 thereof, is expressly excluded from applying to any claim to which s. 1 of the Maritime Conventions Act 1911, applies.

[3] *The Beaconsfield* (1894), 158 U.S. 303; *The Atlas* (1876), 93 U.S. 302.

this sum from the carrying ship.[1] This is an anomalous result because a shipowner is not directly responsible to cargo-owners for damage arising out of negligent navigation, provided that due diligence has been exercised to make the ship seaworthy.[2] Thus if a shipowner is solely to blame for a collision, he is usually under no liability to cargo-owners. But if he is partly to blame, he will become indirectly liable to them, as explained above. Not unnaturally, shipowners felt aggrieved at this result, and in an endeavour to overcome the difficulty they adopted the "both-to-blame collision clause". A specimen clause is reproduced in Appendix B,[3] from which it will be seen that the object is to free the carrying ship from liability.

In 1952 the legality of the clause was tested in the United States in a case where a bill of lading, *not issued under a charter-party*, contained the clause. The Supreme Court decided that the clause was invalid as being a violation of the rule which in general forbids carriers from stipulating against the negligence of themselves or their employees.[4] But it may be that the decision would be different in the case of a charter-party with bills of lading thereunder, and for this reason the clause is still being used.

(10) *All the perils, dangers, and accidents of the sea.* This exception covers all occurrences which are peculiarly incident to a sea voyage and "which could not be foreseen and guarded against by the shipowner or his servants as necessary or probable incidents of the adventure".[5]

---

[1] *The Chattahoochee* (1899), 173 U.S. 540.

[2] Harter Act 1893, s. 3; (United States) Carriage of Goods by Sea Act 1936, s. 4 (2).

[3] See pp. 255–256, *post*.

[4] *United States of America* v. *Atlantic Mutual Insurance Co.*, [1952] 1 T. L. R. 1237. See also *Vendo International* v. *M/T "Frances Hammer" and Oxyness Shipping Co. Inc., M. V. "Simba" and A/S Det Ostasiatiske Kompagni* (*The "Frances Hammer"*), [1975] 1 Lloyd's Rep. 305, District Court, Southern District of New York.

[5] *Scrutton on Charter-parties* (18th edn. 1974), Art. 108, p. 225; *Falconbridge Nickel Mines, Ltd., Janin Construction, Ltd. and Hewitt Equipment, Ltd.* v. *Chimo Shipping, Ltd., Clarke S.S. Co., Ltd. and Munro Jorgensson Shipping, Ltd.*, [1973] 2 Lloyd's Rep. 469, Supreme Court of Canada; *Charles Goodfellow Lumber Sales, Ltd.* v. *Verreault Hovington and Verreault Navigation Inc.*, [1971] 1 Lloyd's Rep. 185, Supreme Court of Canada, where the authorities were reviewed by RITCHIE, J., *ibid.*, at pp. 187–90.

The occurrence need not be a rare nor an extraordinary one. Thus, it is not rare for rough seas to beat into a ship nor for a vessel to strand on rocks during fog; but both these would be within the exception, unless there was negligence on the part of those in charge of the ship. On the other hand, damage caused under ordinary climatic conditions by water entering the vessel, owing to the decayed state of her timbers, is not within the exception.[1]

But an incident which might equally well occur on land will not be covered, *e.g.* consumption of part of the cargo by vermin, or the bursting of boilers or steam-pipes.[2]

Thus, fire is not a peril of the sea,[3] nor does the term "sea accident" include a fire at sea.[4]

In order to bring himself within this exception, it is not necessary for the shipowner to prove exactly how the loss was caused; it is sufficient if he shows that it was due to some unexpected occurrence of a kind to which a maritime adventure as such is subject.[5]

(11) *Loss or damage from any neglect of the servants of the carrier.* When this exception, commonly known as the "negligence clause", is included in the contract, its effect is to protect the shipowner from liability even though he or nis servants have been negligent.

(12) *Insufficiency of packing.* It has been held that the carrier is protected by this exception[6] even when the loss is due to the insufficient packing of goods other than those actually damaged.[7] If, however, the insufficiency of the packing was apparent on

---

[1] *Sassoon v. Western Assurance Co.*, [1912] A. C. 561.

[2] *Thames and Mersey, etc., Co. v. Hamilton* (1887), 12 App. Cas. 484.

[3] *Hamilton, Fraser & Co. v. Pandorf & Co.* (1887), 12 App. Cas. 518, at p. 523 (*per* Lord BRAMWELL).

[4] *Oricon Waren-Handels G.m.b.H. v. Intergraan N.V.*, [1967] 2 Lloyd's Rep. 82, Q. B. D. (Commercial Court) (a case concerning a c.i.f. contract). See especially the judgment of ROSKILL, J., *ibid.*, at pp. 97–8.

[5] *The Stranna*, [1938] 1 All E. R. 458; [1938] P. 69.

[6] See e.g. *Stelwyre, Ltd. v. Kawasaki Kisen K.K.: The "Masashima Maru"*, [1974] 2 Lloyd's Rep. 394, Ontario Supreme Court, where the shipowners failed to show that a cargo of galvanised wire which arrived in a damaged condition had been insufficiently wrapped.

[7] *Goodwin, Ferreira & Co., Ltd. v. Lamport and Holt*, [1929] All E. R. Rep.

reasonable inspection, the shipowner cannot rely upon the exception;[1] presumbaly the same principle would apply where a carrier claimed the benefit of the exception "insufficiency or inadequacy of marks".

(13) *Act, neglect or default of the master, etc., in the navigation or management of the ship.*

(14) *Fire.*

The effect of negligence on the exceptions. If the shipowner has been guilty of negligence, he cannot rely on the "excepted perils". Thus, in *Siordet* v. *Hall,*[2]

goods were shipped under a bill of lading excepting "acts of God". On the night before she was to sail the ship's boiler was filled, and, owing to frost, a pipe connected with the boiler burst, damaging the goods. *Held*, although frost was an "act of God", negligence in filling the boiler overnight excluded the exception.

Again, where a clause in a charter-party stated that the liability of the shipowner "for rot, decay or deterioration", and a cargo of potatoes arrived in a deteriorated condition, it was held that the clause could not be relied on by the shipowner because he was guilty of negligence.[3]

Negligence on the part of the shipowner or his agent defeats the exception of barratry, as where the master could by reasonable care have prevented the crew from wrongfully damaging the cargo. But negligence itself is not barratry.[4]

The exception of jettison does not cover cases where goods which were improperly stowed were afterwards jettisoned, for the improper stowage amounts to negligence.[5]

Further, if the shipowner has negligently taken as part of the cargo goods which are likely to cause a seizure, he is liable to

---

[1] *Silver and Layton* v. *Ocean S.S. Co.*, [1930] 1 K. B. 416; [1929] All E. R. Rep. 611.

[2] (1828), 6 L. J. C. P. 137.

[3] *Ismail* v. *Polish Ocean Lines: The "Ciechocinek"*, [1975] 2 Lloyd's Rep. 170, Q. B. D. (Commercial Court); *reversed* on other grounds: (1976) *Times*, February 5, C. A.

[4] *Per* CHANNELL, J., in *Briscoe* v. *Powell* (1905), 22 T. L. R., at p. 130.

[5] *Royal Exchange S. Co.* v. *Dixon* (1886), 12 App. Cas. 11.

other shippers for delay arising from such a seizure, and cannot claim the benefit of the exception of "restraints of princes".[1]

The shipowner cannot plead that a loss has been caused by "the Queen's enemies" unless he has used reasonable care, *e.g.* to avoid capture by the enemies' cruisers. He is justified in deviating when there is reasonable danger of capture.[2]

But the shipowner can rely on the "excepted perils" even if he has been negligent as long as "negligence" itself is one of the "excepted perils". Thus, in *Blackburn* v. *Liverpool, etc., S.N. Co.,*[3]

sugar was stored in a tank at the bottom of the ship. The engineer negligently let salt water into the tank. *Held*, the shipowner was not liable because the bill of lading contained an exception of perils of the sea whether arising from the negligence of the engineers or otherwise.

But, of course, the negligence of a third party will not expose the shipowner to liability. Thus, in *The Xantho,*[4]

where salt water entered the ship and damaged the cargo owing to a collision caused solely by the negligence of *another* ship, the owner of the first vessel was *held* not to be liable to the shipper.

The construction of the exceptions has sometimes been confused by placing upon a wrong basis the distinction between their effect in a bill of lading and the operation of the same phrases (*e.g.* "perils of the sea") in a contract of marine insurance. On the part of the insurer, a contract of marine insurance is a positive undertaking to indemnify the shipowner in the event of the loss of his vessel from certain specified causes such as perils of the sea. Consequently, it is sufficient to entitle the shipowner to claim the indemnity that he should show that the vessel was lost by perils of the sea. On the other hand, the exceptions in a bill of lading are merely limitations exempting the shipowner from the "absolute liability of a common carrier".[5] They relate to certain undertakings implied by law on the part of the shipowner, and, in the absence of express agreement to the contrary, he cannot claim the

---

[1] *Dunn* v. *Currie*, [1902] 2 K. B. 614.
[2] *The Teutonia* (1872), L. R. 4 P. C. 171.
[3] [1902] 1 K. B. 290.
[4] (1887), 12 App. Cas. 503.
[5] *Per* WILLES, J., in *Notara* v. *Henderson* (1872), L. R. 7 Q. B., at p. 235.

benefit of them if he has been guilty of negligence causing the loss complained of.[1]

The effect of an unjustifiable deviation on the exceptions. We have seen already that unless the contract has been affirmed, a shipowner whose vessel has unjustifiably deviated cannot rely on the "excepted perils".[2]

The effect of unseaworthiness on the exceptions. We have already alluded to the rule that, even if his vessel was unseaworthy, a shipowner can still rely on the "excepted perils" if the loss has not been caused by unseaworthiness.[3]

The effect of a fundamental breach. An exception clause cannot be relied on where there has been a fundamental breach of contract.[4]

Excepted perils and overcarrying. Sometimes the contract expressly gives to the carrier the right to carry the goods beyond their destination, provided that he tranships them and sends them back. In such case she will be entitled to the protection of the exceptions even after the transhipment.[5]

But, once again, negligence defeats the exceptions. Thus, in *Searle v. Lund*,[6]

owing to the negligence of the shipowners' servants, it was necessary to carry goods beyond their destination in order to avoid undue detention.

---

[1] *The Xantho*, (*supra*).
[2] See pp. 22–23, *ante*.
[3] See pp. 16–17, *ante*.
[4] *The "Berkshire"*, [1974] 1 Lloyd's Rep. 185, Q. B. D. (Admiralty Court), where the shipowners discharged the goods at a port short of the destination into another vessel not owned or operated by them and were held to have made such a fundamental departure from the contract contemplated by the parties at the time when it was made that they could not rely on an exception in the bill of lading relieving them from personal liability. (See the judgment of BRANDON, J., *ibid.*, at p. 190); *Suisse Atlantique Société d'Armement Maritime S.A.* v. *N.V. Rotterdamsche Kolen Centrale* [1966] 2 All E. R. 61; [1967] 1 A. C. 361, H. L.
[5] *Broken Hill Co.* v. *P. & O.*, [1917] 1 K. B. 688.
[6] (1904), 20 T. L. R. 390.

Although the bill of lading gave permission to overcarry to avoid undue delay, it was *held* that negligence prevented the shipowner from claiming the benefit of the exception.

The burden of proof where damage has been caused by an excepted peril

If the shipowner relies on an excepted peril, he must prove that the loss or damage was caused thereby.[1] Thus, if it is clear that the damage must have arisen either from bad stowage or from "perils of the sea", and the latter are excepted, in order to escape liability the shipowner must show that the damage arose from "perils of the sea". If the shipowner proves that *prima facie* the cause of the damage was excepted, the burden shifts to the shipper, who must show that the real cause of the damage was something not excepted, *e.g.* negligence or unseaworthiness. Thus, in *The Glendarroch*,[2]

cement was shipped under a bill of lading excepting "perils of the sea". The vessel went ashore, and there was no evidence indicating negligence on the part of the shipowner's servants. It was *held* that the burden of proving such negligence was on the cargo-owner.

Again, where such evidence of negligence on the part of the shipowner as the shipper has produced is not sufficient to turn the scale, but is sufficient to leave the matter in doubt, the burden is once more shifted back to the shipowner, who must prove absence of negligence.[3]

If the shipowner can only show that some part of the damage to the goods was due to a cause within the exception, he must also show how much of the damage is comprised in that part, otherwise he is liable for the whole.[4]

Causa proxima non remota spectatur

Where damage has been caused by several agencies, this rule must be observed in considering whether it was caused by an

---

[1] *The Xantho* (1887), 12 App. Cas. 503.
[2] [1894] P. 226.
[3] *Travers* v. *Cooper*, [1915] 1 K. B. 73. Cf. *The Kite*, [1933] P. 154.
[4] *Ceylon Government* v. *Chandris*, [1965] 2 Lloyd's Rep. 204, Q. B. D. (Commercial Court), at p. 216 (*per* MOCATTA, J.).

excepted peril.[1] The shipowner is not excused by the fact that a *remote* cause of the loss was an excepted peril. But it is clear that, even if the *proximate* cause was an excepted peril, the court is not precluded from ascertaining whether this cause was brought into operation by the shipowner's default; if it was, he will be liable.

Thus, in *The Thrunscoe*,[2]

where the ventilators of the hold had to be kept closed owing to bad weather, and heat from the engines and boilers injured the cargo, the severity of the weather was regarded as the direct cause of the damage, and this was accordingly held to be a "peril of the sea".

Again, in *Standard Oil Co. of New York v. Clan Line Steamers, Ltd.*,[3]

the master of a turret ship, not having been instructed by his owners as to the peculiarities of a turret ship, so handled her that she capsized. The loss was immediately due to perils of the sea which overwhelmed her when she capsized, liability for which was excepted, but the dominant cause was her unseaworthiness in that her master, though otherwise efficient, was inefficient in not being aware of the special danger.

(C) By Statute

Certain statutory provisions exempt the shipowner from being liable. These are contained in:

(1) The Merchant Shipping Act 1894.[4]

(2) The Carriage of Goods by Sea Act 1924.

(3) The Carriage of Goods by Sea Act 1971.

(1) *The Merchant Shipping Act 1894*

(a) *Dangerous goods.* If dangerous goods have been thrown overboard by the shipowner or the master, neither can be made liable for their loss.[5]

---

[1] *The Xantho* (1887), 12 App. Cas. 503; *Hamilton v. Pandorf* (1887), 12 App. Cas. 518; Chorley and Tucker's *Leading Cases* (4th edn. 1962), p. 298.

[2] *The Thrunscoe*, [1897] P. 301.

[3] [1924] A. C. 100.

[4] As amended by the Merchant Shipping (Liability of Shipowners and Others) Act 1958.

[5] Merchant Shipping Act 1894, s. 448 (2). See generally p. 24, *ante*.

(b) *Loss or damage due to fire, and loss of or damage to valuables.*
The Merchant Shipping Act 1894, s. 502[1] provides that the owner[2] of a British ship shall not be liable to make good any loss due to fire, or any theft of valuables the true nature and value of which were not declared in writing at the time of shipment, if the loss arose "without his actual fault or privity".

The fault or privity of his servants (*e.g.* officers on board) is not sufficient to render the shipowner liable. Where the shipowner is a company, the fault or privity must be that of "the person who is really the directing mind and will of the corporation, the very *ego* and centre of the personality of the corporation".[3]

Thus, in *Lennard's Carrying Co., Ltd.* v. *Asiatic Petroleum Co., Ltd.*,[4]

A ship was sent to sea in an unseaworthy state, and as a result she stranded and her cargo was destroyed by fire. The vessel belonged to a limited company of which a Mr. Lennard was a director. He took an active part in her management. *Held*, that Lennard was the *"alter ego"* of the company and not merely a servant. The company could not therefore exclude its liability for loss by fire under the Merchant Shipping Act 1894, s. 502, for it had not shown that the loss had occurred "without its actual fault or privity". The action of Lennard was the very action of the company, and he was at fault.

"Fault or privity" of the shipowner includes culpable acts of omission on the part of a managing owner.[5]

Concerning fire, it is noticeable that, where the undertaking of seaworthiness is absolute, there may be an innocent breach of it which will not amount to "fault or privity" within the above section. Moreover, the shipowner will not be deprived of the benefit of the section merely because the fire was due to unseaworthiness.

---

[1] As amended by the Merchant Shipping (Liability of Shipowners and Others) Act 1958. See Appendix D, *post*.

[2] The section also protects a charterer and any person interested in or in possession of the vessel and, in particular, any manager or operator of her: Merchant Shipping (Liability of Shipowners and Others) Act 1958, s. 3.

[3] *Per* HALDANE, L.C., in *Lennard's Carrying Co., Ltd.* v. *Asiatic Petroleum Co., Ltd.*, [1915] A. C., at p. 713.

[4] *Supra.*

[5] *Lennard's Carrying Co., Ltd.* v. *Asiatic Petroleum Co., Ltd.*, [1915] A. C. 705.

Thus, in *Louis Dreyfus & Co., Ltd.* v. *Tempus Shipping Co., Ltd.*,[1]

A vessel was sent to sea with bad bunker coal on board. The coal caught fire, and she went to a port of refuge to have the fire extinguished. Part of the cargo was damaged. The shipowners maintained that they were not liable by reason of the exception of "fire" stated in s. 502 of the Merchant Shipping Act 1894, for the loss had occurred "without their actual fault or privity". *Held*, that they could still plead the benefit of this section although the fire was due to the unseaworthy condition of the vessel.

But an agreement by the shipowner to waive his right to the benefit of the section will be implied from a specific undertaking in the contract to be liable for fire resulting from unseaworthiness.[2] In the absence of such an agreement, however, the section must be read as though it said "a British ship, be she seaworthy or unseaworthy".

Sometimes "fire" is one of the perils excepted in the contract of affreightment.[3] In some respects such an express exception is narrower than the statutory exception. The express exception will not excuse the shipowner where the fire is caused by the negligence of his servants;[4] whereas the statutory exception applies in all cases except where the shipowner is personally at fault. Moreover, as we have seen, the statutory exception may apply although there has been a breach of the undertaking as to seaworthiness.

It is to be observed that s. 502 applies, with necessary modifications to Crown ships.[5] Further, the section is expressly kept alive by the Carriage of Goods by Sea Act, 1924, and is therefore not excluded from operation in cases to which the 1924 Act applies.[6] It is also kept alive by the Carriage of Goods by Sea Act 1971[7] in cases to which that Act applies.[8]

---

[1] [1931] A. C. 726.
[2] Compare *Virginia, etc., Co.* v. *Norfolk S.S. Co.*, [1912] 1. K. B. 229, with *Ingram* v. *Services Maritimes*, [1914] 1 K. B. 541.
[3] See p. 155, *ante*.
[4] See pp. 155–157, *ante*.
[5] The Crown Proceedings Act 1947, s. 5.
[6] Section 6 (2). (See Appendix E, *post*).
[7] Section 6 (4). *The Act is not yet in force.* See p. 76, *ante*.
[8] See pp. 77–79, *ante*.

(2) *The Carriage of Goods by Sea Act 1924*

(a) *Dangerous goods.* The Act provides that, in cases to which it applies,[1] goods of an inflammable, explosive or dangerous nature to the shipment whereof the carrier, master or agent of the carrier, has not consented, with knowledge of their nature and character, may at any time before discharge be landed at any place or destroyed or rendered innocuous by the carrier without compensation.[2]

(b) *Loss or damage due to "excepted perils".* The Act provides that in cases to which it applies[3] neither the carrier nor the ship[4] shall be liable for loss or damage arising or resulting from certain causes.[5] These correspond, in general, to those considered above which are commonly excluded in charter-parties and those bills of lading to which the Act of 1924 does not apply.[6]

The list of "excepted perils". The list of "excepted perils" is as follows:

    (i) act, neglect or default of the master, mariner, pilot, or the servants of the carrier in the navigation[7] or in the management[8] of the ship;

    (ii) fire, unless caused by the actual fault or privity of the carrier;

---

[1] See pp. 67–79, *ante.*

[2] Carriage of Goods by Sea Act 1924, Sched. Art. IV, r. 6.

[3] See pp. 67–69, *ante.*

[4] A lash barge is not a "ship": *Wirth, Ltd.* v. *S.S. "Acadia Forest" and Lash Barge "CG 204" : The "Acadia Forest"*, [1974] 2 Lloyd's Rep. 563, District Court, Eastern District of Louisiana.

[5] Carriage of Goods by Sea Act 1924, Sched. Art. IV, r. 2.

[6] See pp. 147–155, *ante.*

[7] *President of India* v. *West Coast S.S. Co.; The Portland Trader*, [1964] 2 Lloyd's Rep. 443, U.S. Court of Appeals (negligent navigation resulting in vessel grounding on reef in Sulu Sea).

[8] *E.g.* failure to take soundings of the water level in the hold: *Riverstone Meat Co. Pty., Ltd.* v. *Lancashire Shipping Co., Ltd.*, [1958] 3 All E. R. 261, at p. 272; [1959] 1 Q. B. 74, at p. 100 (*per* McNAIR, J.); failure to get rid of water in the hold after collision: *Leval & Co. Inc.* v. *Colonial Steamships, Ltd.*, [1961] 1 Lloyd's Rep. 560 (Supreme Court of Canada); failure to use locking bars on the hatches at sea in heavy weather: *International Packers London, Ltd.* v. *Ocean S.S. Co., Ltd.*, [1955] 1 Lloyd's Rep. 218; failure to adjust the metacentric height of a vessel: *Georgia-Pacific Corporation* v. *"Marilyn L.", Elvapores Inc., Evans Products Co. and Retla S.S. Co. : The "Marilyn L."*, [1972] 1 Lloyd's Rep. 418, District Court for the Eastern District of Virginia, Norfolk Division.

[*continued opposite*

(iii) perils, dangers and accidents of the sea or other navigable waters;[1]

In *Leesh River Tea Co., Ltd.* v. *British India Steam Navigation Co., Ltd., The "Chyebassa"*, [1966] 2 Lloyd's Rep. 193, C. A., it was held that where the cargo had been damaged owing to stevedores stealing a storm valve cover plate at a port of call, the stevedores' act was not "an act, neglect or default in the management of the ship". In *Falconbridge Nickel Mines, Ltd., Janin Construction, Ltd. and Hewitt Equipment, Ltd.* v. *Chimo Shipping Ltd., Clarke S.S. Co., Ltd. and Munro Jorgensson Shipping, Ltd.*, [1973] 2 Lloyd's Rep. 469, Supreme Court of Canada, a failure to secure the cargo on a barge to keep it from sliding and a failure to tether the barge to the vessel were held not to be an "act, neglect or fault in the management of the ship"; *International Produce Inc. and Greenwich Mills Co.* v. *S.S. "Frances Salman", Swedish Gulf Line A/B and Companhia de Navegacao Maritima Netumar: The "Frances Salman"*, [1975] 2 Lloyd's Rep. 355, District Court, Southern District of New York, where the failure to drain the fresh water system which might have caused the parting of a pipe was not an "act, neglect or default in the management of the ship".

[1] In *Leesh River Tea Co., Ltd.* v. *British India Steam Navigation Co., Ltd., The "Chyebassa" (supra)*, it was held that the entry of sea water was a peril of the sea, but that this defence would fail if the cover plate had been removed in circumstances in which the shipowners were responsible for the stevedores' servants who removed it. See the judgment of SELLERS, L.J., *ibid.*, at pp. 199–200, and that of SALMON, L.J., *ibid.*, at pp. 202–3. In *G. E. Crippen and Associates, Ltd.* v. *Vancouver Tug Boat Co., Ltd.*, [1971] 2 Lloyd's Rep. 207, Exchequer Court, British Columbia Admiralty District, where a cargo of peat moss was found to be damaged, it was held that the loss was not due to perils of the sea for the weather was normal for the time of year. See the judgment of WALSH, J., *ibid.*, at p. 216. In *United States of America* v. *Eastmount Shipping Corp.: The "Susquehanna"*, [1975] 1 Lloyd's Rep. 216, District Court, Southern District of New York, the weather was not so severe or unusual as to be classed as a "peril of the sea". (See the judgment of FRANKEL, D.J., *ibid.*, at p. 219.) In *Bruck Mills Ltd.* v. *Black Sea S.S. Co.: The "Grumant"*, [1973] 2 Lloyd's Rep. 531, Federal Court of Canada, Trial Division, the escape of apple concentrate in plastic containers was held not to be due to "perils of the sea". In *William D. Branson, Ltd. and Tomas Alcazar S.A.* v. *Jadranska Slobodna Plovidba (Adriatic Tramp Shipping): The "Split"*, [1973] 2 Lloyd's Rep. 535, Federal Court of Canada, the loss of a cargo of melons stowed in crates 17 high without air circulating in the hold was held not to have been caused by "perils of the sea". In *Falconbridge Nickel Mines, Ltd., Janin Construction, Ltd. and Hewitt Equipment Ltd.* v. *Chimo Shipping, Ltd., Clarke S.S. Co., Ltd. and Munro Jorgensson Shipping, Ltd.*, [1973] 2 Lloyd's Rep. 469, Supreme Court of Canada, where the loss of a tractor and generating set was held not to be due to "perils of the sea", but to a failure to secure the cargo on a barge to keep it from sliding and a failure to tether the barge to the vessel. In *International Produce Inc. and Greenwich Mills Co.* v. *S.S. "Frances Salman", Swedish Gulf Line A/B and Companhia de Navegacao Maritima Netumar: The "Frances Salman"*, [1975] 2 Lloyd's Rep. 355, District Court, Southern District of New York, the cargo was held to be damaged by bad stowage near a leaking sanitary water pipe and not by "perils of the sea".

(iv) act of God;

(v) act of war;

(vi) act of public enemies;

(vii) arrest or restraint of princes, rulers or people, or seizure under legal process;

(viii) quarantine restrictions;

(ix) act or omission of the shipper or owner of the goods, his agent or representative;

(x) strikes or lock-outs or stoppage or restraint of labour from whatever cause, whether partial or general;

(xi) riots and civil commotions;

(xii) saving or attempting to save life or property at sea;

(xiii) wastage in bulk or weight or any other loss or damage arising from inherent defect, quality or vice of the goods;[1]

---

[1] *Easwest Produce Co.* v. *The Ship S.S. Nordnes*, (1956) Ex C. R. 328 (onions); *Shaw, Savill and Albion Co., Ltd.* v. *R. Powley & Co., Ltd.*, [1949] N. Z. L. R. 668 (brandy). *Wm. Fergus Harris & Son, Ltd.* v. *China Mutual Steam Navigation Co., Ltd.*, [1959] 2 Lloyd's Rep. 500 (timber); *Albacora S.R.L.* v. *Westcott and Laurance Line, Ltd.*, [1966] 2 Lloyd's Rep. 53, H. L. (wet salted fish); *Jahn (Trading as C. F. Otto Weber)* v. *Turnbull Scott Shipping Co., Ltd. and Nigerian National Line, Ltd., The "Flowergate"*, [1967] 1 Lloyd's Rep. 1 (cocoa); *Chris Foodstuffs (1963), Ltd.* v. *Nigerian National Shipping Line, Ltd.*, [1967] 1 Lloyd's Rep. 293, C. A. (coco yams). But in *David McNair & Co., Ltd. and David Oppenheimer, Ltd. & Associates* v. *The "Santa Malta"*, [1967] 2 Lloyd's Rep. 391 (Exchequer Court, British Columbia Admiralty District), where a cargo of melons, garlic and onions was stowed in the same hold as a cargo of fishmeal and became tainted thereby, it was held that the loss was due to bad stowage and lack of ventilation, and not due to inherent vice. In *G. E. Crippen and Associates, Ltd.* v. *Vancouver Tug Boat Co., Ltd. (supra)*, the damage to a cargo of peat moss was held not to be due to the inherent defect of uneven compression, for this defect would not by itself have caused the damage if the cargo had not been stowed four pallets high and if dunnage had not been used. See the judgment of WALSH, J., [1971] 2 Lloyd's Rep. at p. 216. In *William D. Branson, Ltd. and Tomas Alcazar S.A.* v. *Jadranska Slobodna Plovidba (Adriatic Tramp Shipping): The "Split"*, [1973] 2 Lloyd's Rep. 535, Federal Court of Canada, Trial Division, the loss of a cargo of melons packed in crates 17 high without air circulating in the hold was held to be due not to "inherent defect" but to improper stowage. In *Nissan Automobile Co. (Canada) Ltd.* v. *Owners of the Vessel "Continental Shipper": The "Continental Shipper"*, [1974] 1 Lloyd's Rep. 482, Federal Court of Canada, Trial Division, the damage to uncrated cars was found to be due to their being stowed too closely together and not to "inherent vice". In *Crelinsten Fruit Co. and William D. Branson, Ltd.* v. *Maritime Fruit Carriers Co., Ltd.: The "Lemoncore"*, [1975] 2 Lloyd's Rep. 249, Federal Court of Canada, Trial Division, the loss of a cargo of apples and pears carried in a refrigerated vessel was held not to be due to "inherent vice" but to bad stowage since it was a block stow without dunnage.

(xiv) insufficiency of packing;[1]

(xv) insufficiency or inadequacy of marks;[2]

(xvi) latent defects not discoverable by due diligence;

(xvii) any other cause arising without the actual fault or privity of the carrier, or[3] without the fault or neglect of the agents or servants of the carrier, but the burden of proof shall be on the person claiming the benefit of this exception to show that neither the actual fault or privity of the carrier nor the fault or neglect of the agents or servants of the carrier contributed to the loss or damage.[4]

It must be borne in mind that, where the Act applies, no exception which does not appear in the foregoing list can be included, except where a special contract is permitted in the case of the coasting trade[5] or unusual shipments of particular goods;[6] for to incorporate some further exception would be to increase the carrier's immunity and diminish his responsibility.

Cases where the "excepted perils" cannot apply. The shipowner cannot rely on the "excepted perils" if he has not carried out his obligation under Art. III, r. 1 to exercise due diligence to make

---

[1] In *G. E. Crippen and Associates, Ltd.* v. *Vancouver Tug Boat Co., Ltd.* (*supra*) the damage to the cargo of peat moss was held not to be due to insufficiency of packing. See the judgment of WALSH, J., [1971] 2 Lloyd's Rep. at p. 216. In *Nissan Automobile Co. (Canada), Ltd.* v. *Owners of the Vessel "Continental Shipper": The "Continental Shipper"* (*supra*) the damage to the cars was also held not to be due to "insufficiency of packing".

[2] See *British Imex Industries, Ltd.* v. *Midland Bank, Ltd.*, [1958] 1 All E. R. 264; [1958] 1 Q. B. 542.

[3] The word "or" here must be construed as meaning "and": see *Brown & Co.* v. *Harrison* (1927), 43 T. L. R. 633; *Paterson Steamships, Ltd.* v. *Canadian Co-operative Wheat Producers, Ltd.*, [1934] A. C. 538, at p. 549; *Leesh River Tea Co., Ltd.* v. *British India Steam Navigation Co., Ltd., The "Chyebassa"*, [1966] 2 Lloyd's Rep. 193, C. A., at p. 202 (*per* SALMON, L.J.).

[4] *E.g.* as in *Leesh River Tea Co., Ltd.* v. *British India Steam Navigation Co., Ltd., The "Chyebassa"* (*supra*), where the shipowners were held not to be liable for damage to the cargo owing to the stevedores stealing a storm valve cover plate at a port of call; *G. E. Crippen and Associates, Ltd.* v. *Vancouver Tug Boat Co., Ltd.* (*supra*) where it was held that the damage to a cargo of peat moss had arisen without privity or fault on their part or fault or neglect of their agents or servants, for there was no negligence in stowing the cargo in the state of knowledge at the time with regard to the proper method of stowing that type of cargo. See the judgment of WALSH, J., [1971] 2 Lloyd's Rep. at p. 217.

[5] See p. 75, *ante.*

[6] See pp. 74–75, *ante.*

the ship seaworthy and its non-fulfilment causes the damage,[1] nor can he do so if the vessel makes a deviation not permitted by Art. IV, r. 4.[2]

Burden of proof of absence of negligence. The question as to the burden of proving the absence of negligence is an unsettled one.

In a High Court decision it has been held that the shipowner will be liable for the loss or damage to the goods even if this is due to "excepted perils", unless he can prove that he has taken proper care of them whilst they were in his custody,[3] *i.e.* has fulfilled his duties under Art. III, r. 2.[4]

But in a case in the House of Lords, Lord PEARSON stated that there was no express provision, and in his opinion no implied provision, in the Hague Rules that the shipowner was debarred from relying on an exception unless he proved absence of negli-

---

[1] *Maxine Footwear Co., Ltd.* v. *Canadian Government Merchant Marine, Ltd.*, [1959] 2 All E. R. 740; [1959] A. C. 589, P. C. See also Carriage of Goods by Sea Act 1924, Sched. Art. IV, r. 1 and *Robin Hood Flour Mills, Ltd.* v. *N. M. Paterson & Sons, Ltd., The "Farrandoc"*, [1967] 2 Lloyd's Rep. 276 (Exchequer Court of Canada), at p. 283 (*per* NOEL, J.). *Fisons Fertilizers, Ltd. and Fisons, Ltd.* v. *Thomas Watson (Shipping), Ltd.*, [1971] 1 Lloyd's Rep. 141, Mayor's and City of London Court, where a cargo was damaged due to a valve in the forward hold suction line being jammed, and it was shown that the defect occurred before the beginning of the voyage; *Charles Goodfellow Lumber Sales, Ltd.* v. *Verreault Hovington and Verreault Navigation Inc.*, [1971] 1 Lloyd's Rep. 185, Supreme Court of Canada, where it was shown that the vessel's hull was not sufficiently strong to withstand the voyage, and the shipowners were held not to have discharged their duty under Art. III, r. 1, and accordingly could not plead that the loss was due to "perils of the sea." See the judgment of RITCHIE, J., *ibid.*, at p. 188; *United States of America* v. *Eastmount Shipping Corp.: The "Susquehanna"*, [1975] 1 Lloyd's Rep. 216, District Court, Southern District of New York, where the shipowners could not rely on the exception of "perils of the seas" because the vessel had not sufficient bunkers on board at the beginning of the voyage. (See the judgment of FRANKEL, D.J., *ibid.*, at p. 219.); *American Smelting & Refining Co.* v. *S.S. "Irish Spruce" and Irish Shipping Ltd.: The "Irish Spruce"*, [1976] 1 Lloyd's Rep. 63, District Court, Southern District of New York, where the shipowners could not rely on the exception of a fault in navigation because the vessel was unseaworthy as she did not have on board the latest Admiralty List of Radio Signals.

[2] *Stag Line, Ltd.* v. *Foscolo, Mango & Co., Ltd.*, [1932] A. C. 328; [1931] All E. R. Rep. 666, H. L., p. 89, *ante*.

[3] *Svenska Traktor Aktiebolaget* v. *Maritime Agencies (Southampton), Ltd.*, [1953] 2 All E.R. 570; [1953] 2 Q. B. 295; *J. Kaufman, Ltd.* v. *Cunard S.S. Co., Ltd.*, [1965] 2 Lloyd's Rep. 564 (Exchequer Court, Quebec Admiralty District) (furs delivered in wet condition).

[4] See pp. 70–72, *ante*.

gence on his part. But he did have to prove that the damage was caused by an excepted peril or excepted cause, and in order to do that he might in a particular case have to give evidence excluding causation by his negligence.[1]

(c) *Loss or damage when value mis-stated*

Neither the carrier nor the ship is responsible in any event for loss or damage to or in connection with the goods if their nature or value has been knowingly misstated by the shipper in the bill of lading.[2]

(3) *The Carriage of Goods by Sea Act 1971*[3]

Where the Carriage of Goods by Sea Act 1971 applies,[4] the same provisions concerning

(a) dangerous goods;[5] and

(b) the "excepted perils"[6]

as are set out in the Schedule to the Act of 1924 can be relied on by the carrier seeking to avoid liability for loss or damage to the goods.

The defence that the peril is excepted applies in any action against the carrier in respect of loss or damage to the goods whether the action is founded in contract or in tort.[7]

If such action is brought against a servant or agent of the carrier (such servant or agent not being an independent contractor), such servant or agent is entitled to avail himself of the defences which the carrier is entitled to invoke under the Act.[8]

---

[1] *Albacora S.R.L.* v. *Westcott and Laurance Line, Ltd.,* [1966] 2 Lloyd's Rep. 53, at p. 64, H. L. See further the speech of Lord PEARCE, *ibid.,* at p. 61. In *Jahn (Trading as C. F. Otto Weber)* v. *Turnbull Scott Shipping Co., Ltd. and Nigerian National Line, Ltd., The "Flowergate",* [1967] 1 Lloyd's Rep. 1, Q. B. D. (Commercial Court), ROSKILL, J., said (*ibid.,* at p. 8) that he proposed to follow Lord PEARSON's view, leaving it open to the cargo owners, if they so desired, to argue to the contrary in a higher Court.

[2] Carriage of Goods by Sea Act 1924, Sched. Art. IV, r. 5. *Frank Hammond Pty., Ltd.* v. *Huddart Parker, Ltd.* [1956], V.L.R. 496.

[3] *This Act is not yet in force.* See p. 76, *ante.*

[4] See pp. 77–79, *ante.*

[5] See p. 162, *ante.*

[6] See pp. 162–165, *ante.*

[7] Carriage of Goods by Sea Act 1971, Sched. Art. IV *bis,* r. 1.

[8] *Ibid.,* Sched. Art. IV *bis,* r. 2.

But the servant or agent is not entitled to do so if it is proved that the damage resulted from an act or omission on his part done with intent to cause damage or recklessly and with knowledge that damage would probably result.[1]

THE LIMITATION OF LIABILITY

Although the shipowner may be responsible for the loss of or damage to the goods, his liability may be limited by

(A) the terms of the contract;
(B) by statute.

(A) By the Terms of the Contract

In the case of a charter-party and of a bill of lading to which the Carriage of Goods by Sea Act, 1924, does not apply,[2] a shipowner is entitled to limit his liability to any sum which he thinks fit. But in some cases he cannot rely on a limitation clause, *e.g.* where the loss was due to unseaworthiness, and liability for loss by unseaworthiness was not excepted.[3]

Where the Carriage of Goods by Sea Act, 1924, applies,[4] the shipowner cannot limit his liability to a sum less than £100 per package or unit.[5] Any clause purporting to do so will be void.[6] Thus, a clause limiting a claim to the invoice value of the goods was held invalid.[7]

The general rule is that only the shipowner who is entitled to limit his liability, for any person who is not a party to the charter-party or bill of lading has no rights under it.

---

[1] *Ibid.*, Sched. Art. IV *bis.*, r. 4.
[2] See pp. 67–69, *ante.*
[3] *Tattersall* v. *National S.S. Co.* (1884), 12 Q. B. D. 297, p. 84, *ante.*
[4] See pp. 67–69, *ante.*
[5] Carriage of Goods by Sea Act 1924, Sched. Art. IV, r. 5. See pp. 173–176, *post.*
[6] *Ibid.*, Sched. Art. III, r. 8.
[7] *Nabob Foods, Ltd.* v. *The "Cape Corso"*, [1954] 2 Lloyd's Rep. 40 (Exchequer Court of Canada).

Thus, in *Scruttons, Ltd.* v. *Midland Silicones, Ltd.,*[1]

Shipowners issued to the shippers of a drum containing chemicals a bill of lading, by the terms of which they were entitled to limit their liability if the goods were damaged through their negligence. The drum was damaged during its loading by stevedores. The shippers sued the stevedores, who claimed to be entitled to limit their liability in accordance with the terms of the bill of lading. *Held*, that they were not entitled to do so, because they were not parties to the bill of lading, and so were liable to pay in full for the damage which had been caused.

But if the carrier contracts as an agent for a third party, e.g. a stevedore, the third party can enforce the terms of the bill of lading against the shipper if

(i) the bill of lading makes it clear that the stevedore is intended to be protected by the provisions in it which limit liability;

(ii) the bill of lading makes it clear that the carrier, in addition to contracting for these provisions on his own behalf, is also contracting as agent for the third party that those provisions should apply to the third party;

(iii) the carrier has authority from the third party to do that (or perhaps later ratification by the third party would suffice); and

(iv) any difficulties about consideration moving from the third party would be overcome.[2]

---

[1] [1962] 1 All E. R. 1; [1962] A. C. 446, H. L. In the United States it has been held that the parties to a bill of lading may extend any contractual benefit to a third party by clearly expressing their intent to do so: *Carle and Montanari Inc.* v. *American Export Isbrandtsen Lines Inc. and John W. McGrath Corporation*, [1968] 1 Lloyd's Rep. 260, District Court (Southern District of New York), where a stevedore, although not a party to the bill of lading, was held to be entitled to the benefit of a provision in it enabling the carrier to limit his liability; *Cabot Corpn.* v. *The "Mormascan": Moore-McCormack Lines Inc. and John W. McGrath Corpn.*, [1971] 2 Lloyd's Rep. 351, U.S. Ct. of Appeals, Second Circuit; *Rupp* v. *International Terminal Operating Co. Inc., S.S. Mormacstar, Moore–McCormack Lines Inc. and American Scantic Line: The "Mormacstar"*, [1973] 2 Lloyd's Rep. 485, U.S. Court of Appeals, Second Circuit; *Tessler Brothers (B.C.), Ltd.* v. *Italpacific Line and Matson Terminals Inc.*, [1975] 1 Lloyd's Rep. 210, U.S. Court of Appeals, Ninth Circuit.

[2] *Scruttons, Ltd.* v. *Midland Silicones, Ltd.*, [1962] 1 All E. R. 1, at p. 10 (*per* Lord REID).

Thus, in *New Zealand Shipping Co., Ltd.* v. *A. M. Satterthwaite & Co., Ltd.: The "Eurymedon"*,[1]

A bill of lading in respect of a drilling machine stated that the carrier acted as agent "for all persons who are or might be his servants or agents from time to time" and that the limitation of liability provisions in the bill of lading were available to such servant or agent. The machine was damaged whilst being discharged by stevedores. The stevedores contended that they were entitled to limit their liability under the clause in the bill of lading. *Held,* by the Judicial Committee of the Privy Council, that they were so entitled. The bill of lading brought into existence a unilateral bargain which became a full contract when the stevedores discharged the goods.[2] The discharge of the goods for the benefit of the shipper was the consideration for the agreement by the shipper that the stevedores should have the benefit of the limitation provisions in the bill of lading.[3] To give the stevedores the benefit of the limitation provisions was to give effect to the clear intentions of a commercial document.[4]

(B) By Statute

The shipowner is entitled to limit his liability under:

(1) The Merchant Shipping Act 1894.

(2) The Carriage of Goods by Sea Act 1924.

(3) The Carriage of Goods by Sea Act 1971.[5]

(1) *Under the Merchant Shipping Act 1894.* By the Merchant Shipping Act 1894, s. 503[6] the owner of a ship, whether British or foreign, is entitled to limit his liability where any loss of or damage to any goods, merchandise, or other things whatsoever on board the vessel is caused, if the loss or damage has occurred "without his actual fault or privity". The maximum sum for

---

[1] [1974] 1 Lloyd's Rep. 534, P. C.
[2] *Ibid.,* at p. 539 (*per* Lord WILBERFORCE).
[3] *Ibid.,* at p. 539 (*per* Lord WILBERFORCE).
[4] *Ibid.,* at p. 540 (*per* Lord WILBERFORCE).
[5] *This Act is not yet in force. See p. 76, ante.*
[6] As amended by the Merchant Shipping (Liability of Shipowners and Others) Act 1958.

which he can be made liable is £37.06 for each ton of the ship's registered tonnage.[1]

The owner can also limit his liability where loss of life or personal injury is caused, and the maximum amount payable will be £114.89 per ton.[2] Where there are claims both for loss of life and personal injury as well as for loss of, or damage to, goods, the former claims fall upon the £77.83 (the greater sum minus the smaller) per ton. If this fund is insufficient, they rank *pari passu* with the latter claims against £37.06 per ton in respect of the balance unpaid out of the £77.83 per ton.[3]

Although the main business of the shipowners may be that of brewers, in their capacity as shipowners they must be judged by the standard of conduct of the ordinary reasonable shipowner in the management and control of vessels.[4]

Thus, in *The "Lady Gwendolen"*,[4]

A firm of brewers also engaged in acting as shipowners for the carriage of stout from Dublin to Liverpool in a vessel which they owned. A collision occurred due to their failure to impress upon the master the urgency of the use of radar in fog. *Held*, that they could not limit their liability because they had failed to show that the collision had occurred without their actual fault or privity. A company, whose shipping activities were merely ancillary to its main business, could be in no better position than one whose main business was that of shipowning.[5]

---

[1] This sum represents the sterling equivalent of 1,000 gold francs which is the figure mentioned in the Act of 1958, s. 1 (1) (b). See Merchant Shipping (Limitation of Liability) (Sterling Equivalents) Order 1975 (S. I. 1975, No. 1615).

[2] This sum represents the sterling equivalent of 3,100 gold francs which is the the figure mentioned in the Act of 1958, s. 1 (1) (a). See Merchant Shipping (Limitation of Liability) (Sterling Equivalents) Order 1975 (S. I. 1975, No. 1615).

[3] *The Victoria* (1888), 13 P. D. 125 decided under the Merchant Shipping Act, 1862, s. 54. See generally Marsden, *The Law of Collisions at Sea* (11th edn. 1961), para. 213.

[4] *The "Lady Gwendolen"*, [1965] 1 Lloyd's Rep. 335, C. A.

[5] See the judgment of WILLMER, L.J., where he said (*ibid.*, at p. 346): "It seems to me that any company which embarks on the business of shipowning must accept the obligation to ensure efficient management of its ships if it is to enjoy the very considerable benefits conferred by the statutory right to limitation." See also the judgment of SELLERS L.J., *ibid.*, at p. 339.

The owner can also limit his liability where loss or damage to property other than goods on board his vessel has been caused as a result of the "act or omission of any person in the navigation or management of the ship".[1] But this matter is outside the scope of this work.[2]

The right to limit liability in connection with the ship is also extended to charterers and any person interested in or in possession of the vessel and, in particular, any manager or operator of her.[3]

The provisions of the Merchant Shipping Acts which limit the amount of the liability of shipowners apply, with necessary modifications, in relation to Crown ships.[4]

It should be observed that the onus is on the shipowner to prove that he is within the terms of the section upon which he relies: it is, therefore, for him to prove absence of actual fault or privity.[5] The fault or privity of the shipowner's servants (*e.g.* officers on

---

[1] Merchant Shipping Act 1894, s. 503, as amended by the Merchant Shipping (Liability of Shipowners and Others) Act 1958, s. 2 (1). An owner who is also the master of the vessel at the time of the loss or damage is entitled to limit his liability under s. 3 (2) of the Act of 1958, even though the loss or damage has been caused by his negligence: *The Annie Hay, Coldwell-Horsfall* v. *West Country Yacht Charters Ltd.*, [1968] 1 All E. R. 657; [1968] 1 Lloyd's Rep. 141.

[2] See generally Marsden, *op. cit.* paras. 182 and 183; *The Athelvictor*, [1946] P. 42; *The Teal* (1949), 82 Ll. L. Rep. 414; *The Anonity*, [1961] 2 Lloyd's Rep. 117, C. A., which were all decided under the similar wording of the Merchant Shipping (Liability of Shipowners and Others) Act 1900.

[3] Merchant Shipping (Liability of Shipowners and Others) Act 1958, s. 3 (1).

[4] Crown Proceedings Act 1947, s. 5. For an attempt to limit liability in respect of one of H.M.'s ships, see *The Truculent, The Admiralty* v. *Divina (Owners)*, [1951] 2 All E. R. 968; [1952] P. 1.

[5] *Standard Oil Co.* v. *Clan Line*, [1924] A. C. 100. *The Empire Jamaica*, [1956] 2 Lloyd's Rep. 119, H.L. *City Steam Fishing Co. (Owners of the Motor Trawler Hildina)* v. *Robertson; The Hildina*, [1957] 2 Lloyd's Rep. 247. *Northern Fishing Co. (Hull)* v. *Eddom, The Norman*, [1960] 1 Lloyd's Rep. 1, H. L. *The "Lady Gwendolen"*, [1965] 1 Lloyd's Rep. 335, C. A. (failure of shipowners to impress upon master urgency of use of radar in fog). *The "Dayspring"*, [1968] 2 Lloyd's Rep. 204 P. D. A. (failure of shipowners to ensure that there should be a look-out on deck in addition to the helmsman, for the forward visibility of the helmsman was restricted by the forecastle); *Rederij Erven H. Groen and Groen* v. *The "England" (Owners)*, [1973] 1 Lloyd's Rep. 373, C. A. (failure to instruct master that in trading to the port of London he must have a copy of the by-laws); *Marpole Towing, Ltd.* v. *British Columbia Telephone Co.: The "Chugaway II"*, [1973] 2 Lloyd's Rep. 159, Supreme Court of Canada (practice to estimate height of water by counting how many planks on bridge were visible).

board) is not sufficient to deprive the shipowner of his right to limit his liability.[1]

Where the shipowner is a company, the fault or privity must be that of the person who is really the directing mind and will of the company, the *very* ego and centre of the personality of the company, in order to render the company unable to limit its liability.[2]

Thus, where the assistant managing director of a brewery company was responsible for the operation of the vessels which it owned, he was held to be the *alter ego* of the company, and the problem of radar installed in them merited his personal attention. Since he had failed in this duty, the company could not limit its liability in respect of a collision, for this had not occurred "without its actual fault or privity".[3]

One other point to be noticed is that the provisions of s. 503 of the Merchant Shipping Act 1894, are expressly kept alive by the Carriage of Goods by Sea Act 1924,[4] and are therefore not excluded from operation in cases to which the 1924 Act applies.

(2) *Under the Carriage of Goods by Sea Act 1924.* In cases to which the 1924 Act applies,[5] a limit of "£100 per package or unit" is set by the Act to the total liability of a carrier in respect of any parcel of goods, "unless the nature and value of such goods have been declared by the shipper before shipment and inserted in the bill of lading".[6]

---

[1] *Lennard's Carrying Co., Ltd.* v. *Asiatic Petroleum Co., Ltd.*, [1915] A. C. 705. *Beauchamp* v. *Turrell*, [1952] 1 All E. R. 719; [1952] 2 Q. B. 207.

[2] *The "Lady Gwendolen"* (*supra*).

[3] *Ibid.*

[4] Section 6 (2) (see Appendix E, *post*).

[5] See pp. 67–69, *ante*.

[6] Sched. Art. IV, r. 5. Actual insertion of the value in the bill of lading is necessary. The fact that the shipowner knows the value is immaterial: *Anticosti Shipping Co.* v. *Viateur St. Amand*, [1959] 1 Lloyd's Rep. 352 (Supreme Court of Canada). For a case where there was no means prescribed for making a declaration in excess of the value of U.S. $500, see *Sommer Corporation* v. *Panama Canal Co.*, [1974] 1 Lloyd's Rep. 287, U.S. Court of Appeal Fifths, Circuit.

The word "package" has been held to cover 6 cartons of 40 television tuners strapped to pallet boards,[1] a 42 ft. cruiser carried in a cradle,[2] and a bundle containing 22 tin ingots.[3]

But where the shipowners chose to classify an uncrated yacht as "unpacked", it could not be regarded as a "package", and they could not limit their liability.[4]

An electrical transformer bolted to a skid,[5] and "lift-on lift-off tanks" supplied by the shipowner for the carriage of liquid latex,[6] have been held not to be "packages".

Difficulty has been experienced where goods are loaded into a container for shipment. Sometimes each separate item has been regarded as a "package",[7] whereas at other times it is the container

---

[1] *Standard Electrica, S.A.* v. *Hamburg Suderamerikanische Dampfschiffahrts-Gesellschaft and Columbus Lines Inc.*, [1967] 2 Lloyd's Rep. 193, U.S. Court of Appeals, Second Circuit. Cf. *International Factory Sales Service, Ltd.* v. *The Ship "Aleksandr Serafimovich" and Far Eastern S.S. Co.: The "Aleksandr Serafimovich"*, [1975] 2 Lloy'ds Rep. 346, Federal Court of Canada, Trial Division, where sewing machine heads shipped in cartons fixed to pallets, and it was held that each carton was a package, for the description of the goods in the bill of lading, the numbering of the cartons and their visibility from outside the pallet showed that this was the intention of the parties. (See the judgment of Deputy Judge SMITH, *ibid.*, at p. 355.) As to the growing practice of carriers to receive cargo from shippers in a "palletised" form or a "containerised" form, see the judgment of LUMBARD, Ct. J., in *Standard Electrica, S.A.* v. *Hamburg Suderamerikanische Dampfschiffahrts-Gesellschaft and Columbus Lines Inc.* (*supra*) at p. 195.

[2] *Island Yachts Inc.* v. *Federal Pacific Lakes Line*, [1972] 1 Lloyd's Rep. 426, District Court, Northern District of Illinois (Eastern District).

[3] *Primary Industries Corporation* v. *Barber Lines A/S and Skilos A/S Tropic: The "Fernland"*, [1975] 1 Lloyd's Rep. 461, Civil Court of City of New York.

[4] *Van Breems* v. *International Terminal Operating Co. Inc. and Holland America Line: The "Prinses Margriet"*, [1974] 1 Lloyd's Rep. 599, District Court, Southern District of New York.

[5] *Hartford Fire Insurance Co.* v. *Pacific Far East Line Inc.: The "Pacific Bear"*, [1974] 1 Lloyd's Rep. 359, U.S. Court of Appeals, Ninth Circuit.

[6] *Shinko Boeki Co., Ltd.* v. *S.S. "Pioneer Moon" and United States Line Inc.: The "Pioneer Moon"*, [1975] 1 Lloyd's Rep. 199, U.S. Court of Appeals, Second Circuit

[7] *Leather's Best Inc.* v. *The "Mormaclynx" Moore-McCormack Lines Inc., Tidewater Terminal Inc. and Universal Terminal and Stevedoring Corporation*, [1971] 2 Lloyd's Rep. 476 (see the judgment of FRIENDLY, Ct. J., *ibid.*, at pp. 485–486); *J. A. Johnston Co., Ltd.* v. *The Ship "Tindefjell", Sealion Navigation Co. S.A. and Concordia Line A/S: The "Tindefjell"*, [1973] 2 Lloyd's Rep. 253, Federal Court of Canada, Trial Division, where it was also held that the container was not a unit but merely a modern method of carrying goods.

itself which has been held to constitute the "package",[1] and the
carrier has been entitled to limit his liability to the much smaller
sum involved.

Where a tractor and generating set were shipped on board a
vessel and lost overboard whilst being discharged, each was
held to be a "unit".[2]

The carrier is entitled to limit his liability to £100 per package
or unit even if he has failed to exercise due diligence to make the
vessel seaworthy,[3] but he cannot do so if he has loaded the cargo
on deck for this constitutes a quasi-deviation.[4]

It is further provided that "the monetary units mentioned in
these Rules are to be taken to be gold value".[5]

Doubts have arisen as to how this limit of "£100 gold value"

---

[1] *Royal Typewriter Co. Division Litton Business Systems Inc.* v. *M.V.
"Kulmerland" and Hamburg-Amerika Linie: The "Kulmerland"*, [1973] 2
Lloyd's Rep. 428, U.S. Court of Appeals, Second Circuit, where it was held
that where the shipper's own packing units were not "functional", i.e. usable
for overseas shipment, the burden was on the shipper to show why the container should not be treated as a package (see the judgment of OAKES, Ct. J.,
ibid., at p. 431); *Lufty Ltd.* v. *Canadian Pacific Railway Co.: The "Alex"*,
[1974] 1 Lloyd's Rep. 106, Federal Court of Canada, Trial Division; *Rosenbruch*
v. *American Export Isbrandtsen Lines Inc.: The "Container Forwarder"*, [1974]
1 Lloyd's Rep. 119, District Court, Southern District of New York, where the
shipper's household goods were stowed in a container supplied by the carrier,
who had nothing to do with the packing, and it was held that it was the shipper's
intention that the container should constitute a "package"; *Sperry Rand Corp.*
v. *Norddeutscher Lloyd: The "Bischofstein"*, [1974] 1 Lloyd's Rep. 122, District
Court, Southern District of New York, where the bill of lading stated the number
of packages as "one container" and gave no idea of the number of cartons
inside; *Cameco Inc.* v. *"American Legion" and United States Lines Inc.*, [1975]
1 Lloyd's Rep. 295, U.S. Court of Appeals, Second Circuit, where the "functional" test was applied and OAKES, Ct. J. said (*ibid.*, at p. 304): "To hold in all
cases is to defeat the purpose of COGSA which is to protect shippers from the
overreaching of carriers through contracts of adhesion and to provide incentive
for careful transport and delivery"; *Insurance Co. of North America* v. *S/S
Brooklyn Maru, Japan Line Ltd.: The "Brooklyn Maru"*, [1975] 2 Lloyd's Rep.
512, District Court, Southern District of New York, where the container was
packed by the shipper.

[2] *Falconbridge Nickel Mines, Ltd., Janin Construction, Ltd. and Hewitt
Equipment, Ltd.* v. *Chimo Shipping, Ltd., and Munro Jorgensson Shipping Ltd.*,
[1973] 2 Lloyd's Rep. 469, Supreme Court of Canada.

[3] *Iligan Integrated Steel Mills Inc.* v. *S.S. "John Weyerhauser", Weyerhauser
Co. and New York Navigation Co. Inc.: The "John Weyerhauser"*, [1975] 2
Lloyd's Rep. 439, U.S. Court of Appeal, Second Circuit. (See the judgment of
FRIENDLY, Ct. J., *ibid.*, at p. 442.)

[4] *Jones* v. *Flying Clipper*, [1954] A. M. C. 259.

[5] Carriage of Goods by Sea Act 1924, Sched. Art. IX.

should be calculated, and to overcome this difficulty an agreement was concluded in August 1950, between the British underwriters', shipowners' and merchants' organisations who are members of the British Maritime Law Association. Clause 2 of the agreement provides that "the shipowner's liability (whether contested or not) in respect of any such claim shall be limited to £200 sterling lawful money of the United Kingdom per package or unit of cargo (unless the nature and value of such cargo have been declared by the shipper before loading and inserted in the bill of lading) notwithstanding that some other monetary limit is laid down by the legislation to which the contract of carriage is subject". This agreement is, of course, binding only on the parties to it or on those who become parties to it.

By agreement between the carrier and the shipper a higher maximum may be fixed.[1] But the carrier cannot reduce the maximum amount laid down by the Act.[2]

(3) *Under the Carriage of Goods by Sea Act 1971*.[3] In cases to which the Act of 1971 applies,[4] unless the nature and value of the goods have been declared by the shipper before shipment and inserted in the bill of lading, neither the carrier nor the ship shall in any event be or become liable for any loss or damage to or in connection with the goods in an amount exceeding the equivalent of 10,000 francs per package or unit or 30 francs per kilo of gross weight of the goods lost or damaged, whichever is the higher.[5]

The declaration made by the shipper, if embodied in the bill of lading, is *prima facie* evidence, but is not binding or conclusive on the carrier.[6]

---

[1] *Ibid.,* Art. IV, r. 5.

[2] *Ibid.*

[3] *The Act is not yet in force.* See p. 76, *ante.*

[4] See pp. 77–79, *ante.*

[5] Carriage of Goods by Sea Act 1971, Sched. Art. IV, r. 5 (a). A franc means a unit consisting of 65·5 milligrammes of gold of millesimal fineness 900: *ibid.,* Sched. Art. IV, r. 5 (d). The date of conversion of the sum awarded into national currencies is governed by the law of the Court seized of the case: *ibid.,* Sched. Art. IV, r. 5 (d). The Secretary of State may from time to time by order made by statutory instrument specify the amount in sterling which is to be taken as equivalent to the sum expressed in francs: *ibid.,* s. 1 (5).

[6] *Ibid.,* Sched. Art. IV, r. 5 (f).

The total amount recoverable is fixed by reference to the value of the goods at the place and time at which they are discharged from the ship in accordance with the contract or should have been so discharged.[1]

The value is fixed according to the commodity exchange price, or, if there is no such commodity exchange price or current market price, by reference to the normal value of goods of the same kind and quality.[2]

Where a container, pallet or similar article of transport is used to consolidate goods, the number of packages or units enumerated in the bill of lading as packed in such article of transport are deemed to be the number of packages or units in calculating the amount beyond which the carrier or the ship is not liable. Where the number of packages or units is not enumerated in the bill of lading, the article of transport is considered to be the package or unit, and the amount is calculated accordingly.[3]

By agreement between the carrier and the shipper a higher maximum may be fixed.[4] But the carrier cannot reduce the maximum laid down by the Act.[5]

If an action is brought against a servant or agent of the carrier (such servant or agent not being an independent contractor), the servant or agent is entitled to avail himself of the defences and limits of liability which the carrier is entitled to invoke under the Act.[6] But the aggregate of the amounts recoverable from the carrier and such servants and agents can in no case exceed the limit stated in the Act.[7] Further, a servant or agent of the carrier cannot limit his liability if it is proved that the damage resulted from an act or omission of the servant or agent done with intent to cause damage or recklessly and with knowledge that damage would probably result.[8]

---

[1] *Ibid.*, Sched. Art. IV, r. 5 (b).
[2] *Ibid.*, Sched. Art. IV, r. 5 (b).
[3] *Ibid.*, Sched. Art. IV, r. 4 (c).
[4] *Ibid.*, Sched. Art. IV, r. 5 (g).
[5] *Ibid.*, Sched. Art. IV, r. 5 (g)
[6] *Ibid.*, Sched. Art. IV *bis*, r. 2.
[7] *Ibid.*, Sched. Art. IV *bis*, r. 3.
[8] *Ibid.*, Sched. Art. IV *bis*, r. 4.

CHAPTER 8

The Master

The master of a ship may be said be to regarded by the law as two persons rolled into one. He is the agent of the shipowner, and the agent of the owner or owners of the cargo. In each of these capacities he has certain duties and a certain authority.

THE DUTIES OF THE MASTER

At Common Law

The duties of the master, which arise from his having charge of the ship and possession of the cargo, may be stated as follows:

(1) His first duty to the cargo-owners is to carry the cargo to its destination in the same ship.[1]

(2) He must take all reasonable care of the cargo, both during the ordinary course of the voyage and where some accident has exposed the cargo to danger.[2] In doing so he must always act with a view to the benefit of the cargo-owners. If he acts reasonably, with that end in view, his conduct is justifiable, irrespective of the result.[3]

(3) In case of necessity, where extraordinary measures must be taken, *e.g.* a sale of part of the cargo, he must first communicate with the cargo-owners for instructions; where communication with them is impossible, he must take such extraordinary action as will be for their ultimate benefit.[4]

---

[1] *Notara* v. *Henderson* (1872), L. R. 7 Q. B. 225.
[2] *Ibid.*
[3] *Benson* v. *Chapman* (1849), 2 H. L. Cas., at p. 720, and see *per* Sir MONTAGUE SMITH in *Cargo ex Argos* (1873), 42 L. J. Adm., at p. 56.
[4] See *The Hamburg* (1864), 2 Moo. P. C. N. S., at p. 323.

(4) He must collect general average contributions for the benefit of those entitled to them, be they cargo-owners or shipowner, exercising the shipowner's lien on the cargo, where necessary, until they are paid.[1]

(5) He must allow a reasonable time to the consignees of the cargo for taking delivery.[2]

(6) He must proceed on the voyage without unjustifiable deviation and with reasonable despatch.[3]

(7) He must do everything else which is necessary for the performance of the contract.[4]

By Statute

(i) *Under the Carriage of Goods by Sea Act 1924.* Under this Act, a shipper who furnishes the carrier with written information concerning

(a) the leading marks necessary for identification of the goods, and

(b) either the number of packages or pieces, or the quantity or weight, as the case may be,

has a right to insist upon the master or other agent of the carrier issuing a bill of lading incorporating the information so furnished.[5]

It should, however, be observed that the master is not bound to show *both* the number of packages *and* the weight; if the number is stated, the phrase "weight unknown" may properly be inserted, and will have full effect.[6] Moreover, the master can refuse to incorporate in the bill the statements required by the Act if either he has reasonable grounds for suspecting that the information given by the shipper is inaccurate, or he has had no reasonable

---

[1] *Strang* v. *Scott* (1889), 14 App. Cas. 601.

[2] *Bourne* v. *Gatliff* (1844), 11 Cl. & Fin., at p. 70.

[3] See pp. 18–23, *ante*.

[4] *The Turgot* (1886), 11 P. D. 21.

[5] Carriage of Goods by Sea Act 1924, Sched. Art. III, r. 3 (see Appendix E, *post*). There is, however, a partial exception in the case of bulk cargoes: see s. 5.

[6] *Pendle and Rivet* v. *Ellerman Lines* (1927), 33 Com. Cas. 70.

means of checking it.[1] And, in the case of the leading marks, the master may refuse to show these in the bill of lading if the goods or their containers are not clearly marked "in such a manner as should ordinarily remain legible until the end of the voyage".[2]

Further, under the 1924 Act, any shipper can insist upon the bill of lading incorporating a statement as to the "apparent order and condition" of the goods.[3]

(ii) *Under the Carriage of Goods by Sea Act 1971.* The duties of the master are the same under the Carriage of Goods by Sea Act 1971,[4] where it applies,[5] as his duties under the Carriage of Goods by Sea Act 1924.[6]

The Authority of The Master

His Authority in Ordinary Circumstances

It is now necessary to consider what are the limits set by the law to the ordinary authority of the master, as distinct from a consideration of what he may do in extraordinary circumstances, *e.g.* in time of grave peril. One broad principle must never be lost sight of: that is that, even in the absence of express instructions (by which, of course, he might be authorised to do anything), the authority of the master of a ship is very large and extends to all acts that are usual and necessary for the employment of the ship.[7]

He may make contracts for the hire of the ship, and enter into agreements to carry goods for freight. Apart from notice to the contrary, persons dealing with the master may assume that he is a general agent having authority to bind the owners for the purposes and on the terms on which the vessel is usually employed.

---

[1] Carriage of Goods by Sea Act, 1924, Sched. Art. III, r. 3 (see Appendix E, *post*).

[2] Carriage of Goods by Sea Act 1924, Sched. Art. III, r. 3 (see Appendix E, *post*).

[3] *Ibid.*

[4] *This Act is not yet in force.* See p. 76, *ante*.

[5] See pp. 77–79, *ante*.

[6] See pp. 179–180, *ante*.

[7] *Per* Jervis, C.J., in *Grant* v. *Norway* (1851), 20 L. J. C. P., at p. 98.

The master has no power to carry goods freight-free[1] nor to sign bills of lading for a lower rate of freight than the owner has contracted for.[2] He must not assume "any other authority than the indispensable and necessary one of procuring a freight for the vessel according to the ordinary terms".[3] "The authority of the captain to bind his owners by charter-party only arises when he is in a foreign port and his owners are not there and there is difficulty in communicating with them".[4] Further, the authority of a master of a foreign ship to contract on behalf of his owners is usually limited by the law of the ship's flag.[5]

The master has no authority to cancel or alter contracts already made by the owners.[6] Thus, he cannot alter the port of discharge or the amount of the freight. But where the other party refuses to perform the original contract, the master may make the best arrangement possible for the employment of the ship. Thus, in *Pearson* v. *Goschen,*[7]

the charterers became insolvent after part of the homeward cargo had been loaded. Their agents refused to load the rest of the cargo, and the master then agreed, under protest, to carry the whole homeward cargo at 30*s.* per ton. The shipowners claimed freight at 90*s.* per ton as originally agreed. *Held,* as to the cargo shipped after the insolvency, the new agreement was valid; but as to that already on board, the original freight of 90*s.* per ton was payable.

Where a master knew the load capacity of the ship's derrick, and that the shipper's cargo of machinery was too heavy for the derrick, but he still accepted the load, it was held that the action of the master was the effective cause of the damage to the derrick. The master's lack of authority to alter the terms of the contract of carriage did not transfer responsibility for that action from the shipowner to the shipper. Consequently the shipper was not to blame for the damage caused.[8]

---

[1] *Ibid.*

[2] *Pickernell* v. *Jauberry* (1862), 3 F. & F. 217.

[3] *Per* Dr. LUSHINGTON in *The Sir Henry Webb* (1849), 13 Jur. 639.

[4] *Per* BRETT, L.J., in *The Fanny, etc.* (1883), 48 L. T., at p. 775.

[5] *Lloyd* v. *Guibert* (1865), L. R. 1 Q. B. 115.

[6] *Grant* v. *Norway (supra).*

[7] (1864), 17 C. B. N. S. 352.

[8] *Brown and Root, Ltd.* v. *Chimo Shipping, Ltd.,* [1967] 2 Lloyd's Rep. 398 (Supreme Court of Canada).

The master is presumed to be the servant of the registered owner of the ship. On a change of ownership, the master's original authority and instructions are valid until he receives notice of the change; and, though the new owners may not be bound by his contracts, if they recognise his act in receiving goods on board, they must accept the terms upon which he received them.[1]

The master often signs bills of lading and charter-parties in his own name, without words showing that he is merely acting as agent for the owners. In such cases the other party can treat either the master or the shipowner as the person liable on the contract. As in the case of any other form of agency, judgment against the master is a bar to an action on the same cause against the owners of the ship.[2]

The master may himself sue on contracts made in his own name, but not where he acted merely as servant of the owner. Thus, in *Repetto* v. *Millar's Karri, etc. Forests,*[3]

where the charter provided that the master should sign bills of lading and these incorporated the terms of the charter-party, it was *held* that he could not sue the charterers for freight. His signature to the bills of lading was not a fresh contract, but merely a means of carrying out the charter-party.

The master may bind the shipowner or charterer by doing such things as are necessary on the part of the one or of the other to carry out the contract. Such necessaries for the voyage as the shipowner is bound by the contract to provide must, if purchased by the master on his behalf, be paid for by him, as also must such necessaries as were needed in order that the ship might sail, where it was in the shipowner's interest that the ship should sail;[4] and the charterer is similarly liable *mutatis mutandis.*[5] But where the master has not disclosed to the suppliers of necessaries that under an existing time-charter the charterer is liable for the particular disbursements in question, the shipowner will be

---

[1] *Per* BRAMWELL, B., in *Mercantile Bank* v. *Gladstone* (1868), 37 L. J. Ex. 130.
[2] *Priestly* v. *Fernie* (1865), 3 H. &. C. 977.
[3] [1901] 2 K. B. 306.
[4] *The Turgot* (1886), 11 P. D. 21.
[5] *The Beeswing* (1885), 53 L. T. 554.

liable to such suppliers to that extent.[1] The term "necessaries" has a wide meaning, extending even to quay rent and the cost of destroying putrid cargo where the ship is liable for such charges and *could* be prevented from sailing for their non-payment.[2]

The mere presence of the owner's authorised agents, even where the owners are domiciled abroad and the agents are in England, does not oust the authority of the master to make disbursements.[3]

Again, the master may, if nobody presents a bill of lading or offers to give an indemnity in its place, land cargo on arrival, or, if prevented from so doing by the port authorities, he may (and indeed it is his duty to[4]) deal with it as a reasonable man would, with a view to protecting the shipowner's interests by preserving the lien for freight, and in the best interests of the cargo-owner.[5]

Further, the master has certain statutory powers of landing goods in the United Kingdom under the Merchant Shipping Act 1894.[6]

His authority to bind the shipowner by admissions in the bill of lading has already been noted.[7]

He is entitled to jettison dangerous goods or destroy them or render them innocuous.[8]

His Authority in Extraordinary Circumstances

The principles involved. In cases of emergency the master *may* become the agent of the cargo-owners to take special measures to preserve the cargo or to minimise the loss arising from damage

---

[1] *The Tolla*, [1921] P. 22.

[2] *The Arzpeitia* (1921), 126 L. T. 29.

[3] *The Equator* (1921), 152 L. T. Jo. 259.

[4] See p. 234, *post*.

[5] *Erichsen* v. *Barkworth* (1858), 3 H. & N. 894; *Cargo ex Argos* (1873), 42 L. J. Adm. 49.

[6] Sections 492–501 (see Appendix D, *post*).

[7] See pp. 57–65, *ante*.

[8] Merchant Shipping Act 1894, ss. 446–50 (See Appendix D, *post*): Carriage of Goods by Sea Act 1924, Sched. Art. IV, r. 6 (see Appendix E, *post*): Carriage of Goods by Sea Act 1971, Sched. Art IV, r. 6 (See Appendix H, *post*). *This Act is not yet in force. See p. 76, ante.*

which has already been suffered. Such emergency *only* arises, however, when extraordinary action is necessary, *and* communication with his principals, be they shipowners or cargo-owners, is impracticable. Here, again, the standard set up by the law is the same as holds good in other cases; that is to say, action will be deemed to have been necessary when, *in the interests of the whole of the adventure of the principals concerned*, it would have appeared to a reasonable and prudent man to be so.[1]

The master's authority to act in the interests of the cargo-owner is part of his general authority as servant of the shipowner, and therefore the latter will be liable if the master abuses his powers. Thus, if the master improperly jettisons goods, the shipowner will be liable; for such an act is within the scope of his functions as servant of the shipowner.[2] But it must never be forgotten that the master has no authority to take *extraordinary* measures for the cargo-owner if the latter or his representative can be communicated with.[3] If this can be done, he must obtain instructions from the owner of the goods and must obey them.[4] Where charterer and shipowner agreed on instructions which were ambiguous and were misinterpreted in good faith by the master, it was held that the charterer could not make the shipowner liable.[5]

Further, supposing unforeseen circumstances to have arisen, if the master delays unreasonably before deciding on what action he must take, and the cargo suffers from such delay, the shipowner will be liable to the cargo-owners for the damage, for it is, as we have seen, part of the *duty* of the master, as agent of the shipowner, to take all reasonable precautions to preserve the cargo.[6]

---

[1] *Atlantic Mutual Insurance Co.* v. *Huth* (1880), 16 Ch. D. 474.

[2] See e.g. *Federal Commerce and Navigation Co., Ltd.* v. *Eisenerz G.m.b.H.* : *The "Oak Hill"*, [1975] 1 Lloyd's Rep. 105, Supreme Court of Canada, where the master in unloading the cargo after the vessel had stranded was held to be representing the shipowner but still to have an overriding duty to care for the cargo.

[3] *Cargo ex Argos* (1873), 42 L. J. Adm., at p. 56.

[4] *Acatos* v. *Burns* (1878), 47 L. J. Ex. 566.

[5] *Miles* v. *Haslehurst* (1906), 12 Com. Cas. 83.

[6] *Hansen* v. *Dunn* (1906), 11 Com. Cas. 100.

Examples of Extraordinary Action

Such extraordinary action as may be taken under this principle is as follows:

(1) *Affecting the whole adventure:*

(A) Delay and/or deviation from the proper route.[1]

(B) Hypothecation of ship and cargo by giving a bottomry bond.[2]

The authority of the master to hypothecate the ship and cargo is a general rule of maritime law. BRETT, L.J., explained it in this way:[3]

"It arises from the necessity of things; it arises from the obligation of the shipowner and the master to carry the goods from one country to another, and from it being inevitable from the nature of things that the ship and cargo may at some time or other be in a strange port where the captain may be without means, and where the shipowner may have no credit because he is not known there, that, for the safety of all concerned and for the carrying out of the ultimate object of the whole adventure, there must be a power in the master not only to hypothecate the ship but the cargo."

The purpose of a bottomry bond is to enable the ship to complete the voyage. If she does not arrive at her destination, the lender loses his money. Consequently where several bonds have been given, a later bond takes priority over an earlier one. The later bond is given at a time of necessity when the earlier one would otherwise be frustrated, and the later is therefore entitled to be satisfied before the bond of earlier date.

A bottomry bond confers upon the person advancing money under it a maritime lien on the ship, freight and cargo.[4]

---

[1] See pp. 20–23, *ante.*
[2] *The Karnak* (1869), L. R. 2 P. C. 505.
[3] *The Gaetano and Maria* (1882), 7 P. D., at p. 145.
[4] See Chapter 12, *post.*

The cargo cannot be resorted to in satisfaction of a bottomry bond unless the ship and freight are insufficient to satisfy the charge. If it was unnecessary to charge the cargo at all, the bottomry bond will be invalid as against the cargo-owner. Where expenditure is incurred for repairs to the ship of a more extensive character than were necessary, the bond will be valid against the cargo only to the extent to which such repairs were necessary for the purpose of the voyage.[1]

(C) Conclusion of a salvage agreement.[2]

(D) General average sacrifices and expenditure.[3]

(E) Sale of ship and cargo.[4]

(2) *Affecting the cargo only:*

(A) Sale of damaged goods at a port of call.[5]

It is to be noted that purchasers of a cargo from the master of a ship do not get a good title "unless it is established that the master used all reasonable efforts to have the goods conveyed to their destination, and that he could not by any means available to him carry the goods, or procure the goods to be carried, to their destination as merchantable articles, or could not do so without an expenditure clearly exceeding their value after their arrival at their destination".[6]

The fundamental rule that the master's authority to act for the cargo-owner arises from *necessity*, and cannot be exercised if the cargo-owner can be communicated with, is applied here with strictness. Thus, in *Acatos* v. *Burns*,[7]

---

[1] *The Onward* (1873), 42 L. J. Adm., at p. 70.

[2] *The Renpor* (1883), 8 P. D. 115.

[3] See Chapter 9.

[4] But see *Cannan* v. *Maeburn* (1823), 2 L. J. C. P. 60.

[5] *Australasian S. Nav. Co.* v. *Morse* (1872), L. R. 4 P. C. 222.

[6] *Per* COTTON, L.J., in *Atlantic Mutual Insurance Co.* v. *Huth* (*supra*), at p. 481.

[7] (1878), 47 L. J. Ex. 566.

a cargo of maize which had become heated was sold at an intermediate port. The jury found that it was impossible to carry the cargo to its destination and that a sale was prudent under the circumstances, but that the necessity for a sale was not so urgent as to prevent communication with the cargo-owner. *Held*, the shipowner was liable to the cargo-owner for selling without his consent. BAGGALLAY, L.J., said: "In order to justify the sale under the circumstances, there must be not only an absolute necessity but an inability to communicate with the owner of the cargo".[1]

(B) Transhipment of the cargo.[2]

(C) Conclusion of a salvage agreement, where the ship herself is not in danger but only the cargo, or part of it.

(D) General average sacrifices and expenditure, *e.g.* jettison.

(E) Reconditioning of damaged goods, as by landing them to dry them when one of the holds is flooded.

(F) Hypothecation of the cargo by giving a respondentia bond.[3]

But the master has no authority to charge the cargo for such an advance unless the interests of the cargo-owner require it, and the ship and freight are an insufficient security for the sum required,[4] and he cannot obtain the necessary money in any other way.

The charge created by a respondentia bond becomes payable only in the event of the ship's safe arrival. If the ship is lost, the loan is not recoverable.

It is essential to the validity of a bottomry[5] or respondentia bond that a maritime risk should be involved, but the fact that the loan has been insured does not affect the character of the bond.[6]

A respondentia bond confers upon the person advancing the money a maritime lien on the cargo only.[7]

---

[1] *Ibid.*, at p. 568.
[2] *The Soblemsten* (1866), L.R. 1 A. & E. 293.
[3] See *Cargo ex Sultan* (1859), Sw. 504.
[4] *The Onward* (1873), 42 L. J. Adm. 61.
[5] *The Indomitable* (1859), Sw. 446.
[6] See *The Dora Forster*, [1900] P. 241.
[7] See Chapter 12, p. 238, *post*.

CHAPTER 9

General Average

PARTICULAR AND GENERAL AVERAGE

The invariable result of particular average is that the loss falls on the owner of the particular property which has suffered the damage, whether that damage was due to a deliberate sacrifice or to an accident. Thus, if owing to heating, it becomes necessary to sell the cargo at an intermediate port, the cargo-owner will have to bear the loss arising from such a sale. The same principle applies to extraordinary expenditure during the voyage. If, owing to bad weather, the ship has to put in for repairs, the expense of such repairs must be borne by the shipowner.

But where ship and cargo are exposed to a common danger and some part of the cargo or of the ship is intentionally sacrificed, or extra expenditure is incurred, to avert that danger, such loss or expense will be the subject of a general average contribution. It will be apportioned between ship and cargo in proportion to their saved values. This is a very ancient rule of maritime law. It found its way from the law of Rhodes into the Digest of Justinian, and through the usage of commerce it has become a part of the Common Law of England.

Very commonly a clause is inserted in the contract incorporating the York-Antwerp Rules, which are a standard set of rules relating to general average. The name, "York-Antwerp", is derived from the places where conferences were held which brought the Rules into existence. The title "York-Antwerp" was first given to rules formulated in 1877. They have been revised on several occasions, and the present ones are those of 1974.[1] But they do not constitute a complete or self-contained code and need to be supplemented by

---

[1] See Appendix G.

bringing into the gaps provisions of the general law which are applicable to the contract.[1]

The Carriage of Goods by Sea Act 1924 expressly provides that nothing therein "shall be held to prevent the insertion in a bill of lading of any lawful provision regarding general average".[2] The Carriage of Goods by Sea Act 1971[3] is to the same effect.[4]

For a sacrifice or expenditure to be the subject of general average contribution[5] the following conditions must obtain:

(1) *There must be a danger common to the whole adventure.*

The danger must be in fact a real one, not merely imagined to exist by the master, however reasonable such fear may be.[6] Thus, in *Nesbitt* v. *Lushington*,[7]

> a ship was stranded on the coast of Ireland during a period of great scarcity. The inhabitants compelled the captain to sell wheat, which was on board, at less than its value. As they intended no injury to the vessel, there was no common danger, and it was *held* that this was not a general average loss.

But the fact that a part of the cargo has already been discharged will not preclude the owners of the rest, under all circumstances, from claiming a general average con-

---

[1] *Goulandris Bros.* v. *B. Goldman & Sons*, [1957] 3 All E. R. 100; [1958] 1 Q. B. 74; *Federal Commerce and Navigation Co., Ltd.* v. *Eisenerz G.m.b.H.: The "Oak Hill"*, [1975] 1 Lloyd's Rep. 105, Supreme Court of Canada, where RITCHIE, J., said (*ibid.*, at p. 110): "It would, in my opinion, be wrong to assume that . . . the York-Antwerp Rules are to be treated as a code governing the rights of the parties concerned to the exclusion of other rights and obligations created by the contract of carriage".

[2] Sched. Art. V (See Appendix E, *post*).

[3] *The Act is not yet in force.* See p. 76, *ante*.

[4] Sched. Art. V (See Appendix H).

[5] A claim for a general average contribution is barred after 6 years from the date of the occurrence of the general average loss: *Chandris* v. *Argo Insurance Co., Ltd.*, [1963] 2 Lloyd's Rep. 65, Q. B. D. (Commercial Court). The period of limitation does not run from the time when the general average statement is completed: *ibid.* See further *Arthur L. Liman, as trustee in bankruptcy of A. H. Bull S.S. Co.* v. *India Supply Mission: The "Beatrice"*, [1975] 1 Lloyd's Rep. 220, District Court, Southern District of New York.

[6] *Per* BRETT, L.J., in *Whitecross Wire Co.* v. *Savill* (1882), 8 Q. B. D. 653, at p. 662. See also *Watson* v. *Firemen's Fund Co.*, [1922] 2 K. B. 355.

[7] (1792), 4 Term Rep. 783.

tribution from the shipowner. Thus, in *Whitecross Wire Co.*
v. *Savill*,[1]

> where, most of the cargo having been discharged, a fire broke out
> on the ship, and the remainder of the cargo was damaged by
> water used in putting out the fire, it was *held* that the shipowner
> must contribute in respect of this damage.

But under the York-Antwerp Rules it is sufficient if "the extraordinary sacrifice or expenditure . . . is . . . reasonably made . . .".[2]

(2) *The sacrifice or expenditure must be real and intentional.*

Where the thing abandoned is already lost, there is no
real sacrifice, and consequently no claim for contribution,
e.g. cutting away a mast which is already virtually useless.[3]
But in *Johnson* v. *Chapman*,[4]

> where deck cargo had broken loose in a storm so that it was
> a source of danger, and interfered with the working of the pumps,
> it was *held* that the cargo was not virtually lost and its jettison
> amounted to a real sacrifice.

Under the York-Antwerp Rules the sacrifice or expenditure
must be "intentionally" made.[5] They also provide that "loss or
damage caused by cutting away wreck or parts of the ship which
have been previously carried away or are effectively lost by
accident shall not be made good as general average."[6]

(3) *The sacrifice or expenditure must be necessary.*

Generally the duty of deciding whether a sacrifice or
expenditure is necessary rests with the master of the ship.
But it appears that the actual order may be given by some

---

[1] *Supra.*

[2] Rule A. See, *e.g. Federal Commerce and Navigation Co., Ltd.* v. *Eisenerz
G.m.b.H.: The "Oak Hill"* (*supra*), where the master's decision to unload the
cargo after the vessel had stranded was held to be reasonable and made for the
benefit of the ship and cargo alike.

[3] *Shepherd* v. *Kottgen* (1877), 2 C. P. D. 585.

[4] (1865), 19 C. B. N. S. 563; Chorley and Tucker's *Leading Cases* (4th edn.
1962), p. 309.

[5] Rule A.

[6] Rule IV.

other person, provided that the master sanctions it. Thus, in *Papayanni* v. *Grampian Steamship Co.*,[1]

a fire broke out on board, and the master put into port. The fire increased, and the captain of the port ordered that the ship be scuttled. The master believed this course to be best in the interests of ship and cargo, so he raised no objection. It was *held* that he had sanctioned the scuttling of the ship, and that the loss must be adjusted as a general average sacrifice.

(4) *The danger must not have arisen through the fault of the person claiming contribution, where such fault would expose such person to legal liability for the damage done.*

In order to prevent a person recovering general average contribution on the ground that he was in fault, the fault must be something which constitutes an actionable wrong.[2] Thus, in *Greenshields, Cowie & Co.* v. *Stephens*,[3]

during the voyage, a cargo of coal took fire by spontaneous combustion. The shippers were *held* entitled to contribution from

---

[1] (1896), 1 Com. Cas. 448.

[2] See, *e.g. Gesellschaft fur Getreidchandel A.G., Hugo Mathes and Schurr KG, Herman Schrader, E. Kampffmeyer, Jurt A. Becher, Getreide-Import-Gesellschaft m.b.H.* v. *The "Texas" and Wilh. Wilhemsen, The "Texas"*, [1970] 1 Lloyd's Rep. 175, District Court, Eastern District of Louisiana, New Orleans Division, where the shipowners were held not to be entitled to a general average contribution because they were at fault in allowing the vessel to sail with smoke in her hold. See the judgment of CASSIBRY, D.J., *ibid.*, at p. 176; *Diestelskamp* v. *Baynes (Reading), Ltd., The "Aga"*, [1968] 1 Lloyd's Rep. 431, Q. B. D. (Commercial Court), where the shipowners were held not to be entitled to a general average contribution because they had not exercised due diligence to make the vessel seaworthy; *Wirth, Ltd.* v. *S.S. "Acadia Forest" and Lash Barge "CG 204": The "Acadia Forest"*, [1974] 2 Lloyd's Rep. 563, District Court, Eastern District of Louisiana, where barge owners could not claim a general average contribution because they failed to disprove unseaworthiness; *United States of America* v. *Eastmount Shipping Corporation: The "Susquehanna"*, [1975] 1 Lloyd's Rep. 216, District Court, Southern District of New York, where no general average contribution could be claimed by the shipowners because the vessel was unseaworthy in that she had failed to have sufficient bunkers on board for the intended journey (see the judgment of FRANKEL, D.J., *ibid.*, at p. 219); *Gemini Navigation Inc.* v. *Philipp Brothers Division of Minerals and Chemicals, Philipp Corporation and Royal Insurance Co., Ltd.: The "Ionic Bay"*, [1975] 1 Lloyd's Rep. 287, U.S. Court of Appeals, Second Circuit, where a general average contribution was not payable to the shipowners because the cargo had been improperly stowed. (See the judgment of WATERMAN, Ct. J., *ibid.*, at pp. 294–295.)

[3] [1908] A. C. 431.

the shipowner in respect of damage to the coal in extinguishing the fire. There had been no negligence on the part of the shippers, and it was assumed that both parties were equally familiar with the liability of coal to spontaneous combustion in a climate like that of India.

But where the contract of carriage makes certain exceptions to the liability which would otherwise fall on one of the parties, it prevents the grounds of such liability being imputed as a fault to the party in whose favour the exceptions are made. Hence, if negligence of the shipowner is excepted in the contract, he can recover in respect of loss or expense incurred for the common good even though his negligence made the loss or expense necessary.[1] So also, where a general average sacrifice is incurred by reason of fire due to unseaworthiness, if the shipowner can invoke the Merchant Shipping Act 1894, s. 502,[2] so as to avoid liability for the fire, he can recover a general average contribution.[3]

The "amended Jason clause" should be inserted in all bills of lading for voyages to and from the United States. The necessity for it arises because of an important difference between American law and English law. Briefly, the history of the subject in the United States is as follows. The Harter Act 1893, s. 3, provides that if a shipowner exercises due care to make his vessel seaworthy, neither he, the vessel, her agent, nor her charterer shall be liable for damage or loss arising from (*inter alia*) faults or errors in navigation, or in the management of the vessel. After this Act was passed, it was assumed that since it exempted a shipowner from liability for losses arising from negligent navigation, he was entitled to recover in general average for the ship's sacrifices

---

[1] *The Carron Park* (1890), 15 P. D. 203; *Milburn* v. *Jamaica Fruit Co.*, [1900] 2 Q. B. 540; *Federal Commerce and Navigation Co., Ltd.* v. *Eisenerz G.m.b.H.: The "Oak Hill"*, [1975] 1 Lloyd's Rep. 105, Supreme Court of Canada, where the charter-party exempted the shipowners from liability for loss caused by negligent navigation.

[2] See p. 160, *ante*, and Appendix D, *post*.

[3] *Louis Dreyfus & Co.* v. *Tempus Shipping Co.*, [1931] A. C. 726.

which had minimised the greater loss for which he was now relieved from liability.[1] Nevertheless, the Supreme Court of the United States held in *The Irrawaddy*[2] that the exemption in the Act did *not* entitle a shipowner to claim a contribution for a general average loss due to the negligence of his servants. In English law there is not, and never has been, any rule corresponding with that laid down in *The Irrawaddy*. To overcome the difficulty, it became usual to insert a clause in bills of lading for vessels trading to and from the United States, expressly declaring that the shipowner could recover in general average in the event of negligence, provided that due diligence had been exercised to make the ship in all respects seaworthy. The legality of the clause was questioned, and it was eventually decided by the Supreme Court of the United States in *The Jason*[3] that the clause was valid. Thereafter it became known as the "Jason clause". Subsequent decisions[4] necessitated certain changes in the drafting of the clause. The one now in use is generally called the "amended Jason clause" and is reproduced in Appendix B.[5]

But suppose goods have been jettisoned to avert a common danger caused by negligent navigation: can the owners of those goods claim against the owners of the rest of the cargo? It has been decided that they can.[6] The owners of the jettisoned goods "were not privy to the master's fault and were under no duty, legal or moral, to make a

---

[1] Lowndes and Rudolf's *Law of General Average and the York-Antwerp Rules* (10th edn. 1975), para. 84.

[2] (1897), 171 U.S. 187.

[3] (1912), 225 U.S. 32.

[4] For details, see Lowndes and Rudolf, *op. cit.*, para. 84, footnote 29. See also *Drew Brown, Ltd.* v. *The "Orient Trader" and Owners: The "Orient Trader"*, [1973] 2 Lloyd's Rep. 174, Supreme Court of Canada; *Gemini Navigation Inc.* v. *Philipp Brothers Division of Minerals & Chemicals, Philipp Corporation and Royal Insurance Co., Ltd.: The "Ionic Bay"*, [1975] 1 Lloyd's Rep. 287, United States Court of Appeals, Second Circuit, where it was held that the shipowners were not entitled to a general average contribution in respect of the expenses of the restowage of a cargo which they had stowed improperly.

[5] See p. 256, *post*.

[6] *Strang* v. *Scott* (1889), 14 App. Cas. 601.

gratuitous sacrifice of their goods for the sake of others to avert the consequences of his fault".[1]

The York-Antwerp Rules provide that,

"Rights to contribution in general average shall not be affected though the event which gave rise to the sacrifice or expenditure may have been due to the fault of one of the parties to the adventure; but this shall not prejudice any remedies or defences which may be open against or to that party in respect of such fault".[2]

The effect of the first part of the Rule is that the average adjustment is compiled on the assumption that the casualty has not been caused by anybody's fault.[3] The second part operates as a proviso qualifying the first part. The rights may be nullified or defeated or diminished or otherwise affected by the remedies.[4] For this purpose a "fault" is a legal wrong which is actionable as between the parties at the time when the general average sacrifice or expenditure is made.[5]

(5) *The property which was in danger must have been actually benefited by the sacrifice.*[6]

(6) *Only direct losses are recoverable.*

The York-Antwerp Rules provide that:[7]

"Only such losses, damages or expenses which are the direct consequence of the general average act shall be allowed as general average.

Loss or damage sustained by the ship or cargo through delay, whether on the voyage or subsequently, such as

---

[1] *Per* Lord WATSON, in *Strang* v. *Scott* (1889), 14 App. Cas., at p. 609.

[2] Rule D. *Westfal-Larsen & Co. A/S* v. *Colonial Sugar Refining Co., Ltd.,* [1960] 2 Lloyd's Rep. 206 (Supreme Court of New South Wales).

[3] *Goulandris Bros.* v. *B. Goldman & Sons, Ltd.,* [1957] 3 All E. R. 100; [1958] 1 Q. B. 74; *Federal Commerce and Navigation Co., Ltd.* v. *Eisenerz G.m.b.H.: The "Oak Hill",* [1975] 1 Lloyd's Rep. 105, Supreme Court of Canada.

[4] *Goulandris Bros.* v. *B. Goldman & Sons Ltd.* (*supra*), at p. 106 and p. 93.

[5] *Ibid.,* at p. 114 and p. 104.

[6] *Pirie* v. *Middle Dock Co.* (1881), 44 L. T. 426. See also *Chellew* v. *Royal Commission, etc.,* [1922] 1 K. B. 12.

[7] Rule C. See p. 201, *post.*

demurrage,[1] and any indirect loss whatsoever, such as loss of market, shall not be admitted as general average".

GENERAL AVERAGE SACRIFICE

There are three interests involved in a maritime venture—the cargo, the ship, and the freight. Consequently general average loss may arise from:

(1) *Sacrifice of cargo.* The commonest instance of a general average sacrifice is jettison. The mere washing overboard of part of the cargo will not give rise to a general average contribution: nor will the throwing overboard of cargo by the crew or passengers out of private malice.

To give rise to a general average contribution, the cargo jettisoned must have been stowed in a proper place. Generally it is not proper to stow cargo on deck; and, in the absence of a special custom or the consent of the other interests in the adventure, the owner of deck cargo has no claim for a general average contribution if it is jettisoned.[2] If the shipowner has agreed to receive deck cargo, the ship and freight must contribute to the loss, provided the owner of the jettisoned goods is the sole cargo-owner. But where there are other cargo-owners who have not consented to the stowing on deck, no contribution can be obtained from them or from the shipowner.[3]

But where goods are stowed on deck without the shipper's consent, the shipowner is alone responsible for their loss by jettison, because he has placed them in a dangerous position in violation of his undertaking to carry them safely.[4]

Again, cargo may sometimes have to be used as fuel to keep the engines and pumps going, where the ship has been delayed by a hurricane; or damage may be done to the cargo by pouring water on to it to extinguish a fire. In both cases the damage is a general average sacrifice.

---

[1] As to demurrage, see Chapter 10.
[2] *Strang* v. *Scott* (1889), 14 App. Cas., at p. 608.
[3] *Wright* v. *Marwood* (1881), 7 Q. B. D. 62.
[4] *Royal Exchange Co.* v. *Dixon* (1886), 12 App. Cas. 11.

The York-Antwerp Rules provide that

"No jettison of cargo shall be made good as general average unless such cargo is carried in accordance with the recognised custom of the trade."[1]

"Damage done to a ship and cargo, or either of them, by or in consequence of a sacrifice made for the common safety, and by water which goes down a ship's hatches opened or other opening made for the purpose of making a jettison for the common safety, shall be made good as general average."[2]

"Damage done to a ship and cargo, or either of them, by water or otherwise, including damage by beaching or scuttling a burning ship, in extinguishing a fire on board the ship, shall be made good as general average; except that no compensation shall be made for damage by smoke or heat however caused."[3]

(2) *Sacrifice of ship or tackle.* Where any sacrifice of the ship, her stores or tackle is necessary to avert a common danger, it will be the subject of a general average contribution, unless it was incurred in fulfilling the shipowner's original contract to carry the goods safely to their destination. All *ordinary* losses sustained by the ship must be borne by the shipowner: but sacrifices to meet the particular emergency, such as loss of the ship's tackle through using it for unusual purposes in order to secure her safety in specially difficult circumstances, will be the subject of a general average contribution.[4] Similarly, where spare parts were cut up for fuel to keep a pump going, their value was held to be the subject of contribution, because this was not the use they were intended for and the ship would have gone down if the pumping had not been maintained.[5] But where the tackle is insufficient for the ordinary needs of the ship, the shipowner cannot claim in respect of things destroyed to make up the deficiency.

If the ship is in danger of sinking, and the master deliberately runs her ashore for the purpose of saving the cargo and possibly also the ship, the loss of or damage to the ship is probably a general average sacrifice. The difficulty lies in the fact that, if the ship is practically certain to go down, there is no real sacrifice in stranding her.[6] Still, the policy of our Courts is to encourage the master

---

[1] Rule I.
[2] Rule II.
[3] Rule III.
[4] See *Birkley* v. *Presgrave* (1801), 1 East 220.
[5] *Harrison* v. *Bank of Australasia* (1872), L. R. 7 Exch. 39.
[6] See *Shepherd* v. *Kottgen* (*supra*).

to act impartially in the interest of *all* concerned, and to hold otherwise would be to encourage him to hazard ship and cargo in preference to incurring certain damage to the ship by stranding her to save the cargo. "It would defeat the main utility of general average if at a moment of emergency the captain's mind were to hesitate as to saving the adventure through fear of casting a burden on his owners."[1]

The York-Antwerp Rules provide that,

"When a ship is intentionally run on shore for the common safety, whether or not she might have been driven on shore, the consequent loss or damage shall be allowed in general average."[2]
"Damage caused to any machinery and boilers of a ship which is ashore and in a position of peril, in endeavouring to refloat, shall be allowed in general average when shown to have arisen from an actual intention to float the ship for the common safety at the risk of such damage; but where a ship is afloat no loss or damage caused by working the propelling machinery and boilers shall in any circumstances be made good as general average."[3]
"When a ship is ashore and cargo and ship's fuel and stores or any of them are discharged as a general average act, the extra cost of lightening, lighter hire and reshipping if incurred and the loss or damage sustained thereby, shall be admitted as general average."[4]
"Ship's materials and stores, or any of them, necessarily burnt for fuel for the common safety at a time of peril shall be admitted as general average, when and only when an ample supply of fuel had been provided; but the estimated quantity of fuel that would have been consumed calculated at the price current at the ship's last port of departure at the date of her leaving, shall be credited to the general average."[5]

(3) *Sacrifice of freight.* Where freight is payable on delivery, a jettison of the goods involves not only sacrifice of the goods themselves but also a loss of the freight on them. Accordingly the person to whom the freight would have been payable, whether charterer or shipowner, is entitled to claim a contribution from the owners of the interests saved. Thus, in *Pirie* v. *Middle Dock Co.*,[6]

cargo damaged by a general average sacrifice had to be discharged at an intermediate port. It was *held* that a general average contribution was due from the cargo-owner in respect of the freight thus lost.

---

[1] *Per* GROVE, J., in *Shepherd* v. *Kottgen* (1877), 47 L. J. C. P., at p. 69.
[2] Rule V.
[3] Rule VII.
[4] Rule VIII.
[5] Rule IX.
[6] (1881), 44 L. T. 426.

But where freight is payable in advance, it does not depend upon the safe arrival of the goods, and a claim to a general average contribution in respect of freight cannot arise.

The York-Antwerp Rules provide that,

"Loss of freight arising from damage to or loss of cargo shall be made good as general average, either when caused by a general average act, or when the damage to or loss of cargo is made good. Deduction shall be made from the amount of gross freight lost of the charges which the owner thereof would have incurred to earn such freight, but has, in consequence of the sacrifice, not incurred."[1]

GENERAL AVERAGE EXPENDITURE

Where extraordinary expenditure is incurred for the purpose of avoiding a common danger which threatens ship and cargo, such expenditure is the subject of a general average contribution in the same way as a loss voluntarily incurred by a sacrifice of the ship, cargo, or freight. At the same time, it must be borne in mind that the shipowner is under an obligation to defray such expense as may be necessary to complete the voyage. It is sometimes difficult to determine whether expenditure is the subject of a general average contribution or has been incurred merely in fulfilment of the contractual obligation of the shipowner.

Payments for salvage services may or may not be general average expenditure. The liability to pay salvage attaches to the property saved in proportion to its value in the same way as general average claims attach. Where expense is incurred in saving both ship and cargo, as in refloating a ship that has sunk or gone aground with her cargo, this is treated as a general average expense.[2] But where the cargo has been safely discharged and further operations are directed to getting the ship afloat and towing her into a port for repairs, the further expense thus incurred will fall on the shipowner alone.[3]

---

[1] Rule XV.
[2] *Kemp* v. *Halliday* (1865), 34 L. J. Q. B. 233.
[3] *Job* v. *Langton* (1856), 26 L. J. Q. B. 97.

The York-Antwerp Rules state that

"Expenditure incurred by the parties to the adventure on account of salvage, whether under contract or otherwise, shall be allowed in general average to the extent that the salvage operations were undertaken for the purpose of preserving from peril the property involved in the common maritime adventure."[1]

When a ship puts into a port of refuge to repair damage done *by a general average sacrifice*, the cost of repairing the ship, together with other charges incidental thereto, is the subject of general average.[2] Such incidental charges would include the cost of reloading the cargo if it had to be unloaded in order to effect the repairs. But this is not the case where the damage to be repaired arises in the ordinary course of the voyage. Thus, in *Svendsen* v. *Wallace*,[3]

a ship sprang a leak under no special stress of weather beyond the ordinary perils of the sea. Acting for the safety of the whole adventure, the master put into a port of refuge for repairs. It was necessary to unload the cargo in order to effect the repairs. *Held*, the expenses of entering the port and of discharging the cargo were general average expenditure; but the warehousing charges, the expenses of the repairs, the cost of reloading the goods and the pilotage and harbour dues on leaving the port were not general average expenditure, because when they were incurred the adventure was no longer in danger.[4]

Where by reason of an impending peril it has become unsafe for ship and cargo to continue the voyage, deviation to a port of refuge is a general average act. But if the deviation was rendered necessary by the unseaworthiness of the ship, the shipowner cannot recover general average contributions in respect of the port of refuge expenses.[5] Furthermore, it has been held that deviation ordered by the Admiralty for strategic reasons in wartime does not amount to a general average act, because the masters

---

[1] Rule VI.

[2] *Atwood* v. *Sellar* (1880), 5 Q. B. D. 286.

[3] (1885), 10 App. Cas. 404.

[4] It is important to note that this Common Law rule does not apply in cases where the York-Antwerp Rules operate. See Rule X in Appendix G, *post*.

[5] *Schloss* v. *Heriot* (1863), 14 C. B. N. S. 59.

obeying the order had no opportunity of exercising their own judgment or discretion.[1]

But unjustified deviation will debar the shipowner from claiming a general contribution, unless the cargo-owner has elected to affirm the contract.[2]

In *Morrison S.S. Co., Ltd.* v. *Greystoke Castle (Cargo Owners)*,[3] the question arose whether the master of a ship incurs general average expenditure as agent of the ship alone or as agent also of the cargo-owners. In this case,

Two ships collided, one being one-fourth to blame and the other three-fourths. The latter had to put into port, and a general average expenditure was incurred. The owners of cargo on that ship became liable to their shipowners for a general average contribution, and brought an action against the owners of the other ship, claiming (*inter alia*) one-fourth of this contribution. *Held*, that the claim succeeded. The obligation of the cargo-owners to contribute to general average expenditure arose from the act of the master in incurring that expenditure on their behalf. Had the cargo-owners been merely liable to indemnify their shipowners, only the latter could have sued.

Under the York-Antwerp Rules,

"When a ship shall have entered a port or place or refuge, or shall have returned to her port or place of loading in consequence of accident, sacrifice or other extraordinary circumstances which render that necessary for the common safety, the expenses of entering such port or place shall be admitted as general average; and when she shall have sailed thence with her original cargo, or part of it, the corresponding expenses of leaving such port or place consequent upon such entry or return shall likewise be admitted as general average."[4]

Further, they state that,

"The cost of handling on board or discharging cargo, fuel or stores whether at a port or place of loading, call or refuge, shall be admitted as general average when the handling or discharge was necessary for

---

[1] *Athel Line, Ltd.* v. *Liverpool and London War Risks Insurance Association, Ltd.*, [1944] 1 All E. R. 46; [1944] 1 K. B. 87.

[2] *Hain S.S. Co.* v. *Tate and Lyle*, [1936] 2 All E. R. 597.

[3] [1946] 2 All E. R. 696; [1947] A. C. 265.

[4] Rule X (a).

the common safety or to enable damage to the ship caused by sacrifice or accident to be repaired, if the repairs were necessary for the safe prosecution of the voyage."[1]

The wages and maintenance of the crew and other expenses incurred in entering the port of refuge and in staying there are also allowed as general average expenditure under the Rules.[2]

Any extra expense incurred in place of another expense which would have been allowable as general average shall be deemed to be general average and so allowed without regard to the saving, if any, to other interests, but only up to the amount of the general expense avoided.[3]

The York-Antwerp Rules provide that,[4]

"Only such loss, damages or expenses which are the direct consequence of the general average act shall be allowed as general average."

Thus, in *Australian Coastal Shipping Commission* v. *Green,*[5]

A vessel was in distress and a tug was employed to tow her to a port of safety. The towage contract included a clause whereby the owners of the vessel agreed to indemnify the tugowners for any loss of the tug. The tow rope parted and fouled the tug's propellers, and the tug became a total loss. The tugowners claimed damages from the owners of the vessel, who incurred expenses in defending the action.
Held, these expenses were general average expenditure, for the towage contract was a "general average act" under Rule A of the York-Antwerp Rules 1950, and the expenses were the direct consequence of such general average act.

---

[1] Rule X (b).
[2] Rule XI.
[3] Rule F. See *Western Canada Steamship Co., Ltd.* v. *Canadian Commercial Corporation*, [1960] 2 Lloyd's Rep. 313 (Supreme Court of Canada) (replacement of broken tailshaft flown out by air as extra expense).
[4] Rule C.
[5] [1971] 1 All E.R. 353, C. A. See the judgment of Lord DENNING, M.R., *ibid.*, at pp. 358–359. See further, *Federal Commerce and Navigation Co., Ltd.* v. *Eisenerz G.m.b.H. : The "Oak Hill"*, [1975] 1 Lloyd's Rep. 105, Supreme Court of Canada, where the expenses incurred in handling cargo which was unloaded after a vessel had stranded was held to be a "direct consequence" of the general average act. But the negligence of the master and of the surveyors and of the stevedores who caused the damage to the cargo was not attributable to the general average act and was not the "direct consequence" of it. (See the judgment of RITCHIE, J., *ibid.*, at p. 114.)

DAMAGE DONE TO PROPERTY OF THIRD PARTIES

Damage done to the property of persons *not* concerned in the adventure can be the subject of general average. Thus, in *Austin Friars* v. *Spillers and Bakers*,[1]

a ship had been stranded and was leaking badly. The master and pilot knew that in taking the ship into a dock they were liable to cause damage. Nevertheless, their action was *held* to be reasonable and prudent in the interests of ship and cargo, and the damage done to the dock to be the subject of general average.

ADJUSTMENT OF GENERAL AVERAGE CONTRIBUTION

Unless it is specially agreed otherwise, the adjustment of the claims to contribution takes place after the conclusion of the voyage and is governed by the law of the place of delivery of the cargo.[2] The shipowner cannot claim contribution from the cargo-owners if, after general average expenditure has been incurred, the ship and cargo are lost before the conclusion of the voyage.[3]

The York-Antwerp Rules provide that,

"General average shall be adjusted as regards both loss and contribution upon the basis of values at the time and place when and where the adventure ends."[4]

Further they state that,

"Repairs to be allowed in general average shall not be subject to deductions in respect of "new for old" where old material or parts are replaced by new unless the ship is over fifteen years old in which case there shall be a deduction of one third. The deductions shall be regulated by the age of the ship from the 31st December of the year of completion of construction to the date of the general average act, except for insulation, life and similar boats, communications and navigational apparatus and equipment, machinery and boilers for which the deductions shall be regulated by the age of the particular parts to which they apply.

---

[1] [1915] 3 K. B. 586.
[2] *Simonds* v. *White* (1824), 2 B. & C. 805.
[3] *Chellew* v. *Royal Commission on Sugar Supply*, [1921] 2 K. B. 627; affirmed, [1922] 1 K. B. 12.
[4] Rule G.

The deductions shall be made only from the cost of the new material or parts when finished and ready to be installed in the ship.

No deduction shall be made in respect of provisions, stores, anchors and chain cables.

Drydock and slipway dues and costs of shifting the ship shall be allowed in full.

The costs of cleaning, painting or coating of bottom shall not be allowed in general average unless the bottom has been painted or coated within the twelve months preceding the date of the general average act in which case one half of such costs shall be allowed."[1]

They also provide that,

"The contribution to a general average shall be made upon the actual net value of the property at the termination of the adventure except that the value of cargo shall be the value at the time of discharge, ascertained from the commercial invoice rendered to the receiver or if there is no such invoice from the shipped value. The value of the cargo shall include the cost of insurance and freight unless and insofar as such freight is at the risk of interests other than the cargo, deducting therefrom any loss or damage suffered by the cargo prior to or at the time of discharge. The value of the ship shall be assessed without taking into account the beneficial or detrimental effect of any demise or time charterparty to which the ship may be committed.

To these values shall be added the amount made good as general average for property sacrificed, if not already included, deduction being made from the freight and passage money at risk of such charges and crew's wages as would not have been incurred in earning the freight had the ship and cargo been totally lost at the date of the general average act and have not been allowed as general average; deduction being also made from the value of the property of all extra charges incurred in respect thereof subsequently to the general average act, exept such charges as are allowed in general average.

Where cargo is sold short of destination, however, it shall contribute upon the actual net proceeds of sale, with the addition of any amount made good as general average.

Passenger's luggage and personal effects not shipped under Bill of Lading shall not contribute in general average."[2]

---

[1] Rule XIII.
[2] Rule XVII.

CHAPTER 10

Demurrage
and Despatch Money

(A) DEMURRAGE

It is first necessary to define "demurrage" and "damages for detention" and to show the difference between them. A number of lay days are allowed to the charterer. It is important to notice when these commence, and to notice the effect of lay time being fixed. It is necessary to ascertain when loading is complete, what the rate of demurrage is and the persons by whom demurrage is payable.

THE DIFFERENCE BETWEEN DEMURRAGE AND DAMAGES FOR DETENTION

A charter-party generally fixes a number of days called "lay days" in which the ship is to be loaded or discharged, as the case may be.

"Demurrage" is a sum named in the charter-party to be paid by the charterer as *liquidated* damages for delay beyond such lay days.[1]

The shipowner is entitled to sue for "damages for detention" if

   (i) the lay days have expired and demurrage has not been provided for; *or*

  (ii) the time for loading or discharge is not agreed, and a reasonable time for loading or discharge has expired; *or*

---

[1] In the United States it has been held in *Randall* v. *Sprague*, (1896) 74 F. 27 that demurrage is a form of liquidated damages payable whether or not the shipowner suffers actual damage. But later cases do not support this view: *The "S.S. Hartismere"*, (1937) 18 F. Supp. 767; *D'Amico Mediterranean Pacific Line Inc.* v. *Proctor & Gamble Manufacturing Co.: The "Giovanni D'Amico"*, [1975] 1 Lloyd's Rep. 202, District Court, Northern District of California.

(iii) demurrage is only to be paid for an agreed number of days and a further delay takes place.

In the case of a claim for "damages for detention" the damages are *unliquidated, i.e.* for the Court to assess what loss has been suffered by the shipowner by his vessel being detained in port. As a general rule the measure of such damages is the rate agreed on for demurrage, if any.[1] But where a breach of some other term of the contract, such as the obligation to load a full and complete cargo, is thereby caused, any additional damage referable to such breach may also be recovered, unless, on the true construction of the contract, the shipowner is precluded from claiming more than the agreed rate.[2]

THE NUMBER OF LAY DAYS

Where the charter-party names a number of "days" or "running days", these mean consecutive days including Sundays and holidays.[3] The word "day" usually means a calendar day, and not a period of 24 hours calculated from the moment of the vessel's arrival.[4]

If the term "working day" is used, this means the days on which work is normally done in the port,[5] and "weather working

---

[1] *Inverkip S.S. Co.* v. *Bunge & Co.*, [1917] 2 K. B. 193; *Suisse Atlantique Société D'Armement Maritime S.A.* v. *N.V. Rotterdamsche Kolen Centrale*, [1966] 2 All E. R. 61; [1967] A. C. 361, H. L.

[2] *Akt. Reidar* v. *Arcos*, [1927] 1 K. B. 352.

[3] *Nielsen* v. *Wait* (1885), 16 Q. B. D. 67, at p. 72 (*per* Lord E[1]HER, M.R.).

[4] *The Katy*, [1895] P. 56, C. A.

[5] *Westfal-Larsen (A/S)* v. *Russo-Norwegian Transport Co.* (1931), 40 Ll. L. Rep. 259; *Reardon Smith Line, Ltd.* v. *Ministry of Agriculture, Fisheries and Food*, [1963] 1 All E. R. 545; [1963] A. C. 691, H. L.; *The Chief Controller of Chartering of the Government of India* v. *Central Gulf Steamship Corporation*, [1968] 2 Lloyd's Rep. 173, Q. B. D. (Commercial Court), where it was held that Saturday in the port of Lake Charles, Louisiana, was a working although not a regular working day (see the judgment of DONALDSON, J., *ibid.*, at p. 179); *Primula Compania Naviera S.A.* v. *Finagrain Cie Commerciale Agricole et Financière S.A.: The "Point Clear"*, [1975] 2 Lloyd's Rep. 243, Q. B. D. (Commercial Court), where it was held that a Saturday in the port of Rotterdam counted as a lay day; *Tramp Shipping Corporation* v. *Greenwich Marine Inc.: The "New Horizon"*, [1975] 2 Lloyd's Rep. 314, C. A., where it was the custom for crane and sucker drivers, if requested to do so by the stevedore companies, to work in shifts for 24 hours a day.

days" are working days on which the weather allows work to be done.[1]

Thus, in *Compania Naviera Azuero S.A.* v. *British Oil and Cake Mills, Ltd.*,[2]

A charter-party provided that a certain number of "weather working days" should be allowed for discharge. There were several periods during which rain was heavy enough to stop or prevent discharge. In fact, however, no unloading was prevented, for the charterer had not planned to unload during these periods even if the weather had been fine. *Held*, that in calculating the lay time deductions should be made in respect of the periods in which the rain fell, for a "weather working day" was to be determined solely by the state of the weather on that day, although no plans had been made for working at the relevant time.

A reasonable apportionment of the day must be made according to the incidence of the weather upon the length of day that the parties were working or might be expected to have been working at the time.[3] Such apportionment is entirely a question of fact.[4]

Sometimes the number of lay days allowed is not directly specified in the charter-party, but has to be calculated by reference to a daily rate of loading or discharge, *e.g.* 500 tons of the cargo per weather working day.[5]

COMMENCEMENT OF THE LAY DAYS

Usually[6] the lay days commence when:

(1) the vessel is an "arrived ship";

---

[1] *Alvion S.S. Corporation of Panama* v. *Galban Lobo Trading Co. S.A. of Havana*, [1954] 3 All E. R. 324; [1955] 1 Q. B. 430; *Compania Naviera Azuero S.A.* v. *British Oil and Cake Mills, Ltd.*, [1957] 2 All E. R. 241; [1957] 2 Q. B. 293: *Compania Crystal de Vapores of Panama* v. *Herman and Mohatta* (*India*), *Ltd.*, [1958] 2 All E. R. 508; [1958] 2 Q. B. 196.

[2] *Supra.*

[3] *Reardon Smith Line, Ltd.* v. *Ministry of Agriculture, Fisheries and Food*, [1963] 1 All E. R. 545; [1963] A. C. 691, H. L.

[4] *Ibid.*

[5] See *Compania de Navigacion Zita S.A.* v. *Louis Dreyfus & Compagnie*, [1953] 2 All E. R. 1359, where the cargo was to be loaded "at an average rate of not less than 150 tons per available working hatch per day"; *Lodza Compania de Navigacione S.A.* v. *Government of Ceylon, The "Theraios"*, [1971] 1 Lloyd's Rep. 209, C. A., where the cargo was to be loaded "at the average rate of 120 metric tons per hatch per weather working day".

[6] But sometimes the charter-party states that "time lost in waiting for a berth is to count as loading time", *i.e.* even before the vessel is an "arrived

ship". See *North River Freighters* v. *H. E. The President of India*, [1956] 1 All
E. R. 50; [1956] 1 Q. B. 333; *Roland-Linie Schiffahrt* v. *Spillers, Ltd.*, [1956] 3
All E. R. 383; [1957] 1 Q. B. 109; *Carga del sur Compania Naviera, S.A.* v.
Ross T. Smyth & Co. Ltd., *The Seafort*, [1962] 2 Lloyd's Rep. 147. See further,
Sociedad Carga Oceanica S.A. v. *Idolinoele Vertriebagesellschaft m.b.H.*, *The
Angelos Lusis*, [1964] 2 Lloyd's Rep. 28, Q. B. D. (Commercial Court), where
the charterers' obligation was to nominate a "reachable place where the vessel
could load" at the point whether within or outside the fiscal or commercial
limits of the port where, in the absence of such nomination, she would be held
up; *Metals & Ropes Co., Ltd.* v. *Filia Compania Limitada, The Vastric,*
[1966] 2 Lloyd's Rep. 219, Q. B. D. (Commercial Court), where it was held
that time ran from the arrival of the vessel outside the port of Genoa, and
not from the earliest time discharging time would have commenced if a berth
had been available; *Compania Naviera Termar S.A.* v. *Tradax Export S.A.,*
[1966] 1 Lloyd's Rep. 566, H. L., where it was held that laytime started when
the vessel reached the anchorage off Spurnhead, and there was nothing to
stop laytime continuing except a provision excepting time which was occupied
in shifting her from the anchorage to her discharging berth at Hull; *Inca
Compania Naviera S.A. and Commercial and Maritime Enterprises Evanghelos
P. Nomikos S.A.* v. *Mofinol Inc., The President Brand*, [1967] 2 Lloyd's Rep.
338, Q. B. D. (Commercial Court), where it was held that laytime started
when the vessel arrived at the pilot station at Lourenco Marques, even though
that station was not within the commercial limits of the port; *President of
India* v. *Edina Compania Naviera S.A., The Stamatios G. Embiricos*, [1965]
1 Lloyd's Rep. 574, Q. B. D. (Commercial Court), where it was held that
overtime worked before laytime started was to count as laytime; *Navico A. G.*
v. *Vrontados Naftiki Etairia P.E.: The "Costis"*, [1968] 1 Lloyd's Rep. 379,
Q. B. D. (Commercial Court), where the question was whether the period
from the anchoring of the vessel off the port to the giving of notice of readiness
to load counted as time used in loading; *Ionian Navigation Co. Inc.* v. *Atlantic
Shipping Co. S.A.: The "Loucas N"*, [1971] 1 Lloyd's Rep. 215, C. A., where
the time lost in waiting for berths at Caen and Houston counted as loading
time, and the "time lost" provisions in the charter-party were independent
of a strike clause; *Shipping Developments Corporation S.A.* v. *V/O Sojuzneftexport, The "Delian Spirit"*, [1971] 1 Lloyd's Rep. 506, C.A., where the charterers were to indicate a place or dock reachable on the vessel's arrival and it
was held that they were entitled to their full laytime from the moment when
notice of readiness to load and after the expiry of the laytime were liable for
demurrage, but were not additionally liable for damages in failing to indicate the
place or dock at which she was to load. See the judgment of Lord DENNING,
M.R., *ibid.*, at p. 510; *Aldebaran Compania Maritima S.A.* v. *Aussenhandel
A.G.: The "Darrah"*, (1975), *Times*, 21st November, C. A., where it was held
that a clause stating "time lost in waiting for berth to count as lay time" was
not independent of the laytime provisions; *Agios Stylianos Compania Naviera
S.A.* v. *Maritime Associates International, Ltd. Lagos: The "Agios Stylianos"*,
[1975] 1 Lloyd's Rep. 426, Q. B. D. (Commercial Court), where the question
was whether the charterer of a vessel carrying cement which was overstowed
by cargo belonging to a third party was liable for the time lost by the vessel in
waiting for a berth; *Nea Tyhi Maritime Co., Ltd. of Piraeus* v. *Compagnie
Grainière S.A. of Zurich: The "Finix"*, [1975] 2 Lloyd's Rep. 415, Q. B. D.
(Commercial Court), where the word "berth" was held to mean the relevant
berth at which the vessel was to discharge.

(2) she is ready to load or discharge; and

(3) the shipowner has given notice of readiness to load.[1]

But no notice of readiness to *discharge* is necessary,[2] unless there is an express provision to the contrary in the charter-party.

There is an implied term that the charterer must act with reasonable dispatch and in accordance with the ordinary practice of the port in doing those acts which he must do to enable the vessel to become an arrived ship.[3] The burden of proving breach of this term lies on the shipowners.[4]

Whether a ship is an "arrived ship" will depend on whether the charter-party is:

(a) a port charter-party; or

(b) a berth charter-party.

(1) An "Arrived Ship"

(a) *Port charter-parties.* The rule is that where the charter-party names a *port* simply, without further particularity or qualification, the ship is an "arrived ship" when, if she cannot proceed immediately to a berth, she has reached a position within the port where she is at the immediate and effective disposition of the charterer. If she is at the place where waiting ships usually lie, she is in such a position unless there are some extraordinary circumstances, proof of which lies on the charterer. If the vessel is waiting at some other place in the port, it is for the shipowner to prove that she is as fully at the disposition of the charterer as she would be if she were in the vicinity of the berth for loading or discharge.[5]

---

[1] See p. 114, *ante.*

[2] See pp. 128–129, *ante.*

[3] *Sunbeam Shipping Co., Ltd.* v. *President of India : The "Atlantic Sunbeam"*, [1973] 1 Lloyd's Rep. 482, Q. B. D. (Commercial Court) at p. 488 (*per* KERR, J.).

[4] *Ibid.*, at p. 488 (*per* KERR, J.).

[5] *E. L. Oldendorff & Co. G.m.b.H.* v. *Tradax Export S.A. : The "Johanna Oldendorff"*, [1973] 2 Lloyd's Rep. 285, H. L. (See especially the judgment of Lord REID, *ibid.*, at p. 291, and that of Lord DILHORNE, *ibid.*, at p. 299.)

Thus, in *E. L. Oldendorff & Co. G.m.b.H.* v. *Tradax Export S.A. : The "Johanna Oldendorff"*,[1]

A vessel carrying grain under a port charter-party anchored at the Bar anchorage at Liverpool. The anchorage was 17 miles from the usual discharging berth, but was the usual place where grain vessels lay whilst awaiting a berth. *Held*, by the House of Lords that she was an "arrived ship" when she reached the anchorage, for she was then at the immediate and effective disposition of the charterer.

Again, where a vessel reached the intersection anchorage at Buenos Aires, and was at a place where vessels customarily waited their turn for admission to a berth by the port authorities, she was held to be an "arrived ship".[2]

If the voyage has not ended and the vessel is not waiting, she is not an "arrived ship" even though she may be in a commercial and legal sense within the port when she is off a quay.

Thus, in *Federal Commerce and Navigation Co., Ltd.* v. *Tradax Export S.A. : The "Maratha Envoy"*[3]

A vessel carrying grain anchored at the Weser Light vessel on December 8, 1970, while waiting for a berth at the port of Brake. On that day and she made an excursion to Brake, turned there and went back to the light vessel. On December 12 she made a similar excursion, turned at Brake and went back to the light vessel. *Held*, by Q. B. D. (Commercial Court), that she was not an arrived ship on December 8 or December 12 for the voyage had not ended nor was she waiting. She had merely been on a trip to Brake and back to the light vessel, with no pause other than such as was inherent in the movement of turning. It was immaterial that she was in the port of Brake in a commercial and legal sense when she was off a quay.

If the charterers fail to nominate the port of discharge within the time limited by the charter-party, there is no implied term

---

[1] [1973] 2 Lloyd's Rep. 285, H. L., overruling *Sociedad Financiera de Bienes Raices S.A.* v. *Agrimpex Hungarian Trading Co. for Agricultural Products*, [1960] 2 All E. R. 578; [1961] A. C. 135, H. L. All cases concerning an "arrived ship" decided before 1973 must be read in the light of *E. L. Oldendorff & Co. G.m.b.H.* v. *Tradax Export S.A. : The "Johanna Oldendorff"* (*supra*).

[2] *Venizelos A.N.E. of Athens* v. *Société Commerciale de Cereales et Financière S.A. of Zurich : The "Prometheus"*, [1974] 1 Lloyd's Rep. 350, Q. B. D. (Commercial Court) (See the judgment of MOCATTA, J., *ibid.*, at p. 352.)

[3] [1975] 2 Lloyd's Rep. 222, Q. B. D. (Commercial Court). (See the judgment of DONALDSON, J., *ibid.*, at p. 233.)

that the master may make the nomination himself, and thus cause the vessel to be an "arrived ship".

Thus, in *Zim Israel Navigation Co., Ltd.* v. *Tradax Export S.A. : The "Timna"*,[1]

The charterers were under a duty to nominate a port of discharge. On December 31, 1968 they told the master to "proceed destination Weser". On January 2, 1969, the vessel reached the Weser light vessel, which was about 25 miles off the mouth of the River Weser. No further orders were received so the master moved her to Bremerhaven on January 3, and gave notice of readiness to discharge.
Held, the vessel was never an "arrived ship" at Bremerhaven, and the notice of readiness to discharge was invalid.

(b) *Berth charter-parties.* But where the contract expressly reserves to the charterer the right to name a particular dock or berth, the lay days do not begin until the ship has arrived at that dock or berth. Thus, in *Stag Line, Ltd.* v. *Board of Trade*,[2]

a charter-party required a vessel to proceed to "one or two safe ports East Canada or Newfoundland, place or places as ordered by charterers and/or shippers". She was ordered to the port of Miramichi, and on arrival there was told that she would be required to load at Millbank, a place within the port. As there was not then a berth for her she had to wait for six days, in respect of which the shipowners claimed demurrage. *Held*, that the charter-party gave the charterers an express right to nominate a "place", meaning a berth within the port; therefore the vessel did not become an "arrived ship" until arriving at the berth, and demurrage was not payable.

(2) Ready to Load or Discharge

It should be noted that lay days do not begin to run until the ship is, so far as she is concerned, ready to receive or discharge cargo, unless she would have been ready but for the charterer's default.[3] Hence the charterer is not liable for delay where the

---

[1] *Zim Israel Navigation Co., Ltd.* v. *Tradax Export S.A., The "Timna"*, [1970] 2 Lloyd's Rep. 409, Q. B. D. (Commercial Court). See the judgment of DONALDSON, J., *ibid.*, at p. 413. In the Court of Appeal this aspect of the case was not gone into, and the Court decided the case on other grounds: [1971] 2 Lloyd's Rep. 91, C. A. See the judgment of Lord DENNING, M.R., *ibid.*, at p. 94.

[2] [1950] 1 All E. R. 1105; [1950] 2 K. B. 194.

[3] *Vergottis* v. *Wm. Cory & Son*, [1926] 2 K. B. 344.

ship, in common with all other vessels coming from a prescribed area, has to go into quarantine on her arrival at the port of loading or discharge.[1] But if at the port of discharge the ship comes within quarantine regulations on account of the cargo she is carrying, presumably the charterer is liable. At any rate he is liable for delay in obtaining the necessary customs-house papers for discharging, when the delay arises from the fact that special papers are required for the particular cargo carried.[2]

A vessel is not ready to load[3] or discharge[4] until she is ready in all her holds to give the charterer complete control of every part of her which is available for cargo.

The mere fact that free pratique has not been obtained does not mean that the ship is not ready to load, if, in fact, free pratique can be obtained at any time and without the possibility of delaying the loading.

Thus, in *Shipping Developments Corporation S.A.* v. *V/O Sojuzneftexport: The "Delian Spirit"*,[5]

A vessel reached the commercial area of Tuapse at 0100 hours on February 19. Her master gave notice of readiness to load. She was directed to

---

[1] *White* v. *Winchester S.S. Co.* (1886), 23 Sc. L. R. 342. Nor is he liable if the port which he nominates is strike-bound: *Reardon Smith Line, Ltd.* v. *Ministry of Agriculture, Fisheries and Food*, [1961] 2 All E. R. 577; [1962] 1 Q. B. 42, C. A.

[2] *Hill* v. *Idle* (1815), 4 Camp. 327: *Sociedad Financiera de Bienes Raices S. A.* v. *Agrimpex Hungarian Trading Co. for Agricultural Products*, [1960] 2 All E. R. 578, H. L. (failure to obtain berthing permit); *Sunbeam Shipping Co., Ltd.* v. *President of India: The "Atlantic Sunbeam"*, [1973] 1 Lloyd's Rep. 482, Q. B. D. (Commercial Court) (failure to obtain a document at Calcutta called a jetty challan).

[3] *Armement Adolf Deppe* v. *John Robinson & Co., Ltd.*, [1917] 2 K. B. 204; *N.V. Bodewes Scheepswerven and N.V. Kuva* v. *Highways Construction, Ltd., The "Jan Herman"*, [1966] 1 Lloyd's Rep. 402 (Mayor's and City of London Court); *Compania de Naviera Nedelka S.A.* v. *Tradax International S.A.: The "Tres Flores"*, [1973] 2 Lloyd's Rep. 247, C. A., where the holds of the vessel were infested and required to be fumigated.

[4] *Government of Ceylon* v. *Societe Franco-Tunisienne d'Armement-Tunis*, [1960] 3 All E. R. 797 (charterer's cargo overstowed by other cargo loaded en route); *Agios Stylianos Compania Naviera S.A.* v. *Maritime Associates International, Ltd. Lagos: The "Agios Stylianos"*, [1975] 1 Lloyd's Rep. 426, Q. B. D. (Commercial Court), where a cargo of cement was overstowed by a cargo of vehicles, and it was held that laytime did not begin to run until the cement was accessible.

[5] [1971] 1 Lloyd's Rep. 506, C. A. See the judgment of Lord DENNING, M.R., *ibid.*, at p. 510.

her berth on February 24 and arrived there at 1320 hours. Free pratique was granted at 1600 hours. Loading began at 2150 hours.
Held, the notice of readiness to load was valid because it could have been obtained at any time without the possibility of delaying the loading.

(3) Notice of Readiness

A clause[1] usually provides that the lay days are to commence after the expiry of a specified time after the giving of the notice of readiness to load or discharge, *e.g.*

"Time to commence at 1 p.m. if notice of readiness to load is given before noon and at 6 a.m. next working day if notice given during office hours after noon".[2]

A notice of readiness is not valid unless it indicates that the vessel is ready to load or discharge as the case may be, at the time at which it is given. It is insufficient if the notice merely indicates that she will be ready at a future time.

Thus, in *Christensen* v. *Hindustan Steel, Ltd.*,[3]

At 0900 hours on October 28, 1967 the master gave notice that the vessel would be ready to load on October 29.
Held, that the notice was invalid even if the vessel was in fact ready at the time at which it was given. It was one of anticipated readiness and impliedly reported to the charterers that she was not yet ready.[4]

---

[1] See, *e.g.* "Gencon" form, clause 3 (loading) and clause 4 (discharge) (Appendix B.)

[2] For a case where the lay days for loading and discharging had already expired before the vessel arrived at the discharging port, and it was held that the vessel was on demurrage immediately on her arrival there irrespective of the giving of notice of readiness to discharge, see *R. Pagnan & Fratelli* v. *Tradax Export S.A.*, [1969] 2 Lloyd's Rep. 150, Q. B. D. (Commercial Court). See the judgment of DONALDSON, J., *ibid.*, at p. 154. For a case where notice of readiness to load was given on a public holiday, see *Pacific Carriers Corporation* v. *Tradax Export S.A.*, The *"North King"*, [1971] 2 Lloyd's Rep. 460, Q.B.D. (Commercial Court). For a case where the notice of readiness to discharge was invalid because the vessel had not been entered at the Customs House, see *Venore Transportation Co.* v. *President of India : The "Venore"*, [1973] 1 Lloyd's Rep. 494, District Court, Southern District of New York.

[3] [1971] 1 Lloyd's Rep. 395, Q. B. D. (Commercial Court).

[4] See the judgment of DONALDSON, J., *ibid.*, at pp. 399–400. See further, *Compania de Naviera Nedelka S.A.* v. *Tradax Internacional S.A. : The "Tres Flores"*, [1973] 2 Lloyd's Rep. 247, C. A., where the notice of readiness to load was invalid because it was given at a time when the holds of the vessel were infested and required to be fumigated. (See the judgment of Lord DENNING, M.R., *ibid.*, at p. 249.)

EFFECT OF LAY TIME NOT BEING FIXED

The general principle is that where no definite period of lay days has been agreed on, the charterer is only bound to load and unload the ship within a reasonable time. This obligation is not very stringent, for it allows extraordinary circumstances to be taken into consideration. Thus, in *Hick* v. *Raymond*,[1]

where no time was fixed for the unloading, and the unloading was delayed owing to a strike of dock labourers, it was *held* that the shipowners were not entitled to damages for detention.

But a clause in a charter-party stating that the vessel is to be discharged "with customary steamship dispatch" does not make the charter-party into a fixed lay time charter-party for the purpose of the principle set out above.[2]

EFFECT OF LAY TIME BEING FIXED

Where the time for loading or unloading is fixed by agreement, the only[3] cases in which the charterer is excused for his failure to load or discharge the ship within such time are:

(1) where the delay is due to the shipowner's fault, or that of his servants or agents acting within their authority;[4]

or (2) where the cause of the delay falls within an exceptions clause.

---

[1] [1893] A. C. 22. See further, *Hellenic Lines, Ltd.* v. *Embassy of Pakistan*, [1973] 1 Lloyd's Rep. 263, U.S. Court of Appeals, Second Circuit, where in a freight contract governed by English law it was held that where no time was fixed for the discharge of the cargo, a reasonable time was implied, and "reasonable time" meant what was reasonable in the circumstances then existing. (See the judgment of TIMBERS, Ct. J., *ibid.*, at p. 365.)

[2] *Hulthen* v. *Stewart & Co.*, [1903] A. C. 389, H. L.

[3] See *Benson* v. *Blunt* (1841), 1 Q. B. 870.

[4] But where there has been a deviation, unless the deviation has been waived, the shipowner cannot rely on a provision in a charter-party for loading or unloading in a fixed time: *United States Shipping Board* v. *Bunge y Born Limitada Sociedad*, [1925] All E. R. Rep. 173, H. L. On the effect of deviation, see further *Hain S.S. Co., Ltd.* v. *Tate and Lyle, Ltd.*, [1936] 2 All E. R. 597. See pp. 22–23 *ante*.

(1) Fault of the Shipowner

Where, owing to the voluntary act of the owner, the ship ceases for a period to be ready to receive cargo, such period is excluded in calculating demurrage, *e.g.* if for his own convenience she leaves the berth for the purposes of bunkering.[1]

Again, in *Gem Shipping Co. of Monrovia* v. *Babanaft (Lebanon) S.A.R.L.: The "Fontevivo"*[2]

A vessel arrived at Lattakia, Syria. After her arrival there was aircraft activity near the port. Syrian anti-aircraft guns went into action. The incident did not exceed one hour. About 5 hours later the master yielded to pressure from the crew and decided to leave the port.
Held, by Q. B. D. (Commercial Court) that, on the evidence, the master's action was unjustified and that time did not run against laytime during the period of the vessel's absence from the port.

On the other hand, in *Houlder* v. *Weir*,[3]

during the course of unloading it was necessary to take in ballast to keep the ship upright. This caused the agreed time for discharge to be exceeded. It was *held* that taking in ballast could not be regarded as a default on the part of the shipowner and the charterers were therefore liable for the delay.

(2) Exceptions Clause in Charterer's Favour

Where the time for loading is fixed, and the lay days have once started to run, time will continue to run against the charterer, even though the ship is, by circumstances altogether beyond the control of either party, forced to leave port before loading is completed, unless the ship's departure was due to an exception of which the charterer can claim the benefit.[4]

An exceptions clause protected the charterers in *Steamship "Induna" Co., Ltd.* v. *British Phosphate Commissioners: The Loch Dee*,[5]

---

[1] In *Re Ropner Shipping Co.*, [1927] 1 K. B. 879.
[2] [1975] 1 Lloyd's Rep. 339, Q. B. D. (Commercial Court). (See the judgment of DONALDSON, J., *ibid.*, at p. 343.)
[3] [1905] 2 K. B. 267.
[4] *Cantiere Navale* v. *Russian Agency*, [1925] 2 K. B. 172.
[5] [1949] 1 All E. R. 522; [1949] 2 K. B. 430.

By the terms of a charter-party charterers undertook to discharge cargo at New Zealand ports at the rate of 1,500 tons per working day of twenty-four consecutive hours and to pay demurrage if the time allowed for discharge was exceeded. By an exception, demurrage was not to accrue in the event of delay by reason of, *inter alia*, "intervention of constituted authorities or from any cause whatsoever beyond the control of the charterers". At the time the charter-party was entered into, but unknown to either charterers or shipowners, an order was in force in New Zealand which made it illegal to work between 9 p.m. and 8 a.m., and thus rendered it impossible for the ship to discharge at the prescribed rate. Delay took place, and the shipowners claimed demurrage. *Held*, that the shipowners' claim failed because the exception clause applied.

Again, in *The Amstelmolen*,[1]

Where the charter-party provided that the charterer was not to be liable in the event of a delay caused by an "obstruction", it was *held* that this exception covered a delay caused by other vessels occupying all available berths and so preventing the ship from loading.[2]

If the charter-party states that time is not to count if the cargo cannot be loaded because of obstructions, and the charterer has made all arrangements to load at a customary berth but has not nominated such berth before the vessel is an "arrived ship", he is entitled, on the berth of his choice being obstructed, to a reasonable time within which to make up his mind to load at an alternative berth if one is available and it is commercially practicable to use it.[3]

Once a vessel is on demurrage the exceptions clauses relieving a charterer from liability for delay caused, *e.g.* by a strike do not apply, unless there are clear words to that effect.[4]

Thus, in *Compania Naviera Aeolus S.A.* v. *Union of India*,[5]

---

[1] [1961] 2 Lloyd's Rep. 1, C. A.

[2] In *Ionian Navigation Co. Inc.* v. *Atlantic Shipping Co. S.A.: The "Loucas N"*, [1971] 1 Lloyd's Rep. 215, C. A., Lord DENNING, M.R., said (*ibid.*, at p. 218) that the decision was an unsatisfactory one "which merchants and lawyers try to get out of".

[3] *Venizelos A.N.E. of Athens* v. *Société Commerciale de Cereales et Financière S.A. of Zurich: The "Prometheus"*, [1974] 1 Lloyd's Rep. 350, Q. B. D. (Commercial Court). (See the judgment of MOCATTA, J., *ibid.*, at p. 356.)

[4] *Compania Naviera Aeolus S.A.* v. *Union of India*, [1962] 3 All E. R. 670; [1964] A. C. 868, H. L.

[5] [1962] 3 All E. R. 670; [1964] A. C. 868, H. L.

A vessel had been chartered under a charter-party which contained a strike clause stating that the time for discharging should not count against the charterers during the continuance of a strike. The vessel began to discharge the cargo, but after the lay time had expired a strike took place which interrupted further unloading. *Held*, that the charterers could not rely on the strike clause because it was not sufficiently clearly worded to have the effect of relieving them from the payment of demurrage. Consequently they had to pay demurrage for the whole period after the lay days had expired.

THE COMPLETION OF THE LOADING

Where demurrage is claimed, it may become necessary to decide at what precise time loading was completed. The general rule has been stated as follows: "In most cases, the mere reception or dumping down of the cargo on the ship does not involve completion of loading, because . . . the operation of loading involves all that is required to put the cargo in a condition in which it can be carried".[1] So, in *Argonaut Navigation Co., Ltd.* v. *Ministry of Food*,[2]

where it was necessary, both for the safety of the ship and also to comply with regulations in force at the loading port, for grain carried in the 'tween decks to be stowed in bags, and loose wheat was loaded for bagging on board, it was *held* that loading was not completed until the grain had been bagged and stowed.

If the charterer has loaded the vessel before the lay days expire, he is not entitled to delay her sailing by failing to tender the bills of lading for signature and will be liable in damages if he does so.

Thus, in *Nolisement (Owners)* v. *Bunge and Born*,[3]

A vessel was loaded 19 days before the expiration of the lay days. The charterers could not make up their minds as to what port of call to order her to. So they did not tender immediately the bills of lading for signature by the master, and they did not do so for another 3 days, by which time they had settled the name of the port of call. The vessel was accordingly delayed for these 3 days, and the shipowners sued the charterers for

---

[1] *Svenssons Travaruaktiebolog* v. *Cliffe S.S. Co.*, [1932] 1 K. B. 490, *per* WRIGHT, J., at p. 494.

[2] [1949] 1 All E. R. 160; [1949] 1 K. B. 572.

[3] [1917] 1 K. B. 160.

2 days' delay (since the charterers were entitled by the terms of the charter-party to keep the vessel waiting for 24 hours after loading for the purpose of settling accounts). *Held*, that the action succeeded, for once the vessel was loaded the charterers were under a duty to present the bills of lading for signature.

But the charterer is not obliged to load in a lesser time than the laytime, even if this is possible. Consequently, so long as loading has not been completed, the charterer is entitled to delay the vessel's sailing until the expiration of the laytime.[1]

Thus, in *Margaronis Navigation Agency, Ltd.* v. *Henry W. Peabody & Co. of London, Ltd.*,[2]

The charterer had loaded 12,588 tons, 4 cwt. of a cargo by December 29. Only 11 tons, 16 cwt. remained to be loaded, and loading would only have taken another 40 minutes. The charterer completed loading on January 2, which was within the period of laytime. The shipowner claimed damages for deliberately detaining the vessel, for she could have sailed earlier. *Held*, that the shipowner's claim failed, for the charterer could keep the vessel in port for the whole of the laytime without incurring liability.

RATE OF DEMURRAGE

The rate of demurrage is expressly stated in the charter-party, *e.g.*

"Ten running days on demurrage at the rate of £200 per day or *pro rata* for any part of a day, payable day by day, to be allowed Merchants altogether at ports of loading and discharge".[3]

In certain circumstances only half demurrage may be payable, for the charter-party may provide, *e.g.*

"If there is a strike or lock-out affecting the cargo on or after vessel's arrival at port of discharge and same has not been settled within 48 hours, Receivers shall have the option of keeping vessel waiting until

---

[1] *Margaronis Navigation Agency, Ltd.* v. *Henry W. Peabody & Co. of London, Ltd.*, [1964] 2 All E. R. 296; [1965] 1 Q. B. 300; [1964] 1 Lloyd's Rep. 173; affirmed [1964] 3 All E. R. 333; [1965] 2 Q. B. 430; [1964] 2 Lloyd's Rep. 153, C. A. Another aspect of this case, *viz.* whether the charterer had loaded a full and complete cargo subject to the limits of the *de minimis* rule is considered at p. 120, *ante*.

[2] *Supra*.

[3] See "Gencon" form, Part A, clause 5. (Appendix B, p. 249, *post*.)

such strike or lock-out is at an end against paying half demurrage after expiration of the time prescribed for discharging . . ."[1]

By whom Demurrage is Payable

Usually it will be the charterer who will be liable for the payment of demurrage.

If it is desired to make shippers or consignees other than persons who are parties to the charter-party liable for demurrage agreed on in the charter-party, there must be a clear stipulation to that effect in the bill of lading. The stipulation usually takes the form "freight and all other conditions as per charter".[2]

Even where the ship is not under charter, the bill of lading which is issued may make the shipper, consignee or holder of the bill of lading liable to pay demurrage.[3]

The charter-party or bill of lading often gives the shipowner a lien in respect of demurrage and damages for detention.[4]

The charter-party often contains a "cesser clause"[5] which purports to relieve the charterer from paying demurrage, but in each case it is a question of construction whether it does relieve him in fact.[6]

---

[1] See "Gencon" form, Part B, General Strike Clause (Appendix B, p. 250, *post*). For an example, see *The "Onisilos", Salamis Shipping (Panama) S.A.* v. *Edm. Van Meerbeeck & Co. S.A.*, [1971] 2 All E. R. 497, C. A., where it was held that half demurrage was payable from the end of a strike at the first of three discharging ports until discharge was completed at the third port. See the judgment of Lord Denning, M.R., *ibid.*, at p. 501.

[2] See *Porteus* v. *Watney* (1878), 3 Q. B. D. 534.

[3] Bills of Lading Act 1855, s. 1. (See Appendix C).

[4] See Chapter 12, *post*. For an example, see "Gencon" charter-party, clause 8 (Appendix B).

[5] See, further, on "cesser clauses", p. 231.

[6] See *e.g. Fidelitas Shipping Co., Ltd.* v. *V/O Exportchleb*, [1963] 2 Lloyd's Rep. 113, C. A., where it was held that by reason of the "cesser clause" the charterers were not liable for demurrage at the port of loading; *Overseas Transportation Co.* v. *Mineralimportexport, The "Sinoe"*, [1972] 1 Lloyd's Rep. 201, C. A., where the "cesser clause" gave the shipowner a lien on the cargo for demurrage, but was held not to relieve the charterer from liability because, on the evidence, the lien was not an effective one. See the judgment of Lord Denning, M.R., *ibid.*, at p. 204.

The difficulty in construing "cesser clauses" has arisen mainly on the question whether the charterer is to be relieved of liabilities accrued before completion of the loading, or whether the exemption applies only to liabilities arising after the goods have been shipped. Now, where it appears from the rest of the contract that another remedy is given to the shipowner for the liabilities already incurred by the charterer, he is held to be released from them.

It thus appears that the proper principle is that the exemption granted to the charterer is co-extensive with the lien given to the shipowner.[1]

Where no lien has been given in respect of a particular claim, the Courts will not enforce the exemption, unless there is a clear intention to free the charterer from liability in respect of that claim.[2]

It seems, further, that this principle, carried to its logical conclusion, involves the proposition that the charterer is still liable for damages for undue detention of the ship for the purpose of loading (*i.e.* beyond the period allowed for by the charter-party and covered by the demurrage clause) *despite* the "cesser clause", for it has been decided that, where there is a demurrage clause in the charter-party, the lien for demurrage does not include a lien for damages for detention. Thus, in *Gray* v. *Carr*,[3]

the charter-party provided that the charterer's liability was to cease on shipment of the cargo, allowed ten days' demurrage and gave a "lien for demurrage". The bill of lading provided for "freight and all other conditions or demurrage as per charter". The ship was detained at the port of loading beyond the ten days allowed on demurrage by the charter-party. It was *held* that the shipowner has a lien as against consignees under the bill of lading for the ten days' demurrage, but not for the detention beyond that time.

---

[1] See *Overseas Transportation Co.* v. *Mineralimportexport, The "Sinoe"* [1971] 1 Lloyd's Rep. 514, Q. B. D. (Commercial Court), where DONALDSON, J., observed at p. 516: "Cesser clauses are curious animals because it is now well established that they do not mean what they appear to say, namely that the charterers' liability shall cease as soon as the cargo is on board. Instead, in the absence of special wording . . . they mean that the charterers' liability shall cease if and to the extent that the owners shall have an alternative remedy by way of lien on the cargo." The decision was subsequently affirmed by the Court of Appeal: [1972] 1 Lloyd's Rep. 201.

[2] See *Francesco* v. *Massey* (1873), L. R. 8 Exch. 101; *Dunlop* v. *Balfour* [1892] 1 Q. B. 507.

[3] (1871), L. R. 6 Q. B. 522.

(B) DESPATCH MONEY

If the charterer loads or discharges the vessel in a shorter time than is allowed to him by the lay days, he may be entitled to despatch money. The amount of despatch money payable is often fixed at half the demurrage rate.[1]

---

[1] See e.g. *Fury Shipping Co., Ltd.* v. *State Trading Corporation of India, Ltd. : The "Atlantic Sun"*, [1972] 1 Lloyd's Rep. 509, Q. B. D. (Commercial Court).

CHAPTER 11

Freight

Unless there is evidence to the contrary in one or other of the documents containing or evidencing the contract, freight is construed as bearing its ordinary mercantile meaning, namely the reward payable on arrival of the goods ready to be delivered to the consignee in a merchantable condition.[1] Where the contract is ambiguous, oral evidence as to the intention of the parties is admissible.

THE DIFFERENT TYPES OF FREIGHT

When there is no provision to the contrary, freight is payable on the delivery of the goods, and is calculated on the amount actually delivered. Sometimes, however, the parties agree that a lump sum freight shall be paid irrespective of the amount of cargo carried. A frequent provision is that freight is to be paid in advance. In certain cases a *pro rata* freight is payable. If the consignee does not take delivery of the goods, the shipowner may be entitled to a back freight. If the charterer does not load a full cargo, damages for dead freight may be claimed.

(1) Freight payable on delivery

Payment of freight and delivery of the goods at the port of discharge are, unless otherwise agreed, concurrent conditions. The consignee must, if required, pay the freight as the goods are delivered, and cannot withhold payment until delivery of the whole parcel.[2] It is thus a condition precedent of the shipowner's

---

[1] *Krall* v. *Burnett* (1877), 25 W. R. 305.
[2] *Möller* v. *Young* (1855), 24 L. J. Q. B. 217 (reversed on another point, 25 L. J. Q. B. 94).

right to recover freight that he should have delivered or been ready to deliver the goods. It was said by WILLES, C.J., that

"the true test of the right to freight, is the question whether the service in respect of which the freight was contracted to be paid has been substantially performed; and according to the law of England, as a rule, freight is earned by the carriage and arrival of the goods ready to be delivered to the merchant".[1]

Where a period is fixed during which freight is to be paid, the shipowner must be prepared to deliver the goods throughout the whole of that period if he wishes to claim payment. So in *Duthie* v. *Hilton*,[2]

where the bill of lading stipulated that "freight [was] to be paid within three days after the arrival of ship before the delivery of any portion of the goods", and on the day after arrival an accidental fire necessitated the scuttling of the ship, whereby the cargo of cement was rendered commercially useless, it was *held* that freight was not payable.

It is no defence to a claim for freight to show that the goods are damaged. The shipowner is entitled to full freight if he is ready to deliver at the port of destination the goods which were loaded. The charterer or consignee, as the case may be, cannot deduct from the freight the damage to the goods, but will have a separate cause of action for it, unless it was caused solely by excepted perils, whether excepted by express stipulation or by the operation of the common law. Thus, in *Dakin* v. *Oxley*,[3]

coal shipped under a charter had, through the negligence of the master, so deteriorated as not to be worth its freight. The charterer, therefore, abandoned it to the shipowner. *Held*, he was nevertheless liable for freight, his remedy for damage to the coal being by cross-action.

But freight will not be payable unless the goods are delivered in such a condition that they are substantially and in a mercantile sense the same goods as those shipped. Thus, in *Asfar* v. *Blundell*,[4]

---

[1] *Per* WILLES, C.J., in *Dakin* v. *Oxley* (1864), 10 L. T., at p. 270; *Henriksens Rederi A/S* v. *T. H. Z. Rolimpex: The "Brede"*, [1973] 2 Lloyd's Rep. 333, C. A., where CAIRNS, L.J., said (*ibid.*, at p. 441) that it was unnecessary to justify the rule under modern conditions, and that countless transactions had been entered into on the basis that it existed; *Aries Tanker Corporation* v. *Total Transport Ltd.*, (1975) *Times*, February 10.

[2] (1868), L. R. 4 C. P. 138.

[3] (1864), 10 L. T. 268.

[4] [1896] 1 Q. B. 123. Chorley and Tucker's *Leading Cases* (4th edn. 1962), p. 307.

a ship carrying dates was sunk in the Thames. The dates were recovered, but in a state which rendered them unfit for human food. They were sold for distilling purposes. *Held*, no freight was payable because the goods delivered were, for business purposes, something different from those shipped.

Unless the shipowner carries the goods to the destination agreed on, he is not entitled to any part of the freight. If the goods are lost on the way, *no matter how*, no freight is earned. The excepted perils afford the shipowner a good excuse for non-delivery of the goods, but he cannot earn freight by virtue of one of them. If the ship cannot finish the voyage, the shipowner must forward the goods by some other means or his claim to freight is lost. Thus, in *Hunter* v. *Prinsep*,[1]

where the voyage was from Honduras to London, freight was payable "on a right and true delivery of the homeward bound cargo". After being captured by the enemy, the vessel was recaptured and recommenced the voyage, but owing to bad weather she was driven ashore at St. Kitts. The wreck and cargo were put up for sale without the consent of the cargo-owner. After paying claims for salvage, the master claimed to retain the balance of the proceeds of sale for freight. *Held*, although the ship was prevented by excepted perils from completing the voyage, no freight was payable.

In that case[2] Lord ELLENBOROUGH stated the principles relating to the payment of freight as follows:

"The shipowners undertake that they will carry the goods to the place of destination, unless prevented by the dangers of the seas or other unavoidable casualties; and the freighter undertakes that if the goods be delivered at the place of their destination, he will pay the stipulated freight but it was only in that event, viz., of their delivery at the place of destination, that he, the freighter, engages to pay anything. If the ship be disabled from completing her voyage, the shipowner may still entitle himself to the whole freight, by forwarding the goods by some other means to the place of destination; but he has no right to any freight if they are not so forwarded, unless the forwarding of them be dispensed with, or unless there be some new bargain upon this subject. If the shipowner will not forward them, the freighter is entitled to them without paying anything."

---

[1] (1808), 10 East 378.
[2] *Ibid.*, at p. 394.

But where the shipowner is prevented solely by the act or default of the cargo-owner from carrying the goods to their destination, full freight is payable. Thus, in *Cargo ex Galam*,[1]

the ship was driven ashore at Scilly and the cargo had to be landed and stored there. The charterer wished to alter the port of destination and named Hamburg. But the holders of a respondentia bond on the cargo, payable at Falmouth, obtained an order from the Court for the removal of the cargo to London and its sale there. It was *held* that as the shipowner had not abandoned his intention of completing the voyage, but had been prevented from doing so by the order of the Court, occasioned by the default of the cargo-owner, he was entitled to the freight.

As long as delivery of the goods has been made, the shipowner is still entitled to claim freight even though the vessel has been overloaded in breach of the Merchant Shipping (Safety and Load Line Conventions) Act 1932.[2]

If the vessel unjustifiably deviates from the contractual route, the contractual rate of freight is not payable.[3] But if the goods are delivered safely, he will be entitled to a reasonable remuneration on a *quantum meruit* basis.[4]

Similarly, where a charter-party had been frustrated by the closure of the Suez Canal, a shipowner was entitled to a reasonable remuneration for bringing the goods safely to their destination via the Cape of Good Hope, but could not claim the contractual rate of freight.[5]

---

[1] (1863), 33 L. J. P. M. & A. 97.

[2] *St. John Shipping Corporation* v. *Joseph Rank, Ltd.*, [1957] 1 Q. B. 267; [1956] 3 All E. R. 683.

[3] *Joseph Thorley, Ltd.* v. *Orchis S.S. Co., Ltd.*, [1907] 1 K. B. 660, C. A.

[4] *Hain S.S. Co., Ltd.* v. *Tate and Lyle, Ltd.*, [1936] 2 All E. R. 597, H. L.

[5] *Société Franco Tunisienne d'Armement* v. *Sidermar S.P.A.*, [1960] 2 All E. R. 529; [1961] 2 Q. B. 278. This decision was overruled as to the question of frustration by *Ocean Tramp Tankers* v. *V/O Sofracht*, [1964] 1 All E. R. 161; [1964] 2 Q. B. 226; [1963] 2 Lloyd's Rep. 381, C. A., but not on the point considered above, so presumably on that point the decision at first instance still stands.

(2) Lump Sum Freight

To earn lump sum freight, either the ship must complete the voyage, or else the cargo must be transhipped, or forwarded by some means other than the ship in which it was originally loaded, and delivered by the shipowner or his agents at its destination.[1]

Where the ship fails to complete the voyage and some portion of the cargo is lost, the question arises whether any deduction is to be made from the lump sum agreed on. Thus, in *Thomas* v. *Harrowing S.S. Co.*,[2]

lump sum freight was payable on delivery of a cargo of props. The exception clause included "perils of the sea". Near the port of discharge, the vessel was driven ashore by bad weather and became a total loss. Part of the cargo was washed ashore and was afterwards collected on the beach by the master's directions and deposited on the dock premises, the residue being lost by perils of the sea. *Held*, the shipowners had performed their contract, which was to deliver the cargo so far as they were not prevented by "perils of the sea"; and they were entitled to recover the whole lump sum freight, even though the charter-party stipulated that it should be payable "on unloading *and right delivery* of the cargo".

Where lump sum freight is payable on "right and true delivery" of the cargo, these words do not mean right and true delivery of the whole of the cargo shipped, and accordingly freight becomes due when the cargo which has arrived at the port of discharge has been completely delivered.[3]

Further, it seems that where the ship arrives at her destination, the shipper must pay full lump sum freight even if some of the goods are lost through causes other than expected perils.[4] Again, the cargo delivered need not be that which was agreed upon in the charter-party; for a different cargo may in fact have been loaded.[5]

---

[1] See *per* Lord HALDANE, L.C., in *Thomas* v. *Harrowing S.S. Co.*, [1915] A. C., at p. 63; also *per* TINDAL, C.J., in *Mitchell* v. *Darthez* (1836), 2 Bing. N.C., at p. 569 *et seq.*

[2] [1915] A. C. 58.

[3] *Skibs A/S Trolla and Skibs A/S Tautra* v. *United Enterprises & Shipping (Pte.) Ltd.: The "Tarva"*, [1973] 2 Lloyd's Rep. 385, Singapore High Ct. (See the judgment of CHUA, J., *ibid.*, at p. 387.)

[4] See *per* Sir E. V. WILLIAMS in *The Norway* (1865), 13 L. T., at p. 52.

[5] *Ritchie* v. *Atkinson* (1808), 10 East 295.

Sometimes, however, the contract provides that the lump sum freight must be paid in advance and will not be returnable even if the vessel and/or her cargo are lost.[1]

(3) Advance Freight

Where advance freight is agreed upon, payment does not depend on delivery and must be made even though the ship is lost and the cargo never delivered.[2] If after advance freight has been paid the voyage is abandoned, no part of the freight can be recovered.[3] Advance freight must be paid to the shipowner even if the goods are lost (by excepted perils) before payment, where they are lost after the due date of payment; nor is it recoverable if the goods are so lost after payment.

Where freight is made payable "upon final sailing", the ship must have left the port of departure, with no intention of returning. Thus, in *Roelandts* v. *Harrison*,[4]

the ship was being towed out to sea when she ran aground in a ship-canal leading from the dock to the sea. *Held*, freight payable "on final sailing" was not due. The ship must have got clear of the port and be at sea, ready to proceed on the voyage.

As freight is *prima facie* payable on delivery of the goods, the burden of making out a case for advance freight is on the shipowner. Where freight was "payable in London", it was held that the stipulation referred to the place and not to the time of payment. As the vessel was lost on the voyage, no freight became due.[5]

---

[1] *E.g.* in *Northern Sales, Ltd.* v. *The "Giancarlo Zeta", The "Giancarlo Zeta"*, [1966] 2 Lloyd's Rep. 317 (Exchequer Court, British Columbia Admiralty District), where the charter-party stated: "Freight Rate: A lump sum $130,000 U.S. currency fully prepaid upon surrender of signed bills of lading, discountless and non-returnable vessel and/or cargo lost or not lost, freight deemed earned as cargo loaded on board." As to advance freight, see *infra*.

[2] *De Silvale* v. *Kendall* (1815), 4 M. & S. 37.

[3] *Civil Service Co-operative Society* v. *General Steam Navigation Co.*, [1903] 2 K. B. 756.

[4] (1854), 9 Exch. 441.

[5] *Krall* v. *Burnett* (1877), 25 W. R. 305.

Sometimes there is a proviso that freight is to be paid "ship lost or not lost". This indicates an obligation to pay freight whether the ship is lost or not, provided that the loss is due to an excepted peril.[1] It is thus not quite the same as advance freight.

Again, it is sometimes stipulated that freight shall be payable at a certain fixed time, or on the happening of a certain event, instead of merely "in advance". Thus, in *Oriental S.S. Co.* v. *Tylor*,[2]

one-third of the freight was made payable "on signing bills of lading". The ship and cargo were lost before bills of lading had been signed, and the charterers refused to present them for signature, actually holding them back until the ship had sunk. *Held*, the charterers must pay one-third of the freight charges as damages for breach of contract.

Further, where a clause in a bill of lading stated that freight was to be "completely earned on shipment", it was held that no freight was payable if the goods were never shipped on board.[3]

Advance freight must be distinguished from advances of cash which it is often agreed shall be made by a charterer to meet the current expenses of the ship, and which are usually deducted from the freight if it becomes payable. The latter are simply a loan to the shipowner, and can be recovered in any case. An advance payment will be construed by the Court either as advance freight or as a loan according to the intention of the parties as expressed in the documents.[4] If the charter-party shows that it was the intention of the parties that the charterer making the advances should insure them, that is almost conclusive that the advances are to be on account of freight. Thus, in *Hicks* v. *Shield*,[5]

it was agreed that "cash for ship's disbursements to be advanced to the extent of £300 free of interest, but subject to insurance, and £2 10s. per cent commission". Lord CAMPBELL said: "This mention of insurance seems to me to stamp the transaction indelibly as a payment on account of freight, and not a mere loan; for if the advance was to be insured, it must be an advance of freight which is insurable whereas a loan is not."

---

[1] *Great Indian Peninsular Rail Co.* v. *Turnbull* (1885), 53 L. T. 325.
[2] [1893] 2 Q. B. 518.
[3] *Seald-Sweet Sales Inc.* v. *Finnlines* (*Meriventi Oy*): *The "Finn Forest"*, [1975] 2 Lloyd's Rep. 92, District Court, Eastern District of New York.
[4] *Allison* v. *Bristol Marine Insurance Co.* (1876), 1 App. Cas., at p. 229.
[5] (1857), 7 E. & B. 633.

(4) *Pro Rata* Freight

Sometimes *pro rata* freight is payable, *i.e.* a payment proportionate to the part of the voyage accomplished or to the part of the cargo delivered.

Where the facts warrant an inference that delivery at an intermediate port is to be accepted as part performance of the contract, the law implies a promise to pay *pro rata* freight in proportion to the part of the voyage completed.[1] To raise such an implied promise to pay *pro rata* freight the merchant must have the option of having his goods conveyed to the port of destination. He must exercise a real choice. Thus, a promise to pay *pro rata* freight will not be implied merely from acceptance of the goods at an intermediate port where the master insisted on leaving them,[2] or from acceptance of the proceeds of sale where the master has exercised his discretion to sell the cargo in the interests of the cargo-owner.[3]

It follows that *pro rata* freight is payable only if the shipowner was able and willing to carry the cargo to its destination. Thus, in *Vlierboom* v. *Chapman,*[4]

rice was to be delivered at Rotterdam. During the voyage, some was jettisoned and the rest had to be sold at Mauritius. It was *held* that, as the shipowner could not have delivered at Rotterdam, no fresh agreement for the payment of *pro rata* freight could be inferred.

Sometimes the cargo-owner expressly asks for delivery to be made at an intermediate port. Thus, in *Christy* v. *Row,*[5]

coal was shipped for Hamburg. Owing to the presence of a French army, it was dangerous to get to Hamburg and the cargo-owner asked for delivery at an intermediate port. Part of the cargo was delivered there, but the vessel was then ordered to leave the port. The cargo-owner refused to pay freight. *Held*, there was an agreement to accept delivery at the intermediate port as a substituted performance of the contract, and full freight was payable on the goods delivered there.

---

[1] *Hill* v. *Wilson* (1879), 4 C. P. D. 329.

[2] *Metcalfe* v. *Britannia Ironworks Co.* (1877), 2 Q. B. D. 423.

[3] *Hunter* v. *Prinsep* (*supra*).

[4] (1844), 13 L. J. Exch. 384. See also *St. Enoch S. Co.* v. *Phosphate Mining Co.,* [1916] 2 K. B. 624.

[5] (1808), 1 Taunt. 300.

(5) Back Freight

Normal delivery at the port of destination may sometimes be prevented by some cause beyond the control of the master, such as failure on the part of the cargo-owner to take delivery. In such cases the master may and must deal with the cargo for the benefit of its owners by landing it, carrying it on, or transhipping it, as may seem best. The shipowner may then charge the cargo-owners with "back freight" to cover the expenses thus incurred in their interest.[1]

(6) Dead Freight

Where a charterer has failed to keep his contract to provide a full cargo, the shipowner has a good cause of action against him for "dead freight", *i.e.* damages.[2]

The claim for dead freight being a claim for damages for breach of contract, the shipowner is under a duty, where the charterer fails to load a full and complete cargo, to minimise the damage by obtaining other cargo, provided he acts reasonably in so doing. It follows that "he must also have implied liberty to delay the charter voyage by the period of time reasonably and necessarily occupied in taking in that substituted cargo".[3]

By whom Freight is Payable

The shipowner can claim freight from the following persons:

(1) the shipper of the goods;
(2) the consignee or indorsee of the bill of lading;
(3) a seller who stops the goods *in transitu*;
(4) the charterer.

(1) The Shipper of the Goods

The liability to pay freight reserved in a bill of lading is primarily upon the shipper of the goods, unless he was merely acting as agent and made this clear at the time.

---

[1] *Cargo ex Argos* (1873), 42 L. J. Adm. 49.
[2] See *McLean and Hope* v. *Fleming* (1871), L. R. 2 Sc. & Div. 128.
[3] *Wallems* v. *Muller*, [1927] 2 K. B. 99.

By shipping goods, the shipper impliedly agrees to pay the freight on them. He can be relieved of this obligation:

(1) by the shipowner giving credit to the consignee. Thus, if the master for his own convenience takes a bill of exchange from a consignee who was willing to pay cash, the shipper is discharged;[1]

or (2) by delivery of a bill of lading indorsed with a clause freeing the shipper from liability, the shipowner or his agent knowing, at the time, of the existence of such a clause.[2]

The Bills of Lading Act 1855, s. 2, expressly preserves the shipowner's right to claim freight from the original shipper, so that the shipowner can elect to sue the holder of the bill of lading or the shipper.[3]

(2) The Consignee or Indorsee of the Bill of Lading

The bill of lading usually contains a clause making delivery conditional upon the consignee or his assigns paying freight. The master of the ship is entitled to refuse delivery unless the freight is paid. The mere delivery of goods does not impose a legal liability to pay the freight on them,[4] but is evidence of an implied promise to do so.[5] A custom of the trade, and even former transactions of the same parties, are also admissible as evidence of an implied contract.

The Bills of Lading Act 1855, s. 1,[6] imposes on all consignees or indorsees of a bill of lading, to whom the property in goods passes, the liability to pay freight.

Where the goods have been shipped on a chartered ship, the bills of lading often include a clause stating "freight and all other conditions as per charter". But this clause will not incorporate provisions which are inconsistent with the bill of lading or which

---

[1] *Strong* v. *Hart* (1827), 6 B. & C. 160.
[2] See *Watkins* v. *Rymill* (1883), 10 Q. B. D. 178.
[2] See Appendix C, *post.*
[4] *Sanders* v. *Vanzeller* (1843), 4 Q. B. 260.
[5] *Cock* v. *Taylor* (1811), 13 East 399; see also *per* PARKE, B., in *Möller* v. *Young* (1855), 25 L. J. Q. B., at p. 96.
[6] See Appendix C, *post.*

do not affect the consignees' right to take delivery.[1] Thus, where
the bill of lading specifies an amount to be paid as freight, this
cannot be altered by a general reference to the charter such as in
the clause set out above.

(3) A Seller who stops the goods *in transitu*

A seller who stops *in transitu*[2] is liable to pay freight on the cargo
being delivered to him; if he refuses, he is liable in damages to the
shipowner for the amount of the freight.[3] But he does not, by stop-
ping *in transitu*, become a party to the contract of affreightment.

(4) The Charterer

In the case of a charter-party, the charterer is primarily liable
for freight, and the fact that he has sublet the services of the ship
to persons who have put goods on board under bills of lading
reserving the same freight does not release him. Even if the shipowner delivers goods to such shippers without insisting on payment of freight, he can still recover it from the charterer.[4]

Where the charterer is merely an agent or broker to fill the
ship with the goods of other persons, his liability is made to
cease when the goods are shipped. This is effected by means of a
"cesser clause" inserted in the charter-party and giving the shipowner a lien on the cargo for freight[5] and other claims under the
charter. It seems, however, that a "cesser clause" in the charter-
party will not free a charterer, who is also the shipper and is sued
as such, from liability to pay freight arising on the bill of lading,
and that this is so even though the bill of lading provides for freight
"as per charter-party", since the "cesser clause" protects only
charterers as such and not shippers as such.[6]

---

[1] See *Hogarth S. Co.* v. *Blyth*, [1917] 2 K. B. 534.
[2] See pp. 97–100, *ante*.
[3] *Booth S. S. Co.* v. *Cargo Fleet Iron Co.*, [1916] 2 K. B. 570.
[4] *Shepard* v. *De Bernales* (1811), 13 East 565.
[5] See p. 234, *post*.
[6] *Rederi Aktiebolaget Transatlantic* v. *Board of Trade* (1925), 30 Com. Cas.
117, at pp. 125–6; *Hill S.S. Co.* v. *Hugo Stinnes, Ltd.*, [1941] S. C. 324.

To whom Freight is Payable

To whom freight is payable depends upon the terms of the contract of affreightment, subject to any subsequent dealings, such as assignment of the freight or mortgage of the ship.

Thus, freight may be payable to:

(1) *The shipowner*

The shipowner is, in the case of an ordinary charter-party or bill of lading, *prima facie* entitled to the freight.

or (2) *The master*

Even where the contract was not made between the master and the consignee, "it has been held that [the master] may maintain an action against the consignee upon an implied promise to pay the freight, in consideration of his letting the goods out of his hands before payment".[1] The master cannot, however, sue for freight where he signed the bill of lading merely as the shipowner's agent.[2]

or (3) *The broker*

or (4) *A third person*

It may be that, under the contract, freight was made payable to a third person. Payment of freight to such a person will protect the shipper from an action for freight.

or (5) *The charterer*

Where the charter-party is one of demise, the charterer can sue for freight, for the shipowner was not a party to the contract evidenced by the bill of lading. But it is otherwise if the charter-party is only one of hiring, and the bills of lading covering goods shipped by third persons are signed by the master.[3]

---

[1] *Per* Lord MANSFIELD, C.J., in *Brouncker* v. *Scott* (1811), 4 Taunt., at p. 4.
[2] *Repetto* v. *Millar's, etc., Co.*, [1901] 2 K. B. 306.
[3] *Coker & Co.* v. *Limerick S.S. Co.* (1918), 34 T. L. R. 296.

or (6) *An assignee of the freight (or the ship)*

The right to freight is incidental to the ownership of the ship which earns it, and therefore a transfer of a share in a ship passes the corresponding share in the freight, under an existing charter-party, without the mention of the word "freight". Further, in equity an assignment of freight to be earned is valid.[1]

or (7) *A mortgagee of the ship*

A mortgagee does not acquire a right to the freight unless he has taken actual or constructive possession of the ship; he then becomes entitled to all the freight which the ship is in the course of earning, and which she proceeds to earn after such possession comes into being.[2] This position is to be contrasted with that resulting from the sale of the ship or a share in her; for "the purchaser of a ship takes a right to all accruing freight, to all profits of the ship, from the time of the assignment to him and the transfer of the ship to him".[3] If the shipowner subsequently mortgages the ship, and the mortgagee has no notice of a previous assignment, the mortgagee will have a better claim to the freight than the assignee.[4]

---

[1] *Lindsay* v. *Gibbs* (1856), 22 Beav. 522.
[2] See, however, *Shillito* v. *Biggart*, [1903] 1 K. B. 683.
[3] *Per* MELLISH, L.J., in *Keith* v. *Burrows* (1877), 46 L. J. C. P., at p. 457.
[4] *Wilson* v. *Wilson* (1872), L. R. 14 Eq. 32.

CHAPTER 12

Liens

LIENS AT COMMON LAW

The Common Law grants a lien to two persons:

(1) the shipowner;

(2) the broker or other agent who has arranged shipment of the cargo on behalf of the shipper.

(1) The Shipowner's Lien

At Common Law the shipowner has possessory liens on the cargo for freight (but not dead freight, nor advance freight, nor freight payable after delivery), for general average contributions, and for moneys spent in protecting the cargo.[1]

The shipowner may do what is reasonable to maintain any of these liens in view of the fact that they are possessory liens, *i.e.* they can only be enforced by retaining actual or constructive (*e.g.* in a statutory warehouse) possession of the cargo. He may, of course, waive the lien for freight; on the other hand, it can be exercised against all goods consigned to the same person on the same voyage, even under different bills of lading, but not against goods on different voyages under different contracts.[2] Further, the Common Law lien for freight is not displaced unless the terms of the contract are inconsistent with it.[3]

Where freight is made payable on delivery, there will be a lien for it whether given by the contract or not. But where freight is made payable otherwise than on delivery, there will be no lien unless it is expressly given. Thus, in *Tamvaco* v. *Simpson*,[4]

---

[1] See *per* BLACKBURN, J., in *Hingston* v. *Wendt* (1876), 1 Q. B. D. 367, at p. 373.

[2] *Bernal* v. *Pim* (1835), 1 Gale 17.

[3] *Chase* v. *Westmore* (1816), 5 M. & S. 180.

[4] (1866), L. R. 1 C. P. 363.

half the freight was made payable by a bill of exchange at three months from signing the bills of lading, and the bill of exchange had not become due when the ship reached the port of discharge. It was *held* that there was no lien for this part of the freight, although the shipper had become insolvent.

At Common Law the lien for freight could be enforced only by retaining the goods. The shipowner had no power to sell them in order to pay the freight. But by the Merchant Shipping Act 1894, s. 497,[1] a power to sell the goods is conferred after they have been warehoused for ninety days and the freight and charges on them have not been tendered. In the case of perishable goods, the power of sale may be exercised earlier.

(2) The Broker's Lien

In addition to the shipowner's lien there is at Common Law a broker's lien on the bill of lading for his charges in respect of goods he has shipped. If the lien is not satisfied before they have reached their destination, he may have the goods brought home in order to retain his lien on them, and is not liable to any action for so doing.[2]

On the other hand, a broker who has negotiated a charter-party, as opposed to merely arranging for the shipment of goods under bills of lading, where his commission is due on the execution of the charter-party, has no lien and cannot enforce the payment of such commission by action on the charter-party, for he is not a party to the contract. The difficulty can, however, be overcome by the charterer suing the shipowner, the charterer acting as trustee for the broker.[3]

LIENS BY EXPRESS AGREEMENT

Liens may be created by the contract, where they do not exist at Common Law, as, for example, for dead freight, demurrage,[4] damages for detention or even "all charges whatsoever".

---

[1] See Appendix D, *post*.
[2] *Edwards* v. *Southgate* (1862), 10 W. R. 528.
[3] *Robertson* v. *Wait* (1853), 8 Exch. 299; *Les Affréteurs Réunis* v. *Walford*, [1919] A. C. 801; *Christie and Vesey* v. *Maatschoppij Tot Exploitatie van Schepen en Andere Zaken*; *The "Helvetia"*, [1960] 1 Lloyd's Rep. 540.
[4] *Gray* v. *Carr* (1871), L. R. 6 Q. B. 522. See generally "Gencon" charter-party, clause 8 (Appendix B, *post*).

As against an indorsee of the bill of lading, the word "charges" does not include charges which are specifically mentioned in the charter-party.[1] It seems, however, that, as against the charterer, a lien in respect of expenses properly incurred by the shipowner in warehousing the goods in order to avoid demurrage would be conferred by a clause granting a lien for "freight, demurrage and all other charges whatsoever".[2] But even a very widely worded clause giving a lien for any moneys due to the carrier from either shipper or consignee will not give a right of lien superior to the right of an unpaid seller who stops the goods *in transitu*.[3]

The position of holders of a bill of lading, other than the charterer himself or his agent, where the bill of lading contains a lien clause, may be summarised by saying that

"unless the language used in the bill of lading is wide enough to extend the shipowner's rights, the holder of the bill of lading is entitled to have his goods delivered to him upon payment of the freight reserved by the bill of lading; as against him there is no lien for freight payable under the charter-party in respect of the same or other goods, or for the difference, if any, between the bill of lading freight and the [charter-party] freight,[4] or for dead freight, or for demurrage at the port of loading".[5]

To avoid the operation of this principle it must be made absolutely clear by the bill of lading that such was not the intention of the parties.[6] Mere notice of the charter-party is not sufficient to extend such liens, even where the holder of the bill of lading has himself prescribed, in his capacity as sub-charterer, the form of charter-party to be used.[7]

In the leading case of *Gardner* v. *Trechmann*,[8]

the charter-party reserved freight at 31*s*. 3*d*. per ton. It contained a clause giving "an absolute lien on the cargo for freight, dead freight, demurrage, lighterage at port of discharge, and average". The master

---

[1] *Rederiaktieselskabet Superior* v. *Dewar*, [1909] 2 K. B. 998; *Gardner* v. *Trechmann* (*infra*) was distinguished.

[2] *Harley* v. *Gardner* (1932), 43 Ll. L. Rep. 104.

[3] *United States, etc., Co.* v. *Gt. W. Rly. Co.*, [1916] 1 A. C. 189.

[4] *Gardner* v. *Trechmann* (1884), 15 Q. B. D. 154.

[5] Halsbury's Laws of England (3rd edn.), vol. 35, pp. 472–3, para. 672.

[6] *Pearson* v. *Goschen* (1864), 17 C. B. N. S. 352.

[7] See *Turner* v. *Haji Azam*, [1904] A. C. 826.

[8] *Supra*.

was given power to sign bills of lading at any rate of freight, and provision was made for him to demand payment in advance of the difference between charter-party and bill of lading freight. Bills of lading were signed reserving freight at 22*s.* 6*d.* per ton and containing a clause "other conditions as per charter-party". It was *held*, that the lien for charter-party freight was not preserved as against a consignee (other than the charterer) under the bill of lading. As to the clause "other conditions as per charter-party", it was said: "It brings in only those clauses of the charter-party which are applicable to the contract contained in the bill of lading; and those clauses of the charter-party cannot be brought in which would alter the express stipulations in the bill of lading".[1] Again: "It does not take in the clause of lien as to the charter-party freight."[2]

Where, however, the consignee is also the charterer, the lien can be exercised for the full charter-party freight,[3] unless a new contract evidenced by the bill of lading shows a contrary intention.[4]

MARITIME LIENS

Maritime liens are of a different nature from those we have already noticed, and they operate in a different way. A maritime lien is a privileged claim on a ship, or on her cargo, or on either both of these and the freight, in respect of service done to, or injury caused by, them.[5] A maritime lien cannot generally exist in respect of a foreign State-owned vessel or a vessel compulsorily requisitioned for public purposes by a sovereign State.[6] But where a vessel owned by a foreign State is engaged in ordinary trading, no immunity will be granted to her.[7]

Again, a maritime lien travels with the thing to which it attaches, into whosesoever hands that thing may pass; it is in no way dependent on possession, as are the other liens we have mentioned. "It is inchoate from the moment the claim or privilege attaches, and,

---

[1] *Per* BRETT, M.R., at p. 157.
[2] *Per* COTTON, L.J., at p. 158.
[3] *McLean and Hope* v. *Fleming* (1871), L. R. 2 Sc. & Div. 128.
[4] See *per* WILLES, J., in *Pearson* v. *Goschen* (*supra*), at p. 374.
[5] *The Ripon City*, [1897] P. 226.
[6] *The Parlement Belge* (1880), 5 P. D. 197; *The Porto Alexandre*, [1920] P. 30; *Compania Naviera Vascongada* v. *S.S. Cristina*, [1938] 1 All E. R. 719; [1938] A. C. 485.
[7] *The "Philippine Admiral"*, [1976] 1 All E.R. 78, P. C.

when called into effect by the legal process of a proceeding *in rem*, relates back to the period when it first attached".[1] Further, a maritime lien attaches and remains effective even if only pronounced by a foreign court.

The principal maritime liens recognised by English law are those in respect of disbursements of the master, salvage, wages,[2] and damage done by the ship to another ship or property resulting from want of skill or from negligent navigation.[3]

Maritime liens, if not properly discharged by the owner of the property affected, are enforced by proceedings *in rem*; if necessary, the Court will order the property charged to be sold.

Maritime liens which arise *ex delicto* (*i.e.* as a result of damage done by the thing affected), generally rank before those arising *ex contractu* (*e.g.* in respect of bottomry bonds or salvage), since a sufferer has no option, whereas those who render services take the risk of subsequent claims attaching.[4] But the lien of *subsequent* salvors has priority over a damage lien of *earlier* date, because the salvors have preserved the property for the benefit of the earlier lienee.[5]

Where there is more than one lien arising *ex delicto*, it seems that, if A obtains judgment before B institutes his action, A will have priority; but that, apart from such a case, the several claimants rank *pari passu* with each other.[6]

As between contractual lienees priority depends on a variety of factors which cannot here be examined in detail. One broad principle should, however, be noted: if, after a contractual lien has attached in favour of A, B preserves the security from destruction by rendering services (*e.g.* salvage) which confer on him a lien, B will have priority over A.[7] This principle applies to cases of salvage, to money advanced by mortgagees, and to the crew's lien

---

[1] Halsbury's Laws of England (3rd. edn.), vol. 35, p. 781, para. 1202.
[2] Including arrears of National Insurance contributions: *The Gee-Whiz'* [1951] 1 All E. R. 876; and contributions to a pension fund: *The "Halcyon Skies'*, (1975), *Times*, 2nd December.
[3] But see *The Rene* (1922), 38 T. L. R. 790.
[4] *The Veritas*, [1901] P. 304.
[5] *The Inna*, [1938] P. 148.
[6] *The Stream Fisher*, [1927] P. 73.
[7] *The Veritas* (*supra*).

for wages, all of which, both against other claims and *inter se*, rank in inverse order of attachment.[1]

In some cases there is a statutory right to arrest a ship.[2] For example, where there is a claim for towage or salvage, or where goods or materials have been supplied to a ship for her operation or maintenance,[3] or where there is a dispute as to the ownership of a ship, or where there is a claim by the master or seamen for wages earned, the Court may arrest the ship[4] or a ship in the same ownership[5] until the dispute is determined.

The object of arresting the ship is, of course, to secure her continued presence and to prevent her from slipping away. The right does not, strictly speaking, give rise to a lien, though it is sometimes so described. It should be noted that any maritime liens attaching to the ship at the time of her arrest have priority over the claim for which she was arrested.[6]

---

[1] *The Selina* (1842), 2 Notes of Cases 18; *The Hope* (1873), 1 Asp. M.L.C. 563; *The Veritas (supra)*; *The Mons*, [1932] P. 109.

[2] Administration of Justice Act 1956, ss. 1, 3.

[3] *The Zafiro, John Carlbom & Co. v. Zafiro S.S. (Owners)*, [1959] 2 All E. R. 537; [1960] P. 1.

[4] Administration of Justice Act 1956, s. 3 (4) (a); *The "Andrea Ursula" : Medway Drydock and Engineering Co., Ltd. v. Beneficial Owners of Ship "Andrea Ursula"*, [1971] 1 All E. R. 821; [1971] 2 W. L. R. 681.

[5] Administration of Justice Act 1956, s. 3 (4) (b); *The St. Elefterio, Schwarz & Co. (Grain) v. St. Elefterio ex Arion (Owners)*, [1957] 2 All E. R. 374; [1957] P. 179; *Monte Ulia (Owners) v. The "Banco" (Owners)*, [1971] 1 Lloyd's Rep. 49, C. A.

[6] *Johnson v. Black, The Two Ellens* (1872), L. R. 4 P. C. 161.

CHAPTER 13

Carriage of Goods by Hovercraft

The carriage of goods by hovercraft is governed by the terms of the contract and by the Hovercraft Act 1968, and Orders made under it.[1]

The Act defines a "hovercraft" as "a vehicle which is designed to be supported when in motion wholly or partly by air expelled from the vehicle to form a cushion of which the boundaries include the ground, water or other surface beneath the vehicle".[2]

The Hovercraft (Civil Liability) Order 1971,[3] applies with modifications

(1) the Carriage of Goods by Sea Act 1924, to the carriage of cargo by hovercraft;

(2) Part VIII of the Merchant Shipping Act 1894, and the Merchant Shipping (Liability of Shipowners and Others) Act 1958, in relation to the limitation of liability for damage caused by hovercraft;

(3) the Crown Proceedings Act 1947, to hovercraft owned by the Crown; and

(4) the Maritime Conventions Act 1911, as far as collisions are concerned.

---

[1] By virtue of s. 1 (1) of the Act.

[2] Hovercraft Act, 1968, s. 4 (1). But a "hovercraft" is treated as a "ship" for the purposes of the Harbours Act 1964, which by s. 57 (1) states " 'ship', where used as a noun, includes every description of vessel used in navigation, seaplanes on the surface of the water and hover vehicles, that is to say, vehicles designed to be supported on a cushion of air."

[3] S.I. 1971, No. 720.

(1) Application of the Carriage of Goods by Sea Act 1924

The Order[1] states that the Act is to apply[2] in relation to the carriage of goods[3] by hovercraft (other than passengers' baggage)[4] as it applies to goods on board or carried by ship.

The Act, as modified by the Order, is set out in Sched. 4.

There are minor modifications, *e.g.* the word "hovercraft" is substituted for "ship" wherever that word occurs in the Act of 1924, and "hoverport" is substituted for "port".[5] The words "fit for the voyage" are substituted for "seaworthy".[6]

The limit of liability is the same as under the Act of 1924.

The provisions in the Act of 1924 concerning bulk cargo do not apply.[7]

(2) Application of the Merchant Shipping Act 1894 and the Merchant Shipping (Liability of Shipowners and Others) Act 1958

The Order states that Part VIII of the Act of 1894 and the Act of 1958 shall apply,[8] subject to certain modifications in relation to

(a) personal injury (including loss of life);

(b) loss of or damage of property caused by a person or to property (except passengers or baggage[9] carried by the hovercraft) by an act or omission of any person (whether

---

[1] Hovercraft (Civil Liability) Order 1971, Art. 4 and Sched. 2.

[2] The word "goods" means "goods, wares, merchandises, and articles of every kind whatsoever": *ibid*, Sched. 2. Thus, whereas the Carriage of Goods by Sea Act 1924, does not apply to the carriage by sea of live animals, it does apply when they are carried by hovercraft.

[3] A vehicle and its contents are not treated as baggage, whereas any property of which the passenger takes charge himself is treated as baggage: *ibid.*, Art. 5.

[4] *Ibid.*, Sched. 2.

[5] *Ibid.*, Sched. 2.

[6] *Ibid.*, Sched. 2.

[7] *Ibid.*, Sched. 2.

[8] *Ibid.*, Art. 6 and Sched. 3.

[9] As to the meaning of "baggage", see footnote 3, *supra*. The liability in respect of passengers and baggage carried by hovercraft is governed by the Carriage of Goods by Air Act 1961: *ibid.*, Art. 3 and Sched. 1.

on board the hovercraft or not) in the navigation or management of a hovercraft, in the loading, carriage or discharge of its cargo or in the embarkation, carriage or disembarkation of its passengers, or through any other act or omission of any person on board the hovercraft, as they apply in relation to injury, loss, damage and infringement of rights caused in the navigation or management of a ship.

The Acts, as modified by the Order, are set out in Sched. 4.

The effect of the application of these Acts, as modified, is that the owner of a hovercraft, whether British or foreign, is entitled to limit his liability where any loss of or damage to any goods, merchandise, or other things whatsoever on board the hovercraft is caused if the loss or damage has occurred "without his actual fault or privity". The maximum sum for which he can be made liable is £1 per kg. of the hovercraft's maximum weight.[1]

The owner can limit his liability where loss of life or personal injury is caused and the maximum sum for which he can be made liable is £3·50 per kg. of the hovercraft's maximum weight.[2]

But liability cannot be limited at all unless at the time of the incident causing the damage the hovercraft was on or over navigable water, or on or over the foreshore, or place where the tide normally ebbs and flows, or was proceeding between navigable water and a hoverport, or was on or over a hoverport either preparing for or after such transport.[3]

(3) Application of the Crown Proceedings Act 1947

The Order states that s. 5 of the Crown Proceedings Act 1947, is to be applied in the case of hovercraft as it applies in the case of vessels, *i.e.* the provisions of the Merchant Shipping Acts entitling a shipowner to limit his liability apply in relation to Crown hovercraft.[4]

---

[1] *Ibid.*, Sched. 3.
[2] *Ibid.*, Sched. 3.
[3] *Ibid.*, Sched. 6.
[4] *Ibid.*, Art. 8.

(4) Application of the Maritime Conventions Act 1911

The Order states that ss. 1, 2, 3, 8 and 9 (4) of the Maritime Conventions Act 1911, are to apply as if references therein to vessels included references to hovercraft.[1]

These sections concern

(i) division of loss (*i.e.* the Court may apportion liability according to the degree in which each vessel was at fault);

(ii) damages for personal injuries caused by the fault of two or more vessels;

(iii) the right of contribution (*i.e.* the right of an owner of a vessel, who has paid damages to a third party in excess of the proportion in which the vessel was at fault, to obtain a contribution in respect of the amount of the excess from the owners of the other vessel at fault);

(iv) the period of limitation (which is generally 2 years from the date of the damage or loss or injury); and

(v) the application of the Act of 1911 to various parts of the Commonwealth.

---

[1] *Ibid.*, Art. 7.

APPENDIX A

Specimen Bill of Lading

NOTE

The form appearing opposite is reproduced by courtesy of the New Zealand Tonnage Committee.

APPENDIX B

Specimen Charter-parties

NOTE

The forms commencing on the following page are reproduced by the courtesy of the Baltic and International Maritime Conference. The written insertions are intended merely to make the documents as a whole intelligible to the student and have no reference to any actual transaction.

RECOMMENDED
UNIFORM GENERAL CHARTER
AS REVISED 1922   Code Name:
LAYOUT 1906   **Gencon**

Figures in brackets denote clause numbering in 1922 edition

PART A   Place and date:.   *30th. September 1975*

1. (1) IT IS THIS DAY MUTUALLY AGREED between   *John Doe & Co.*   1

Owners   ~~steam~~ motor-vessel *Alpha*   of   Owners of the ~~steamer~~ 2

Position   carrying about *1800* tons of deadweight cargo, now *2400* tons ~~gross~~ net Register and 3
and expected ready to load under this Charter about *On a passage to Gdynia* and Messrs. 4

20 October 1975 5

Charterers   *Richard Roe Ltd.* of *London.* as Charterers. 6 / 7

Where to load   That the said vessel shall proceed to *Gdynia* 8
or so near thereto as she may safely get 9

Cargo   and lie always afloat, and there load a full and complete cargo (if shipment of deck cargo agreed same to be at Charterers' risk) of 10

Scrap iron 11
12
13

(Charterers to provide all mats and/or wood for dunnage and any separations required, the Owners allowing the use of any 14
dunnage wood on board if required) which the Charterers bind themselves to ship, and being so loaded the vessel shall proceed to 15

Destination   *Cork* 16
17

as ordered on signing Bills of Lading or so near thereto as she may 18
safely get and lie always afloat and there deliver the cargo on being paid freight – on delivered / intaken quantity – as follows: 19

Rate of Freight   20
21
22

Payment of Freight   2. (4) The freight to be paid in cash without discount on delivery of the cargo at mean rate of exchange ruling on day or 23
days of payment, the receivers of the cargo being bound to pay freight on account during delivery, if required by Captain or Owners. 24
Cash for vessel's ordinary disbursements at port of loading to be advanced by Charterers if required at highest current rate of 25
exchange, subject to two per cent. to cover insurance and other expenses. 26

Loading   3. (5) Cargo to be brought alongside in such a manner as to enable vessel to take the goods with her own tackle and to load 27
the full cargo in *five* running working days. Charterers to procure and pay the necessary 28
men on shore or on board the lighters to do the work there, vessel only heaving the cargo on board. 29
If the loading takes place by elevator cargo to be put free in vessel's holds, Owners only paying trimming expenses. 30
Any pieces and/or packages of cargo over two tons weight, shall be loaded, stowed and discharged by Charterers at their risk 31
and expense. 32
Time to commence at 1 p.m. if notice of readiness to load is given before noon and at 6 a.m. next working day if notice given 33
during office hours after noon. 34
The notice to be given to the Shippers, Messrs. *John & Co., Gdynia* 35
36
Time lost in waiting for berth to count as loading time. 37

Discharging   4. (6) Cargo to be received by Merchants at their risk and expense alongside the vessel not beyond the reach of her tackle and to 38
be discharged in *four* running working days. Time to commence at 1 p.m. if notice of 39
readiness to discharge is given before noon, and at 6 a.m. next working day if notice given during office hours after noon. 40
Time lost in waiting for berth to count as discharging time. 41

Demurrage   5. (7) Ten running days on demurrage at the rate of *£500* per day or pro rata for any part 42
of a day, payable day by day, to be allowed Merchants altogether at ports of loading and discharging. 43

Cancelling Clause   6. (11) Should the vessel not be ready to load (whether in berth or not) on or before the *November 15th.* 44
Charterers have the option of cancelling this contract, such option to be declared, if demanded, 45
at least 48 hours before vessel's expected arrival at port of loading. Should the vessel be delayed on account of average or otherwise, 46
Charterers to be informed as soon as possible, and if the vessel is delayed for more than 10 days after the day she is stated to be 47
expected ready to load, Charterers have the option of cancelling this contract, unless a cancelling date has been agreed upon. 48

Agency   7. (14) In every case the Owner shall appoint his own Broker or Agent both at the port of loading and the port of discharge. 49

Brokerage   8. (15) *5* % brokerage on the freight earned is due to *Messrs. Thomas* 50
Brown & Son 51
In case of non-execution at least 1/3 of the brokerage on the estimated amount of freight and dead-freight to be paid by the 53
Owners to the Brokers as indemnity for the latter's expenses and work. In case of more voyages the amount of indemnity to be 54
mutually agreed. 55
9.–15.: as in part B, which constitutes a part of this Charter as though fully set forth herein. 56

Signatures   *John Doe & Co.*
Richard Roe Ltd.

PART B

<table>
<tr><td>Owners' Responsibility Clause</td><td>9. (2) Owners are to be responsible for loss of or damage to the goods or for delay in delivery of the goods only in case the 1
loss, damage or delay has been caused by the improper or negligent stowage of the goods (unless stowage performed by shippers or 2
their stevedores or servants) or by personal want of due diligence on the part of the Owners or their Manager to make the vessel in 3
all respects seaworthy and to secure that she is properly manned, equipped and supplied or by the personal act or default of the Ow- 4
ners or their Manager. 5</td></tr>
</table>

And the Owners are responsible for no loss or damage or delay arising from any other cause whatsoever, even from the neglect 6
or default of the Captain or crew or some other person employed by the Owners on board or ashore for whose acts they would, but 7
for this clause, be responsible, or from unseaworthiness of the vessel on loading or commencement of the voyage or at any time what- 8
soever. 9

Damage caused by contact with or leakage, smell or evaporation from other goods or by the inflammable or explosive nature or 10
insufficient package of other goods not to be considered as caused by improper or negligent stowage, even if in fact so caused. 11

Deviation Clause 10. (3) The vessel has liberty to call at any port or ports in any order, for any purpose, to sail without pilots, to tow and/or 12
assist vessels in all situations, and also to deviate for the purpose of saving life and/or property. 13

Lien Clause 11. (8) Owners shall have a lien on the cargo for freight, dead-freight, demurrage and damages for detention. Charterers shall 14
remain responsible for dead-freight and demurrage (including damages for detention), incurred at port of loading. Charterers shall 15
also remain responsible for freight and demurrage (including damages for detention) incurred at port of discharge, but only to such 16
extent as the Owners have been unable to obtain payment thereof by exercising the lien on the cargo. 17

Bills of Lading 12. (9) The Captain to sign Bills of Lading at such rate of freight as presented without prejudice to this Charterparty, but 18
should the freight by Bills of Lading amount to less than the total chartered freight the difference to be paid to the Captain in cash 19
on signing Bills of Lading. 20

General Average 13. (12) General average to be settled according to York–Antwerp Rules, 1950, Proprietors of cargo to pay the cargo's share 21
in the general expenses even if same have been necessitated through neglect or default of the Owners' servants (see clause 9. [2]). 22

Indemnity 14. (13) Indemnity for non-performance of this Charterparty, proved damages, not exceeding estimated amount of freight. 23

Strike-, War- and Ice-Clauses 15. (10) Strike-Clause, War-Clause and Ice-Clause as below. 24

GENERAL STRIKE CLAUSE

Neither Charterers nor Owners shall be responsible for the consequences of any strikes or lock-outs preventing or delaying the 25
fulfilment of any obligations under this contract. 26

If there is a strike or lock-out affecting the loading of the cargo, or any part of it, when vessel is ready to proceed from her 27
last port or at any time during the voyage to the port or ports of loading or after her arrival there, Captain or Owners may ask Char- 28
terers to declare, that they agree to reckon the laydays as if there were no strike or lock-out. Unless Charterers have given such dec- 29
laration in writing (by telegram, if necessary) within 24 hours, Owners shall have the option of cancelling this contract. If part cargo 30
has already been loaded, Owners must proceed with same, (freight payable on loaded quantity only) having liberty to complete with 31
other cargo on the way for their own account. 32

If there is a strike or lock-out affecting the discharge of the cargo on or after vessel's arrival at or off port of discharge and 33
same has not been settled within 48 hours, Receivers shall have the option of keeping vessel waiting until such strike or lock-out is at 34
an end against paying half demurrage after expiration of the time provided for discharging, or of ordering the vessel to a safe port, 35
where she can safely discharge without risk of being detained by strike or lock-out. Such orders to be given within 48 hours after Cap- 36
tain or Owners have given notice to Charterers of the strike or lock-out affecting the discharge. On delivery of the cargo at such port, 37
all conditions of this Charterparty and of the Bill of Lading shall apply and vessel shall receive the same freight as if she had discharged 38
at the original port of destination, except that if the distance of the substituted port exceeds 100 nautical miles, the freight on 39
the cargo delivered at the substituted port to be increased in proportion. 40

GENERAL WAR CLAUSE

If the nation under whose flag the vessel sails should be engaged in war and the safe navigation of the vessel should thereby 41
be endangered either party to have the option of cancelling this contract, and if so cancelled, cargo already shipped shall be discharged 42
either at the port of loading or, if the vessel has commenced the voyage, at the nearest safe place at the risk and expense of the 43
Charterers or Cargo-Owners. 44

If owing to outbreak of hostilities the goods loaded or to be loaded under this contract or part of them become contraband of 45
war whether absolute or conditional or liable to confiscation or detention according to international law or the proclamation of any of 46
the belligerent powers each party to have the option of cancelling this contract as far as such goods are concerned, and contraband 47
goods already loaded to be then discharged either at the port of loading, or if the voyage has already commenced, at the nearest safe 48
place at the expense of the Cargo-Owners. Owners to have the right to fill up with other goods instead of the contraband. 49

Should any port where the vessel has to load under this Charter be blockaded the contract to be null and void with regard to 50
the goods to be shipped at such port. 51

No Bills of Lading to be signed for any blockaded port, and if the port of destination be declared blockaded after Bills of La- 52
ding have been signed, Owners shall discharge the cargo either at the port of loading, against payment of the expenses of discharge, 53
if the ship has not sailed thence, or, if sailed at any safe port on the way as ordered by Shippers or if no order is given at the nearest 54
safe place against payment of full freight. 55

GENERAL ICE CLAUSE

Port of Loading
a) In the event of the loading port being inaccessible by reason of ice when vessel is ready to proceed from her last port or at 56
any time during the voyage or on vessel's arrival or in case frost sets in after vessel's arrival, the Captain for fear of being 57
frozen in is at liberty to leave without cargo, and this Charter shall be null and void. 58

b) If during loading the Captain, for fear of vessel being frozen in, deems it advisable to leave, he has liberty to do so with 59
what cargo he has on board and to proceed to any other port or ports with option of completing cargo for Owners' benefit 60
for any port or ports including port of discharge. Any part cargo thus loaded under this Charter to be forwarded to desti- 61
nation at vessel's expense but against payment of freight, provided that no extra expenses be thereby caused to the Receivers, 62
freight being paid on quantity delivered (in proportion if lumpsum), all other conditions as per Charter. 63

c) In case of more than one loading port, and if one or more of the ports are closed by ice, the Captain or Owners to be at 64
liberty either to load the part cargo at the open port and fill up elsewhere for their own account as under section b or to 65
declare the Charter null and void unless Charterers agree to load full cargo at the open port. 66

d) This Ice Clause not to apply in the Spring. 67

Port of discharge
a) Should ice (except in the Spring) prevent vessel from reaching port of discharge Receivers shall have the option of keep- 68
ing vessel waiting until the re-opening of navigation and paying demurrage, or of ordering the vessel to a safe and imme- 69
diately accessible port where she can safely discharge without risk of detention by ice. Such orders to be given within 48 70
hours after Captain or Owners have given notice to Charterers of the impossibility of reaching port of destination. 71

b) If during discharging the Captain for fear of vessel being frozen in deems it advisable to leave, he has liberty to do so with 72
what cargo he has on board and to proceed to the nearest accessible port where she can safely discharge. 73

c) On delivery of the cargo at such port, all conditions of the Bill of Lading shall apply and vessel shall receive the same freight 74
as if she had discharged at the original port of destination, except that if the distance of the substituted port exceeds 100 75
nautical miles, the freight on the cargo delivered at the substituted port to be increased in proportion. 76

Adopted by
the Documentary Committee
of the Chamber of Shipping
of the United Kingdom.

Copyright. Published by The Baltic and
International Maritime Conference,
Copenhagen.

Issued 5/2/1909.
Amended 13/3/1911.
Amended 6/3/1912.
Amended 10/6/1920.
Amended 1/3/1939.
Amended 1/1/1950.

THE BALTIC AND INTERNATIONAL MARITIME CONFERENCE
(Formerly The Baltic and White Sea Conference.)

UNIFORM TIME-CHARTER

Code-Name
Baltime
1939.

.....*September 20th*.....19 *75*

Description of Vessel.	It is this Day mutually agreed between *Great Eastern S.S. Co. Ltd.* Owners 1

of the Vessel called *Mary Jane*   of *10339* tons gross Register, 2
classed *Lloyds 100 A1*   of *6300* indicated horse power, 3
carrying about *9131* tons deadweight on Board of Trade summer freeboard inclusive 4
of bunkers, stores, provisions and boiler water, having as per builder's plan *478,000* cubic-feet 5
~~grain~~ bale capacity, exclusive of permanent bunkers, which contain about *950* tons, and fully loaded capable 6
of steaming about *12½* knots in good weather and smooth water on a consumption of ~~about~~ 7
~~tons best Welsh coal,~~ or about *15½* tons oil-fuel, now *at London* 8

Charterers.   and *Central Merchants Ltd.* 9

of *London*   Charterers, as follows : 10

Period.   **1.** The Owners let, and the Charterers hire the Vessel for a period of *24 (twenty-four)* 11

calendar months from the time (not a Sunday or a legal Holiday unless taken over) the Vessel is delivered 12
and placed at the disposal of the Charterers between 9 a.m. and 6 p.m., or between 9 a.m. and 2 p.m. 13
if on Saturday, at *Liverpool* 14

Port of Delivery.

in such available berth where she can safely lie always afloat, as the Charterers 15
may direct, she being in every way fitted for ordinary cargo service. 16

Time for Delivery.   The Vessel to be delivered *not before November 1st* 17

Trade.   **2.** The Vessel to be employed in lawful trades for the carriage of lawful merchandise only 18
between good and safe ports or places where she can safely lie always afloat within the following 19
limits : 20

United Kingdom, Continent, Elbe Brest limits (excluding
Shetland or Orkneys)

No live stock nor injurious, inflammable or dangerous goods (such as acids, explosives, calcium 21
carbide, ferro silicon, naphtha, motor spirit, tar, or any of their products) to be shipped. 22

Owners to provide.   **3.** The Owners to provide and pay for all provisions and wages, for insurance of the Vessel, for all 23
deck and engine-room stores and maintain her in a thoroughly efficient state in hull and machinery 24
during service. 25
The Owners to provide one winchman per hatch. If further winchmen are required, or if the 26
stevedores refuse or are not permitted to work with the Crew, the Charterers to provide and pay 27
qualified shore-winchmen. 28

Charterers to provide.   **4.** The Charterers to provide and pay for all coals, including galley coal, oil-fuel, water for boilers, 29
port charges, pilotages (whether compulsory or not), canal steersmen, boatage, lights, tug-assistance, 30
consular charges (except those pertaining to the Master, Officers and Crew) canal, dock and other dues 31
and charges, including any foreign general municipality or state taxes, also all dock, harbour and 32
tonnage dues at the ports of delivery and re-delivery (unless incurred through cargo carried before delivery 33
or after re-delivery) agencies, commissions, also to arrange and pay for loading, trimming, stowing (includ- 34
ing dunnage and shifting boards, excepting any already on board), unloading, weighing, tallying and 35
delivery of cargoes, surveys on hatches, meals supplied to officials and men in their service and all 36
other charges and expenses whatsoever including detention and expenses through quarantine (including 37
cost of fumigation and disinfection). 38

All ropes, slings and special runners actually used for loading and discharging and any special gear, including special ropes, hawsers and chains required by the custom of the port for mooring to be for the Charterers' account. The Vessel to be fitted with winches, derricks, wheels and ordinary runners capable of handling lifts up to 2 tons.

Bunkers. 5. The Charterers at port of delivery and the Owners at port of re-delivery to take over and pay for all coal or oil-fuel remaining in the Vessel's bunkers at current price at the respective ports. The Vessel to be re-delivered with not less than *4 00* tons and not exceeding *500* tons of ~~coal or~~ oil-fuel in the Vessel's bunkers.

Hire. 6. The Charterers to pay as hire : *£5 per deadweight ton*

per 30 days, commencing in accordance with clause 1 until her re-delivery to the Owners.

Payment. Payment of hire to be made in cash, in *London* without discount, every 30 days, in advance.

In default of payment the Owners to have the right of withdrawing the Vessel from the service of the Charterers, without noting any protest and without interference by any court or any other formality whatsoever and without prejudice to any claim the Owners may otherwise have on the Charterers under the Charter.

Re-delivery. 7. The Vessel to be re-delivered on the expiration of the Charter in the same good order as when delivered to the Charterers (fair wear and tear excepted) at an ice-free port in the Charterers' option in *the United Kingdom*

between 9 a.m. and 6 p.m., and 9 a.m. and 2 p.m. on Saturday, but the day of re-delivery shall not be a Sunday or legal Holiday.

Notice. The Charterers to give the Owners not less than ten days' notice at which port and on about which day the Vessel will be re-delivered.

Should the Vessel be ordered on a voyage by which the Charter period will be exceeded the Charterers to have the use of the Vessel to enable them to complete the voyage, provided it could be reasonably calculated that the voyage would allow re-delivery about the time fixed for the termination of the Charter, but for any time exceeding the termination date the Charterers to pay the market rate if higher than the rate stipulated herein.

Cargo Space. 8. The whole reach and burthen of the Vessel, including lawful deck-capacity to be at the Charterers' disposal, reserving proper and sufficient space for the Vessel's Master, Officers, Crew, tackle, apparel, furniture, provisions and stores.

Master. 9. The Master to prosecute all voyages with the utmost despatch and to render customary assistance with the Vessel's Crew. The Master to be under the orders of the Charterers as regards employment, agency, or other arrangements. The Charterers to indemnify the Owners against all consequences or liabilities arising from the Master, Officers or Agents signing Bills of Lading or other documents or otherwise complying with such orders, as well as from any irregularity in the Vessel's papers or for overcarrying goods. The Owners not to be responsible for shortage, mixture, marks, nor for number of pieces or packages, nor for damage to or claims on cargo caused by bad stowage or otherwise.

If the Charterers have reason to be dissatisfied with the conduct of the Master, Officers, or Engineers, the Owners, on receiving particulars of the complaint, promptly to investigate the matter, and, if necessary and practicable, to make a change in the appointments.

Directions and Logs. 10. The Charterers to furnish the Master with all instructions and sailing directions and the Master and Engineer to keep full and correct logs accessible to the Charterers or their Agents.

Suspension of Hire, etc. 11. (A) In the event of drydocking or other necessary measures to maintain the efficiency of the Vessel, deficiency of men or Owners' stores, breakdown of machinery, damage to hull or other accident, either hindering or preventing the working of the vessel and continuing for more than twenty-four consecutive hours, no hire to be paid in respect of any time lost thereby during the period in which the Vessel is unable to perform the service immediately required. Any hire paid in advance to be adjusted accordingly.

(B) In the event of the Vessel being driven into port or to anchorage through stress of weather, trading to shallow harbours or to rivers or ports with bars or suffering an accident to her cargo, any detention of the Vessel and/or expenses resulting from such detention to be for the Charterers' account even if such detention and/or expenses, or the cause by reason of which either is incurred, be due to, or be contributed to by, the negligence of the Owners' servants.

Cleaning Boilers.

12. Cleaning of boilers whenever possible to be done during service, but if impossible the Charterers to give the Owners necessary time for cleaning. Should the Vessel be detained beyond 48 hours hire to cease until again ready. 92 93 94

Responsibility and Exemption.

13. The Owners only to be responsible for delay in delivery of the Vessel or for delay during the currency of the Charter and for loss or damage to goods on board, if such delay or loss has been caused by want of due diligence on the part of the Owners or their Manager in making the Vessel seaworthy and fitted for the voyage or any other personal act or omission or default of the Owners or their Manager. The Owners not to be responsible in any other case nor for damage or delay whatsoever and howsoever caused even if caused by the neglect or default of their servants. The Owners not to be liable for loss or damage arising or resulting from strikes, lock-outs or stoppage or restraint of labour (including the Master, Officers or Crew) whether partial or general. 95 96 97 98 99 100 101 102

The Charterers to be responsible for loss or damage caused to the Vessel or to the Owners by goods being loaded contrary to the terms of the Charter or by improper or careless bunkering or loading, stowing or discharging of goods or any other improper or negligent act on their part or that of their servants. 103 104 105 106

Advances.

14. The Charterers or their Agents to advance to the Master, if required, necessary funds for ordinary disbursements for the Vessel's account at any port charging only interest at 6 per cent. p.a., such advances to be deducted from hire. 107 108 109

Excluded Ports.

Ice.

15. The Vessel not to be ordered to nor bound to enter : (a) any place where fever or epidemics are prevalent or to which the Master, Officers and Crew by law are not bound to follow the Vessel (b) any ice-bound place or any place where lights, lightships, marks and buoys are or are likely to be withdrawn by reason of ice on the Vessel's arrival or where there is risk that ordinarily the Vessel will not be able on account of ice to reach the place or to get out after having completed loading or discharging. The Vessel not to be obliged to force ice. If on account of ice the Master considers it dangerous to remain at the loading or discharging place for fear of the Vessel being frozen in and/or damaged, he has liberty to sail to a convenient open place and await the Charterers' fresh instructions. Unforeseen detention through any of above causes to be for the Charterers' account. 110 111 112 113 114 115 116 117 118

Loss of Vessel.

16. Should the Vessel be lost or missing, hire to cease from the date when she was lost. If the date of loss cannot be ascertained half hire to be paid from the date the Vessel was last reported until the calculated date of arrival at the destination. Any hire paid in advance to be adjusted accordingly. 119 120 121 122

Overtime.

17. The Vessel to work day and night if required. The Charterers to refund the Owners their outlays for all overtime paid to Officers and Crew according to the hours and rates stated in the Vessel's articles. 123 124 125

Lien.

18. The Owners to have a lien upon all cargoes and sub-freights belonging to the Time-Charterers and any Bill of Lading freight for all claims under this Charter, and the Charterers to have a lien on the Vessel for all moneys paid in advance and not earned. 126 127 128

Salvage.

19. All salvage and assistance to other vessels to be for the Owners' and the Charterers' equal benefit after deducting the Master's and Crew's proportion and all legal and other expenses including hire paid under the charter for time lost in the salvage, also repairs of damage and coal or oil-fuel consumed. The Charterers to be bound by all measures taken by the Owners in order to secure payment of salvage and to fix its amount. 129 130 131 132 133

Sublet.

20. The Charterers to have the option of subletting the Vessel, giving due notice to the Owners, but the original Charterers always to remain responsible to the Owners for due performance of the Charter. 134 135

War.

21. (A) The Vessel unless the consent of the Owners be first obtained not to be ordered nor continue to any place or on any voyage nor be used on any service which will bring her within a zone which is dangerous as the result of any actual or threatened act of war, war, hostilities, warlike operations, acts of piracy or of hostility or malicious damage against this or any other vessel or its cargo by any person, body or State whatsoever, revolution, civil war, civil commotion or the operation of international law, nor be exposed in any way to any risks or penalties whatsoever consequent upon the imposition of Sanctions, nor carry any goods that may in any way expose her to any risks of seizure, capture, penalties or any other interference of any kind whatsoever by the belligerent or fighting powers or parties or by any Government or Ruler. 136 137 138 139 140 141 142 143 144

(B) Should the Vessel approach or be brought or ordered within such zone, or be exposed in any way to the said risks, (1) the Owners to be entitled from time to time to insure their interests in the Vessel and/or hire against any of the risks likely to be involved thereby on such terms as they shall think fit, the Charterers to make a refund to the Owners of the premium on demand ; and (2) notwithstanding the terms of clause 11 hire to be paid for all time lost including 145 146 147 148 149

Appendix B

any loss owing to loss of or injury to the Master, Officers, or Crew or to the action of the Crew 150
in refusing to proceed to such zone or to be exposed to such risks. 151

Section (C) is
optional and
should be
deleted
unless agreed.

(C) In the event of the wages of the Master, Officers and/or Crew or the cost of provisions 152
and/or stores for deck and/or engine room and/or insurance premiums being increased by reason of 153
or during the existence of any of the matters mentioned in section (A) the amount of any increase 154
to be added to the hire and paid by the Charterers on production of the Owners' account therefor, 155
such account being rendered monthly. 156

(D) The Vessel to have liberty to comply with any orders or directions as to departure, 157
arrival, routes, ports of call, stoppages, destination, delivery or in any other wise whatsoever given 158
by the Government of the nation under whose flag the Vessel sails or any other Government or any 159
person (or body) acting or purporting to act with the authority of such Government or by any 160
committee or person having under the terms of the war risks insurance on the Vessel the right to 161
give any such orders or directions. 162

(E) In the event of the nation under whose flag the Vessel sails becoming involved in war, hosti- 163
lities, warlike operations, revolution, or civil commotion, both the Owners and the Charterers may cancel 164
the Charter and, unless otherwise agreed, the Vessel to be re-delivered to the Owners at the port 165
of destination or, if prevented through the provisions of section (A) from reaching or entering it, 166
then at a near open and safe port at the Owners' option, after discharge of any cargo on board. 167

(F) If in compliance with the provisions of this clause anything is done or is not done, such 168
not to be deemed a deviation. 169

Cancelling.
22. Should the Vessel not be delivered by the *twentieth* day of *November* 1975 , 170
the Charterers to have the option of cancelling. 171

If the Vessel cannot be delivered by the cancelling date, the Charterers, if required, to declare 172
within 48 hours after receiving notice thereof whether they cancel or will take delivery of the Vessel. 173

Arbitration.
23. Any dispute arising under the Charter to be referred to arbitration in London (or such 174
other place as may be agreed) one Arbitrator to be nominated by the Owners and the other by the 175
Charterers, and in case the Arbitrators shall not agree then to the decision of an Umpire to be 176
appointed by them, the award of the Arbitrators or the Umpire to be final and binding upon both 177
parties. 178

General
Average.
24. General Average to be settled according to York-Antwerp Rules, 1950. Hire not to contribute 179
to General Average. 180

Commission.
25. The Owners to pay a commission of *5%* to *Messrs. Thomas Brown & Son* 181
on any hire paid under the Charter, but in no case less than is necessary to cover the actual expenses 182
of the Brokers and a reasonable fee for their work. If the full hire is not paid owing to breach 183
of Charter by either of the parties the party liable therefor to indemnify the Brokers against their 184
loss of commission. 185

Should the parties agree to cancel the Charter, the Owners to indemnify the Brokers against any 186
loss of commission, but in such case the commission not to exceed the brokerage on one year's hire. 187

Witness to signature of
Great Eastern S.S. Co. Ltd. } *F. Black*

For Great Eastern S.S. Co. Ltd.
D. Morris
Managing Director

Witness to signature of
Central Merchants Ltd. } *R. White*

For Central Merchants Ltd.
B. Lewis
Chairman

Printed and Sold by S. Straker & Sons Ltd.,
49 Fenchurch Street, London, E.C.3.
by Authority of the Baltic & International Maritime Conference

NOTES

THE "GENVOY" SLIP

The "Gencon" form of charter-party does not contain any reference to the "general paramount clause" (see p. 12, *ante*), the "both-to-blame collision clause" (see pp. 152-153, *ante*) or the "amended Jason clause" (see pp. 192-193, *ante*). In 1946 the Documentary Council of the Baltic and International Maritime Conference issued a slip, usually known as the "Genvoy" slip, setting forth these clauses. The slip is often added to the "Gencon" charter-party. It is reproduced here by the courtesy of the Baltic and International Maritime Conference. The text of the slip is as follows:

BALTIC CONFERENCE ADDENDUM 1946
CODE NAME: "GENVOY"

All Bills of Lading under this Charter shall contain the following clauses:

General Paramount Clause.

"This Bill of Lading shall have effect subject to the provisions of any legislation relating to the carriage of goods by sea which incorporates the rules relating to Bills of Lading contained in the international Convention, dated Brussels 25th August, 1924 and which is compulsorily applicable to the contract of carriage herein contained. Such legislation shall be deemed to be incorporated herein, but nothing herein contained shall be deemed a surrender by the Carrier of any of its rights or immunities or an increase of any of its responsibilities or liabilities thereunder. If any term of this Bill of Lading be repugnant to any extent to any legislation by this clause incorporated, such term shall be void to that extent but no further. Nothing in this Bill of Lading shall operate to limit or deprive the Carrier of any statutory protection or exemption from, or limitation of, liability."

Clause for Shipments between ports in Denmark, Finland, Norway and Sweden.

"Where Par. 122 of the Danish, Finnish, Norwegian and Swedish Maritime Laws apply the Carrier is considered to have taken all such reservation as to the liability and responsibility as he is allowed to do by the sections 122 and 123 of the said Acts."

Both-to-Blame Collision Clause.

"If the Vessel comes into collision with another ship as a result of the negligence of the other ship and any act, neglect or default of the Master, Mariner, Pilot or the servants of the Carrier in the navigation or in the

255

management of the vessel, the owners of the cargo carried hereunder will indemnify the Carrier against all loss or liability to the other or non-carrying ship or her owners in so far as such loss or liability represents loss of, or damage to, or any claim whatsoever of the owners of said cargo, paid or payable by the other or non-carrying ship or her owners to the owners of said cargo and set-off, recouped or recovered by the other or non-carrying ship or her owners as part of their claim against the carrying Vessel or Carrier. The foregoing provisions shall also apply where the owners, operators or those in charge of any ship or ships or objects other than, or in addition to, the colliding ships or objects are at fault in respect of a collision or contract."

Amended Jason Clause.

"In the event of accident, danger, damage, or disaster before or after commencement of the voyage resulting from any cause whatsoever, whether due to negligence or not, for which or for the consequence of which the Carrier is not responsible by statute, contract, or otherwise, the cargo, shippers, consignees, or owners of the cargo shall contribute with the Carrier in General Average to the payment of any sacrifices, losses or expenses of a General Average nature that may be made or incurred, and shall pay salvage and special charges incurred in respect of the cargo. If a salving ship is owned or operated by the Carrier, salvage shall be paid for as fully as if the salving ship or ships belong to strangers."

HISTORY OF THE "GENCON" CHARTER-PARTY AND NOTES ON THE THIRD EDITION

The following article on the "Gencon" charter-party appeared in the Monthly Circular of the Baltic and International Maritime Conference for December 1965, pp. 11836–11838, and is reprinted by the kind permission of that Conference:

"GENCON" CHARTER

History

The first suggestion as to the drafting of a general form of charter was made at a meeting of the Documentary Council of the *Conference* held in Paris on April 10th, 1913. In the Monthly Circular for April 1913, page 101, it was reported that

"Mr. Heinrich F. C. Arp, Hamburg, proposed the formulation of a general form of charter, principally intended for short trades, such as for instance grain from Hamburg and also from near Baltic Ports to French ports.

After some discussion a Committee consisting of

Mr. Heinrich F. C. Arp, Hamburg,
Mr. J. Jantzen, Christiania, and
Mr. D. Lauritzen, Esbjerg.

was appointed with the object of considering the formulation of a general form of charter.

The Committee appointed was authorized to co-opt a fourth member."

Because of the war of 1914/1918, the drafting was delayed. However, even during the war a revision committee discussed the draft. A first rough draft was before a meeting of the revision committee held in Copenhagen on June 3rd, 1915.

With a Special Circular dated Copenhagen, December 6th, 1915, the first edition of the "Gencon" Charter was issued as a "recommended document". In the Special Circular the Revision Committee which had drafted it expressed the hope "that the new charter will receive your unqualified support and that it may prove a useful document."

Next, we find that in the Monthly Circular for September/October, 1918, page 108, there was the following note recommending owners to use the "Gencon" Charter:

"The following letter is to hand from a prominent firm of Norwegian shipowners:

'We beg to suggest that the *Conference* through its Circular should urge upon the owners to insist upon the "Gencon" Charter for such cargoes where this is possible.

'We have ourselves worked in this direction, and we have succeeded in most cases to carry this charter through both for coasting, Scandinavian trade, and woodpulp cargoes to foreign countries.'

"In commending this letter to the attention of our members, we can only express the hope that owners will follow the example of the author of the letter. The 'Gencon' Charter has proved to be a most valuable document, which is best shown by the success it has obtained since its introduction. The 'Gencon' Charter, it should be mentioned, is the first *Conference* document containing the new standard clauses, namely the General Strike Clause, War Clause, Ice Clause and, last but not least, the Owners' Responsibility Clause (to substitute the Negligence Clause)."

In the years following, there were proposals about revising the wording of some of the clauses. On September 1st, 1922, the "Gencon" Charter, as Revised 1922, was issued.

Several clauses followed the principles laid down in the maritime codes of Denmark, Finland, Norway and Sweden, which today are identical.

The "Gencon" Charter has not been revised since.

However, in 1946 the Documentary Council considered whether it would not be advisable to issue an addendum with reference to the

General Paramount Clause,
Both-to-Blame Collision Clause,
Amended Jason Clause.

Subsequently, the Documentary Council agreed on the wording of the

Baltic Conference Addendum 1946. Code Name "Genvoy", popularly known as the "Genvoy" Slip. The wording of the "Genvoy" Slip is given in the Annual Report 1964–1965, page 220.

"Congenbill" Bill of Lading. As no special bill of lading existed to be used with the "Gencon" Charter, the Documentary Council decided in 1946 to issue such a special bill of lading, known as:

Uniform Bill of Lading 1946 (to be used together with charter-parties), code name "Congenbill". The form is available in the old traditional size and also in the modern A4 Format with "E.C.E. Key Layout" to be used with standardized export documents.

F.I.O. Rider. At the request of several members who frequently concluded fixtures on the "Gencon" Charter on "f.i.o." terms, sometimes with separate laytime for loading and discharging and sometimes with total laytime for loading and discharging, the Documentary Council decided in 1962 to issue two separate riders showing the changes required. They were commented upon in the Monthly Circular for December, 1962, pages 9976/9977, and are also repeated in the Annual Report 1964–1965, pages 234/235.

4-Page Edition. The first edition of the "Gencon" Charter was printed on four pages, i.e., the one issued in 1918 and revised in 1922.

8-Page Edition. As some of the *Conference* broker members stated that it would be more convenient for them, and facilitate the duplicating of copies, if a two-page edition was published, the Documentary Council agreed to do so in 1955.

Members were advised accordingly through a note printed on page 5741 of the Monthly Circular for June, 1955. The four-page and the two-page editions are identical, word for word, line for line and clause for clause.

Third Edition

"Gencon" Charter, "Layout 1966". During more recent years two special wishes have been expressed by members, notably by some broker members. The first was that the modern, standard size—the A4 Format (210 mm × 297 mm)—should be used, the second, that all the conditions to be filled in by typewriter should be shown on one page only in order to make it simpler to complete the form.

Several drafts were subsequently placed before the Documentary Council.

At the meeting of the Documentary Council held in Madrid on June 8th, 1965, a sub-committee was appointed to study them. The members were:

> Mr. K. A. Grevesmühl, Stockholm,
> Mr. Stig Lundqvist, Mariehamn,
> The General Manager.

At the meeting of the Documentary Council held in Copenhagen on November 17th, 1965, a proposal for a modern solution was duly approved. A facsimile of the draft will be found on pages 11839/11840.

This new—third—edition of the "Gencon" Charter will be known as "Gencon" Charter, "Layout 1966".

The wording is the same as in the two previous editions, with the exception of line 56 in the new edition which covers a technical point considered desirable in view of the new layout.

The only other difference between the two previous editions of the "Gencon" Charter and the new edition is the heading, which has been modernized. In order to save space the name of the *Conference* and the reference to the Documentary Council have been omitted and the *Conference* crest inserted instead. **All the terms remain the same.**

As will be seen from the facsimile print on pages 11839/11840, the charter is divided into two parts; the first page is called PART A and the second page PART B.

Numbering of Clauses. Moving the clauses and lines to be filled in one page means that in the new edition the clauses will not follow in the same order as in the two previous editions. In the circumstances, while in the new edition the clauses have been given running numbers, behind them is shown in brackets the number of the clauses appearing in the two old editions. Hence the new reference in the heading:

"Figures in brackets denote clause numbering in 1922 edition."

Numbering of Lines. The lines in the new edition have been given running numbers. More words are contained in the lines of the new edition than in the two previous editions. On that account it is not possible to show in brackets the numbering of the lines in the old editions.

In the new edition the lines in the open spaces have been given numbers printed in heavier type than the printed lines, so as to facilitate the filling in.

Filling In. Tabulation System. Likewise, in order to facilitate filling in the form and enable the clerk doing so to make use of the tabulation system of typewriters, the open space in most of the lines commences in the same spot—at the same tabulation setting. Also, at the very top of the first page, short vertical lines have been printed according to which the clerk may set the tabulation.

Payment of Freight. Clause 2 (4) does not have any space to be filled in by typewriter. Nevertheless this clause has been moved to the first page because it may have to be amended or some addition may have to be made in view of special sales conditions or exchange regulations, or because the owners wish the freight to be paid into a certain bank account.

Agency. Clause 7 (14). The stipulation in this clause is sometimes amended or amplified by typewriter and, for that reason, it has been felt practical likewise to show it on the first page.

The clauses with open spaces to be filled in have been shown on the first page under "PART A". All other clauses appear on the second page under "PART B".

In view of the principle that items to be filled in by typewriter should appear only on the first page, space for the signature has been provided at foot of the first page.

In order to ensure that the signature covers all clauses and conditions mentioned in "PART B", the following addition has been made at the end of the printed text of "PART A", line 56:

"9–15: as in part B, which constitutes a part of this Charter as though fully set forth herein."

In order to save space on the first page, the usual reference about the charter being "Adopted by the Documentary Committee of the Chamber of Shipping of the United Kingdom" and concerning "Copyright" are shown in a frame at the end of page 2.

The facsimile print on pages 11839/11840 represents the draft before the Documentary Council at the meeting in Copenhagen on November 17th, 1965.

In the new edition there will be a few changes of a purely editorial nature; for instance, the name "Gencon" will appear in larger type in the heading.

Copyright. The copyright of the three editions of the "Gencon" Charter is held by *The Baltic and International Maritime Conference*, Copenhagen.

Distribution. The new edition is expected to be available at the end of January 1966, from the printers,

> Fr. G. Knudtzon's Bogtrykkeri A/S,
> Toldbodgade 57,
> Copenhagen, K.,
> Denmark.

The companies in other countries stocking the previous editions of the "Gencon" Charter will be invited also to stock and sell the new edition of the "Gencon" Charter, "Layout 1966".

Use of the "Gencon" Charter

Shipowners, charterers, chartering agents and others interested are at liberty to us either the

> four-page
> two-page, or
> "Layout 1966"

edition.

It should be emphasized that the terms of the three editions are exactly the same. If they are maintained, no disputes need arise.

The "Gencon" Charter is known and used the world over. It is eminently suitable, for instance, for cargoes of

Grain	Stones
Fertilizers	Logs
Phosphates	Prefabricated Houses
Ore	Bricks
Potash	Cattle
Salt	Relief Cargoes, etc.
Scrap Iron	

APPENDICES C—H

SUMMARY

APPENDIX C

BILLS OF LADING ACT 1855

(18 & 19 Vict. c. 111)

Whereas, by the custom of merchants, a bill of lading of goods being transferable by endorsement, the property in the goods may thereby pass to the endorsee, but nevertheless all rights in respect of the contract contained in the bill of lading continue in the original shipper or owner; and it is expedient that such rights should pass with the property: And whereas it frequently happens that the goods in respect of which bills of lading purport to be signed have not been laden on board, and it is proper that such bills of lading in the hands of a bona fide holder for value should not be questioned by the master or other person signing the same on the ground of the goods not having been laden as aforesaid:

1. Consignees, and endorsees of bills of lading empowered to sue.—Every consignee of goods named in a bill of lading, and every endorsee of a bill of lading, to whom the property in the goods therein mentioned shall pass upon or by reason of such consignment or endorsement, shall have transferred to and vested in him all rights of suit, and be subject to the same liabilities in respect of such goods as if the contract contained in the bill of lading had been made with himself.

2. Saving as to stoppage in transitu, and claims for freight, etc.— Nothing herein contained shall prejudice or affect any right of stoppage *in transitu*, or any right to claim freight against the original shipper or owner, or any liability of the consignee or endorsee by reason or in consequence of his being such consignee or endorsee, or of his receipt of the goods by reason or in consequence of such consignment or endorsement.

3. Bill of lading in hands of consignee, etc. conclusive evidence of shipment as against master, etc.—Every bill of lading in the hands of a consignee or endorsee for valuable consideration, representing goods to have been shipped on board a vessel, shall be conclusive evidence of such shipment as against the master or other person signing the same, notwithstanding that such goods or some part thereof may not have been so shipped, unless such holder of the bill of lading shall have had actual notice at the time of receiving the same that the goods had not been in fact laden on board: Provided, that the master or other person so signing may exonerate himself in respect of such misrepresentation by showing that it was caused without any default on his part, and wholly by the fraud of the shipper, or of the holder, or some person under whom the holder claims.

MERCHANT SHIPPING ACT 1894

(57 & 58 Vict. c. 60)

PART V. SAFETY.

Dangerous Goods

446. Restrictions on carriage of dangerous goods.—(1) A person shall not send or attempt to send by any vessel, British or foreign, and a person not being the master or owner of the vessel shall not carry or attempt to carry in any such vessel, any dangerous goods, without distinctly marking their nature on the outside of the package containing the same, and giving written notice of the nature of those goods and of the name and address of the sender or carrier thereof to the master or owner of the vessel at or before the time of sending the same to be shipped or taking the same on board the vessel.

(2) If any person fails without reasonable cause to comply with this section he shall for each offence be liable to a fine not exceeding one hundred pounds; or if he shows that he was merely an agent in the shipment of any such goods as aforesaid, and was not aware and did not suspect and had no reason to suspect that the goods shipped by him were of a dangerous nature, then not exceeding ten pounds.

(3) For the purpose of this Part of this Act the expression "dangerous goods" means aquafortis, vitriol, naphtha, benzine, gunpowder, lucifer matches, nitro-glycerine, petroleum, any explosives within the meaning of the Explosives Act 1875, and any other goods which are of a dangerous nature.

447. Penalty for misdescription of dangerous goods.—A person shall not knowingly send or attempt to send by, or carry or attempt to carry in, any vessel, British or foreign, any dangerous goods under a false description, and shall not falsely describe the sender or carrier thereof, and if he acts in contravention of this section he shall for each offence be liable to a fine not exceeding five hundred pounds.

448. Power to deal with goods suspected of being dangerous.—(1) The master or owner of any vessel, British or foreign, may refuse to take on board any package or parcel which he suspects to contain any dangerous goods, and may require it to be opened to ascertain the fact.

(2) When any dangerous goods, or any goods, which in the judgment of the master or owner of the vessel, are dangerous goods, have been sent or brought aboard any vessel, British or foreign, without

being marked as aforesaid, or without such notice having been given
as aforesaid, the master or owner of the vessel may cause those goods
to be thrown overboard, together with any package or receptacle in
which they are contained; and neither the master nor the owner of the
vessel shall be subject to any liability, civil or criminal, in any court for
so throwing the goods overboard.

449. Forfeiture of dangerous goods improperly sent or carried.—
(1) Where any dangerous goods have been sent or carried, or attempted
to be sent or carried, on board any vessel, British or foreign, without
being marked as aforesaid, or without such notice having been given
as aforesaid, or under a false description, or with a false description
of the sender or carrier thereof, any court having Admiralty jurisdiction may declare those goods and any package or receptacle in which
they are contained, to be, and they shall thereupon be, forfeited, and
when forfeited, shall be disposed of as the court direct.

(2) The court shall have, and may exercise, the aforesaid powers of
forfeiture and disposal notwithstanding that the owner of the goods
has not committed any offence under the provisions of this Act relating
to dangerous goods, and is not before the court, and has not notice of the
proceedings, and notwithstanding that there is no evidence to show to
whom the goods belong; nevertheless the court may, in their discretion,
require such notice as they may direct to be given to the owner or shipper
of the goods before they are forfeited.

450. Saving for other enactments relating to dangerous goods.—
The provisions of this Part of this Act relating to the carriage of dangerous
goods shall be deemed to be in addition to and not in substitution for,
or in restraint of, any other enactment for the like object, so nevertheless that nothing in the said provisions shall be deemed to authorise
any person to be sued or prosecuted twice in the same matter.

Part VII. Delivery of Goods.

Delivery of Goods and Lien for Freight.

492. Definitions under Part VII.—In this Part of this Act, unless the
context otherwise requires:

The expression "goods" includes every description of wares and merchandise:

The expression "wharf" includes all wharves, quays, docks, and premises
in or upon which any goods, when landed from ships, may be lawfully
placed:

The expression "warehouse" includes all warehouses, buildings, and
premises in which goods, when landed from ships, may be lawfully
placed:

The expression "report" means the report required by the customs
laws to be made by the master of an importing ship:

The expression "entry" means the entry required by the customs laws to be made for the landing or discharge of goods from an importing ship:

The expression "shipowner" includes the master of the ship and every other person authorised to act as agent for the owner or entitled to receive the freight, demurrage, or other charges payable in respect of the ship:

The expression "owner" used in relation to goods means every person who is for the time entitled, either as owner or agent for the owner, to the possession of the goods, subject in the case of a lien (if any), to that lien:

The expression "wharfinger" means the occupier of a wharf as herein before defined:

The expression "warehouseman" means the occupier of a warehouse as herein before defined.

493. Power of a shipowner to enter and land goods on default by owner of goods.—(1) Where the owner of any goods imported in any ship from foreign parts into the United Kingdom fails to make entry thereof, or, having made entry thereof, to land the same or take delivery thereof, and to proceed therewith with all convenient speed, by the times severally herein-after mentioned, the shipowner may make entry of and land or unship the goods at the following times:

(*a*) If a time for the delivery of the goods is expressed in the charter-party, bill of lading, or agreement, then at any time after the time so expressed:

(*b*) If no time for the delivery of the goods is expressed in the charter-party, bill of lading, or agreement, then at any time after the expiration of seventy-two hours, exclusive of a Sunday or holiday, from the time of the report of the ship.

(2) Where a shipowner lands goods in pursuance of this section he shall place them, or cause them to be placed—

(*a*) if any wharf or warehouse is named in the charter-party, bill of lading, or agreement as the wharf or warehouse where the goods are to be placed and if they can be conveniently there received, on that wharf or in that warehouse; and

(*b*) in any other case on some wharf or in some warehouse on or in which goods of a like nature are usually placed; the wharf or warehouse being, if the goods are dutiable, a wharf or warehouse duly approved by the Commissioners of Customs for the landing of dutiable goods.

(3) If at any time before the goods are landed or unshipped the owner of the goods is ready and offers to land or take delivery of the same, he shall be allowed to do so, and his entry shall in that case be preferred to any entry which may have been made by the shipowner.

(4) If any goods are, for the purpose of convenience in assorting the same, landed at the wharf where the ship is discharged, and the owner of the goods at the time of that landing has made entry and is ready and

offers to take delivery thereof, and to convey the same to some other wharf or warehouse, the goods shall be assorted at landing, and shall, if demanded, be delivered to the owner thereof within twenty-four hours after assortment; and the expense of and consequent on that landing and assortment shall be borne by the shipowner.

(5) If at any time before the goods are landed, or unshipped the owner thereof has made entry for the landing and warehousing thereof at any particular wharf or warehouse other than that at which the ship is discharging, and has offered and been ready to take delivery thereof, and the shipowner has failed to make that delivery, and has also failed at the time of that offer to give the owner of the goods correct information of the time at which the goods can be delivered, then the shipowner shall, before landing or unshipping the goods, in pursuance of this section, give to the owner of the goods or of such wharf or warehouse as last aforesaid twenty-four hours notice in writing of his readiness to deliver the goods, and shall, if he lands or unships the same without that notice, do so at his own risk and expense.

494. Lien for freight on landing goods.—If at the time when any goods are landed from any ship, and placed in the custody of any person as a wharfinger or warehouseman, the shipowner gives to the wharfinger or warehouseman notice in writing that the goods are to remain subject to a lien for freight or other charges payable to the shipowner to an amount mentioned in the notice, the goods so landed shall, in the hands of the wharfinger or warehouseman, continue subject to the same lien, if any, for such charges as they were subject to before the landing thereof; and the wharfinger or warehouseman receiving those goods shall retain them until the lien is discharged as herein-after mentioned, and shall, if he fails so to do, make good to the shipowner any loss thereby occasioned to him.

495. Discharge of lien.—The said lien for freight and other charges shall be discharged—

(1) upon the production to the wharfinger or warehouseman of a receipt for the amount claimed as due, and delivery to the wharfinger or warehouseman of a copy thereof or of a release of freight from the shipowner, and

(2) upon the deposit by the owner of the goods with the wharfinger or warehouseman of a sum of money equal in amount to the sum claimed as aforesaid by the shipowner;

but in the latter case the lien shall be discharged without prejudice to any other remedy which the shipowner may have for the recovery of the freight.

496. Provisions as to deposits by owners of goods.—(1) When a deposit as aforesaid is made with the wharfinger or warehouseman, the person making the same may, within fifteen days after making it, stating in the notice the sums, if any, which he admits to be payable to the shipowner, or, as the case may be, that he does not admit any sum to be so payable, but if no such notice is given, the wharfinger or warehouseman may, at the expiration of the fifteen days, pay the sum deposited over to the shipowner.

(2) If a notice is given as aforesaid the wharfinger or warehouseman shall immediately apprize the shipowner of it, and shall pay or tender to him out of the sum deposited the sum, if any, admitted by the notice to be payable, and shall retain the balance, or if no sum is admitted to be payable, the whole of the sum deposited, for thirty days from the date of the notice.

(3) At the expiration of those thirty days unless legal proceedings[1] have in the meantime been instituted by the shipowner against the owner of the goods to recover the said balance or sum, or otherwise for the settlement of any disputes which may have arisen between them concerning the freight or other charges as aforesaid, and notice in writing of those proceedings has been served on the wharfinger or warehouseman, the wharfinger or warehouseman shall pay the balance or sum to the owner of the goods.

(4) A wharfinger or warehouseman shall by any payment under this section be discharged from all liability in respect thereof.

497. Sale of goods by warehouseman.—(1) If the lien is not discharged, and no deposit is made as aforesaid, the wharfinger or warehouseman may, and, if required by the shipowner, shall, at the expiration of ninety days from the time when the goods were placed in his custody or, if the goods are of a perishable nature, at such earlier period as in his discretion he thinks fit, sell by public auction, either for home use or for exportation, the goods or so much thereof as may be necessary to satisfy the charges herein-after mentioned.

(2) Before making the sale the wharfinger or warehouseman shall give notice thereof by advertisement in two local newspapers circulating in the neighbourhood, or in one daily newspaper published in London, and in one local newspaper, and also, if the address of the owner of the goods has been stated on the manifest of the cargo, or on any of the documents which have come into the possession of the wharfinger or warehouseman, or is otherwise known to him, send notice of the sale to the owner of the goods by post.

(3) The title of a bona fide purchaser of the goods shall not be invalidated by reason of the omission to send the notice required by this section, nor shall any such purchaser be bound to inquire whether the notice has been sent.

498. Application of proceeds of sale.—The proceeds of sale shall be applied by the wharfinger or warehouseman as follows, and in the following order:

    (1) first, if the goods are sold for home use, in payment of any customs or excise duties owing in respect thereof; then

---

[1] An arbitration is a legal proceeding: see Arbitration Act 1950, s. 29 (1).

(ii) in payment of the expenses of the sale; then

(iii) in payment of the charges of the wharfinger or warehouseman and the shipowner according to such priority as may be determined by the terms of the agreement (if any) in that behalf between them; or, if there is no such agreement—

    (*a*) in payment of the rent, rates, and other charges due to the wharfinger or warehouseman in respect of the said goods; goods; and then

    (*b*) in payment of the amount claimed by the shipowner as due for freight or other charges in respect of the said goods;

and the surplus, if any, shall be paid to the owner of the goods.

499. Warehouseman's rent and expenses.—Whenever any goods are placed in the custody of a wharfinger or warehouseman, under the authority of this Part of this Act, the wharfinger or warehouseman shall be entitled to rent in respect of the same, and shall also have power, at the expense of the owner of the goods, to do all such reasonable acts as in the judgment of the wharfinger or warehouseman are necessary for the proper custody and preservation of the goods, and shall have a lien on the goods for the rent and expenses.

500. Warehouseman's protection.—Nothing in this Part of this Act shall compel any wharfinger or warehouseman to take charge of any goods which he would not have been liable to take charge of if this Act had not been passed; nor shall he be bound to see to the validity of any lien claimed by any shipowner under this Part of this Act.

501. Saving for powers under Local Acts.—Nothing in this Part of this Act shall take away or abridge any powers given by any local Act to any harbour authority, body corporate, or persons, whereby they are enabled to expedite the discharge of ships or the landing or delivery of goods; nor shall anything in this Part of this Act take away or diminish any rights or remedies given to any shipowner or wharfinger or warehouseman by any local Act.

PART VIII. LIABILITY OF SHIPOWNERS.[1]

502. Limitation of shipowner's liability in certain cases of loss of, or damage to, goods.— The owner[2] of a British ship, or any share therein, shall not be liable to make good to any extent whatever any loss or damage happening without his actual fault or privity in the following cases; namely:

(i) Where any goods, merchandise, or other things whatsoever taken in or put on board his ship are lost or damaged by reason of fire on board the ship; or

---

[1] This term includes "any charterer and any person interested in or in possession of the ship and, in particular, any manager or operator of the ship": Merchant Shipping (Liability of Shipowners and Others) Act, 1958, s. 3 (1). (*Considerable changes in ss.* 502 *and* 503 *of the Act of* 1894 *were made by the Act of* 1958, *and these sections are set out in this Appendix as thereby amended.*)

[2] *Ibid.*

(ii) Where any gold, silver, diamonds, watches, jewels, or precious stones taken in or put on board his ship, the true nature and value of which have not at the time of shipment been declared by the owner or shipper thereof to the owner or master of the ship in the bills of lading or otherwise in writing, are lost or damaged by reason of any robbery, embezzlement, making away with, or secreting thereof.

503. Limitation of owner's liability in certain cases of loss of life, injury, or damage.— (1) The owners[1] of a ship, British or foreign, shall not, where all or any of the following occurrences take place without their actual fault or privity; (that is to say,)

(a) Where any loss of life or personal injury is caused to any person being carried in the ship;

(b) Where any damage or loss is caused to any goods, merchandise, or other things whatsoever on board the ship;

(c) Where any loss of life or personal injury is caused to any person not carried in the ship through the act or omission of any person (whether on board the ship or not) in the navigation or management of the ship or in the loading, carriage or discharge of its cargo or in the embarkation, carriage or disembarkation of its passengers, or through any other act or omission of any person on board the ship;

(d) Where any loss or damage is caused to any property (other than any property mentioned in paragraph (b) of this subsection) or any rights are infringed through the act or omission of any person (whether on board the ship or not) in the navigation or management of the ship, or in the loading, carriage or discharge of its cargo or in the embarkation, carriage or disembarkation of its passengers, or through any other act or omission of any person on board the ship;

be liable to damages beyond the following amounts; (that is to say,)

(i) In respect of loss of life or personal injury, either alone, or together with such loss, damage or infringement as is mentioned in paragraphs (b) and (d) of this subsection, an aggregate amount not exceeding an amount equivalent to 3,100 gold francs[2] for each ton of their ship's tonnage; and

(ii) In respect of such loss, damage or infringement as is mentioned in paragraphs (b) and (d) of this subsection, whether there be in addition loss of life or personal injury or not, an aggregate amount

---

[1] *Ibid.*

[2] A gold franc shall be taken to be a unit consisting of 65½ milligrams of gold of millesimal fineness 900: Merchant Shipping (Liability of Shipowners and Others) Act 1958, s. 1 (2). The sterling equivalent of 3,100 gold francs is £114·89p: Merchant Shipping (Limitation of Liability) (Sterling Equivalents) Order 1975 (S.I. 1975, No. 1615).

not exceeding an amount equivalent to 1,000 gold francs[1] for each ton of their ship's tonnage.

(3) The limits set by this section to the liabilities mentioned therein shall apply to the aggregate of such liabilities which are incurred on any distinct occasion, and shall so apply in respect of each distinct occasion without regard to any liability incurred on another occasion.

THE MERCHANT SHIPPING (LIABILITY OF SHIPOWNERS AND OTHERS) ACT 1900

(63 & 64 Vict. c. 32)

3. Limitation of liability where several claims arise on one occasion.—The limitation of liability under this Act shall relate to the whole of any losses and damages, which may arise upon any one distinct occasion, although such losses and damages may be sustained by more than one person, and shall apply whether the liability arises at common law or under any general or private Act of Parliament, and notwithstanding anything contained in such Act.

---

[1] For the meaning of gold franc see p. 270, *ante*. The sterling equivalent of 1,000 gold francs is £37·06p.: Merchant Shipping (Limitation of Liability) (Sterling Equivalents) Order 1975 (S.I. 1975, No. 1615).

APPENDIX E

CARRIAGE OF GOODS BY SEA ACT 1924

(14 & 15 Geo. 5, c. 22)

Whereas at the International Conference on Maritime Law held at Brussels in October 1922, the delegates at the Conference, including the delegates representing His Majesty, agreed unanimously to recommend their respective Governments to adopt as the basis of a convention a draft convention for the unification of certain rules relating to bills of lading:

And whereas at a meeting held at Brussels in October 1923, the rules contained in the said draft convention were amended by the Committee appointed by the said Conference:

And whereas it is expedient that the said rules as so amended and as set out with modifications in the Schedule to this Act (in this Act referred to as "the Rules") should, subject to the provisions of this Act, be given the force of law with a view to establishing the responsibilities, liabilities, rights and immunities attaching to carriers under bills of lading:

Be it therefore enacted by the King's most Excellent Majesty, by and with the advice and consent of the Lords Spiritual and Temporal, and Commons, in this present Parliament assembled, and by the authority of the same, as follows:

1. Application of Rules in Schedule.—Subject to the provisions of this Act, the Rules shall have effect in relation to and in connection with the carriage of goods by sea in ships carrying goods from any port in Great Britain or Northern Ireland to any other port whether in or outside Great Britain or Northern Ireland.

2. Absolute warranty of seaworthiness not to be implied in contracts to which Rules apply.—There shall not be implied in any contract for the carriage of goods by sea to which the Rules apply any absolute undertaking by the carrier of the goods to provide a seaworthy ship.

3. Statement as to application of Rules to be included in bills of lading.—Every bill of lading, or similar document of title, issued in Great Britain or Northern Ireland which contains or is evidence of any contract to which the Rules apply shall contain an express statement that it is to have effect subject to the provisions of the said Rules as applied by this Act.[1]

---

[1] Failure to comply with this direction, however, does not of itself render the contract illegal: see *Vita Food Products Inc.* v. *Unus Shipping Co., Ltd.,* [1939] 1 All E. R. 513; [1939] A. C. 277.

4. Modification of Article VI of Rules in relation to coasting trade.— Article VI of the Rules shall, in relation to the carriage of goods by sea in ships carrying goods from any port in Great Britain or Northern Ireland to any other port in Great Britain or Northern Ireland or to a port in the Irish Free State, have effect as though the said Article referred to goods of any class instead of to particular goods and as though the proviso to the second paragraph of the said Article were omitted.

5. Modification of Rules 4 and 5 of Article III in relation to bulk cargoes.—Where under the custom of any trade the weight of any bulk cargo inserted in the bill of lading is a weight ascertained or accepted by a third party other than the carrier or the shipper and the fact that the weight is so ascertained or accepted is stated in the bill of lading, then, notwithstanding anything in the Rules, the bill of lading shall not be deemed to be prima facie evidence against the carrier of the receipt of goods of the weight so inserted in the bill of lading, and the accuracy thereof at the time of shipment shall not be deemed to have been guaranteed by the shipper.

6. Short title, saving, and operation.—(1) This Act may be cited as the Carriage of Goods by Sea Act 1924.

(2) Nothing in this Act shall affect the operation of sections four hundred and forty-six to four hundred and fifty, both inclusive, five hundred and two, and five hundred and three of the Merchant Shipping Act 1894, as amended by any subsequent enactment, or the operation of any other enactment for the time being in force limiting the liability of the owners of seagoing vessels.

(3) These Rules shall not by virtue of this Act apply to any contract for the carriage of goods by sea made before such day, not being earlier than the thirtieth day of June, nineteen hundred and twenty-four, as His Majesty may by Order in Council direct, nor to any bill of lading or similar document of title issued, whether before or after such day as aforesaid, in pursuance of any such contract as aforesaid.

SCHEDULE

RULES RELATING TO BILLS OF LADING

ARTICLE I. DEFINITIONS.

In these Rules the following expressions have the meanings hereby assigned to them respectively, that is to say—

(a) "Carrier" includes the owner or the charterer who enters into a contract of carriage with a shipper:

(b) "Contract of Carriage" applies only to contracts of carriage covered by a bill of lading or any similar document of title, in so far as such document relates to the carriage of goods by sea, including any bill of lading or any similar document as aforesaid issued under or pursuant to a charter-party from the moment at which such bill of lading or similar document of title regulates the relations between a carrier and a holder of the same:

(c) "Goods" includes goods, wares, merchandises, and articles of every kind whatsoever, except live animals and cargo which by the contract of carriage is stated as being carried on deck and is so carried:

(d) "Ship" means any vessel used for the carriage of goods by sea:

(e) "Carriage of goods" covers the period from the time when the goods are loaded on to the time when they are discharged from the ship.

ARTICLE II. RISKS.

Subject to the provisions of Article VI, under every contract of carriage of goods by sea the carrier, in relation to the loading, handling, stowage, carriage, custody, care, and discharge of such goods, shall be subject to the responsibilities and liabilities, and entitled to the rights and immunities hereinafter set forth.

ARTICLE III. RESPONSIBILITIES AND LIABILITIES.

1. The carrier shall be bound, before and at the beginning of the voyage, to exercise due diligence to—

(a) make the ship seaworthy:

(b) properly man, equip, and supply the ship:

(c) make the holds, refrigerating and cool chambers, and all other parts of the ship in which goods are carried, fit and safe for their reception, carriage and preservation.

2. Subject to the provision of Article IV, the carrier shall properly and carefully load, handle, stow, carry, keep, care for and discharge the goods carried.

3. After receiving the goods into his charge, the carrier, or the master or agent of the carrier, shall, on demand of the shipper, issue to the shipper a bill of lading showing among other things—

(a) The leading marks necessary for identification of the goods as the same are furnished in writing by the shipper before the loading of such goods starts, provided such marks are stamped or otherwise shown clearly upon the goods if uncovered, or on the cases or coverings in which such goods are contained, in such a manner as should ordinarily remain legible until the end of the voyage;

(b) Either the number of packages or pieces, or the quantity, or weight, as the case may be, as furnished in writing by the shipper;

(c) The apparent order and condition of the goods:

Provided that no carrier, master or agent of the carrier, shall be bound to state or show in the bill of lading any marks, number, quantity, or weight which he has reasonable ground for suspecting not accurately to represent the goods actually received, or which he has had no reasonable means of checking.

4. Such bill of lading shall be prima facie evidence of the receipt by the carrier of the goods as therein described in accordance with paragraph 3 (*a*), (*b*), and (*c*).

5. The shipper shall be deemed to have guaranteed to the carrier the accuracy at the time of shipment of the marks, number, quantity, and weight, as furnished by him, and the shipper shall indemnify the carrier against all loss, damages, and expenses arising or resulting from inaccuracies in such particulars. The right of the carrier to such indemnity shall in no way limit his responsibility and liability under the contract of carriage to any person other than the shipper.

6. Unless notice of loss or damage and the general nature of such loss or damage be given in writing to the carrier or his agent at the port of discharge before or at the time of the removal of the goods into the custody of the person entitled to delivery thereof under the contract of carriage, or, if the loss or damage be not apparent, within three days, such removal shall be prima facie evidence of the delivery by the carrier of the goods as described in the bill of lading.

The notice in writing need not be given if the state of the goods has at the time of their receipt been the subject of joint survey or inspection.

In any event the carrier and the ship shall be discharged from all liability in respect of loss or damage unless suit is brought within one year after delivery of the goods or the date when the goods should have been delivered.

In the case of any actual or apprehended loss or damage the carrier and the receiver shall give all reasonable facilities to each other for inspecting and tallying the goods.

7. After the goods are loaded the bill of lading to be issued by the carrier, master or agent of the carrier, to the shipper shall, if the shipper so demands, be a "shipped" bill of lading, provided that if the shipper shall have previously taken up any document of title to such goods, he shall surrender the same as against the issue of the "shipped" bill of lading, but at the option of the carrier such document of title may be noted at the port of shipment by the carrier, master, or agent with the name or names of the ship or ships upon which the goods have been shipped and the date or dates of shipment, and when so noted the same shall for the purpose of this Article be deemed to constitute a "shipped" bill of lading.

8. Any clause, covenant or agreement in a contract of carriage relieving the carrier or the ship from liability for loss or damage to or in connection with goods arising from negligence, fault or failure in the duties and obligations provided in this Article or lessening such liability otherwise than as provided in these Rules, shall be null and void and of no effect.

A benefit of insurance or similar clause shall be deemed to be a clause relieving the carrier from liability.

ARTICLE IV. RIGHTS AND IMMUNITIES.

1. Neither the carrier nor the ship shall be liable for loss or damage arising or resulting from unseaworthiness unless caused by want of due diligence on the part of the carrier to make the ship seaworthy, and to secure that the ship is properly manned, equipped and supplied, and to make the holds, refrigerating and cool chambers and all other parts of the ship in which goods are carried fit and safe for their reception, carriage and preservation in accordance with the provisions of paragraph 1 of Article III.

Whenever loss or damage has resulted from unseaworthiness, the burden of proving the exercise of due diligence shall be on the carrier or other person claiming exemption under this section.

2. Neither the carrier nor the ship shall be responsible for loss or damage arising or resulting from—

(a) Act, neglect, or default of the master, mariner, pilot, or the servants of the carrier in the navigation or in the management of the ship:

(b) Fire, unless caused by the actual fault or privity of the carrier:

(c) Perils, dangers and accidents of the sea or other navigable waters:

(d) Act of God:

(e) Act of war:

(f) Act of public enemies:

(g) Arrest or restraint of princes, rulers or people, or seizure under legal process:

(h) Quarantine restrictions:

(i) Act or omission of the shipper or owner of the goods, his agent or representative:

(j) Strikes or lock-outs or stoppage or restraint of labour from whatever cause, whether partial or general:

(k) Riots and civil commotions:

(l) Saving or attempting to save life or property at sea:

(m) Wastage in bulk or weight or any other loss or damage arising from inherent defect, quality, or vice of the goods:

(n) Insufficiency of packing:

(o) Insufficiency or inadequacy of marks:

(p) Latent defects not discoverable by due diligence:

(q) Any other cause arising without the actual fault or privity of the carrier, or without the fault or neglect of the agents or servants of the carrier, but the burden of proof shall be on the person claiming the benefit of this exception to show that neither the actual fault or privity of the carrier nor the fault or neglect of the agents or servants of the carrier contributed to the loss or damage.

3. The shipper shall not be responsible for loss or damage sustained by the carrier or the ship arising or resulting from any cause without the act, fault or neglect of the shipper, his agents or his servants.

4. Any deviation in saving or attempting to save life or property at sea, or any reasonable deviation shall not be deemed to be an infringement or breach of these rules or of the contract of carriage, and the carrier shall not be liable for any loss or damage resulting therefrom.

5. Neither the carrier nor the ship shall in any event be or become liable for any loss or damage to or in connection with goods in an amount exceeding 100*l.* per package or unit, or the equivalent of that sum in other currency, unless the nature and value of such goods have been declared by the shipper before shipment and inserted in the bill of lading.

This declaration if embodied in the bill of lading shall be prima facie evidence, but shall not be binding or conclusive on the carrier.

By agreement between the carrier, master or agent of the carrier and the shipper another maximum amount than that mentioned in this paragraph may be fixed, provided that such maximum shall not be less than the figure above named.

Neither the carrier nor the ship shall be responsible in any event for loss or damage to or in connection with goods if the nature or value thereof has been knowingly misstated by the shipper in the bill of lading.

6. Goods of an inflammable, explosive or dangerous nature to the shipment whereof the carrier, master or agent of the carrier, has not consented, with knowledge of their nature and character, may at any time before discharge be landed at any place or destroyed or rendered innocuous by the carrier without compensation, and the shipper of such goods shall be liable for all damages and expenses directly or indirectly arising out of or resulting from such shipment.

If any such goods shipped with such knowledge and consent shall become a danger to the ship or cargo, they may in like manner be landed at any place or destroyed or rendered innocuous by the carrier without liability on the part of the carrier except to general average, if any.

ARTICLE V. SURRENDER OF RIGHTS AND IMMUNITIES, AND INCREASE OF RESPONSIBILITIES AND LIABILITIES.

A carrier shall be at liberty to surrender in whole or in part all or any of his rights and immunities or to increase any of his responsibilities and liabilities under the Rules contained in any of these Articles, provided such surrender or increase shall be embodied in the bill of lading issued to the shipper.

The provisions of these Rules shall not be applicable to charter-parties, but if bills of lading are issued in the case of a ship under a charter-party they shall comply with the terms of these Rules. Nothing in these Rules shall be held to prevent the insertion in a bill of lading of any lawful provision regarding general average.

Appendix E

ARTICLE VI. SPECIAL CONDITIONS.

Notwithstanding the provisions of the preceding Articles a carrier, master or agent of the carrier, and a shipper shall in regard to any particular goods be at liberty to enter into any agreement in any terms as to the responsibility and liability of the carrier for such goods, and as to the rights and immunities of the carrier in respect of such goods, or his obligation as to seaworthiness, so far as this stipulation is not contrary to public policy, or the care or diligence of his servants or agents in regard to the loading, handling, stowage, carriage, custody, care, and discharge of the goods carried by sea, provided that in this case no bill of lading has been or shall be issued and that the terms agreed shall be embodied in a receipt which shall be a non-negotiable document and shall be marked as such.

Any agreement so entered into shall have full legal effect:

Provided that this Article shall not apply to ordinary commercial shipments made in the ordinary course of trade, but only to other shipments where the character or condition of the property to be carried or the circumstances, terms and conditions under which the carriage is to be performed, are such as reasonably to justify a special agreement.

ARTICLE VII. LIMITATIONS ON THE APPLICATION OF THE RULES.

Nothing herein contained shall prevent a carrier or a shipper from entering into any agreement, stipulation, condition, reservation or exemption as to the responsibility and liability of the carrier or the ship for the loss or damage to or in connection with the custody and care and handling of goods prior to the loading on and subsequent to the discharge from the ship on which the goods are carried by sea.

ARTICLE VIII. LIMITATION OF LIABILITY.

The provision of these Rules shall not affect the rights and obligations of the carrier under any statute for the time being in force relating to the limitation of the liability of owners of sea-going vessels.

ARTICLE IX.

The monetary units mentioned in these Rules are to be taken to be gold value.

COUNTRIES WHICH HAVE ADOPTED THE HAGUE RULES

The following countries have passed legislation giving statutory effect to the Hague Rules:

Algeria
Antigua
Argentina
Ascension
Australia
Bahamas
Bangladesh
Barbados
Belgium
Bermuda
British Honduras
Burma
Cameroons
Canada
Congo
Cyprus
Denmark
Dominica
Egypt
Falkland Islands
Federated Malay
  States
Fiji
Finland
France
Gambia
Germany
Ghana
Gibraltar
Gilbert and Ellice
  Islands
Great Britain and
  Northern Ireland

Grenada
Guyana
Hong Kong
Hungary
Iran
Ireland
Israel
Italy
Ivory Coast
Jamaica
Japan
Kenya
Lebanon
Leeward Islands
Madagascar
Malaya
Malta
Mauritius
Monaco
Montserrat
Nauru
Netherlands
Newfoundland
New Guinea
Nigeria
Non Federated
  Malay States
Norway
Pakistan
Papua and Norfolk
Paraguay
Peru
Poland

Portugal
Rumania
St. Kitts and Nevis
St. Lucia
St. Helena
St. Vincent
Sarawak
Seychelles
Sierra Leone
Singapore
Solomon Islands
Somaliland
South Borneo
Spain
Sri Lanka (Ceylon)
Sudan
Sweden
Switzerland
Syria
Tanzania
Tonga
Trinidad and
  Tobago
Turkey
Turks and Cayman
  Islands
United States of
  America
Virgin Islands
Yugoslavia

THE YORK-ANTWERP RULES 1974

Rule of Interpretation.—In the adjustment of general average the following lettered and numbered Rules shall apply to the exclusion of any Law and Practice inconsistent therewith.

Except as provided by the numbered Rules, general average shall be adjusted according to the lettered Rules.

Rule A.—There is a general average act, when, and only when, any extraordinary sacrifice or expenditure is intentionally and reasonably made or incurred for the common safety for the purpose of preserving from peril the property involved in a common maritime adventure.

Rule B.—General average sacrifices and expenses shall be borne by the different contributing interests on the basis hereinafter provided.

Rule C.—Only such losses, damages or expenses which are the direct consequence of the general average act shall be allowed as general average.

Loss or damage sustained by the ship or cargo through delay, whether on the voyage or subsequently, such as demurrage, and any indirect loss whatsoever, such as loss of market, shall not be admitted as general average.

Rule D.—Rights to contribution in general average shall not be affected, though the event which gave rise to the sacrifice or expenditure may have been due to the fault of one of the parties to the adventure, but this shall not prejudice any remedies or defences which may be open against or to that party in respect of such fault.

Rule E.—The onus of proof is upon the party claiming in general average to show that the loss or expense claimed is properly allowable as general average.

Rule F.—Any extra expense incurred in place of another expense which would have been allowable as general average shall be deemed to be general average and so allowed without regard to the saving, if any, to other interests, but only up to the amount of the general average expense avoided.

Rule G.—General average shall be adjusted as regards both loss and contribution upon the basis of values at the time and place when and where the adventure ends.

This rule shall not affect the determination of the place at which the average statement is to be made up.

Rule I. Jettison of Cargo.—No jettison of cargo shall be made good as general average unless such cargo is carried in accordance with the recognised custom of the trade.

Rule II. Damage by Jettison and Sacrifice for the Common Safety.—Damage done to a ship and cargo, or either of them, by or in consequence of a sacrifice made for the common safety, and by water which goes down a ship's hatches opened or other opening made for the purpose of making a jettison for the common safety, shall be made good as general average.

Rule III. Extinguishing Fire on Shipboard.—Damage done to a ship and cargo, or either of them, by water or otherwise, including damage by beaching or scuttling a burning ship, in extinguishing a fire on board the ship, shall be made good as general average; except that no compensation shall be made for damage by smoke or heat however caused.

Rule IV. Cutting away Wreck.—Loss or damage sustained by cutting away wreck or parts of the ship which have been previously carried away or are effectively lost by accident shall not be made good as general average.

Rule V. Voluntary Stranding.—When a ship is intentionally run on shore for the common safety, whether or not she might have been driven on shore, the consequent loss or damage shall be allowed in general average.

Rule VI. Salvage Remuneration.—Expenditure incurred by the parties to the adventure on account of salvage, whether under contract or otherwise, shall be allowed in general average to the extent that the salvage operations were undertaken for the purpose of preserving from peril the property involved in the common maritime adventure.

Rule VII. Damage to Machinery and Boilers.—Damage caused to any machinery and boilers of a ship which is ashore and in a position of peril, in endeavouring to refloat, shall be allowed in general average when shown to have arisen from an actual intention to float the ship for the common safety at the risk of such damage; but where a ship is afloat no loss or damage caused by working the propelling machinery and boilers shall in any circumstances be made good as general average.

Rule VIII. Expenses Lightening a Ship when Ashore, and Consequent Damage.—When a ship is ashore and cargo and ship's fuel and stores or any of them are discharged as a general average act, the extra cost of lightening, lighter hire and reshipping if incurred and the loss or damage sustained thereby, shall be admitted as general average.

P.—11

Rule IX. Ship's Materials and Stores Burnt for Fuel.—Ship's materials and stores, or any of them, necessarily burnt for fuel for the common safety at a time of peril, shall be admitted as general average, when and only when an ample supply of fuel had been provided; but the estimated quantity of fuel that would have been consumed, calculated at the price current at the ship's last port of departure at the date of her leaving, shall be credited to the general average.

Rule X. Expenses at Port of Refuge etc.

(*a*) When a ship shall have entered a port or place of refuge or shall have returned to her port or place of loading in consequence of accident, sacrifice or other extraordinary circumstances, which render that necessary for the common safety, the expenses of entering such port or place shall be admitted as general average; and when she shall have sailed thence with her original cargo, or part of it, the corresponding expenses of leaving such port or place consequent upon such entry or return shall likewise be admitted as general average.

When a ship is at any port or place of refuge and is necessarily removed to another port or place because repairs cannot be carried out in the first port or place, the provisions of this Rule shall be applied to the second port or place as if it were a port or place of refuge and the cost of such removal including temporary repairs and towage shall be admitted as general average. The provisions of Rule XI shall be applied to the prolongation of the voyage occasioned by such removal.

(*b*) The cost of handling on board or discharging cargo, fuel or stores whether at a port or place of loading, call or refuge, shall be admitted as general average, when the handling or discharge was necessary for the common safety or to enable damage to the ship caused by sacrifice or accident to be repaired if the repairs were necessary for the safe prosecution of the voyage, except in cases where the damage to the ship is discovered at a port or place of loading or call without any accident or other extraordinary circumstance connected with such damage having taken place during the voyage.

The cost of handling on board or discharging cargo, fuel or stores shall not be admissible as general average when incurred solely for the purpose of restowage due to shifting during the voyage unless such restowage is necessary for the common safety.

(*c*) Whenever the cost of handling or discharging cargo, fuel or stores is admissible as general average, the costs of storage, including insurance if reasonably incurred, reloading and stowing of such cargo, fuel or stores shall likewise be admitted as general average.

But when the ship is condemned or does not proceed on her original voyage storage expenses shall be admitted as general average only up to the date of the ship's condemnation or of the abandonment of the voyage or up to the date of completion of discharge of cargo if the condemnation or abandonment takes place before that date.

Rule XI. Wages and Maintenance of Crew and other expenses Bearing up for and in a port of Refuge, etc.

(*a*) Wages and maintenance of master, officers and crew reasonably incurred and fuel and stores consumed during the prolongation of the voyage occasioned by a ship entering a port or place of refuge or returning to her port or place of loading shall be admitted as general average when the expenses of entering such port or place are allowable in general average in accordance with Rule X (*a*).

(*b*) When a ship shall have entered or been detained in any port or place in consequence of accident, sacrifice or other extraordinary circumstances which render that necessary for the common safety, or to enable damage to the ship caused by sacrifice or accident to be repaired, if the repairs were necessary for the safe prosecution of the voyage, the wages and maintenance of the master, officers, and crew reasonably incurred during the extra period of detention in such port or place until the ship shall or should have been made ready to proceed upon her voyage, shall be admitted in general average.

Provided that when damage to the ship is discovered at a port or place of loading or call without any accident or other extraordinary circumstance connected with such damage having taken place during the voyage, then the wages and maintenance of master, officers and crew and fuel and stores consumed during the extra detention for repairs to damage so discovered shall not be admissible as general average, even if the repairs are necessary for the safe prosecution of the voyage.

When the ship is condemned or does not proceed on her original voyage, wages and maintenance of the master, officers and crew and fuel and stores consumed shall be admitted as general average only up to the date of the ship's condemnation or of the abandonment of the voyage or up to the date of completion of discharge of cargo if the condemnation or abandonment takes place before that date.

Fuel and stores consumed during the extra period of detention shall be admitted as general average, except such fuel and stores as are consumed in effecting repairs not allowable in general average.

Port charges incurred during the extra period of detention shall likewise be admitted as general average except such charges as are incurred solely by reason of repairs not allowable in general average.

(*c*) For the purpose of this and the other Rules wages shall include all payments made to or for the benefit of the master, officers and crew, whether such payments be imposed by law upon the shipowners or be made under the terms or articles of employment.

(*d*) When overtime is paid to the master, officers or crew for maintenance of the ship or repairs, the cost of which is not allowable in general average, such overtime shall be allowed in general average only up to the saving in expense which would have been incurred and admitted as general average, had such overtime not been incurred.

Rule XII. Damage to Cargo in discharging, etc.—Damage to or loss of cargo, fuel or stores caused in the act of handling, discharging, storing, reloading and stowing shall be made good as general average, when and only when the cost of those measures respectively is admitted as general average.

Rule XIII. Deductions from Cost of Repairs.—Repairs to be allowed in general average shall not be subject to deductions in respect of "new for old" where old material or parts are replaced by new unless the ship is over fifteen years old in which case there shall be a deduction of one third. The deductions shall be regulated by the age of the ship from the 31st December of the year of completion of construction to the date of the general average act, except for insulation, life and similar boats, communications and navigational apparatus and equipment, machinery and boilers for which the deductions shall be regulated by the age of the particular parts to which they apply.

The deductions shall be made only from the cost of the new material or parts when finished and ready to be installed in the ship.

No deduction shall be made in respect of provisions, stores, anchors and chain cables.

Drydock and slipway dues and costs of shifting the ship shall be allowed in full.

The costs of cleaning, painting or coating of bottom shall not be allowed in general average unless the bottom has been painted or coated within the twelve months preceding the date of the general average act in which case one half of such costs shall be allowed.

Rule XIV. Temporary Repairs.—Where temporary repairs are effected to a ship at a port of loading, call or refuge, for the common safety, or of damage caused by general average sacrifice, the cost of such repairs shall be admitted as general average.

Where temporary repairs of accidental damage are effected in order to enable the adventure to be completed, the cost of such repairs shall be admitted as general average without regard to the saving, if any, to other interest, but only up to the saving in expense which would have been incurred and allowed in general average if such repairs had not been effected there.

No deductions "new for old" shall be made from the cost of temporary repairs allowable as general average.

Rule XV. Loss of Freight.—Loss of freight arising from damage to or loss of cargo shall be made good as general average, either when caused by a general average act, or when the damage to or loss of cargo is so made good.

Deduction shall be made from the amount of gross freight lost, of the charges which the owner thereof would have incurred to earn such freight, but has, in consequence of the sacrifice, not incurred.

Rule XVI. Amount to be made good for Cargo lost or Damaged by Sacrifice.—The amount to be made good as general average for damage to or loss of cargo sacrificed shall be the loss which has been sustained thereby based on the value at the time of discharge, ascertained from the commercial invoice rendered to the receiver or if there is no such invoice from the shipped value. The value at the time of discharge shall include the cost of insurance and freight except insofar as such freight is at the risk of interests other than the cargo.

When cargo so damaged is sold and the amount of the damage has not been otherwise agreed, the loss to be made good in general average shall be the difference between the net proceeds of sale and the net sound value as computed in the first paragraph of this Rule.

Rule XVII. Contributory Values.—The contribution to a general average shall be made upon the actual net value of the property at the termination of the adventure except that the value of cargo shall be the value at the time of discharge, ascertained from the commercial invoice rendered to the receiver or if there is no such invoice from the shipped value. The value of the cargo shall include the cost of insurance and freight unless and insofar as such freight is at the risk of interests other than the cargo, deducting therefrom any loss or damage suffered by the cargo prior to or at the time of discharge. The value of the ship shall be assessed without taking into account the beneficial or detrimental effect of any demise or time charterparty to which the ship may be committed.

To these values shall be added the amount made good as general average for property sacrificed, if not already included, deduction being made from the freight and passage money at risk of such charges and crew's wages as would not have been incurred in earning the freight had the ship and cargo been totally lost at the date of the general average act and have not been allowed as general average; deduction being also made from the value of the property of all extra charges incurred in respect thereof subsequently to the general average act, except such charges as are allowed in general average.

Where cargo is sold short of destination, however, it shall contribute upon the actual net proceeds of sale, with the addition of any amount made good as general average.

Passenger's luggage and personal effects not shipped under Bill of Lading shall not contribute in general average.

Rule XVIII. Damage to Ship.—The amount to be allowed as general average for damage or loss to the ship, her machinery and/or gear caused by a general average act shall be as follows:

(*a*) When repaired or replaced,

The actual reasonable cost of repairing or replacing such damage or loss subject to deduction in accordance with Rule XIII;

(*b*) When not repaired or replaced,

The reasonable depreciation arising from such damage or loss, but not exceeding the estimated cost of repairs. But where the ship is an actual total loss or when the cost of repairs of the damage would exceed the value of the ship when repaired, the amount to be allowed as general average shall be the difference between the estimated sound value of the ship after deducting therefrom the estimated cost of repairing damage which is not general average and the value of the ship in her damaged state which may be measured by the net proceeds of sale, if any.

Rule XIX. Undeclared or Wrongfully declared Cargo.—Damage or loss caused to goods loaded without the knowledge of the shipowner or his agent or to goods wilfully misdescribed at time of shipment shall not be allowed as general average but such goods shall remain liable to contribute, if saved.

Damage or loss caused to goods which have been wrongfully declared on shipment at a value which is lower than their real value shall be contributed for at the declared value, but such goods shall contribute upon their actual value.

Rule XX. Provision of Funds.—A commission of two per cent. of general average disbursements, other than the wages and maintenance of master, officers and crew and fuel and stores not replaced during the voyage, shall be allowed in general average, but when the funds are not provided by any of the contributing interests, the necessary cost of obtaining the funds required by means of a bottomry bond or otherwise, or the loss sustained by owners of goods sold for the purpose, shall be allowed in general average.

The cost of insuring money advanced to pay for general average disbursements shall also be allowed in general average.

Rule XXI. Interest on Losses made good in general average.—Interest shall be allowed on expenditure, sacrifices and allowances charged to general average at the rate of seven per cent. per annum, until the date of the general average statement, due allowance being made for any interim reimbursement from the contributory interests or from the general average deposit fund.

Rule XXII. Treatment of Cash Deposits.—Where cash deposits have been collected in respect of cargo's liability for general average, salvage or special charges, such deposits shall be paid without any delay into a special account in the joint names of a representative nominated on behalf of the shipowner and a representative nominated on behalf of the depositors in a bank to be approved by both. The sum so deposited together with accrued interest, if any, shall be held as security for payment to the parties entitled thereto of the general average, salvage or special charges payable by cargo in respect to which the deposits have been collected. Payments on account of refund of deposits may be made if certified to in writing by the average adjuster. Such deposits and payments or refunds shall be without prejudice to the ultimate liability of the parties.

CARRIAGE OF GOODS BY SEA ACT 1971

(1971 c. 19)

Be it enacted by the Queen's most Excellent Majesty, by and with the advice and consent of the Lords Spiritual and Temporal, and Commons, in this present Parliament assembled, and by the authority of the same, as follows:—

1. Application of Hague Rules as amended.—(1) In this Act, "the Rules" means the International Convention for the unification of certain rules of law relating to bills of lading signed at Brussels on 25th August 1924, as amended by the Protocol signed at Brussels on 23rd February 1968.

(2) The provisions of the Rules, as set out in the Schedule to this Act, shall have the force of law.

(3) Without prejudice to subsection (2) above, the said provisions shall have effect (and have the force of law) in relation to and in connection with the carriage of goods by sea in ships where the port of shipment is a port in the United Kingdom, whether or not the carriage is between ports in two different States within the meaning of Article X of the Rules.

(4) Subject to subsection (6) below, nothing in this section shall be taken as applying anything in the Rules to any contract for the carriage of goods by sea, unless the contract expressly or by implication provides for the issue of a bill of lading or any similar document of title.

(5) The Secretary of State may from time to time by order made by statutory instrument specify the respective amounts which for the purposes of paragraph 5 of Article IV of the Rules and of Article IV bis of the Rules are to be taken as equivalent to the sums expressed in francs which are mentioned in sub-paragraph (*a*) of that paragraph.

(6) Without prejudice to Article X (*c*) of the Rules, the Rules shall have the force of law in relation to—

(*a*) any bill of lading if the contract contained in or evidenced by it expressly provides that the Rules shall govern the contract, and

(*b*) any receipt which is a non-negotiable document marked as such if the contract contained in or evidenced by it is a contract for the carriage of goods by sea which expressly provides that the Rules are to govern the contract as if the receipt were a bill of lading,

but subject, where paragraph (*b*) applies, to any necessary modifications and in particular with the omission in Article III of the Rules of the second sentence of paragraph 4 and of paragraph 7.

(7) If and so far as the contract contained in or evidenced by a bill of lading or receipt within paragraph (*a*) or (*b*) of subsection (6) above applies to deck cargo or live animals, the Rules as given the force of law by that subsection shall have effect as if Article I (*c*) did not exclude deck cargo and live animals.

In this subsection "deck cargo" means cargo which by the contract of carriage is stated as being carried on deck and is so carried.

2. Contracting States, etc.—(1) If Her Majesty by Order in Council certifies to the following effect, that is to say, that for the purposes of the Rules—

> (*a*) a State specified in the Order is a contracting State, or is a contracting State in respect of any place or territory so specified; or
>
> (*b*) any place or territory specified in the Order forms part of a State so specified (whether a contracting State or not),

the Order shall, except so far as it has been superseded by a subsequent Order, be conclusive evidence of the matters so certified.

(2) An Order in Council under this section may be varied or revoked by a subsequent Order in Council.

3. Absolute warranty of seaworthiness not to be implied in contracts to which Rules apply.—There shall not be implied in any contract for the carriage of goods by sea to which the Rules apply by virtue of this Act any absolute undertaking by the carrier of the goods to provide a seaworthy ship.

4. Application of Act to British possessions, etc.—(1) Her Majesty may by Order in Council direct that this Act shall extend, subject to such exceptions, adaptations and modifications as may be specified in the Order, to all or any of the following territories, that is—

> (*a*) any colony (not being a colony for whose external relations a country other than the United Kingdom is responsible),
>
> (*b*) any country outside Her Majesty's dominions in which Her Majesty has jurisdiction in right of Her Majesty's Government of the United Kingdom.

(2) An Order in Council under this section may contain such transitional and other consequential and incidental provisions as appear to Her Majesty to be expedient, including provisions amending or repealing any legislation about the carriage of goods by sea forming part of the law of any of the territories mentioned in paragraphs (*a*) and (*b*) above.

(3) An Order in Council under this section may be varied or revoked by a subsequent Order in Council.

5. Extension of application of Rules to carriage from ports in British possessions, etc.—(1) Her Majesty may by Order in Council provide that section 1 (3) of this Act shall have effect as if the reference therein to the United Kingdom included a reference to all or any of the following territories, that is—

(a) the Isle of Man;

(b) any of the Channel Islands specified in the Order;

(c) any colony specified in the Order (not being a colony for whose external relations a country other than the United Kingdom is responsible);

(d) any associated state (as defined by section 1 (3) of the West Indies Act 1967) specified in the Order;

(e) any country specified in the Order, being a country outside Her Majesty's dominions in which Her Majesty has jurisdiction in right of Her Majesty's Government of the United Kingdom.

(2) An Order in Council under this section may be varied or revoked by a subsequent Order in Council.

6. Supplemental.—(1) This Act may be cited as the Carriage of Goods by Sea Act 1971.

(2) It is hereby declared that this Act extends to Northern Ireland.

(3) The following enactments shall be repealed, that is—

(a) the Carriage of Goods by Sea Act 1924,

(b) section 12 (4) (a) of the Nuclear Installations Act 1965,

and without prejudice to section 38 (1) of the Interpretation Act 1889, the reference to the said Act of 1924 in section 1 (1) (i) (ii) of the Hovercraft Act 1968 shall include a reference to this Act.

(4) It is hereby declared that for the purposes of Article VIII of the Rules section 502 of the Merchant Shipping Act 1894 (which, as amended by the Merchant Shipping (Liability of Shipowners and Others) Act 1958, entirely exempts shipowners and others in certain circumstances from liability for loss of, or damage to, goods) is a provision relating to limitation of liability.

(5) This Act shall come into force on such day as Her Majesty may by Order in Council appoint, and, for the purposes of the transition from the law in force immediately before the day appointed under this subsection to the provisions of this Act, the Order appointing the day may provide that those provisions shall have effect subject to such transitional provisions as may be contained in the Order.

SCHEDULE

The Hague Rules as Amended by the Brussels Protocol 1968

Article I.

In these Rules the following words are employed, with the meanings set out below:—

(a) "Carrier" includes the owner or the charterer who enters into a contract of carriage with a shipper.

(*b*) "Contract of carriage" applies only to contracts of carriage covered by a bill of lading or any similar document of title, in so far as such document relates to the carriage of goods by sea, including any bill of lading or any similar document as aforesaid issued under or pursuant to a charter-party from the moment at which such bill of lading or similar document of title regulates the relations between a carrier and a holder of the same.

(*c*) "Goods" includes goods, wares, merchandise, and articles of every kind whatsoever except live animals and cargo which by the contract of carriage is stated as being carried on deck and is so carried.

(*d*) "Ship" means any vessel used for the carriage of goods by sea.

(*e*) "Carriage of goods" covers the period from the time when the goods are loaded on to the time they are discharged from the ship.

ARTICLE II.

Subject to the provisions of Article VI, under every contract of carriage of goods by sea the carrier, in relation to the loading, handling, stowage, carriage, custody, care and discharge of such goods, shall be subject to the responsibilities and liabilities, and entitled to the rights and immunities hereinafter set forth.

ARTICLE III.

1. The carrier shall be bound before and at the beginning of the voyage to exercise due diligence to—

(*a*) Make the ship seaworthy.

(*b*) Properly man, equip and supply the ship.

(*c*) Make the holds, refrigerating and cool chambers, and all other parts of the ship in which goods are carried, fit and safe for their reception, carriage and preservation.

2. Subject to the provisions of Article IV, the carrier shall properly and carefully load, handle, stow, carry, keep, care for, and discharge the goods carried.

3. After receiving the goods into his charge the carrier or the master or agent of the carrier shall, on demand of the shipper, issue to the shipper a bill of lading showing among other things—

(*a*) The leading marks necessary for identification of the goods as the same are furnished in writing by the shipper before the loading of such goods starts, provided such marks are stamped or otherwise shown clearly upon the goods if uncovered, or on the cases or coverings in which such goods are contained, in such a manner as should ordinarily remain legible until the end of the voyage.

(*b*) Either the number of packages or pieces, or the quantity, or weight, as the case may be, as furnished in writing by the shipper.

(*c*) The apparent order and condition of the goods.

Provided that no carrier, master or agent of the carrier shall be bound to state or show in the bill of lading any marks, number, quantity, or weight which he has reasonable ground for suspecting not accurately to represent the goods actually received, or which he has had no reasonable means of checking.

4. Such a bill of lading shall be prima facie evidence of the receipt by the carrier of the goods as therein described in accordance with paragraph 3 (*a*), (*b*) and (*c*). However, proof to the contrary shall not be admissible when the bill of lading has been transferred to a third party acting in good faith.

5. The shipper shall be deemed to have guaranteed to the carrier the accuracy at the time of shipment of the marks, number, quantity and weight, as furnished by him, and the shipper shall indemnify the carrier against all loss, damages and expenses arising or resulting from inaccuracies in such particulars. The right of the carrier to such indemnity shall in no way limit his responsibility and liability under the contract of carriage to any person other than the shipper.

6. Unless notice of loss or damage and the general nature of such loss or damage be given in writing to the carrier or his agent at the port of discharge before or at the time of the removal of the goods into the custody of the person entitled to delivery thereof under the contract of carriage, or, if the loss or damage be not apparent, within three days, such removal shall be prima facie evidence of the delivery by the carrier of the goods as described in the bill of lading.

The notice in writing need not be given if the state of the goods has, at the time of their receipt, been the subject of joint survey or inspection.

Subject to paragraph 6 *bis* the carrier and the ship shall in any event be discharged from all liability whatsoever in respect of the goods, unless suit is brought within one year of their delivery or of the date when they should have been delivered. This period may, however, be extended if the parties so agree after the cause of action has arisen.

In the case of any actual or apprehended loss or damage the carrier and the receiver shall give all reasonable facilities to each other for inspecting and tallying the goods.

6 *bis.* An action for indemnity against a third person may be brought even after the expiration of the year provided for in the preceding paragraph if brought within the time allowed by the law of the Court seized of the case. However, the time allowed shall be not less than three months, commencing from the day when the person bringing such action for indemnity has settled the claim or has been served with process in the action against himself.

7. After the goods are loaded the bill of lading to be issued by the carrier, master, or agent of the carrier, to the shipper shall, if the shipper so demands, be a "shipped" bill of lading, provided that if the shipper shall have previously taken up any document of title to such goods, he

shall surrender the same as against the issue of the "shipped" bill of lading, but at the option of the carrier such document of title may be noted at the port of shipment by the carrier, master, or agent with the name or names of the ship or ships upon which the goods have been shipped and the date or dates of shipment, and when so noted, if it shows the particulars mentioned in paragraph 3 of Article III, shall for the purpose of this article be deemed to constitute a "shipped" bill of lading.

8. Any clause, covenant, or agreement in a contract of carriage relieving the carrier or the ship from liability for loss or damage to, or in connection with, goods arising from negligence, fault, or failure in the duties and obligations provided in this article or lessening such liability otherwise than as provided in these Rules, shall be null and void and of no effect. A benefit of insurance in favour of the carrier or similar clause shall be deemed to be a clause relieving the carrier from liability.

ARTICLE IV.

1. Neither the carrier nor the ship shall be liable for loss or damage arising or resulting from unseaworthiness unless caused by want of due diligence on the part of the carrier to make the ship seaworthy, and to secure that the ship is properly manned, equipped and supplied, and to make the holds, refrigerating and cool chambers and all other parts of the ship in which goods are carried fit and safe for their reception, carriage and preservation in accordance with the provisions of paragraph 1 of Article III. Whenever loss or damage has resulted from unseaworthiness the burden of proving the exercise of due diligence shall be on the carrier or other person claiming exemption under this article.

2. Neither the carrier nor the ship shall be responsible for loss or damage arising or resulting from—

(a) Act, neglect, or default of the master, mariner, pilot, or the servants of the carrier in the navigation or in the management of the ship.

(b) Fire, unless caused by the actual fault or privity of the carrier.

(c) Perils, dangers and accidents of the sea or other navigable waters.

(d) Act of God.

(e) Act of war.

(f) Act of public enemies.

(g) Arrest or restraint of princes, rulers or people, or seizure under legal process.

(h) Quarantine restrictions.

(i) Act or omission of the shipper or owner of the goods, his agent or representative.

(j) Strikes or lockouts or stoppage or restraint of labour from whatever cause, whether partial or general.

(*k*) Riots and civil commotions.

(*l*) Saving or attempting to save life or property at sea.

(*m*) Wastage in bulk or weight or any other loss or damage arising from inherent defect, quality or vice of the goods.

(*n*) Insufficiency of packing.

(*o*) Insufficiency or inadequacy of marks.

(*p*) Latent defects not discoverable by due diligence.

(*q*) Any other cause arising without the actual fault or privity of the carrier, or without the fault or neglect of the agents or servants of the carrier, but the burden of proof shall be on the person claiming the benefit of this exception to show that neither the actual fault or privity of the carrier nor the fault or neglect of the agents or servants of the carrier contributed to the loss or damage.

3. The shipper shall not be responsible for loss or damage sustained by the carrier or the ship arising or resulting from any cause without the act, fault or neglect of the shipper, his agents or his servants.

4. Any deviation in saving or attempting to save life or property at sea or any reasonable deviation shall not be deemed to be an infringement or breach of these Rules or of the contract of carriage, and the carrier shall not be liable for any loss or damage resulting therefrom.

5. (*a*) Unless the nature and value of such goods have been declared by the shipper before shipment and inserted in the bill of lading, neither the carrier nor the ship shall in any event be or become liable for any loss or damage to or in connection with the goods in an amount exceeding the equivalent of 10,000 francs per package or unit or 30 francs per kilo of gross weight of the goods lost or damaged, whichever is the higher.

(*b*) The total amount recoverable shall be calculated by reference to the value of such goods at the place and time at which the goods are discharged from the ship in accordance with the contract or should have been so discharged.

The value of the goods shall be fixed according to the commodity exchange price, or, if there be no such price, according to the current market price, or, if there be no commodity exchange price or current market price, by reference to the normal value of goods of the same kind and quality.

(*c*) Where a container, pallet or similar article of transport is used to consolidate goods, the number of packages or units enumerated in the bill of lading as packed in such article of transport shall be deemed the number of packages or units for the purpose of this paragraph as far as these packages or units are concerned. Except as aforesaid such article of transport shall be considered the package or unit.

(*d*) A franc means a unit consisting of 65·5 milligrammes of gold of millesimal fineness 900. The date of conversion of the sum awarded into national currencies shall be governed by the law of the Court seized of the case.

(*e*) Neither the carrier nor the ship shall be entitled to the benefit of the limitation of liability provided for in this paragraph if it is proved that the damage resulted from an act or omission of the carrier done with intent to cause damage, or recklessly and with knowledge that damage would probably result.

(*f*) The declaration mentioned in sub-paragraph (*a*) of this paragraph, if embodied in the bill of lading, shall be prima facie evidence, but shall not be binding or conclusive on the carrier.

(*g*) By agreement between the carrier, master or agent of the carrier and the shipper other maximum amounts than those mentioned in sub-paragraph (*a*) of this paragraph may be fixed, provided that no maximum amount so fixed shall be less than the appropriate maximum mentioned in that sub-paragraph.

(*h*) Neither the carrier nor the ship shall be responsible in any event for loss or damage to, or in connection with, goods if the nature or value thereof has been knowingly mis-stated by the shipper in the bill of lading.

6. Goods of an inflammable, explosive or dangerous nature to the shipment whereof the carrier, master or agent of the carrier has not consented with knowledge of their nature and character, may at any time before discharge be landed at any place, or destroyed or rendered innocuous by the carrier without compensation and the shipper of such goods shall be liable for all damages and expenses directly or indirectly arising out of or resulting from such shipment. If any such goods shipped with such knowledge and consent shall become a danger to the ship or cargo, they may in like manner be landed at any place, or destroyed or rendered innocuous by the carrier without liability on the part of the carrier except to general average, if any.

ARTICLE IV BIS.

1. The defences and limits of liability provided for in these Rules shall apply in any action against the carrier in respect of loss or damage to goods covered by a contract of carriage whether the action be founded in contract or in tort.

2. If such an action is brought against a servant or agent of the carrier (such servant or agent not being an independent contractor), such servant or agent shall be entitled to avail himself of the defences and limits of liability which the carrier is entitled to invoke under these Rules.

3. The aggregate of the amounts recoverable from the carrier, and such servants and agents, shall in no case exceed the limit provided for in these Rules.

4. Nevertheless, a servant or agent of the carrier shall not be entitled to avail himself of the provisions of this article, if it is proved that the

damage resulted from an act or omission of the servant or agent done with intent to cause damage or recklessly and with knowledge that damage would probably result.

ARTICLE V.

A carrier shall be at liberty to surrender in whole or in part all or any of his rights and immunities or to increase any of his responsibilities and obligations under these Rules, provided such surrender or increase shall be embodied in the bill of lading issued to the shipper. The provisions of these Rules shall not be applicable to charter-parties, but if bills of lading are issued in the case of a ship under a charter-party they shall comply with the terms of these Rules. Nothing in these Rules shall be held to prevent the insertion in a bill of lading of any lawful provision regarding general average.

ARTICLE VI.

Notwithstanding the provisions of the preceding articles, a carrier, master or agent of the carrier and a shipper shall in regard to any particular goods be at liberty to enter into any agreement in any terms as to the responsibility and liability of the carrier for such goods, and as to the rights and immunities of the carrier in respect of such goods, or his obligation as to seaworthiness, so far as this stipulation is not contrary to public policy, or the care or diligence of his servants or agents in regard to the loading, handling, stowage, carriage, custody, care and discharge of the goods carried by sea, provided that in this case no bill of lading has been or shall be issued and that the terms agreed shall be embodied in a receipt which shall be a non-negotiable document and shall be marked as such.

Any agreement so entered into shall have full legal effect.

Provided that this article shall not apply to ordinary commercial shipments made in the ordinary course of trade, but only to other shipments where the character or condition of the property to be carried or the circumstances, terms and conditions under which the carriage is to be performed are such as reasonably to justify a special agreement.

ARTICLE VII.

Nothing herein contained shall prevent a carrier or a shipper from entering into any agreement, stipulation, condition, reservation or exemption as to the responsibility and liability of the carrier or the ship for the loss or damage to, or in connection with, the custody and care and handling of goods prior to the loading on, and subsequent to the discharge from, the ship on which the goods are carried by sea.

ARTICLE VIII.

The provisions of these Rules shall not affect the rights and obligations of the carrier under any statute for the time being in force relating to the limitation of the liability of owners of sea-going vessels.

ARTICLE IX.

These Rules shall not affect the provisions of any international Convention or national law governing liability for nuclear damage.

ARTICLE X.

The provisions of these Rules shall apply to every bill of lading relating to the carriage of goods between ports in two different States if:

(a) the bill of lading is issued in a contracting State,
or

(b) the carriage is from a port in a contracting State,
or

(c) the contract contained in or evidenced by the bill of lading provides that these Rules or legislation of any State giving effect to them are to govern the contract,

whatever may be the nationality of the ship, the carrier, the shipper, the consignee, or any other interested person.

[*The last two paragraphs of this article are not reproduced. They require contracting States to apply the Rules to bills of lading mentioned in the article and authorise them to apply the Rules to other bills of lading.*]

[*Articles* 11 *to* 16 *of the International Convention for the unification of certain rules of law relating to bills of lading signed at Brussels on 25th August,* 1924 *are not reproduced. They deal with the coming into force of the Convention, procedure for ratification, accession and denunciation, and the right to call for a fresh conference to consider amendments to the Rules contained in the Convention.*]

Index

297

R

RECEIPT
bill of lading as,
  as to condition, 60
    leading marks, 58, 64
    quality, 65
    quantity, 58
  generally, 57, 274, 291
coasting trade carriage, 75, 273, 278
mate's, comparison of bill of lading
    with, 100
    purpose of, 8
"particular goods", for, in lieu of
  bill of lading, 75, 278, 295

REDELIVERY
ship, of, by charterer, 40
    cost of necessary repairs
      on, 40
    hire, when payable, 41

REPAIRS
deductions from cost of, in adjust-
  ing claims, 284
ship, to, to be borne by shipowner,
  188

REPRESENTATIONS
shipowner, by, inducing charterer
  to sign contract, 43

RESPONDENTIA BOND
charge payable only on ship's safe
  arrival, 187
generally, 7, 187
lien conferred by, 187

RESTRAINTS OF PRINCES
excepted peril, as, by statute, 164,
  276, 292
exclusion of shipowner's liability
  for, 149
meaning, 149

RIOT
excepted peril, as, under statute,
  164, 276, 293

ROBBERS
exclusion of shipowner's liability
  for acts of, 149

RUNNING DAYS
meaning, 7

RUST
clause in bill of lading, 63

S

SACRIFICE
general average. *See* GENERAL
  AVERAGE.

SAFE PORT
charterer, agreement by, to use, 25
"or so near thereto as she may
  safely get", effect of clause, 126
what constitutes, 28, 125

SAILS
damage to or loss of, 281

SALE
ship and cargo, of, master's authority, 186

SALE OF GOODS ACT, 1893
insolvency of buyer defined, 98
rescission, effect of stoppage *in
  transitu* on, 99
stoppage *in transitu*, not affected by
  other sale, etc., 99
transfer of document of title
  defeats, 99

SALVAGE
clause in charter-party, 253
meaning, 8
payment for services, generally, 198

SALVAGE AGREEMENT
conclusion of, master's authority,
  186

SEAWORTHINESS
abolition of absolute warranty of,
  70, 79, 272
carrier to exercise due diligence, 84
certificate of, production of, burden
  of proof, as to, 87
clause in time charter-party, 26
condition precedent, undertaking
  as, 14
duty, no absolute, 26n
express and implied undertakings
  as to, 17
    undertaking does not dis-
    place undertaking implied
    by law, 17
fitness to receive cargo as test of, 15
ignorance of defect no defence, 14
implied undertaking of, 14, 83
includes cargoworthiness, 83
law, undertaking implied by, 17, 18
limitation of liability for, 86
no absolute undertaking, under
  1971 Act, 88
"seaworthy trim", 130
seaworthy vessel, undertaking to
  provide, when broken, 15

Printed in Great Britain by Chapel River Press, Andover, Hants.